Female Desires

BETWEEN MEN ~ BETWEEN WOMEN

Lesbian and Gay Studies

Lillian Faderman and Larry Gross, Editors

Female Desires

Same-Sex Relations and Transgender Practices Across Cultures

Edited by *Evelyn Blackwood and Saskia E. Wieringa*

Withdrawn

Columbia University Press

New York

Columbia University Press
New York   Chichester, West Sussex
Publishers Since 1893

Library of Congress Cataloging-in-Publication Data
Female desires : same-sex relations and transgender practices
   across cultures / edited by Evelyn Blackwood and Saskia E. Wieringa.
      p.   cm. — (Between men—between women)
   Includes bibliographical references and index.
   ISBN 0-231-11260-2 (cloth) — ISBN 0-231-11261-0 (paper)
   1. Lesbianism—Cross-cultural studies. 2. Homosexuality—Cross-
cultural studies. 3. Lesbianism—Developing countries—Cross-
cultural studies. 4. Homosexuality—Developing countries—Cross-
cultural studies. I. Blackwood, Evelyn. II. Wieringa, Saskia.
1950–   . III. Series.
HQ75.5.F43   1999
306.76'6—dc21
                                              98-37847
                                              CIP

Columbia University Press books are printed on permanent and durable acid-free paper.
Printed in the United States of America
c 10 9 8 7 6 5 4 3 2 1
p 10 9 8 7 6 5 4 3

1712- 104- 1253

Contents

Preface

While there is a vast body of scholarship on lesbian, gay, and queer issues in Europe and America and a growing literature on same-sex experiences of male-bodied individuals outside the "West," there are few studies that deal with the same-sex desires, experiences, and lifestyles of women outside the "West." As editors, our desire is to put an end to the so-called invisibility of lesbians (invisible to whom?) across the world and to fill the gap in cross-cultural studies of "homosexuality" by providing an anthology devoted to the exploration of female same-sex relationships and transgender practices. By paying particular attention to the problematic of female bodies in the cultural construction of gendered and sexed individuals, we envision this anthology as an effort to make gender an integral part of sexuality studies. At the same time we want to problematize the categories of "homosexuality," "lesbianism," and "woman" by questioning whether they have any coherent, unifying meanings across cultures. In this way we hope to move beyond some of the categories and issues dominant in Western lesbian and gay studies.

In titling this volume *Female Desires* rather than "women's" or "lesbian" desires, we do not mean to highlight the biological aspects of desires but to raise questions about identities and genders that are too easily subsumed under the categories of woman or lesbian. What is common to all these case studies are *female* bodies (this, however, does not mean that the latter necessarily share any predetermined set of traits, feelings, or experiences). The title is meant to highlight the way female bodies are assigned certain cultural meanings that then affect the ways those females (as women, lesbians, and transgendered females) constitute their relations with women. This volume is not only about lesbians or women-loving women; it is about the production and expression of varied and rich cultural identities and same-sex practices between those with female bodies.

Lesbianism is widely seen as a Western phenomenon. Yet there is a growing presence of self-identified lesbians in various national and international settings. Their voices are heard in debates on women's sexual rights; the most well-known example is the speech a Black South African woman, Beverly Ditsie, gave at the Fourth World Women's Conference held in Beijing in 1995 (see the introduction to this volume). There are also many transgendered females and women, both cross-culturally and historically, whose lives do not fit within a narrow definition of lesbianism. Due to the multiple layers of oppression in which heteropatriarchal systems have tried to silence the voices of these women, their experiences have often been ignored or neglected. In this anthology we stress the plurality of their experiences and the multiple ways in which they have shaped their lives. The material collected here raises many questions about issues concerning embodied desires and cultural constructions as well as about the relationship between sexed bodies, gender, and transgendered identities.

As editors we do not speak with a single voice; we put different emphases on issues related to bodies, desires, and cultures. Likewise, the contributors to this volume have different views on the issues mentioned. We have tried not to impose a single theoretical perspective throughout the text. Instead, we have preserved the variety of views expressed by the activists and scholars who speak in the following pages. In addition, each of the authors addresses issues of subjectivity by situating herself in relation to her study and her "subjects" and by paying attention to the problems related to doing fieldwork on women's sexuality.

This volume is divided into several parts. In our first introductory essay we present some of the main theoretical views in studies of sexuality. In the second essay we look more closely at the reasons for the silences about women and then present an overview of the development of lesbian studies in anthropology. Together these two essays provide a history of the issues and theories concerning women's sexuality. They also situate work in lesbian studies, including the present volume, within the theoretical debates that have been at the forefront in studies of sexuality. If theory can be seen as the sediment of experiences, then the virtual absence of women's voices from outside the "West" seriously hampers the development of theoretical positions on women's sexuality and issues of lesbianism and queer studies. This book then fills a significant gap in transnational studies and theories of sexuality and gender.

The first section, "Indigenous Histories, Colonial Legacies," presents case studies from India and Native North America that analyze the effects of encounters with the "colonial other" on representations of and possibilities for women's sexuality. The historical depth of these two essays provides a provocative glimpse of prepatriarchal and precolonial female desires. The growing homophobia and invisibility of female same-sex eroticism recorded in these essays is one of the results of colonial legacies, a theme that appears in several other contributions as well. The second section, "Erotic Intimacies and Cultural Identities," presents in-depth ethnographic accounts that question the very categories of identity and sexuality. The problematic of applying Eurocentric categories to women's sexual practices is prominent in this section.

The third section, "Doing Masculinity: Butches, Female Bodies, and Transgendered Identities," highlights the relationship between desires and cultures with its focus on female-bodied gender transgressors. Although we use the term *transgendered* in this section, we are not suggesting that these cases are necessarily analogous to that category in the U.S. or Western Europe or that all transgendered females are attracted to women. Instead we point to the way sex/gender systems give rise to particular sexualities. We are not interested here in recreating bounded categories, but in recognizing the considerable slippage between transgendered and lesbian identities occurring in the contemporary transnational context.

The final section, "Nationalism, Feminism, and Lesbian/Gay Rights Movements," deals with postcolonial nations and their response to the rise of movements for women's sexual rights. These articles look at how emerging states have used attacks on lesbian/gay or transgendered individuals to project an ideal national identity. Recent national debates on "Asian values" and the "un-Africanness" of homosexuality point to a rethinking of the relation between nationalism, culture, and sexuality.

This volume will be of interest to a wide audience of both activists and researchers. Activists will find fuel for their arguments through the indigenous histories of sexualities presented here. The in-depth accounts of gender and sexual practices and histories will enrich the views of anthropologists and theoreticians on sexuality. Among other things, these case studies demonstrate that women have not always been passive victims of male domination and compulsory heterosexuality but have created a wide range of rich social and cultural spaces in which to live their desires.

This book has its origins in a session that we organized during the 13th International Congress of Anthropological and Ethnological Sciences in Mexico City in 1993. The idea behind this session was to bring together both activists and researchers to discuss the variety of women's same-sex experiences. Some of the authors of the present volume presented papers at that meeting, including Giti Thadani, Norma Mogrovejo, and Saskia Wieringa. The contributions of the other participants during that session, Margarita Pisano, Dafna Argov, BJD. Gayatri, and Moshe Shokeid helped in shaping our thoughts. Other contributors were either unable to attend that meeting or joined us during the long process of preparing this book. Some of the papers were presented at the American Anthropological Association meetings in San Francisco in 1996. The end result is a number of contributions from Asian, Latin American, European, and North American researchers presenting case studies from a broad range of geographical locations. The length of the process attests to the difficulties both of scholarly research on the topic and of finding adequate support for such work. Most of our contributors had very little or no funding for their research, and in many cases the personal desire to uncover this knowledge and make it available has been the only driving force behind their work.

The Dutch Ministry of Development Cooperation provided some of the travel funds for the Third World participants of the ICAES session in 1993. The Institute of Social Studies in The Hague allowed Wieringa to spend a considerable part of her research time to work on this collection. The Department of Sociology and Anthropology at Purdue University provided both financial and secretarial assistance in the preparation of the manuscript. During the last phase of editing the book Tokyo's Ochanomizu University provided the space for Wieringa to work on this collection.

Evelyn Blackwood would like to thank several people for their support over the years, in particular, Mina Davis Caulfield, who provided the initial encouragement to write about lesbian relations; John DeCecco for his faith in asking her to put together a special issue of the *Journal of Homosexuality* on anthropology and homosexual behavior; Bonnie Zimmerman, Ellen Lewin, and Bill Leap, who encouraged Blackwood to write on cross-cultural lesbian studies again; and Jeff Dickemann and Deborah Elliston for numerous, ever provocative discussions.

Saskia Wieringa first discussed issues of sexuality and anthropology in the Women's Group Anthropology Amsterdam, from the mid-1970s onward. Particularly the discussions with Marion den Uyl and Britt Fontaine proved insightful over the years. In the Institute of Social Studies in The Hague several colleagues have stimulated the development of Wieringa's ideas on sexuality and desire, particularly Thanh-Dam Truong, Amrita Chhachhi, and Virginia Vargas.

We greatly appreciated the enthusiasm and confidence of Ann Miller of Columbia University Press in this project. The comments of the anonymous reviewers were extremely helpful. We are also grateful to Deb Amory who provided her apartment for us one weekend so we could hash out the introductory chapters. We express our heartfelt thanks to all the contributors who continued revising their essays as we kept coming up with new questions, and who kept faith in this project.

Last, we as editors have to thank ourselves. We had never met each other before we entered into what turned out to be the intensely intellectual and emotional experience of editing this book. Our ongoing discussions, mostly via e-mail and with only two actual meetings, have enriched both our works. In the process we have become such good colleagues and friends that this intercontinental project has survived the inevitable setbacks, lost mail, and long silences that editing a volume with contributors from all over the world entails. It is a testament to our desire to do this work and our faith in each other that this book was nourished and completed in a period that has spanned a most challenging and mobile time in both our careers, as we moved among such different places as San Francisco, Honolulu, Lafayette, The Hague, Surinam, and Tokyo.

Notes on Contributors

Margrete Aarmo was born in Oslo, Norway, in 1955. Active in the lesbian movement in Oslo and Copenhagen in the 1970s and 1980s, she has also been a social worker with children and youth and worked with immigrant and refugee projects in Copenhagen. With a degree in the history of ideas and in anthropology from the University of Oslo, she finished her postgraduate degree in social anthropology in the autumn of 1998. She has published several articles on immigration and gender questions in Danish and Norwegian.

Evelyn Blackwood is an American anthropologist who divides her work between research on the matrilineal Minangkabau of West Sumatra and studies of female same-sex relations outside the "West." She has written essays on Native American two-spirit females and the anthropology of lesbianism as well as edited *The Many Faces of Homosexuality: Anthropological Approaches to Homosexual Behavior* (1986). She received her Ph.D. in anthropology from Stanford University in 1993 and is currently assistant professor in both anthropology and women's studies at Purdue University.

Deborah A. Elliston received her Ph.D. in anthropology from New York University and has held teaching positions at New York University and Cornell University. Her research and publications document her specializations in feminist theory, queer anthropology, semiotic social theory, Oceanic ethnography, gender and nationalism, and the study of globalization. She is currently at work revising her dissertation "En/Gendering Nationalism: Colonialism, Sex, and Independence in French Polynesia" (1997) into a manuscript on gender, nationalism, and modernity.

Kendall is professor and head of the Department of Drama at the University of Natal in Pietermaritzburg, South Africa. She is the editor of Mpho Nthunya's autobiography, *Singing Away the Hunger* (Indiana, 1997), of *Basali! Stories by and about Women in Lesotho* (University of Natal Press, 1995), and *Of Love and Thunder! Plays by Women in The Age of Queen Anne* (Methuen, 1988). She was born and educated in the USA and has lived in southern Africa since 1992.

Sabine Lang, born in 1958, received her Ph.D. in anthropology from the University of Hamburg, Germany, in 1990. She has done fieldwork on gender variance and homosexuality in Native American communities and has written numerous articles in German and English on Native American gender variance and sexuality. Her most recent publications include *Two-Spirit People: Native American Gender Identity, Sexuality and Spirituality* (1997, ed. with Sue-Ellen Jacobs and Wesley Thomas) and *Men as Women, Women as Men: Changing Gender in Native American Cultures* (1998). Lang is an independent researcher, currently living near Hamburg.

Norma Mogrovejo, a Peruvian feminist residing in Mexico, is a pioneer in several areas. She initiated the first feminist group in her native city Arequipa seventeen years ago, was a lawyer, now sociologist, researcher, and latinoamericanist. She emigrated to Mexico to continue her studies and for political reasons: to live freely her sexual-affective option. She is a student of Latin America's lesbian history and proposes to investigate, provide, and provoke a collective discussion of a regional lesbian theory. Mogrovejo teaches at the National University of Mexico.

Alison J. Murray was born in Cyprus in 1961 and studied geography at Oxford (B.A., M.A.). She has a Ph.D. in human geography from Australian National University; her thesis was published as *No Money No Honey: Street Traders and Prostitutes in Jakarta*. She has been a lecturer in Asian Studies at Sydney University, a peer educator with Sex Workers Outreach Project in Sydney, and a research fellow at ANU working on sexual subcultures and AIDS discourses in the Asia-Pacific region, which has resulted in the forthcoming volume, *Of Peers and Queers*. Her current work is a reassessment of women's tattoos in headhunting societies in Borneo and the Philippines.

Tan beng hui has been working with the women's movement in Malaysia since 1990. She recently completed her M.A. in Women and Development at the Institute of Social Studies in The Hague, The Netherlands, and is currently working on a project with the Women's Development Collective researching women's history in Malaysia.

Giti Thadani is an independent researcher working in New Delhi on issues of women's sexuality. She is a founding member of *Sakhi*, the lesbian archives in Delhi, and the author of *Sakhiyani: Lesbian Desire in Ancient and Modern India* (Cassell, 1996).

Gloria Wekker completed her Ph.D. in sociocultural anthropology at the University of California, Los Angeles, in 1992. She works at the Institute for Media and Representation at Utrecht University, the Netherlands. She has published poetry, prose, and scholarly books and articles. Her current research is on black and white hetero- and homosexual relationships in the Netherlands.

Saskia E. Wieringa is a Dutch anthropologist whose major work has been on the communist women's movement in Indonesia. She coordinated several research projects on women's movements and organizations and is a founder of the Women and Development program of the Institute of Social Studies in The Hague. She has published widely on issues of women's empowerment, public policy, and sexuality and has written a travelogue on lesbian relations in several Third World countries, entitled *Dora D.*

Female Desires

Saskia E. Wieringa and Evelyn Blackwood

Introduction

125th Street and Abomey

Head bent, walking through snow
I see you Seboulisa
printed inside the back of my head
like marks of the newly wrapped akai
that kept my sleep fruitful in Dahomey
and I poured on the red earth in your honor
those ancient parts of me
most precious and least needed
my well-guarded past
the energy-eating secrets
I surrender to you as libation
mother, illuminate my offering
of old victories
over men over women over my selves
who has never before dared
to whistle into the night
take my fear of being alone
like my warrior sisters
who rode in defense of your queendom
disguised and apart
give me the woman strength
of tongue in this cold season

Half earth and time splits us apart
like struck rock.

A piece lives elegant stories
too simply put
while a dream on the edge of summer
of brown rain in nim trees
snail shells from the dooryard
of King Toffah
bring me where my blood moves
Seboulisa mother goddess with one breast
eaten away by worms of sorrow and loss
see me now
your severed daughter
laughing our name into echo
all the world shall remember.

—Audre Lorde, *The Black Unicorn*

This volume brings together a number of anthropological, historical, and sociological studies on female same-sex relations in a variety of cultural settings, including South and Southeast Asia, Polynesia, Africa, Latin America, and Native North America. Although there are currently a growing number of works in lesbian and gay studies, these are almost completely devoted to Western culture and society. As "Western" lesbian and gay culture becomes globalized, the predominance of works about gays and lesbians in the "West" and of the gay movement "liberating" indigenous queers runs the risk of re-instituting the dichotomy between the "West" and the rest. By bringing together a number of case studies from around the world, this anthology seeks to defuse the dominance of the West in lesbian and gay studies and to expand theories of sexuality beyond the cultural problematics of the West. It seeks to question the categories with which we think about sexuality, identity, and culture and so to move beyond debates about identity politics and performativity to more productive means of understanding sexuality and gender. This anthology is of necessity embedded in the discourse of the "West," written by scholars and activists who are mostly educated in Western thought and coming from the countries concerned as well as from Europe and America, but it seeks to transcend this discourse. Our desire in putting this volume together is to help create transnational studies of sexuality and gender through the discussion of identities that are not simply indigenous (or "pure") or "Western"-influenced but complex expressions of female sexualities and genders.

The case studies presented here offer in-depth perspectives on gender and sexual practices and histories. The variety and intensity of women's emotional and erotic experiences presented in these case studies (and in earlier works discussed in the next chapter) will counter the arguments that women, particularly "non-Western" women, have always been passive victims of male domination and compulsory heterosexuality. Although motherhood and reproduction are vital markers for the identity of many of the women discussed here, the various expressions of women's sexuality and the range of their emotional ties with other women demonstrate that their lives cannot be reduced to their reproductive capacities. Given the broad range of cultures and identities included in this anthology, we do not strive for unanimity either in theoretical perspective or terminology. The contributions to this volume indicate that there are no easy answers to many of the questions asked. Rather, our desire is to reflect the diversity of perspectives in lesbian studies.

In this introduction and the following chapters we discuss a number of theoretical issues concerning cultures, sexualities, and identities. Some of the issues we examine in this essay include the complex relationship of gender, race, and class to the construction of sexuality and identity. We raise questions about the relevance of theories on women's oppression to studies of female sex practices and ask whether the category "woman" is inclusive or exclusive of the experiences represented here. We explore the ways in which concepts such as "lesbian," "homosexual," "third sex," and "queer" are used in feminist and queer theory and assess their relevance for the study of female sexual and gender identities. The next essay provides a history of methodological problems and silences in the study of lesbian and female transgender practices as well as a history of lesbian studies in anthropology.

We also revisit the debates over essentialist versus social constructionist theories of sexuality. Early ethnographers worked from an essentialist perspective developed by sexologists such as Ellis, Krafft-Ebing, and Hirschfeld. Present-day scholars of sexuality reject the biological determinism of earlier theories in favor of a social construction perspective. Social construction theory has been a major step forward that allows us to discuss sexuality in its sociohistorical context. Yet it leaves certain questions unexplored. For instance, how does one account for "deviant," rebellious desires? Is it possible to engage in transhistorical, cross-cultural research? What is the relationship between political agency and self-identity? Finally we devote attention to the human rights perspective of women-loving-women in the light of recent debates on, for example, "Asian values" or the "un-Africanness" of homosexuality.

Western or Native Eyes?

In putting together this anthology we have had to come to terms with questions of ethnocentrism and lesbian and gay imperialism. It has been argued that the "Western eyes" of anthropologists, and those of Western feminists, necessarily produce distorted, universalizing, ethnocentric views of "non-Western" women (Mohanty 1991). Does the "standpoint" position (Haraway 1991) of a black woman anthropologist automatically qualify her to produce "better" data on black women's same-sex relations? This is what Amadiume argues in her otherwise fine study of "female husbands and male daughters" in her native region in Nigeria. On the issue of same-sex practices between the partners of a woman-marriage she fulminates against the lesbian African-American poet Audre Lorde, arguing that in her desire to search for African roots of her sexual orientation Lorde has fallen prey to white ethnocentric biases:

> There are already some indications that Black lesbians are using such prejudiced interpretations of African situations to justify their choices of sexual alternatives which have roots and meaning in the West. Black lesbians are, for example, looking into African women's relationships and interpreting some as lesbian. What prejudices and assumptions are they imposing on African material? How advantageous is it for African women to interpret such practices as woman-to-woman marriages as lesbian (see Lorde 1984)? Such interpretation of for example the cases cited in this book would be totally inapplicable, shocking and offensive to Nnobi women, since the strong bonds and support between them do not imply lesbian sexual practices.
>
> (Amadiume 1987:7)

However, Lorde does not refer to the Nnobi of Nigeria; in her 1984 collection of speeches, called "Sister Outsider," she refers to the Fon of Dahomey, citing Herskovits. As the poem at the beginning of this introduction indicates, Lorde draws her inspiration from the Amazon warriors of Dahomey[1] and from the woman-marriages some wealthy and powerful Fon women contracted. Also, Lorde quotes a beautiful example of an erotic friendship among Efik-Ibibio women in Nigeria (1984:49–50), the reference for which she provides. Thus, Lorde does not "bend facts" or "impose her own wishes and fantasies," in the way Amadiume suggests (Amadiume 1987:7).

Amadiume is guilty of the same sins she so rightly denounces in other anthropologists' work, that of universalizing and imposing her own assumptions, in this case her homophobia, on the work of others. It may very well be that the partners in the woman-marriages of the Nigerian Nnobi never engage in same-sex erotic practices, but Lorde referred to the Fon of Dahomey and to a case in Efik-Ebibio, not to the Nnobu. It is not possible to decide on the basis of one ethnographic case, that of the Nigerian Nnobi, that "lesbianism" is un-African.

The issue of whether or not the partners in some African woman-marriages engaged in sexual activity has been widely debated.[2] Apart from Amadiume, Krige (1974), Oboler (1980), and O'Brien (1977) state emphatically that a female husband does not engage in sexual interaction with her wife. Their claims must be tempered with the fact that woman-marriage takes many forms. Krige based her assertion on work among the Lovedu in South Africa, a group that practices "daughter-in-law" marriage, a form in which lesbian relations are highly unlikely. In this form of woman-marriage a married woman who has not borne a son herself marries the daughter-in-law who was destined for her "son" so that children borne to the daughter-in-law (through an appointed lover) will be recognized as heirs of the "son" (Krige 1938, 1974). The form of woman-marriage relevant here is the marriage in which a woman of some means, either married (to a man) or unmarried, pays bride-price for a wife and establishes her own compound, of which she is the head. This form was practiced by the Fon of Dahomey and studied by Herskovits. He recorded that among the Fon, such women are usually independently wealthy and may even take several wives to increase their family size and holdings. Herskovits asserted that this type of marriage "does not imply a homosexual relationship . . . though it is not to be doubted that occasionally homosexual women who have inherited wealth or have prospered economically establish compounds of their own and at the same time utilize the relationship in which they stand to the women whom they 'marry' to satisfy themselves" (1937:338).

We are inclined to give more weight to the observations of Herskovits, which are corroborated by Machadi's present-day account of woman-marriages in Zimbabwe (1996).[3] Obbo (1976), who conducted research in East Africa, does not take a clear stance on the subject of woman-marriage. She does state, however, that women who marry other women do so for more than economic reasons, suggesting it is because they "are unable to lead satisfying lives in a male/female marriage" (1976:372). In this volume Kendall and Aarmo discuss different patterns of African women's same-sex relationships. Although probably most woman-marriages were conducted either to get offspring for a male relative[4] or for reasons related to the status enhancement of the "female husbands," sexuality between the partners cannot be ruled out. It would be surprising if same-sex practices between African women occurred only in the African diaspora (see Lorde 1982, 1984; Silvera 1992; Wekker this volume) or outside of woman-marriages.

Several contributors to the present volume relate their own experiences and positionality in their fieldwork in order to highlight problematics of subjectivity and method. Raising questions only about the perspectives and subjectivities of nonnative scholars is not sufficient, however. Assuming that native scholars represent the authentic native voice is another form of essentializing. Native scholars also speak from particular positions of class, rank, and education—positions that need to be articulated. Impersonal, "objective" accounts of the complex world in which we find ourselves are not possible. The best we can aim for is to disclose where we come from, so that our readers can trace the paths through which we arrive at our conclusions.

Sex, Gender, and Transgender

This anthology raises many theoretical issues relating to the correlation between culture, sexuality, and identity. One of the central questions posed by these articles is the meaning of sexuality itself. The definition of "sexuality" between women may differ between indigenous women and (Western) observers. Kendall (this volume) relates her experiences with Lesotho women. It took her a long time to realize that "sex" in the Lesotho context was associated exclusively with a penis: "no penis, no sex." Gay (1986) was confronted with a similar problem during her investigation of mummy-baby relations among Lesotho girls. When she asked about people of the same sex "making love like a man and a woman," many people denied it, saying that mummy-baby intimacies are different (1986:105). Shostak describes another situation among Kung San women. Nisa, her informant, told her that girls often played sexually, but that they were rather confused about what this meant: "Do we have penises to have sex with each other with? Can two vaginas screw?" (Shostak 1983:117).

Many acts that have no specific sexual connotation in certain African constructions, such as "mutual masturbation," would immediately be classified as sexual in the West. For instance, Rich postulated a "lesbian continuum" that included a whole range of relations between women, starting from women's friendships to their intimate relationships (1980). Her work has been useful in exposing the heteronormativity of most societies and in expanding the concept of sexuality. However, her romantic view is open to various points of criticism. Classifying any deep friendship between women as "lesbian" disregards the anxieties many women may feel about becoming sexual with each other. It also ignores the cultural context that shapes the relationship. Is it appropriate to classify women as "lesbians" who would not identify themselves as such? Further, does this classification recognize women who have or have had sexual relations with men for economic, social, or procreative reasons as well as having deep erotic friendships with women? Wekker's discussion of the Surinamese *mati* in this volume is enlightening in this respect. As her article and others suggest, women in various social and historical situations identify themselves based on different aspects of their sexual and emotional lives. In some cases (Aarmo; Mogrovejo this volume) women self-consciously adopt a "lesbian" identity. Other women see themselves in a different light, although they may be engaged in similar activities (Lang; Wekker this volume).

One concern in this volume is how to conceptualize female erotic friendships and transgender practices in ways that are not biologically reductionist yet allow for a discussion of passion and desire. There are many forms of transgender practices in which females do not conform to the gender roles assigned to members of their anatomical sex. Analyzing these practices yields fascinating insights into the plasticity of mechanisms regulating sex and desire. Yet most analyses ignore questions about the embodied, prediscursive elements of these social forms as well as about the impulses that prompt specific individuals to "choose" a "deviant" way of life, accepting the enormous risks that are at times associated with their lifestyles, including social marginalization, suicide, and even death at the hand of others.

Another problematic is how to conceptualize the gendered and sexed experiences and lifestyles pertaining to female bodies. It is immediately clear by our choice of terminology that we do not consider our topic to be simply "women's" gendered and sexed experiences. "Woman" is a socially constructed category referring to the attributes of "femininity" assigned to female bodies. Lesbian studies in general is not just about "women" or "lesbians" since it includes transgendered men (female-to-male transsexuals, female two-spirits, Balkan sworn virgins). Not all the case studies in this volume pertain to "women" or "lesbians," either; some concern *tombois* and female *māhū*. Rather than conceptualizing our subject as "woman," as we discuss later, we focus on bodies marked as female and the cultural processes in which they are shaped and negotiated. Thus we start with material female bodies that are physically marked by genitals and reproductive capabilities and examine the consequences of that marking for cultural processes such as status, identity, sexuality, and gender.

To ground these problematics we discuss some concerns related to social constructionism, the dominant paradigm for much of the contemporary work on sexuality. Then we discuss certain concepts that have been used to encode sexual and gender practices. Some of these concepts, such as "homosexual," "lesbian," and "queer" have a wider currency in the West and in urban centers worldwide. Others, such as "gender reversal" and "third sex/gender," have of late been used to discuss primarily "non-Western" experiences or those belonging to socially marginalized groups or specific historical situations.

Social Construction and Women's Same-Sex Relations

For over twenty years social construction theory has been the dominant paradigm both in feminist anthropology and in gay/lesbian studies. Developed to redress perceived flaws in essentialism, especially biological determinism and a moralizing discourse on the "normality" of heterosexuality and male domination, constructionism set out to assess the impact of the social upon such domains as sexual patterns and desires. With the work of a number of early feminists and gay scholars, the pendulum swung away from essentializing discourses to those exposing the dominance of the social.[5] Some scholars feared the other extreme of cultural determinism and the loss of the body. Here we chart the terrain that these debates cover and discuss some questions arising out of the material presented in this anthology.

Beginning with Mead, anthropologists have been baffled by the enormous variations in gender practices. Theories that focus on the social relations of gender are mainly embraced by English and American theorists, while French feminists, such as Irigaray and Cixous, prefer theories that stress sexual difference (see Braidotti 1991a; Marks and De Courtivron 1981). The French feminist Simone de Beauvoir (1947) is generally seen as the precursor of gender theories in the present wave of feminism in the West although she herself did not use the concept. She formulated a critique of biological determinism, pointing out the distinction between "natural" sex and "cultural" sex roles (gender) that became the basis for later sex/gender theories.[6] The famous adage that "woman is not born but made" is based on her work.

Starting in the 1970s in the U.S., one of the developing feminist perspectives (which coalesced under the term "radical feminist" and gained notoriety in the sex wars) articulated the position that sexuality was defined by patriarchal institutions and as such was oppressive to women. This proved to be a powerful, albeit limiting, theory of the social construction of sexuality. According to this perspective, women's sexuality was not the natural product of biologically given drives but the result of a long period of male dominance in which men, who had greater power over women, defined and controlled women's sexuality.[7] The scholars advocating that theory argued that in patriarchal societies sexuality is a tool used by men to dominate and oppress women through their sexual objectification (Ferguson 1984). Feminists disagreed on whether this long period of patriarchy was a product of history or a transhistorical phenomenon, but they generally agreed that women's sexuality had long been defined by men (Lerner 1986). The term "patriarchy" itself was used to identify all societies that were thought to be male dominated, and in some views the term seemed to encompass all of world history, as in the feminist materialist perspective of Delphy (1984). The project of these scholars became one of erasing men's sexual inscriptions from women's bodies and psyches and eradicating men's sexual control over women. Feminists such as Cixous denounced patriarchy as the practice of which phallologocentrism[8] was the theory. The feminist answer was a radical break with the logic of exclusion and domination that equated rationality with masculinity.

In one of the early and formative anthropological works in the study of sexuality, Rubin (1975) suggested that women's oppression arises in systems of kinship in which women are exchanged in marriage. Drawing on Marx, Freud, and Lévi-Strauss, she argued that this system of exchange gave men rights in women that women did not have in themselves, ensuring heterosexual unions by creating an obligatory heterosexuality. Arguing against the assertion of Lévi-Strauss that the principle of exchange (originating in the incest taboo) constitutes the origin of culture, Rubin locates women's oppression in culture and history. Many writers, however, took Rubin's argument as explanation of the origins of a universal and transhistorical repression of women's sexuality by men and men's institutions, overlooking the historical dimension of her thesis.

As feminists continued to develop the social construction argument, they refined the important insight that the forms of sexuality are ideologically produced. Some insisted that this ideological production was controlled by men. Janeway argued that the polar split in Western sexuality between woman as Eve and woman as Mary was not a product of female being but of "masculine emotions at work in a male-dominated society" (1980:575). Women learn this model, she argued, as a means of survival, but it does not come from women. According to the early radical feminists in the U.S., men had appropriated women's sexuality through their laws, customs, and other institutions. "The new feminist analysis" argued that women therefore needed to take control of their sexuality (Shulman 1980). Although veering close to an essentialist view, the insistence by radical feminists on women's ability to take control and redefine their sexuality highlighted the social construction of gender.

Drawing on anthropology and the work of radical feminists, Adrienne Rich (1980) reinforced the idea of the transhistorical nature of women's sexual oppression. She argued provocatively that heterosexuality was a political institution that disempowers women. Using Gough's (1975) analysis of sexual inequality in "archaic states" and capitalist nations, Rich made the challenging assertion that not just inequality but heterosexuality was being enforced by men "in archaic and contemporary cultures" (1980:638). Citing a long list of customs aimed at controlling women's sexuality including arranged and child marriages, bride-price, foot-binding, purdah, the veil, the chastity belt, clitoridectomies, and female infanticide, she highlighted the cultural constraints and sanctions that "historically, have enforced or insured the coupling of women with men" (1980:636). "Whatever its origins," she stated, "the enforcement of heterosexuality for women" was "a means of assuring male right of physical, economical and emotional access" (1980:647). The weight of cases from a wide range of cultures and historical eras provided strong support for her argument that women's history has been the history of compulsory heterosexuality.

By the late 1970s and early 1980s, the radical feminists' notion of patriarchy and compulsory heterosexuality as an unchanging force throughout history was entrenched (Philipson 1984). Their view of sexuality as danger and their attack against pornography was countered by feminists who were called "libertarian" or "pro-sex" (Ferguson 1984; Philipson 1984) and who emphasized the potentially liberating aspects and pleasures of sexuality. Even the "pro-sex" side, however, seemed to uphold the view that society had long been in the business of suppressing sexuality. With their emphasis on sexuality and repression, both perspectives underscored the need to reclaim sexuality from men's hands. Thus, many feminists viewed nonheterosexual forms of sexuality as forms of resistance, achieved at great risk, to compulsory heterosexuality. Rich, for instance, saw lesbianism as the breaking of a taboo, the struggle by some women for an independent, woman-connected existence (1980:635). Because few feminists were aware of the extent and variety of lesbian practices in non-Western cultures, most assumed that it was either absent in many cultures or heavily suppressed.

As gay and lesbian studies started to take shape in the U.S. and Europe, several prominent scholars articulated a social construction theory of gay/lesbian identity. Mary McIntosh was the first to reflect on the historical construction of the "homosexual role" in England, but her 1968 article was generally ignored. Weeks (1981) elaborated the thesis that historically a distinction must be made between homosexual behavior that, he maintained, was universal and a homosexual identity that has only developed since the end of the nineteenth century. He used social construction theory to argue that sexuality can only be understood within its sociohistorical context. This view was a major step forward from sexologists such as Havelock Ellis or Kinsey who were unable to account for the great variation in sexual practices historically and cross-culturally. It was not possible to account for the proliferation of sexual practices and identities in, for example, present-day Thailand or Amsterdam, on the basis of a theory that sees "natural drives" as the foundation upon which social relations are built. If the "natural" unfolded itself so unproblematically, what was the basis for the sexual variation that Krafft-Ebing so meticulously described in his *Psychopathia Sexualis* (1868)?

Ethnographic insights into the plasticity of cultural sexual practices (Malinowski 1929; Mead 1928) as well as feminist critiques of biological determinism helped to discredit early medico-biological essentialism. The domain of sexuality came to be seen as deeply embedded in (patriarchal) structures of regulation and control. These views became more popular in the European and American world after the translation of Foucault's landmark study on the methodology of research on sexuality in 1978.[9] Foucault, who was distinctly unconcerned with feminist theories of patriarchy, writes: "Homosexuality appeared as one of the forms of sexuality when it was transposed from the practice of sodomy onto a kind of interior androgyny, a hermaphroditism of the soul. The sodomite[10] had been a temporary aberration, the homosexual was now a species" (1978:43). Foucault thus posited an epistemological break when, through the development of a complex political technology, certain sexual behaviors came to be seen as constituting one's whole identity. He also made a distinction between sexuality as a strategy of power and the "creation" of the homosexual in a process of "medicalization" (see also Hekma 1987; Weeks 1981). In unraveling the power relations underlying the production of sexuality Foucault argued:

> Sexuality must not be thought of as a kind of natural given which power tries to hold in check, or as an obscure domain which knowledge tries gradually to uncover. It is the name that can be given to a historical construct: not a furtive reality that is difficult to grasp, but a great surface network in which the stimulation of bodies, the intensification of pleasures, the incitement to discourse, the formation of special knowledges, the strengthening of social controls and resistances are linked to one another in accordance with a few major strategies of knowledge and power. (1978:105–106)

Foucault's work received considerable attention both in Europe and the U.S. and as a result became one of the foundational works in gay and lesbian studies.

Although the distinction between sexual acts and the social meanings given to those acts is a critical insight, the actual historical construction of the gay/lesbian identity in nineteenth-century Europe through a process of "medicalization" deserves some critical attention. It implies that women who in different historical and sociocultural constructions engaged in same-sex practices (such as the Chinese sisters, the Carriacou *zami*, the Surinamese *mati*, African female husbands, or self-identified lesbians of Lima, Zimbabwe, Delhi, and Jakarta, see chapter 2) cannot be unproblematically classified as "lesbian." Is it possible to even speak of European and American women engaged in same-sex behavior as "lesbian" before the sexologists wrote their books? Were the "mannish lesbians" of the nineteenth century in Europe and the U.S. the product of an earlier history of female cross-dressing[11] and sapphism (Meer 1991; Newton 1984; Trumbach 1993) or the product of the writings of the sexologists?

Vicinus (1992) has argued that the writings of Havelock Ellis and Krafft-Ebing were descriptions of contemporary, literary, and historical examples and that the only "new" element they added was a different label. Where before these women's acts were condemned as "immoral choices" (especially if they transgressed men's prerogative of penetrating their women lovers), they were now said to have "innate characteristics." These masculine, cross-dressing, women-loving women existed side by side with women involved in "romantic friendships" and "Boston marriages." Faderman (1981) maintains that these were nonsexual relationships that preceded and were transformed by the sexologists writing about lesbianism. Trumbach, however, argues that these romantic friendships "seem to have approached sapphism in some regards" (1993:134). Hansen (1996), who analyzed the erotic "romantic friendship" of two nineteenth-century African-American women, doubts that all these friendships were nonsexual. The social meanings of women's same-sex behavior have changed from the eighteenth to the twentieth centuries, but that is not the same as saying that the identities of the early tribades were not to a large extent influenced by their same-sex practices: a historical change cannot be equated with an epistemological break.[12]

Sex Versus Gender

A continuing question in feminist and gay/lesbian studies is the relationship between sex, sexuality, and gender. Where does the realm of biological sex, with its chromosomes, external morphology, and reproductive organs end and the sociopsychological attributes of gender begin? What is the relationship between sexual behavior and social meaning? What is natural about erotic arousal and affectionate preferences?

For anthropologists these questions have a special edge. Trained as they are in providing descriptions seen through the eyes of their informants, in "speaking of" instead of "speaking for" the people they work with, they cannot avoid validating the naturalizing characterizations and categories given to them by their informants. If someone says "I don't belong to my gender, I am a member of the third sex," does that mean such a category exists? As we discuss below, what are the boundaries between sex and gender?

Gayle Rubin was the first to articulate a nonessentialist relation between biological sex and gender. She defined the concept "sex/gender system" as "the set of arrangements upon which a society transforms biological sexuality into products of human activity and in which these transformed sexual needs are satisfied" (1975:159). Although in a later article (1984) Rubin suggested that sexuality (lust) and gender should be seen as analytically separate, Rubin's early views on the sex/gender system are still widely debated. Nicholson (1995) argues that earlier formulations such as Rubin's present a "coatrack" theory of gender where the body is seen as stable, natural, unchanging; differences have to be accounted for by analyzing what has been hung over it in various sociohistorical contexts. Nicholson argues that our "knowledge about sexual difference cannot be isolated from its discursive context" (1995:39); that is, the body is not the stable category that earlier feminists assumed it was. In her postmodern view we cannot "know" our bodies in some pure form, for every form of knowledge is a product of the discourse in which it is constructed. We can only "see" our bodies through lenses that are always already social. In this view gender refers to the sexually differentiated body, which is discursively constructed. Sexuality is then subsumed under sexual difference.

Wittig and Butler take social construction theory to its extremes, albeit with different emphases. Wittig (1992) argues that women's bodies as well as their minds are the products of "manipulation" and that these "deformed" bodies are then called "natural." In her view only lesbians, as not-women and not-men, are resisting heteropatriarchy's programming.

Butler is not so optimistic about the ability of lesbians to wage a successful guerrilla warfare. She thinks lesbian identity is as unstable as any other gender category, be it women or men. To her all gender categories are a "kind of imitation for which there is no original" (1990:21). Gender, according to Butler, is always performative, although she concedes that "choosing one's gender" is not as straightforward as donning a coat for the day (1993:x). Because she ignores the "materiality of sex," Butler cannot escape the impression that she sees a person's gender identity as almost an artificial and dispensable phenomenon. Although performance theory is interested in unraveling the workings of gender, it cannot explain how people of different races, classes, and cultures and in different historical periods experience their bodies and their sexuality.[13]

For Butler, sex itself, the "materiality of the body," disappears. Although she concedes that there must be "some kind of necessity" that accompanies bodily functions, such as eating, feeling pain or pleasure, bodies "only appear, only endure, only live within the productive constraints of certain highly gendered regulatory schemas." These "gendered schemas" not only produce the "domain of intelligible bodies," but also that of the "unthinkable, abject, unlivable bodies." This latter domain is not intelligible and perhaps, Butler suggests, constructionist feminist theory is unable to venture into that realm. For, Butler argues, "to claim that sex is already gendered, already constructed, is not yet to explain in which way the 'materiality' of sex is forcibly produced" (Butler 1993:xi).

Ironically, several radical feminist theorists now deplore the turn "strong" constructionism has taken. Barry (1996), for instance, argues that by disconnecting physical sex from gender, theory has become divorced from politics. There is no longer any room for attention to issues such as sexual behavior and desire, battering, rape, incest, reproductive violence, or femicide. This perspective is especially clear in the research undertaken by the gender and development school. That school's focus on gender relations has led to a depoliticization of women's issues and made invisible women's sexual oppression (see, for example, Kabeer 1994; Moser 1993; Young 1993). These scholars' reductionist and economistic treatment of gender issues has led to an emphasis on socioeconomic aspects at the expense of research on body politics (Wieringa 1997a). In doing so these theorists have actually reinforced the gap between the South and the North. By ignoring issues of sexuality, they imply these issues are not relevant to the South. Northern women have body politics, Southern women have "gender and development." The case studies presented here refute these arguments: body politics are of great historical and contemporary concern to women worldwide.

Despite problems in locating the material body, the "unfixing" of gender, sexuality, and sexed bodies in feminist studies and social construction theory has important consequences for analyses of women's same-sex relations. Rather than viewing women's sexuality as a product of natural desire, it allows us to ask what social processes produce particular sexual and gender practices. It allows us to attend to the meanings of certain practices rather than assuming a commonality among all practices labeled "homosexual," whether they are between a tomboi and "hir" normative woman partner (see Blackwood this volume) or between two lipstick lesbians. Gender viewed as cultural process allows us to investigate the process through which certain identities (gender, ritual, or occupational) are produced as naturalized representations of bodies and to explore the way individuals create and negotiate those identities. As the case studies in this volume indicate, female-bodied individuals derive their identities from differing and sometimes contradictory gender ideologies (indigenous, national, and transnational) and employ a range of strategies to carve out their lifestyles in sometimes hostile environments, of which cross-dressing, engaging in ritualized behaviors, and performing activities belonging to the opposite gender—whether they can be called transgendered or passing—may be some expressions.

The adoption of an identity, a process that may involve enormous suffering and defiance, always implies the closing off of other options. In this way an identity gets a fixed character that, once adopted, does not change easily, blurring even for the individuals themselves any distinction between possible innate propensities (that, once expressed, are labeled in certain ways), one's sexual behavior, and the social category into which one has been slotted. Further, adopting a "lesbian" identity, and the naturalizing discourse associated with it by many gay and lesbian activists in Europe and America at this time, carries with it the risk of essentializing, an essentializing that is also employed by the heterosexual culture one wants to challenge.

"Deviant" Desires

Social construction theory is a major step forward compared to the essentialism of the early sexologists in that it allows scientists to ask new questions and to explore the link between sexual acts and social systems. In the study of women's same-sex relations the advantages of social constructionism over earlier medico-biological discourses are clear. Theoretically it allows scholars to analyze the relations between sexual acts, identities, and communities and to relate sexual object choice to given sociohistorical settings. Social constructionism is not a unified body of theories (Vance 1989); there are degrees in what can be imagined to be constructed. In its strongest, most radical form its adherents maintain that there is no inherent "sex drive" or "lust." In this view, sexual impulses are created not only within social contexts, but by social forces.

Yet at the same time that social construction theory insists on social explanation, it becomes difficult to analyze sexuality and "deviant" forms of desires as an embodied experience. Some argue that for all its rejection of essentialism, constructionism actually reproduces the sexual dimorphism of nineteenth- and twentieth-century essentialism: the focus on the cultural and the neglect of the material, embodied elements of the cultural reinforce the split between the social and the physical. This bipolar model is further strengthened because of the polarity between "natural" sex and "cultural" gender that many constructionists maintain (see Vance 1989).

There is a wide range of positions among scholars who take a constructionist or an essentialist perspective. In this volume we find Blackwood arguing that sexual desire itself is socially constructed, produced by a number of processes, including local and national gender ideologies. In like manner, both Aarmo and Elliston in this volume suggest that the construction of gender is not tied to sex but that in fact gender may produce sexuality. In contrast, Wieringa argues that social construction theory makes it problematic to analyze forms of rebellious passions. In a comparison of butch-femme cultures in Jakarta and Lima, Wieringa (this volume) discusses the inability of Foucault to deal with sexual desires that radically depart from dominant heterosexual patterns, even if these desires are shaped by social forces such as gender relations. Wieringa maintains that for an understanding of deviant desires and the embodied origins of defiant sexual cultures bodily processes need to be seen as interacting with social processes. The relationship between sexual desire and sociocultural systems is infinitely more complex than can be captured in a bipolar model built on the distinction between "natural" sex and "cultural" gender. She maintains that individuals may be endowed with a varying range of sexual possibilities that, mediated by cultural patterns, may produce particular fantasies, desires, behaviors, and identities.

Despite our differences, we both agree that there is no sexual desire outside of a cultural ontology that mediates between bodies and culture, and there is no culture that is disembodied. Individuals negotiate their identities in this dense maze of imbricating sociohistorical, political, and cultural relations and embodied motivations.

The analysis of transgendered practices is a focal point for debates about embodied genders and "deviant" desires. Cross-cultural analysis demonstrates both that there is a great variety in degrees of bimorphism as well as a certain degree of transhistorical and transcultural likeness, although those behaviors may have different meanings in different cultural and historical settings (Wieringa 1989). Yet many social construction theorists argue that it is precisely with the transgendered category that the separation of biological sex from cultural gender becomes so apparent (Bolin 1994; Cromwell 1997; Shapiro 1991; Stone 1991). If gender attributes were naturally produced by biology (hormones, etc.), then only ambiguous or defective bodies would produce transgendered individuals. But because gender is a cultural product, learned by all individuals, some individuals learn the gender of the other sex. Blackwood (1984) showed that some Native American cross-gender females learned the man's role, living their lives as social men and being treated as such, suggesting that sexed bodies do not determine the gender of bodies. There is no convincing evidence that, for instance, all two-spirits or *banci* are differently wired genetically, although many cultures and many transgendered people assert just such an argument for their gender. Other cultures, such as many Native American cultures, attribute gender to visions or dreams.

Recent work suggests the process is even more complex. Gender involves not just learning an identity; the process of gendering sexed bodies is a constant shifting, reworking, and reauthorizing of one's identity undertaken against or with local, state, and transnational discourses (see Donham 1998; Elliston; Lang this volume). Even with the influence of social construction theory, there is a need for yet greater attention to the way social processes produce sexual and gender meanings and the way embodied social agents interpret and negotiate these meanings as they construct themselves.

Constructionism has made it possible to see the historicity of the body and sexuality. Without returning to an essentialist model of biological determinism, an important direction for sexuality and gender studies to take is to critically rethink the relationship between the body and the social.[14] Patterns of desires are always mediated ("strong" constructionists will say: produced) by the specific sociocultural sites in which they appear, as suggested in this volume, but consideration needs to be given to the embodied nature of social structures. So far biological models have been simplistic, conflating biological, psychological, and social categories of sex, gender, and sexual behavior (Paull 1993). Yet, learning experiences can influence brain physiology and chemistry. Paull argues that biology does play an important role in developing a sexual orientation but that a linear cause-and-effect model is doomed to failure (1993:51) since neither masculinity nor femininity nor sexual orientation nor, we should add, sexual practices are necessarily consistent over the life cycle. Feminist biologists Birke and Vines (1987) have also argued for a reevaluation of the ways in which biology and the sociopolitical environment interact. Models in which the body and the social are seen as processes engaged in interactions seem to offer the most fruitful way of viewing the link between them.

One possible way to think about transgendered expressions of desire would be that they are based on a range of psychobiological "scripts" that can only be "known" in specific sociocultural settings—on the identities formed in these imbricating layers of power relations and these "scripts." But distinguishing between psychobiological scripts and cultural scripts about those bodies is a difficult task. Bodies and desires can be studied only in their cultural expression and in interaction between the psychobiological and the sociohistorical spheres in which both are reshaped. Desires are not essential, ahistoric, natural patterns; rather, "desirability" of specific bodies is constructed, as we can see by a comparison of Rubens's nudes and the sexual imagery Madonna projects or by studying the desire of eighteenth-century European upper-class men for sex with lower-class men (Meer 1994).

Lesbian or Queer?

The implication of social construction theory is that persons who engage in same-sex behaviors outside of the contemporary European and American sociohistorical context do not have a gay or lesbian identity because those identities have a particular meaning that is not shared in other cultures (see Elliston's 1995 critique of the concept of ritualized homosexuality). The case studies presented here give rise to further reflections on this point. The women described by Kendall (Lesotho, this volume) and Wekker (the Surinamese *mati*, this volume) do not see themselves as "lesbians"; they may have sex with each other, but their erotic attachments are not constructed as "lesbian" but as part of a wider framework of women's sexuality. Relations with others, including husbands, boyfriends, and children, are part of their identity as women. In other cases women consciously adopt a "lesbian" identity as a political act of defiance, at times employing a naturalizing terminology (Mogrovejo; Wieringa this volume). Indonesian butches cling tenaciously to their self-styled social identity (in contrast to other groups of women-loving women in Indonesia). Prepatriarchal, pre-Vedic Indian cultures were based on triadic constellations of same-sex erotic relations between women (Thadani 1996 and this volume). Appropriations and meanings become more intertwined as indigenous peoples move between local and urban contexts where Euro-American lesbian and gay categories are known or dominant (Aarmo; Blackwood; Lang this volume).

Other examples point to historical and cultural flexibility in the development of identities, for instance, the various forms in which "butch-femme" relations appear. Apart from the contributions in this anthology, such forms have been documented for Thailand, where a proliferation of identities and sexual preferences has sprung up in recent decades, including the "tom-dee" lesbian relations ("toms" are the butches, "dee" is derived from "la-dy," Jackson 1997; Morris 1994); in Jamaica "man royals" are also described as "sodomites" (Silvera 1992).

How far is it possible, then, to apply the label "lesbian" to the cases described here and in general to transgendered females and women engaged in same-sex erotic or deeply emotional relations? Making "lesbian" a global category is problematic because it imposes the Eurocentric term "lesbian," a term usually used to refer to a fixed sexual identity, on practices and relationships that may have very different meanings and expectations in other cultures. As Ferguson argued, women cannot be said to be "lesbian" if such cultural categories are not present (1981:166). In contrast, Blackwood (1986a) used this term widely, referring to Chinese "sisters" and to women engaged in "mummy-baby" relations as lesbians. Cavin (1985), writing around the same time about "lesbian origins," does so likewise, applying the term to ancient and African Amazons to African woman-marriages to present-day androgynous urban lesbians. Is this generalizing usage still appropriate?

When applied cross-culturally, the term "lesbian" (and the term "homosexual") invokes an essential linkage among practices whose connections may be tenuous at best. What is assumed by including erotic dances, initiation practices, Chinese sisters, and transgendered men under the umbrella of lesbianism? In the 1970s and 1980s European and American lesbians and transgendered men were proudly reclaimed as "women" who resisted patriarchy (Katz 1976; Rich 1980; San Francisco Lesbian and Gay History Project 1989). Butches were made over into "real" women, not imitation men, while transgendered men were said to be "women" who passed. This categorization assumed that having a female body created a natural link, which was defined as "woman."

Feminist theorists who have been central in efforts to deconstruct the category "woman" point to the diversity of gender representations of women, arguing for multiplicity and difference, not homogeneity. Even within one culture, women are represented and represent themselves in many forms. In white America Eve and Mary represent two ideal and contrasting types (Janeway 1980); the mammie, matriarch, and jezebel represent black women in America (Collins 1991). From this perspective the notion of one "gender" with similar characteristics falls apart. Lesbians have historically been repre-sented by two "genders" (butch and femme), but those categories fall far short of encompassing all possibilities (see Weston 1996). Many female-to-male (FTM) transgendered activists refuse both labels, woman and lesbian, asserting the depth of their identity as men and defining their sexual prac-tices accordingly (heterosexual or gay male). Some, refusing surgery, have also refused all bipolar gender and sexual identities (Bornstein 1994; Bul-lough, Bullough, and Elias 1997). Transgendered females in some cultures identify themselves not as women but as the men they are (Blackwood this volume). Can the term "lesbian" contain the transgendered man, or the tomboi, because they are female, despite their rejection of the categories "woman" or "lesbian"? In some locales, such as San Salvador, two male trans-vestites who live together are called "lesbians."[15] How stable is the category "lesbian" even in relation to a person's morphology? Following Butler's (1991) line of reasoning, how do we know whether such divergent personal-ities as for instance President Mugabe, notorious for his homophobia (see below), and a present-day lipstick lesbian hold remotely similar ideas when using the word "lesbian"?

Does the category "queer" resolve the problems associated with a term as culturally and historically specific as "lesbian"? Butler's poststructuralist cri-tique of the major regulatory symbolic structures that support gender hier-archies and compulsory heterosexuality (1990, 1993) has become the theo-retical basis of theories and political practices of "queer" performativity. As Butler notes, the term "queer" was reappropriated by a part of the lesbian/gay community in the U.S. in the late 1980s. Formerly it was used as "the mundane interpellation of pathologized sexuality," as a regulatory practice to stigmatize lesbians and gay men. It was reappropriated in an effort to rewrite history and to lay claim to the power to name oneself and determine the conditions under which that name is used. As such, the term is used as "a point of departure for a site of historical reflections and futural imaginings" (Butler 1993:228).

It is doubtful, however, whether "queering" lesbian and gay identity in the West has much relevance for the historical and present-day cultures dis-cussed in this anthology. Many of the identities and practices described in-volve not so much derision or disgust at women's same-sex relations, but ac-ceptance and incorporation into a specific social fabric. Some of the case studies presented here are not about a self-conscious postmodern parody on either an essentialized image of gender or the cultural symbols pertaining to those roles. In many cases the price for social acceptance is conformity to particular cultural symbols and practices, not a behavior imitating or criticizing existing gender categories (although see Blackwood; Murray this volume). Further, the term "queer" does not allow for a recognition of gender hierarchies and women's oppression. A term lumping together lesbians and gays denies that lesbians are differently located within their societies. Vicinus (1996), following Weston and Martin, argues that even in the West the category "queer" is not sensitive to class and race differences.

Consequently, despite the problems associated with the use of particular Western-identified terms, we think it is critical at this point in lesbian studies to refuse the ungendered category, whether "queer" or "homosexual," while at the same time refusing reductive definitions or artificial boundaries for lesbian studies. Within the U.S. there is a movement by some lesbian scholars to maintain the visibility of the term. As Vicinus notes, " There may be no core, no fixed definition, but lesbian subjects exist" (1996:1). The term also remains current in Zimmerman and McNaron's *New Lesbian Studies* (1996) as well as in the *Encyclopedia of Homosexuality: Lesbian Histories and Identities* (Zimmerman forthcoming). Zimmerman and McNaron pointedly continue to use the term "lesbian studies" because, despite the diversity of identities and perspectives that are included in their anthology, they argue that "it remains a meaningful political marker" (1996:xv) that keeps its subject from becoming invisible. In the globally oriented *Encyclopedia*, the use of the term "lesbian" is a political move to maintain visibility and independence as well as a refusal to limit the boundaries of the topic.

As long as gender, race, and sexual practice are used to mark people, we cannot ignore the consequences or simply wish away the categories because they are constructs. Despite the problems of misrecognition and ethnocentrism that use of the term "lesbian" occasions, this term needs to remain visible for Western and non-Western audiences alike. Studies of "lesbians" have for too long been submerged in studies of homosexuality in the West. "Lesbian" remains the sole signifier that distinguishes female/women's same-sex eroticism from men's. "Lesbian" carries political meaning because it demands recognition for women's differences. Thadani in this volume self-consciously uses the word "lesbian" as a political weapon in her struggle for the recognition of the inviolable human rights of women-loving-women. In Zimbabwe and Mexico too the term "lesbian" is widely used, as Aarmo and Mogrovejo point out.

Although it falls far short of expressing the diversities of female gender and sexual identities (as will any single category), we claim the term "lesbian" even as we problematize it. It stands both as a signifier of women's difference and as a term recognized globally (and adopted by many activists while rejected by many government officials) for women's same-sex eroticism. While adopting it as a general term, we argue that it cannot stand in for transgendered females or for women who do not identify as lesbians. Consequently, we use the term "female same-sex relations" as the more inclusive term or use local terms where appropriate. Wekker (this volume), for instance, uses the term *mati* that Creole women call themselves. In his work on gays in Indonesia Oetomo leaves untranslated the Indonesian word *banci* in order to avoid distorting its meaning (1996:259). Native American activists and scholars insist on using the term "two-spirit," which became popular in annual gatherings of two-spirit people, and they also use the particular terms of each culture for a two-spirit person (Jacobs, Thomas, and Lang 1997; Lang this volume)[16].

Third Sex/Gender?

Another possible formulation for understanding the relation between sexed bodies and gender is Herdt's (1993) "third sex/gender" category. He posits this category as a way to produce a more flexible and coherent analysis of the relations between nature and culture, between sex and gender, and between male and female. Herdt argues that this category disrupts the dominant paradigm of dimorphism in gender studies: it opens the discussion on flexibility in gender relations and helps to break analytically and conceptually the rigid boundaries between sex and gender, male and female, and homosexual and heterosexual.

The renewed debate on a "third sex/gender" is interesting, for in the late nineteenth century this was one of the first issues the sexologists occupied themselves with. The German jurist Ulrichs proclaimed in 1864 the existence of a third sex consisting of those men who had a female soul in their bodies (Meer 1994). His theory became the basis for the congenital origin of "Uranism," as he called male homosexuality, and for the shift from the consideration of sodomy as an "unmentionable vice" to homosexuality as a form of "moral insanity" (Foucault 1978; Hekma 1987; Weeks 1981). Interestingly, at the same time this usage points to the fact that theories of "third sex/gender" are constructed on male bodies.

What does Herdt mean when he talks of "third sex/gender"? Herdt refuses to be trapped in a categorization of either sex and gender and therefore speaks consistently of "third sex and/or third gender." As Herdt argues, the category of "third sex/gender" is more than a matter of erotic arousal and more than the commitment to the social function of gendered roles or sexual hierarchies, although these may be included (1993:79). Herdt's conceptualization of the category "third sex/gender" is sufficiently vague and all-encompassing to include a number of widely varying social customs, but it is not quite clear on what criteria each case is included. Would cases such as the *mustergil* in southern Iraq (Westphal-Hellbusch 1997) or the female husbands in African woman-marriages fit the category? Herdt may be correct that a more fluid system of sexual/social categorization is needed to capture and analyze the diversity of human experiences, but there are several problems with his "third sex/gender" model. Herdt's analysis does not take into account the different ways in which persons with a female or with a male body are classified in this world. This conceptual blurring of male and female makes it impossible to theorize the different experiences persons with a genitally female or male body have in relation to a "third sex/gender" category.

The limitations of this category become apparent when we compare experiences of male and female transgendered individuals. If the "third sex/gender" category is useful, it should be possible to apply it to both, persons with a male body and those with a female body. In present-day Indonesia male-bodied *banci* (or *waria*) are to be found in the modern cities of Java, such as Surabaya and Jakarta. They see themselves very clearly as belonging to a separate gender, which is neither male nor female (Oetomo 1996). Can cross-dressing, transgendered females in Indonesia who have sex with women be put in the same category? Oetomo, a major source on *banci*, is ambivalent on this point. On the one hand, he writes that the term *banci* is used for cross-dressing girls, who are also called tomboi (1996:261). On the other hand, a few pages later he contradicts this, when he writes that though there are gender-nonconforming or transsexual lesbians "as a rule they do not consider themselves *banci* nor are they considered such by *banci* or gay men" (1996:265).

According to Wieringa (1997b), Jakartan butches have many characteristics in common with Indonesian *waria*. Born with a female body, they decide early on in life that the feminine gender does not fit them. As do the *waria*, they believe being transgendered is caused by "natural" factors: they employ a medical, naturalized discourse about themselves, asserting that they are born like this. They see themselves as neither women nor men. They are clearly perceived as transgendered persons and take the masculine role in lovemaking; they are in appearance, behavior, and dress more conforming to the male than to the female gender. However much the butches conform to men's gender behavior, many of them do not define themselves as men; their relation to their bodies is rather ambiguous. At times they define themselves as a third sex, which is nonfemale, at other times they see themselves as women. In contrast, tombois and other transgendered females speak of being men and wanting to be seen as men (Blackwood this volume); they do not situate themselves as third sex/gender.

The differences between *waria* and butches point out other problems. These differences are perceived by both the *waria* and by the butches themselves. Although both at times refer to themselves as belonging to a "third sex/gender," they do not see themselves as belonging to the same "third sex/gender" category. Unlike in the *waria*, the sexual orientation of the butches is always toward members of the same sex. Their primary motivation is sexual: they want to make love to feminine women and are not particularly happy about the way their female bodies somehow make that difficult. Butches seem to have a harder time than the *waria* have. The butches are socially less visible, and their transgression of accepted gender borders is less accepted. As a result they face severe harassment and are socially and economically marginalized (apart from the few who are lovers of successful female artists).[17]

What does the above mean for the applicability of the category "third sex/gender"? For cases of hermaphroditism (Herdt mentions cases in New Guinea and the Dominican Republic) it certainly does seem to be an important category. But these cases are rare, and the concept used to discuss them, hermaphroditism, seems adequate. The usefulness of the concept "third sex/gender" seems to lie more in its destabilizing of the dominant bipolar model of gender than in its analytical applicability. We can point to a multiplicity of genders that are not represented in the model, for instance, the femme partners of butches. These women do not see themselves as heterosexual, as partners of the *banci* may. Further, an undifferentiated "third sex/gender" category does not take into account the particular system of women's subordination in the culture concerned. In that sense this theory may depoliticize and ultimately deny or even legitimate the oppression persons with a female body face. Thus we feel the concept is too analytically unstable and too insensitive to gender subordination to be applicable to women's erotic friendships or transgendered females.

Rather than creating more categories, we return to the discussion of "woman" and "gender" and the relevance of these concepts to understanding sexuality and gender. As scholars have continued to deconstruct the category "woman," and even "women," invoking the differences among women, the essentiality of gender or "woman" as a core metaphor begins to slip away. The cases presented in this anthology destabilize the idea that lesbians, transgendered females, and women can all be subsumed under one category "woman." The proliferation of lesbian and transgender identities suggests that neither gender nor sexuality are unifying markers cross-culturally. Is there then any connection among female bodies that produces shared meaning when some of these bodies may have never produced milk, never accepted a penis, never borne offspring? If the gender category "woman" is unstable, is there a reason to distinguish between female and male bodies theoretically?

It may be fruitful to consider the cultural ontology of sex and gender and the location of the female body in particular social and historical contexts. We need to be able to capture the specific experiences that gender transgression brings for persons with an originally female or male body. Theory cannot ignore the burden of invisibility and enforced silence transgendered females face, nor the way individuals with female bodies are strongly socialized into conformity to prescribed gender roles. Why is it that male-bodied individuals transgress gender boundaries more freely than female-bodied individuals, or take the label "third sex" as the Indonesian *banci* do, rather than calling themselves "women"? Cultural ideologies of gender have much to tell us about these differences. Recently, Rubin's sex/gender system has been reinvoked in order to emphasize the ideological connection between systems of bodies (sex) and systems of gender (Morris 1994). Many societies refuse the split between sexed bodies and social gender (see, for instance Blackwood, this volume). Thadani (this volume) describes patriarchal India's gender ideology as an inseparable configuration of male/penis/masculinity and female/reproduction/femininity. In such cases female bodies have cultural meaning and significance as potential reproducers that makes the transgressive female extremely threatening and seriously marginalized. Consequently, the female body retains its ideological significance in the negotiation and transgression of gender categories. We argue that the female body is the source of identity among all these different categories of sexuality and gender, whether lesbian, transgender, femme, or butch. Female bodies thus constitute the unifying concept for the work in this volume and for our conceptualization of lesbian studies.

Lesbian Rights are Human Rights

In many places around the world women engaged in same-sex erotic relations, whatever their material reality or social identity, face repression. Issues of sexuality and sexual identity cannot be separated from the oppressive sociocultural contexts in which they are lived. Several chapters in this volume discuss issues related to homophobia and women organizing against it. Particularly those women who are asserting a lesbian identity are beginning to demand international attention. In September 1995 Palesa Beverley Ditsie from Soweto, South Africa, made a powerful statement during the United Nations Fourth World Conference on Women. Some excerpts follow:

> The Universal Declaration of Human Rights recognizes the "inherent dignity and . . . the equal and inalienable rights of all members of the human family," and guarantees the protection of the fundamental rights and freedoms of all people "without distinction of any kind, such as race, color, sex, language . . . or other status" (art. 2). Yet every day, in countries around the world, lesbians suffer violence, harassment and discrimination because of their sexual orientation. . . . No woman can determine the direction of her own life without the ability to determine her sexuality. . . . Anyone who is truly committed to women's human rights must recognize that every woman has the right to determine her sexuality free of discrimination and oppression.

This was the first time a lesbian spoke openly about her sexual orientation at a UN conference. At the Huairou NGO Forum, which was organized parallel to the official conference, the Lesbian Tent attracted a large audience, which included Chinese security personnel, who snatched away all propaganda material in Chinese and tried to film and tape what was going on there. Hundreds of women participated in a demonstration demanding women's sexual rights. Yet in spite of the wide publicity given to the issue of women's sexual rights, an alliance of conservative forces, led by the Holy See and Iran, succeeded in removing a clause guaranteeing women's rights to decide on their sexual orientation from the draft text of the platform for action.[18]

A recent report by Amnesty International (1997) documents human rights violations based on sexual orientation. Reinfelder (1996) and Rosenbloom (1996) have also collected documents on the abuses experienced by women engaged in same-sex relations. Women who engage in same-sex behaviors face staggering oppression; some have been murdered, raped, forced into heterosexual marriages, or sent to psychiatric institutions. Some have committed suicide, been denied custody of their children, and the right to adopt children. They have been denied access to their lovers because of discriminatory clauses in laws regulating immigration or asylum. They are denied access to the pensions or inheritances of their deceased lovers, and cannot possess land or houses. In Iran women caught making love to each other for the fourth time can be sentenced to death. In order to avoid social stigmatization, imprisonment, or loss of jobs, lesbians have encapsulated themselves behind a wall of silence (see also Gayatri 1997). Only a few countries have recognized the right to asylum for lesbians on account of the violation of their human rights (Amnesty International 1997:49–53; Wieringa 1997c).

One of the most pernicious accusations against homosexual people in "non-Western" contexts is that they have imported their sexual orientation from the "perverse, decadent" West. These allegations are made by leaders who object to the universal application of human rights in general. In Asia the (ex) presidents of Malaysia, Singapore, and Indonesia maintain that their countries are characterized by "Asian values," in which the patriarchal (heterosexual) family and state have priority over the individual rights of human beings.[19] In China homosexuality is denounced as offending "socialist morality."

As discussed above, the concept "lesbian" may be of Western origin, especially in the context of women affirming their identity as "being lesbian" (Faderman 1992; Weeks 1985). However, Asian women have found ways to form relationships with each other, such as the Chinese antimarriage sisterhoods and women's erotic bonding in pre-Vedic India (Thadani this volume). Present-day lesbians in Thailand (Jackson 1997), the Philippines, Malaysia, Singapore, and Indonesia (Blackwood; Wieringa this volume) do not see any contradiction in combining their sexual choices and their national identity, apart from the oppression they face.

In Africa President Mugabe of Zimbabwe has declared that homosexuality is "un-African" (Aarmo this volume). Mugabe was supported by his colleagues Moi in Kenya and Nujoma in Namibia,[20] who denounced homosexuality as "immoral" and "un-African." However, reports from Nujoma's own country testify to the existence of women's erotic friendships in precolonial times. Around 1900 the ethnographer Fritsch reported that the Herero, one of the major ethnic groups in Namibia, had a special custom, called *oupanga* or *omapanga*. He gives two meanings: when men engage in an oupanga relation, they have sexual access to each other's wives. Women who are each other's omapanga, however, have sex with each other, which is known and approved of by their elders. These omapanga or oupanga relationships were long-term ties, involving loving care as well as sex among women, and were approved of by society. It is not women's same-sex relationships that are "un-African," but homophobia, as Kendall (this volume) concludes for nearby Lesotho as well. President Mandela from South Africa is a striking exception to the homophobia of his colleagues. The South African constitution specifically condemns discrimination on the basis of sexual orientation.[21]

Women's right to engage in lesbian or same-sex relations can be supported in various ways. In the first place, organizations of lesbians, such as those described by Mogrovejo, and Thadani in this volume, need assistance with legal reforms where necessary,[22] consciousness-raising campaigns, and support to individual women who are victims of hate crimes against lesbians or who are faced with discrimination in their jobs, housing situation, or education. It is important to stress that the initiative for any outside support should always lie with the national groups. Even when activists are sensitive to the local situation, their actions may contradict the interests of those who prefer to maintain the "walls of silence" they have built around themselves and that at least offer some protection. Tolerance for women living together may at times rest on their not being associated with the word "lesbian."

Second, research documenting the variety of women's relations with each other, both historically and in the present time should be supported. Researchers should be very sensitive to distinguish between sexual acts and the meaning given to those acts as well as to the contexts in which these behaviors take place. Third, sexuality should be a topic of public debate, as is any other issue. The AIDS epidemic has demonstrated painfully the results of ignorance and the refusal to discuss sexuality publicly. Homophobia should be treated with the seriousness it merits in general campaigns on sexual reforms, as it is often strongest where sexuality is a taboo topic.[23] It needs to be deconstructed and contextualized, for women who engage in same-sex practices do not face discrimination because of their choices but because of the homophobic reactions to their decisions.

This volume provides not only an insight into the multiple ways in which women have sought and are seeking to express their erotic and sexual attachment to each other, it also makes possible an analysis in which the normalizing model of heterosexuality is exposed. Why are the desires analyzed here seen as "deviant" by many present-day people, even though such desires were socially embedded in society in other times and places? Why do women's sexual practices become suspect when they are endowed with "lesbian" meaning? Why are the cultural identities described in the following case studies under increasing pressure and why are their histories being distorted? Answers to these kinds of questions may lead to the analytical and political destabilizing of compulsory heterosexuality, exposing its construction as a "naturalized" immutability.

NOTES

1. Karsch-Haack mentions that these Amazons, who were not allowed to marry and have children, had hetaerae at their disposal to serve them sexually

(1911:480). See chapter 2 of this volume for a further discussion of the material on the Amazons of Dahomey.

2. A parallel can be drawn to the "romantic friendships" between women that have been documented widely in the Anglo-Saxon world of the nineteenth century and are discussed later.

3. In the old days, Machadi writes, young women went to the meadows to have sex with each other. If women stubbornly refused to marry, they were considered to "possess a male spirit." The spirit demanded to marry another woman, or more, as long as the male-spirited woman could afford to pay the *lobola* (bride-price). This belief has become obsolete, but recently a woman bribed a healer to tell her parents she had a male spirit. In due course the spirit was celebrated, *lobola* was paid, and the couple lived together happily. The female husband has three wives now and four children (Machadi 1996:118–120).

4. See also Tietmeyer (1985) for a discussion of the role of the female husband as father, while another man is the progenitor of the child, and for woman-marriages rich widows contract.

5. For relevant literature arguing and refining the social construction perspective on gender and sexuality, see Plummer (1981), D'Emilio (1983), Ross and Rapp (1981), Padgug (1979), Vance (1989), Blackwood (1986a,b), Caplan (1987), Epstein and Straub (1991), Ortner and Whitehead (1981), Rapp (1975), Foucault (1978), Weeks (1981, 1985), and Laqueur (1990).

6. A weakness with de Beauvoir's theories is that she does not attack patriarchy as such, although she attempts to deconstruct women's "otherness." In her view the way out for women would be to transcend their otherness and become subjects of history and knowledge, just as men have done. De Beauvoir located the site of women's "otherness" in women's bodies, that is in sexuality and motherhood. She did not problematize the body and biology as such, as postmodernist feminists do. "Woman" remained the problem, the deviant one, the one to be explained, while "man" was the norm (see also Braidotti 1991b; Flax 1990).

7. Relevant works include Barry (1979), MacKinnon (1979), Griffin (1978), Dworkin (1974), Brownmiller (1975), Daly (1978), Firestone (1970), Millett (1969), Rubin (1975), and Rich (1980).

8. Phallologocentrism is defined as the view that organizes a material as well as a libidinal economy "where the law is upheld by a phallic symbol that operates by constructing differences and organizing them hierarchically" (Braidotti 1991a:213).

9. The translated title is Introduction to the History of Sexuality but the original French title, La Volonté de Savoir, stresses both the indebtedness of the author to Nietzsche and the epistemological intention of the book.

10. As Trumbach explained, in seventeenth-century Europe all persons were thought capable of desiring both men and women. Such acts became illegal and were defined as sodomy only when the patriarchal code was violated. This code

entailed that penetration should only take place by men who performed this act on women. Sodomy thus took place only when adult men allowed themselves to be penetrated and when women penetrated other women (1993:112–3).

11. Wheelwright (1989), Dekker and van de Pol (1989), and Vicinus (1992) have studied premodern cross-dressing women. The major reasons they noted why women cross-dressed were to go into the military, to earn a living, or to marry and defraud other women.

12. In a similar fashion George Chauncey's (1989) study of early twentieth-century New England sailors suggests that it was not medicalization that created a new identity based on sexual acts. He argues that these men invested their acts with new meaning.

13. For another critique of Butler see also Weston's (1993) analysis of lesbian identities in the 1980s in San Francisco.

14. Some preliminary efforts include Suggs and Miracle (1993) and Abramson and Pinkerton (1995), but they are limited by their inability to incorporate gender, race, and other social categories into their analyses.

15. Don Kulick, personal communication, San Francisco, November 1997. Manual Hernandez corroborated this remark for the case of Honduras: two _culeros_, "passive" homosexuals, having sex together is described as "lesbian sex."

16. They have rejected the term "berdache" used by Western ethnographers (see Lang this volume).

17. This is also the case for neighboring Malaysia. Peletz notes that the male cross-dressing, transgendered _pondan_ are treated with considerable respect in the rural community in which he worked. However, he knows of no female _pondan_ and fears that local attitudes towards _pondan_ "might well be decidedly less accommodating if the majority of _pondan_ and other gender crossers were female" (1996:130). See Tan (this volume) for discussion of a cross-dressing woman in Malaysia.

18. Ditsie's speech is included in the Spring/Summer 1996 issue of Women's Studies Quarterly, which also includes the complete text of the Platform for Action adopted at the Fourth United Nations Conference on Women.

19. Not only movements advocating women's sexual rights are the target of attacks of these leaders. Democratic movements in general are the focus of their displeasure, especially in Singapore and Indonesia. Democracy, however, is not a Western invention either. Southeast Asia is home to some of the most democratic communities in the world, such as the Minangkabau (Kahn 1993; Blackwood 1993; Wieringa 1995).

20. See the reaction to Nujoma's address to the SWAPO Women's Council Congress in Gobabia in Sister Namibia 9 (1): 4–9 (1997). Beverley Ditsie from Feminist Lesbians of Witwatersrand in South Africa stated that in her culture "the traditional leader is a queen, who always had wives. A queen could have 10 or 20 wives. It seems that the more we get educated or 'civilized,' the more the

generations want to close down our herstory. The only explanation I can think of is that this is a fear of female power" (quoted in Reinfelder 1996:3).

21. For the situation of gays and lesbians in South Africa, see Gevisser and Cameron (1995).

22. An infamous example of a recent legal change criminalizing homosexuality is the introduction of law no. 150 in Nicaragua, in which it is stipulated that "anyone who induces, promotes, propagandizes or practices in scandalous form sexual intercourse between persons of the same sex commits the crime of sodomy and shall incur one to three years' imprisonment." The Nicaraguan Supreme Court upheld the law in 1994, arguing that "sodomy is a threat to the holy institution of matrimony and procreation." (from an Amnesty International pamphlet, October 1994).

23. The AIDS epidemic strikes most strongly where women are sexually disempowered and are unable to even demand a condom. See also Vangroenweghe (1997).

REFERENCES

Abramson, Paul and Steven Pinkerton, eds. 1995. *Sexual Nature, Sexual Culture.* Chicago: University of Chicago Press.

Amadiume, Ifi. 1987. *Male Daughters, Female Husbands: Gender and Sex in an African Society.* London: Zed Books.

Amnesty International. 1997. *Breaking the Silence: Human Rights Violations Based on Sexual Orientation.* London: Amnesty International.

Barrett, Michèle. 1991. *The Politics of Truth: From Marx to Foucault.* Cambridge: Polity Press.

Barry, Kathleen. 1979. *Female Sexual Slavery.* Englewood Cliffs, NJ: Prentice-Hall.

———. 1996. "Deconstructing Deconstructionism (or, Whatever Happened to Feminist Studies?)." In Diane Bell and Renate Klein, eds., *Radically Speaking: Feminism Reclaimed*, pp. 188–193. London: Zed Books.

Beauvoir, Simone de. 1953. *The Second Sex.* Paris: Gallimard, 1947. Reprint, New York: Knopf.

Birke, Lynda and Gail Vines. 1987. "Beyond Nature versus Nurture: Process and Biology in the Development of Gender." *Women's Studies International Forum* 10 (6): 555–570.

Blackwood, Evelyn. 1984. "Sexuality and Gender in Certain Native American Tribes: The Case of Cross-gender Females." *Signs: Journal of Women in Culture and Society* 10:27–42.

———. 1986a. "Breaking the Mirror: The Construction of Lesbianism and the Anthropological Discourse on Homosexuality." In Evelyn Blackwood, ed., *The Many Faces of Homosexuality: Anthropological Approaches to Homosexual Behavior*, pp. 1–17. New York: Harrington Park Press.

——, ed. 1986b. *The Many Faces of Homosexuality: Anthropological Approaches to Homosexual Behavior.* New York: Haworth.

——. 1993. "The Politics of Daily Life: Gender, Kinship, and Identity in a Minangkabau Village, West Sumatra, Indonesia." Ph.D. diss., Stanford University.

Bolin, Anne. 1994. "Transcending and Transgendering: Male-to-Female Transsexuals, Dichotomy, and Diversity. In Gilbert Herdt, ed., *Third Sex, Third Gender: Beyond Sexual Dimorphism in Culture and History,* pp. 447–485. New York: Zone Books.

Bornstein, Kate. 1994. *Gender Outlaw: On Men, Women, and the Rest of Us.* New York: Routledge.

Braidotti, Rosi. 1991a. *Patterns of Dissonance: A Study of Women in Contemporary Philosophy.* Cambridge: Polity Press.

——. 1991b. *Theories of Gender.* Utrecht: University of Utrecht Press.

Brownmiller, Susan. 1975. *Against Our Will: Men, Women, and Rape.* New York: Simon and Schuster.

Bullough, Bonnie, Vern Bullough, and John Elias, eds. 1997. *Gender Blending.* Amherst, NY: Prometheus Books.

Butler, Judith. 1990. *Gender Trouble: Feminism and the Subversion of Identity.* New York: Routledge.

——. 1991. "Imitation and Gender Insubordination." In Diana Fuss, ed., *Inside/Out: Lesbian Theories, Gay Theories,* pp. 13–31. New York: Routledge.

——. 1993. *Bodies that Matter: On the Discursive Limits of "Sex."* New York: Routledge.

Caplan, Pat, ed. 1987. *The Cultural Construction of Sexuality.* London: Tavistock.

Carey, Peter and Vincent Houben. 1987. "Spirited Srikandhis and Sly Sumbadras: The Social, Political, and Economic Roles of Women at the Central Javanese Courts in the 18th and Early 19th Centuries." In Elsbeth Locher-Scholten and Anke Niehof, eds., *Indonesian Women in Focus,* pp. 12–43. Dordrecht: Foris.

Cavin, Susan. 1985. *Lesbian Origins.* San Francisco: ISM Press.

Chauncey, George Jr. 1989. "Christian Brotherhood or Sexual Perversion? Homosexual Identities and the Construction of Sexual Boundaries in the World War I Era." In Martin Duberman, Martha Vicinus, and George Chauncey, eds., *Hidden from History: Reclaiming the Gay and Lesbian Past,* pp. 294–317. New York: Meridian.

Collins, Patricia Hill. 1991. *Black Feminist Thought: Knowledge, Consciousness, and the Politics of Empowerment.* New York: Routledge.

Coward, Rosalind. 1983. *Patriarchal Precedents: Sexuality and Social Relations.* London: Routledge & Kegan Paul.

Cromwell, Jason. 1997. "Traditions of Gender Diversity and Sexualities: A Female-to-Male Transgendered Perspective." In Sue-Ellen Jacobs, Wesley Thomas, and Sabine Lang, eds., *Two-Spirit People: Native American Gender Identity, Sexuality, and Spirituality,* pp. 119–142. Urbana: University of Illinois Press.

Daly, Mary. 1978. *Gyn/Ecology: The Metaethics of Radical Feminism*. Boston: Beacon.

Dekker, Rudolf M. and Lotte C. van de Pol. 1989. *The Tradition of Female Transvestism in Early Modern Europe*. London: MacMillan.

Delphy, Christine. 1984. *Close to Home: A Materialist Analysis of Women's Oppression*. Amherst: University of Massachusetts.

D'Emilio, John. 1983. *Sexual Politics, Sexual Communities: The Making of a Homosexual Minority in the United States, 1940–1970*. Chicago: University of Chicago Press.

Donham, Donald L. 1998. "Traveling Identities: The 'Modernization' of Male Sexuality in Soweto." *Cultural Anthropology* 13 (1).

Dworkin, Andrea. 1974. *Woman Hating*. New York: Plume.

Elliston, Deborah. 1995. "Erotic Anthropology: 'Ritualized Homosexuality' in Melanesia and Beyond." *American Ethnologist* 22 (4): 848–867.

Evans-Pritchard, E. E. 1970. "Sexual Inversion among the Azande." *American Anthropologist* 72:1428–1434.

Epstein, Julia and Kristina Straub, eds. 1991. *Body/Guards: The Cultural Politics of Gender Ambiguity*. New York: Routledge.

Faderman, Lilian. 1981. *Surpassing the Love of Men: Romantic Friendship and Love between Women from the Renaissance to the Present*. New York: Morrow.

——. 1992. *Odd Girls and Twilight Lovers: A History of Lesbian Life in Twentieth-Century America*. Hammondsworth: Penguin.

Ferguson, Ann. 1981. "Patriarchy, Sexual Identity, and the Sexual Revolution." *Signs: Journal of Women in Culture and Society* 7 (1): 158–172.

——. 1984. "Sex War: The Debate between Radical and Libertarian Feminists." *Signs: Journal of Women in Culture and Society* 10 (1): 106–112.

Firestone, Shulamith. 1970. *The Dialectic of Sex: The Case for Feminist Revolution*. New York: Morrow.

Flax, Jane. 1990. *Thinking Fragments: Psychoanalysis, Feminism, and Postmodernism in the Contemporary West*. Berkeley: University of California Press.

Foucault, Michel. 1978. *History of Sexuality*. Vol. 1, *An Introduction*. New York: Pantheon.

Fuss, Diana. 1989. *Essentially Speaking: Feminism, Nature, and Difference*. New York: Routledge.

Gay, Judith. 1986. "'Mummies and Babies' and Friends and Lovers in Lesotho." In Evelyn Blackwood, ed., *The Many Faces of Homosexuality: Anthropological Approaches to Homosexual Behavior*, pp. 97–116. New York: Harrington Park Press.

Gayatri, BJD. 1997. *[Come] Outed but Remaining Invisible: A Portrait of Lesbian in Jakarta*. Unpublished ms. Jakarta.

Gevisser, Mark and Edwin Cameron, eds. 1995. *Defiant Desire: Gay and Lesbian Lives in South Africa*. New York: Routledge.

Gough, Kathleen. 1975. "The Origin of the Family." In Rayna R. Reiter, ed., *Toward an Anthropology of Women*, pp. 51–76. New York: Monthly Review Press.

Griffin, Susan. 1978. *Woman and Nature: The Roaring Inside Her*. New York: Harper & Row.

Hansen, Karen V. 1996. "'No Kisses Is Like Youres': An Erotic Friendship between Two African-American Women during the Mid-Nineteenth Century." In Martha Vicinus, ed., *Lesbian Subjects*, pp. 178–209. Bloomington: Indiana University Press.

Haraway, Donna J. 1991. *Simians, Cyborgs, and Women: The Reinvention of Nature*. London: Free Association Books.

Hekma, Gert. 1987. *Homoseksualiteit: Een Medische Reputatie, de Uitdoktering van de Homoseksueel in Negentiende Eeuws Nederland*. Amsterdam: SUA

Herdt, Gilbert. 1993. "Introduction." In Gilbert Herdt, ed., *Third Sex, Third Gender: Beyond Sexual Dimorphism in Culture and History*, pp. 21–85. New York: Zone Books.

Herskovits, Melville J. 1937. "A Note on 'Woman Marriage' in Dahomey." *Africa* 10 (3): 335–341.

Jackson, Peter. 1997. "An Explosion of Thai Identities, 1960–1985." Paper presented at "Beyond Boundaries: Sexuality Across Culture," Amsterdam.

Jacobs, Sue-Ellen, Wesley Thomas, and Sabine Lang, eds.1997. *Two-Spirit People: Native American Gender Identity, Sexuality, and Spirituality*. Urbana: University of Illinois Press.

Janeway, Elizabeth. 1980. "Who is Sylvia? On the Loss of Sexual Paradigms. *Signs: Journal of Women in Culture and Society* 5 (4): 573–589.

Kabeer, Naila. 1994. *Reversed Realities: Gender Hierarchies in Development Thought*. London: Verso.

Kahn, Joel S. 1993. *Constituting the Minangkabau: Peasants, Culture, and Modernity in Colonial Indonesia*. Oxford: Berg.

Karsch-Haack, Ferdinand. 1911. *Das Gleichgeschlechtiche Leben der Naturvölker*. Munich: Reinhardt.

Katz, Jonathan. 1976. *Gay American History: Lesbians and Gay Men in the U.S.A.* New York: Avon.

Krafft-Ebing, R. von. 1868. *Psychopathia Sexualis, mit besonderer Berücksichtigung der Conträren Sexualempfindung*. Stuttgart.

Krige, Eileen Jensen. 1938. "The Place of the Northeast Transvaal Sotho in the Southern Bantu Complex." *Africa* 11 (3): 265–293.

——. 1974. "Woman-Marriage, with Special Reference to the Lovedu: Its Significance for the Definition of Marriage." *Africa* 44:11–36.

Laqueur, Thomas. 1990. *Making Sex: Body and Gender from the Greeks to Freud*. Cambridge: Harvard University Press.

Lerner, Gerda. 1986. *The Creation of Patriarchy*. Oxford: Oxford University Press.

Lorde, Audre. 1978. *The Black Unicorn: Poems*. New York: Norton.

——. 1982. *Zami: A New Spelling of my Name*. Trumansberg: The Crossing Press.

——. 1984. *Sister Outsider: Essays & Speeches*. Trumansberg: The Crossing Press.

Machadi, Tina. 1996. "Sisters of Mercy." In Monika Reinfelder, ed., *Amazon to Zami: Towards a Global Lesbian Feminism*, pp. 118–130. London: Cassell.

MacKinnon, Catherine. 1979. *Sexual Harassment of Working Women: A Case of Sex Discrimination*. New Haven: Yale University Press.

Malinowski, Bronislav. [1929] 1941. *The Sexual Life of Savages in North-Western Melanesia*. New York: Halcyon House.

Marks, Elaine and Isabelle de Courtivron, eds. 1981. *New French Feminisms: An Anthology*. Brighton: Harvester Press.

McIntosh, Mary. 1968. "The Homosexual Role." *Social Problems* 16:182–192.

Mead, Margaret. 1928. *Coming of Age in Samoa*. New York: Morrow.

Meer, Theo van der. 1991. "Tribades on Trial: Female Same-Sex Offenders in Late Eighteenth-Century Amsterdam." *Journal of the History of Sexuality* 1 (3): 424–445.

——. 1994. "Sodomy and the Pursuit of a Third Sex in the Early Modern Period." In Gilbert Herdt, ed., Third Sex, Third Gender: Beyond Sexual Dimorphism in Culture and History, pp. 137–212. New York: Zone Books.

Millett, Kate. 1969. *Sexual Politics*. New York: Ballantine.

Mohanty, Chandra. 1991. "Under Western Eyes: Feminist Scholarship and Colonial Discourses." In Chandra Mohanty, Ann Russo, and Lourdes Torres, eds., *Third World Women and the Politics of Feminism*, pp. 51–81. Bloomington: Indiana University Press.

Morris, Rosalind. 1994. "Three Sexes and Four Sexualities: Redressing the Discourses on Gender and Sexuality in Contemporary Thailand." *Positions: East Asia Cultures Critique* 2 (1): 15–43.

Moser, Caroline. 1993. *Gender Planning and Development: Theory, Practice, and Training*. London: Routledge.

Newton, Esther. 1984. "The Mythic Mannish Lesbian: Radclyffe Hall and the New Woman." *Signs: Journal of Women in Culture and Society* 9 (4): 557–576.

Nicholson, Linda. 1995. "Interpreting Gender." In Linda Nicholson and Steven Seidman, eds., *Social Postmodernism: Beyond Identity Politics*, pp. 39–68. Cambridge: Cambridge University Press.

Obbo, Christine. 1976. "Dominant Male Ideology and Female Options: Three East African Case Studies." *Africa* 46:361–389.

Oboler, Regina Smith. 1980. "Is the Female Husband a Man? Woman/Woman Marriage among the Nandi of Kenya." *Ethnology* 19 (1): 69–88.

O'Brien, Denise. 1977. "Female Husbands in Southern Bantu Societies." In Alice Schlegel, ed., *Sexual Stratification: A Cross-Cultural View*, pp. 109–126. New York: Columbia University Press.

Oetomo, Dédé. 1996. "Gender and Sexual Orientation in Indonesia." In Laurie J.

Sears, ed., *Fantasizing the Feminine in Indonesia*, pp. 259–270. Durham: Duke University Press.

Ortner, Sherry B. and Harriet Whitehead. 1981. *Sexual Meanings: The Cultural Construction of Gender and Sexuality*. Cambridge: Cambridge University Press.

Padgug, Robert A.1979. "Sexual Matters: On Conceptualizing Sexuality in History." *Radical History Review* 20:3–23.

Paull, Jay P. 1993. "Childhood Cross-Gender Behavior and Adult Homosexuality: The Resurgence of Biological Models of Sexuality." *Journal of Homosexuality* 24 (3/4): 41–55.

Peletz, Michael G. 1996. *Reason and Passion: Representations of Gender in a Malay Society*. Berkeley: University of California Press.

Philipson, Ilene. 1984. "The Repression of History and Gender: A Critical Perspective on the Feminist Sexuality Debate." *Signs: Journal of Women in Culture and Society* 10 (1): 113–118.

Plummer, Kenneth. 1981. *The Making of the Modern Homosexual*. Totowa, NJ: Barnes and Noble.

Reinfelder, Monika, ed. 1996. *Amazon to Zami: Towards a Global Lesbian Feminism*. London: Cassell.

Reiter, Rayna R. 1975. *Towards an Anthropology of Women*. New York: Monthly Review Press.

Rich, Adrienne. 1980. "Compulsory Heterosexuality and Lesbian Existence." *Signs: Journal of Women in Culture and Society* 5 (4): 631–660.

Rosenbloom, Rachel, ed. 1996. *Unspoken Rules: Sexual Orientation and Women's Human Rights*. London: Cassell.

Ross, Ellen and Rayna Rapp. 1981. "Sex and Society: A Research Note from Social History and Anthropology." *Comparative Study of Society and History* 23:51–72.

Rubin, Gayle. 1975. "The Traffic in Women: Notes on the Political Economy of Sex." In Rayna Rapp, ed., Towards an *Anthropology of Women*, pp. 157–211. New York: Monthly Review Press.

———. 1984. "Thinking Sex." In Carole Vance, ed., *Pleasure and Danger: Exploring Female Sexuality*, pp. 267–320. New York: Routledge & Kegan Paul.

San Francisco Lesbian and Gay History Project. 1989. "'She Even Chewed Tobacco': A Pictorial Narrative of Passing Women in America." In Martin Duberman, Martha Vicinus, and George Chauncey, Jr., eds., *Hidden from History: Reclaiming the Gay and Lesbian Past*, pp. 183–194. New York: Penguin.

Sankar, Andrea. 1986. "Sisters and Brothers, Lovers and Enemies: Marriage Resistance in Southern Kwangtung." In Evelyn Blackwood, ed., *The Many Faces of Homosexuality: Anthropological Approaches to Homosexual Behavior*, pp. 69–83. New York: Harrington Park Press.

Scott, Joan W. 1989. "Gender: A Useful Category of Historical Analysis." In Elizabeth Weed, ed., *Coming to Terms: Feminism, Theory, Politics*, pp. 81–101. New York: Routledge.

Shapiro, Judith. 1991. "Transsexualism: Reflections on the Persistence of Gender and the Mutability of Sex." In Julia Epstein and Kristina Straub, eds., *Body/Guards: The Cultural Politics of Gender Ambiguity*, pp. 248–279. New York: Routledge.

Shostak, Marjorie. 1983. *Nisa: The Life and Words of a ¡Kung Woman*. New York: Vintage Books.

Shulman, Alix Kates. 1980. "Sex and Power: Sexual Bases of Radical Feminism." *Signs: Journal of Women in Culture and Society* 5 (4): 590–604.

Silvera, Makeda. 1992. "Man Royals and Sodomites: Some Thoughts on the Invisibility of Afro-Caribbean Lesbians." *Feminist Studies* 18 (3): 521–532.

Stone, Sandy. 1991. "The 'Empire' Strikes Back: A Posttranssexual Manifesto." In Julia Epstein and Kristina Straub, eds., *Body/Guards: The Cultural Politics of Gender Ambiguity*, pp. 280–304. New York: Routledge.

Suggs, David and Andrew Miracle, eds. 1993. *Culture and Human Sexuality*. Pacific Grove, CA: Brooks/Cole.

Thadani, Giti. 1996. *Sakhiyani: Lesbian Desire in Ancient and Modern India*. London: Cassell.

Tietmeyer, Elisabeth. 1985. *Frauen Heiraten Frauen: Studien zur Gynaegamie in Afrika*. Höhenschäftlarn: Renner.

Trumbach, Randolph. 1993. "London's Sapphists: From Three Sexes to Four Genders in the Making of Modern Culture." In Gilbert Herdt, ed., *Third Sex, Third Gender: Beyond Sexual Dimorphism in Culture and History*, pp. 111–137. New York: Zone Books.

Vance, Carole S. 1989. "Social Construction Theory: Problems in the History of Sexuality." In Dennis Altman et al., eds., *Homosexuality, Which Homosexuality?*, pp. 13–35. London: GMP.

Vangroenweghe, Daniel. 1997. *AIDS in Afrika*. Berchem: Epo.

Vicinus, Martha. 1992. "They Wonder to Which Sex I Belong: The Historical Roots of the Modern Lesbian Identity." *Feminist Studies* 18 (3): 467–497.

——, ed. 1996. *Lesbian Subjects: A Feminist Studies Reader*. Bloomington: Indiana University Press.

Weeks, Jeffrey. 1981. *Sex, Politics, and Society: The Regulation of Sexuality since 1800*. Harlow: Longman.

——. 1985. *Sexuality and its Discontents: Meanings, Myths, and Modern Sexualities*. London: Routledge.

Weston, Kath. 1993. "Do Clothes Make the Woman? Gender, Performance Theory, and Lesbian Eroticism." *Genders* 17:1–22.

——. 1996. *Render Me, Gender Me: Lesbians Talk Sex, Class, Color, Nation, Studmuffins*. New York: Columbia University Press.

Westphal-Hellbusch, Sigrid. 1997. "Institutionalised Gender-Crossing in Southern Iraq." In Stephen O. Murray and Will Roscoe, eds., *Islamic Homosexualities: Culture, History, and Literature*, pp. 233–244. New York: New York University Press.

Wheelwright, Julie. 1989. *Amazons and Military Maids*. London: Pandora.

Wieringa, Saskia. 1989. "An Anthropological Critique of Constructionism: Berdaches and Butches." In D. Altman et al., eds., *Homosexuality, Which Homosexuality?* pp. 215–230. London: GMP.

———. 1993. "Feminist Anthropology since the Mid-Seventies: From Monocausality to Diversity, A Personal View." In Marlis Krueger, ed., *Was Heisst Hier Eigentlich Feministisch?* pp. 139–151. Bremen: Donat.

———. 1995. "Matrilinearity and Women's Interests: The Minangkabau of Western Sumatra." In Saskia Wieringa, ed., *Subversive Women: Women's Movements in Africa, Asia, Latin America, and the Caribbean*, pp. 241–269. New Delhi and London: Kali for Women/Zed Books.

———. 1997a. "Gender: A Critical Discussion on Theory and Practice." In *Tagungsdokumentation Mit Gender in die Zukunft*. Gelnhausen.

———. 1997b. *"Jakarta's Butches: Transgendered Women or Third Gender?"* Paper presented at "Beyond Boundaries: Sexuality Across Culture." Amsterdam.

———. 1997c. *"Homosexuele Vrouwen in Ontwikkelingslanden: Een Literatuuronderzoek."* Report for Ministry of Foreign Affairs, The Netherlands.

Wittig, Monique. 1992. *The Straight Mind and Other Essays*. New York: Harvester.

Young, Kate. 1993. *Planning Development With Women: Making a World of Difference*. London and Basingstoke: MacMillan.

Zimmerman, Bonnie and Toni McNaron. 1996. *The New Lesbian Studies: Into the Twenty-First Century*. New York: Feminist Press.

Zimmerman, Bonnie. Forthcoming. *Encyclopedia of Homosexuality*. 2d ed. Vol. 1, *Lesbian Histories and Cultures*. New York: Garland Press.

2

Evelyn Blackwood and Saskia E. Wieringa

Sapphic Shadows:
Challenging the Silence in the Study of Sexuality

In this essay we raise a number of methodological issues related to the study of female same-sex relations and transgender practices.[1] These practices have been less studied and documented than male homosexual practices. Although researchers have suggested that the invisibility of emotional and sexual/erotic associations between women is due to a paucity of data on women's same-sex relations, there are several other reasons. Lack of data is due to problems in collection and interpretation as well as to the silence of Western observers and scholars on the topic of female sexuality. In the first part of this essay we discuss the history of the study of lesbian and female same-sex practices and investigate the reasons for its invisibility. Then we provide an overview of the theoretical contributions of lesbian studies to the study of sexuality as a way to situate the work presented in this volume.

Documentation of Female Same-Sex Relations

The study of sexuality in general and female same-sex relations in the non-Western world in particular has been neglected by anthropologists and other social scientists alike. As Vance notes, the study of sexuality is not viewed as a "legitimate area of study," an attitude that "casts doubts not only on the research but on the motives and the character of the researcher" (1991:875). Before the Second World War only a handful of anthropologists gathered material on women's same-sex practices. Although some of the most well-known anthropologists, such as Malinowski, Benedict, and Mead, considered sexuality as a legitimate field of study, they devoted little attention to same-sex relations.[2] The taboo on homosexuality in the West weighed heavily on them.

The rise of structural-functionalism in Great Britain made anthropologists ignore the question of sexuality, while in the United States the culture-and-personality school, founded by Benedict, sustained only a limited interest in the topic of sexuality (Caplan 1987).

In her autobiography published in 1972 Margaret Mead did not mention her female lovers, among whom was Ruth Benedict, whose "remote beauty" (Bateson 1984) enthralled Mead. Mead honored Benedict by writing two biographical books about her, *An Anthropologist at Work: Writings of Ruth Benedict* (1959) and *Ruth Benedict* (1974). In neither of these books is any mention made of their love relationship, although a deep friendship and strong professional cooperation between them is clear. After Mead's death her daughter, Mary Catherine Bateson, felt that in order to understand the work of her mother it was important to uncover this aspect of her life as well. In her biography of Margaret Mead and her father, Gregory Bateson, she maintains that "Margaret continued throughout her life to affirm the possibility of many kinds of love with both men and women, rejecting neither. . . . Through the major parts of her life she sustained an intimate relationship with a man and another with a woman . . . this was both satisfying for her . . . but it also created a kind of isolation . . . an isolation of secrecy" (Bateson 1984:118).

The academic stigma associated with anthropological research on women's same-sex relations was also very strong in the Netherlands until well into the 1980s. At a national conference of feminist anthropologists in 1983, Wieringa's proposal to do fieldwork on women engaged in same-sex relations met with disapproval; such women could not be found in the Third World, she was told; besides the major issue for women in those parts of the world was their economic deprivation. Wieringa published her first short stories on her encounters with lesbians in Jakarta and Lima under a pseudonym (Wieringa 1987, 1990, and this volume). Self-censorship played an important role in this decision. She feared that any publicity about her sexual orientation might jeopardize the research project she was coordinating at the time (Wieringa 1993).

Other anthropologists who observed female same-sex relations decided to publish their findings only after their retirement. Evans-Pritchard published his article on "sexual inversion among the Azande" in 1970, forty years after his fieldwork. Van Lier, who did his fieldwork in Paramaribo, Surinam, in 1947, became interested in the *mati* relations among lower-class Creole women. He stopped his interviews with them after he discovered that this topic was frowned upon. He published his work on the Surinamese *mati* nearly forty years later (Lier 1986), calling them "Tropical Tribades."[3]

The bias against research on sexuality was compounded by difficulties that predominantly European and American men researchers faced in getting access to such information. Part of the reason for the invisibility of lesbian or female same-sex practices, Blackwood observed, was "more likely due to the limitations of the observers than to the conditions of women's lives" (1986:9). Some of these limitations included men's reticence or inability to ask questions of women or get answers about women's practices as well as their ignorance of sexual diversity. For many ethnographers, travelers, and colonial authorities, the possibility of married women engaging in non-heterosexual sex practices was unthinkable (Blackwood 1986). They could imagine it only in places where women were "deprived" of access to men. Where there were plenty of men available as sexual partners, it was assumed, as Firth (1936) did for the Tikopia of Melanesia, that lesbianism did not exist. Many also assumed that homosexuality resulted only from sex-segregated conditions (a theory that persists even today). It was indeed predominantly in all-female harems and polygynous households that researchers noted or assumed lesbianism occurred.

The assumption that women engage in same-sex practices because of "heterosexual deprivation" operates in the accounts of travelers who reported on Middle Eastern harems. Homosexual activity was said to be widespread in "harems of Muslim societies around the world" (Carrier 1980:118), although no outsiders ever had access to these areas of royal palaces. Most reports of lesbianism in harems were greatly exaggerated, a product of the imaginations of European travelers and writers who projected their own sexual fantasies of "the Orient" on the forbidden women of the harem (see Blackwood in press, also Murray and Roscoe 1997). An example of deprivation theory as an explanation of relations between women comes from the analysis of a "lesbian scandal" at the central Javanese court of Surakarta in 1824. In this case the presumption of deprivation was not from the original reporter, Winter, but the two present-day historians, Carey and Houben (1987), who project onto this incident their disbelief that women could actually enjoy same-sex practices unless forced to by the absence of men. Winter (1902) describes the case of a woman who is discovered playing the masculine role sexually with other royal women in the court of Surakarta during the reign of Pakubuwana V. Carey and Houben locate this "series of lesbian relationships" in the context of "frustrated royal concubines" (1987:20). However, the Dutch translator Winter makes no mention of any frustrations among the women. To the contrary he writes, "Ever since he (Pakubuwana V) had discovered when the women would be lying beside each other in various places, that among their indecencies, by way of a piece of wax which had been shaped in the form of the private parts of men they would be amidst each other, he had it made into law that to prevent this harmful practice, as they might never be interested in love with men any more, he would never allow his permanent servants to sleep at night out of his view, so all of them had to lie in front of the door of his room, in a row, six feet from each other" (Winter 1902:39). According to Winter's account, the issue was not the frustrations of the ladies, but the fear of the ruler that the ladies might like the game with their piece of wax too much. Gayatri's comments on *keputren* (1997) corroborate the suggestion that the court women took pleasure in intimate relations with other women.

Inadequate reporting was another reason sexual relations between women remained invisible. In remarking on a public scandal involving homosexual acts between European men and "native" boys in the Dutch East Indies of the 1930s, Kerkhof states that in Bali "the more enterprising boys [sexually] pursued European men on bicycles" (Kerkhof 1992:203). In a footnote to this sentence Kerkhof adds that "such contacts" were also common between women, but then notes that that subject was beyond the framework of his article. What does his comment refer to? Does he really mean to say that in the 1930s Balinese girls were riding around on bicycles, soliciting older European ladies?

The difficulties involved in getting access to information on women's same-sex relations are not just particular to men, however. On Wieringa's recent field trip to Benin, the former Dahomey, both she and native scholars met with considerable resistance to their questions about women. When Wieringa inquired into the custom of woman-marriages (marriage between two women), everyone denied that it had ever existed in Dahomey. Although Herskovits's (1937) work was well known and respected by the historians and lawyers Wieringa spoke with on the topic, they insisted that Herskovits must have erred on this issue because of "language problems." At the end of her trip Wieringa met a woman who had done research on the woman warriors of the king of the Fon. This woman had shown great perseverance in her research in the face of her husband's threats to cut her up with his machete if she pursued such an infamous topic. She carried on anyway and is divorced now with four kids, in a society that looks down on divorced women. When asked, she affirmed that she greatly admired Herskovits's work, although she herself did not know of his essay on woman-marriages. When Wieringa inquired whether she knew anything about this topic, she was silent for a long time. Finally she looked up and said that her own grandmother had had two wives. Unfortunately she had died before her granddaughter had been able to interview her on the topic.

This case suggests another reason for the difficulties in uncovering lesbian relations. Stories such as those about the warrior women of the king of the Fon, who were called the Amazons of Dahomey, remain in people's memories, but the precise circumstances under which those women lived, loved, and worked are not generally known or have been suppressed as a result of both colonial and postcolonial interventions. The Amazon camp is now being reconstructed on the vast terrain where the palaces of the kings of Abomey are located (it is now a UNESCO site). What is known is that the Amazon army was disbanded after the French conquest of Abomey in 1894 (Garcia 1988). The relatives and descendants of the Fon Amazons have kept the warrior dance alive. This dance is still performed by the girls in a missionary school nearby, accompanied by an all-female percussion band. The girls dress in Amazon costume and move in the same impressive, warriorlike way as their forebears did. They display the same mixture of gender elements that frightened the Amazons' adversaries. The Amazons fought in battle and were renowned for their prowess; it was said that no Amazon ever died with a wound in her back. The most attractive of them seduced enemy chiefs for reconnaissance purposes.[4] Karsch-Haack mentions that these Amazons, who were not allowed to marry and have children, had hetaerae (female attendants or courtesans) at their disposal to serve them sexually (1911:480).

There are many other examples of colonial suppression of lesbian sexuality (Lang this volume; Povinelli 1994). In some cases it was not due to colonial practices or anthropological neglect. Female same-sex eroticism was nearly erased or rewritten following conquests by patriarchal cultures and religions of earlier indigenous groups (Gayatri 1997; Thadani this volume). Yet despite the apparent silences in the ethnographic record, documentation on women's same-sex relations existed, mainly observations made by early ethnographers, missionaries, and travelers, who noted down customs they witnessed or were told about. These accounts have to be read with great care. The "colonial gaze" of these observers tended to portray the "natives" they came in contact with as "primitive" and "pagan." Their emphasis on sexual customs served as proof of how "close to nature" these groups were. The exotization of colonized peoples was achieved by the eroticization of their lives.[5] Apart from the biases of early observers, informants may have had their own motives in telling tales of certain sexual customs. Hypersexualizing others was not only done by travelers and missionaries but may also have been a way, for instance, in which informants expressed interethnic tensions.[6]

Travelers' accounts and "scientific" reports were often characterized by serious biases about their subjects. In many cases the authors had little direct access to women. Further, many accounts may have been colored by the misogyny of their authors and that of their men informants and interpreters. Yet they do provide invaluable information about aspects of the social and sexual lives of the people they encountered. Based on these accounts Karsch-Haack wrote his monumental compilation on same-sex love in 1911. A "special section" called "Tribadie bei den Naturvölkern" (Tribadism among primitive peoples) contains a wealth of details on female same-sex practices based on accounts by these earlier travelers and observers. Karsch-Haack gives several examples of cross-dressing or transvestite females. He reports, for instance, that in Java the term *wandu* is used for both transgendered males and females, while in Bali cross-dressed women perform temple services (1911:489, 490). Belo later corroborated that finding, noting that the "crossing of the sex roles" for females is "one of the possibilities afforded by" Balinese culture (1949:58).

Deeper into the Silence

In the post–World War II era, men social scientists who investigated sexual practices in other cultures focused on male homosexuality. Their attention to men, they said, was due to the paucity of data on lesbian practices. According to these scholars, lesbianism was cross-culturally less well developed, less common, and less visible than male homosexuality (Ford and Beach 1951; Gebhard 1971), a belief these scholars underwrote by their very silence on the topic. This belief persisted into the 1970s and 1980s as works on homosexuality continued the emphasis on men and men's sexual practices.

An apparent lack of evidence did not stop these researchers from theorizing about female homosexuality, however. Some simply assumed that lesbianism must be the mirror image of male homosexuality; the theories that applied to men were said to apply to women as well (Blackwood 1986). As Mary McIntosh noted in her formative article, "the assumption always is that we can use the same theories and concepts for female homosexuality and that, for simplicity, we can just talk about men and assume it applies to women" (1981:45). According to Blackwood (1986), men scholars mistakenly conflated male and female homosexuality because they assumed that a structurally analogous sexual practice, i.e., sex with a member of one's own sex, somehow meant the same for both men and women. Consequently, masculinist theories of female homosexuality were limited and often misplaced attempts to understand practices that were inadequately explored and analyzed.[7]

One of the main problems in the study of homosexuality in countries other than the United States and Europe was that it concentrated primarily on evidence of male-male sex practices. In "Homosexuality in History," a history of male homosexuality in the imagined West from ancient Greece to the Victorian era, Karlen (1980) noted that "some Greek literature and art portrayed sexual relations between two women or two men" (1980:79). Despite the existence of Sappho's love poetry and other well-known stories of love between goddesses and mortal women (Dover 1978; Foster 1958), he did not discuss this material further. The possible implications of women's engagement in same-sex practices for an understanding of Greek sexuality and gender were never considered. Karlen suggested that there might be a relationship between women's "status" and the incidence of Greek male homosexuality, a relationship he thought might be correlated to an increasing improvement in women's social status (Karlen 1980). How ancient Greek sexuality would look, however, if attention were paid to portrayals of women's same-sex love in art and literature (particularly Sappho) was not explored.

In an important attempt to theorize homosexuality cross-culturally Carrier (1980) concluded that there were two significant "sociocultural factors" connected with the expression of homosexual behavior: cultural attitudes and proscriptions (acceptance or disapproval of homosexual behavior) and availability of sex partners. Carrier suggested that the absence of the other sex, due to the value of virginity (for women), segregation of men in initiatory camps, men's migration, and polygyny (marriage to more than one woman), all increased homosexual behavior. In this scenario segregation and consequent lack of partners of the other sex was liable to result in homosexual practices for men as well as women.

One of Carrier's contributions to the study of homosexuality was to explain why some cultures accommodate what he called cross-gender behavior (more recently labeled transgender), while others disapprove of it. Although his discussion centered on males rather than females, he asserted that the "same concordance" applied to females.[8] Concerning societies that "disapproved" of cross-gender behavior, Carrier noted that "too little is known" about female homosexuality in these societies to include them in the discussion.

Carrier's conclusion that homosexuality does not always have the same meaning in all cultures stands today as an important insight in lesbian and gay studies. But the lack of attention to female sexuality raises questions about the usefulness of his hypotheses about women. Carrier concluded that "male homosexual behavior generally appears to be more regulated . . . than female homosexual behavior" (1980:118). He suggested that this difference might be due to "the higher status accorded men than women in most societies; in particular, to the defense role that men have historically played in protecting women and children" (1980:103). Carrier's assertion that men's higher status and women's subordinate status was the reason for the greater evidence and visibility of male homosexuality has some bearing in patriarchal societies, but it is less plausible as a general theory. His suggestion that "females [are] less likely than males to engage in homosexual activity" (1980:118) raises the possibility of a biological difference between women and men, but there are no data to support such a conclusion. His final suggestion that perhaps there simply was not enough data to provide an adequate explanation made the most sense given the limited data he was familiar with.

Masculinist work in the 1980s continued the silence on female same-sex practices. Following on earlier researchers' efforts at cataloging variant sex practices, several typologies of homosexuality were propounded (see Adam 1986; Greenberg 1988; Herdt 1988; Murray 1992). The typologies emphasized genital sexual activity between males as the link among all varieties of male sex and gender practices.[9] Most typologies include three types, transgenderal or gender-differentiated relations (partners occupy different genders), transgenerational or age-differentiated relations (partners belong to different generations), and egalitarian relations (partners occupy same status category). Greenberg (1988) adds a class-differentiated type to account for relations between members of different classes, and Herdt (1988) adds a role-specialized category, which includes shamans who have spiritual sanction to engage in homosexual acts. Although these typologies are usually said to apply to both men's and women's sexual practices, in actuality they are based on men's homosexual practices. Data on female sexuality rarely enter into the analysis. The standard phrases that females "were also known to" (engage in whatever is being discussed) or "no examples of females are known" are typical of these writings (see, for example, Herdt 1988).

Greenberg's massive work on the construction of (male) homosexuality includes cases of female homosexuality, but his analysis of these cases is hedged with statements about the lack of information on women. Echoing the words of his predecessors, he claims that "we know far less about lesbianism than about male homosexuality" (1988:19) and that it "is less common and less tolerated" (1988:74). As others before him, the few examples he mentions include erotic acts among women in Greek literature, in harems (lumping all of the Near East and India together), and between Azande cowives. Despite the fact that Greenberg pays little attention to women's same-sex relations, he, too, attempts to find some reason for the difference between men's and women's sexual practices. He concludes that in "kinship-based" societies women tend more often than men to have egalitarian lesbian relations "possibly because women are not socialized to compete for status with other women, or to dominate" (1988:73). This hypothesis is interesting but unsupportable since "age-structured relationships" between women of unequal status do occur in kin-based societies, including woman-marriage in Africa, *madivines* in Carriacou, and mummies and babies in Lesotho. Regarding the societies he labeled "early civilizations," he concludes that lack of independence made lesbian relations less possible (1988:183). Although "lack of independence" as a causal explanation hints at the conclusions drawn by feminists doing research on lesbians, this conclusion is speculative at best due to a lack of evidence presented.

Adam's article on "homosexual relations" makes little excuse for not theorizing about female homosexuality. He claims that his category of "age-structured sexuality" is "predominantly a male form of same-sex bonding" (1986:20), citing examples of youthful homosexuality in bachelorhood and that between older and younger men (Melanesia, Greece, Africa). He too overlooks similar types of relationships among women. Adam does mention the sexual relations of Azande cowives (1986:24), but he does not assign them to a category, noting only that their relationship does not parallel the "warrior homosexuality" of Azande men. Adam mentions the occurrence of sex between female cross-cousins in Australian groups, but he does so in the context of his discussion of age-graded relations, and this example has no bearing on the larger question at hand. Adam's article carries the study of homosexuality more strongly into the cultural domain without, however, providing the same level of analysis for the cases of female same-sex relations he mentions.

Like women in mainstream anthropology texts before the 1970s, female homosexuality is nearly invisible in the anthropology of homosexuality written by men scholars. So complete is the invisibility of female same-sex practices in these works and in gay studies in general, the editors of *Hidden from History* felt confident in asserting that "the data for women are still far too sketchy to allow for even preliminary generalizations" about lesbians in non-Western societies (Duberman et al. 1989:10). There was, however, a substantial number of works available, as we will show in the next section. We now turn to the work on female same-sex practices and transgender relations that developed in the 1980s, work that exploded the myth of invisibility and argued for a feminist analysis of female homosexuality.

Culture and Female Same-Sex Relations

Lesbian feminist work in the 1980s argued for the importance of distinguishing between female and male homosexual practices and experiences. Adrienne Rich was emphatic in her rejection of any correspondences between male and female homosexuality. She argued that "any theory . . . that treats lesbian existence . . . as the mirror image of either heterosexual or male homosexual relations is profoundly weakened thereby, whatever its other contributions" (1980:632). In the introduction to the first anthropological anthology on homosexuality, Blackwood added support to this position. She argued that "because men's and women's roles are structured differently in all cultures, . . . the structure of female homosexuality must be examined as well. A one-sided discourse on homosexuality does not adequately comprehend the complex interplay of factors which shape homosexual behavior, male or female" (1986:6). Further, because sexualities are informed by and embedded in gender hierarchies and gender ideologies that impose different constraints on women and men, sexual roles, behaviors, meanings, and desires are different for women and men. The importance of analytically separating the study of female sexuality from male sexuality is a primary motivation behind this volume. Next to nothing can be gained from collapsing female and male homosexual or transgender practices into one category because they are not simply sexual practices but practices that have meaning only within particular cultural contexts. As we explain more fully later, we argue that the factors shaping sexualities and identities are appropriated and created differently by females and males because of the way sexed bodies are culturally interpreted and defined.

Cultural accounts of female same-sex relations in the 1980s focused on women's experiences and lives in order to understand the relationship of gender and sexuality to homosexual practices. Despite the silences in other texts, information on female same-sex relations has never been as limited as has been suggested. We have already mentioned several reports of female same-sex relations and transgender practices in early ethnographic and colonial reports, particularly Karsch-Haack's (1911) compilation. In this section we flesh out more fully the extent of research and theory on female same-sex practices.

In a survey of primarily English-language anthropological and historical texts on lesbian relations Blackwood (1984a) found evidence of female transgender and same-sex practices that greatly exceeded previous estimates by American researchers.[10] Ford and Beach's (1951) survey of the Human Relations Area Files placed the number of societies with homosexual behavior at seventy-six, with only seventeen accounts of lesbianism. Blackwood (1984a) located reports of female same-sex practices in ninety-five societies. Given the methodological problems cited earlier, neither of these estimates are definitive, but the number of cases in Blackwood's study raises considerable doubt about the "absence" or rarity of lesbianism. Among the early ethnographic reports by English speakers, the most notable (and rarely cited) are an account of Solomon Islander women's erotic same-sex dances celebrating first menstruation and marriage rites of young women (Blackwood 1935), an intriguing note that lesbian relations among adult women in Malekula and the Big Nambas in Melanesia were commonly practiced (Deacon 1934), and reports of erotic ritual practices and cross-cousin affairs among Australian aboriginal women (Kaberry 1939; Roheim 1933). Although many of the reports were brief, they provided provocative hints of nonheterosexual forms of female sexuality.

The most extensive ethnographic reports by British and American scholars on lesbians, same-sex sexuality, and transgendered practices prior to 1980 includes Schaeffer's (1965) biography of a Kutenai "female *berdache*," a Native American female two-spirit of the nineteenth century; Hart's (1968) article on "butch-femme" women, *lakin-on* and their partners, in the Negros Islands of the Philippines; and Evans-Pritchard's (1970) report on "sexual inversion among the Azande," intimate friendships between married women. Evans-Pritchard provides the most explicit description of a sexual relationship between women partners. Bond friendships between women were ritualized through a ceremony called *bagburu*. The following story was told to him by Kisanga, one of his most important informants: After two women had concluded the *bagburu* ceremony, they were vigorously making love. One partner was the junior wife of a husband who had agreed to the ceremony but was not happy with their sexual intercourse. When he heard them, he wanted to intervene, but was stopped by his senior wife who told him not to meddle in "woman's affairs" (1970:1433).

Early feminist work began with Lorde's (1984) note about African woman-marriage (which formed the basis for her poem in the epigraph to the introduction) and with Allen's (1981) study of Native American women's sexualities.[11] Her work was the first to question the academic discourse on

Native American "berdaches" from a feminist and native perspective. She argued strongly against calling Native American women in same-sex relations "berdaches," a pejorative colonial term usually applied to males, and claimed "lesbian" as the appropriate term for all Native American women-loving women. Other work on lesbians included a study of "mummy-baby" relations in South Africa, an institutionalized friendship between older and younger adolescent girls (Gay 1986); work on Chinese sisterhoods (Sankar 1986; Topley 1975); a study of wealthy Muslim women in Mombasa, Kenya, who were were said to have younger women lovers (Shepherd 1987); an article on Cuban lesbians (Arguelles and Rich 1985); and several works on Native American female two-spirits (previously "berdache"), females who are social men (Blackwood 1984b; Grahn 1986; Medicine 1983; Midnight Sun 1988).

The most well-known Asian example of institutionalized same-sex relations among women are the Chinese sisterhoods. In the southern Chinese province of Guangdon in the nineteenth century a movement existed of thousands of women who entered into relations with other women by forming sisterhoods.[12] The following account refers to the most common form of sisterhood. The hairdressing ritual used to sever the women's association with men resembled the one traditionally performed before a heterosexual marriage. They vowed to the goddess Guan Yin never to marry a man. The women concerned were mostly silk workers whose income allowed them economic independence. They formed sisterhoods with such names as "Golden Orchid Association" or "Association for Mutual Admiration." The sisters lived in cooperative houses and helped each other in cases of illness or death. Some houses were vegetarian halls where the eating of meat and heterosexual contacts were forbidden. In these houses women led a religious life, but not as strictly as in a Buddhist nunnery. Sexual relations among the women occurred, just as in the other category, the so-called "spinster halls." These halls were not so strictly religious and vegetarian; however, heterosexual contacts were not allowed either (Honig 1985; Sankar 1986; Smedley 1976; Topley 1975). The sisterhoods were banned as "feudal remnants" after the victory of the Red Army in 1949, and many sisters fled to Malaysia, Singapore, Hong Kong, and Taiwan.

The issue of sexuality and eroticism between women in these sisterhoods has been a matter of controversy for observers describing their relations. Smedley's account (1976) is telling in this respect. The male guide with whom she visited some sisters in the 1930s showed great hostility toward these women who refused to marry, a habit that was caused, he felt, because they earned too much. Smedley herself was more interested in the successful strikes the silk workers had conducted than in their social and erotic bonds. Honig (1985), in describing Shanghai sisterhoods, focuses on their position as workers as well, stressing the need to band together for protection against hoodlums who might rob or rape them. Only Topley (1975) and Sankar (1986) specifically refer to "lesbian practices," which they relate to a distaste for heterosexual relations as well as the religious advantage (heterosexual) celibacy would have. Sankar noted that "larger sisterhoods may have contained several couples or ménage à trois" (1986:78). Wieringa (1987) conducted interviews with sisters living in a Buddhist temple in Singapore. The abbess and the nuns talked freely of their sexual relations and described their choice to enter a "vegetarian life" as a positive decision.

Following feminist anthropology in the 1980s all of these studies underscored the importance of gender ideologies in the construction of women's sexuality. Because women and men are situated differently in all cultures, the factors that may be significant in the construction of male same-sex practices might not pertain to female same-sex practices (Blackwood 1986). It is by now well known that the semen practices of New Guinea have no correlate among women. These practices are explicitly linked to the ritual development of masculinity in young boys. Girls, being viewed as having inherent femininity and reproductive competence, have no such need to be given their femininity ritually (Herdt 1981). Similarly, the oppressive conditions of marriage for women in China, which gave rise to marriage resistance and sisterhoods, had no parallel among Chinese men, who were entitled to control wives and family property. Both cases lack a mirror image of the male or female practice because cultural ideals of gender shape sexual practices. In the New Guinea case a cultural practice rooted in an ideology of gender antagonism and the efficacy of fluids legitimates particular sexual behaviors between men and boys. In China the ideology of male dominance and sexual control of women produced public resistance to oppressive marital and economic conditions.

These studies argued that male-dominated gender ideologies controlled and limited the expression of women's sexuality. Rubin argued that in systems where men have greater control over women than vice versa, "homosexuality in women would be subject to more suppression than in men" (1975:183). This statement was echoed by other lesbian feminists who equated the invisibility of lesbianism with the presence of male-dominated societies (societies where women had "low status"). Following that perspective, Blackwood (1986) suggested that it was precisely within societies stratified by class and gender that evidence of women's same-sex practices is lacking or limited to clandestine relations (in harems) or marginalized groups (the Chinese sisterhoods). Nonheterosexual relations for women were neither publicly tolerated nor legitimated. In contrast, Sankar (1986) argued that the Chinese in Kwangtung province tacitly condoned lesbianism as long as it did not threaten the reproduction of the patrilineage. Her assertion raises the question of whether sisterhoods were the exception in Chinese society since they were the product of a fairly localized economic system (silk production) in which women earned sufficient income to be independent. Evidence from foraging and horticultural groups, Blackwood (1986) argued, suggests that the absence of oppressive gender ideologies correlated with the presence of institutionalized or culturally sanctioned female same-sex practices, such as among the !Kung of south Africa, the indigenous peoples of Australia, and certain native North American groups. Other works in the 1980s suggested a number of other factors that influence the construction and/or presence of particular sexualities and genders, including marriage and kinship norms, gender polarity, control of fertility and sexuality, social stratification, and economics. Most of these explanations were closely tied to a socialist feminist analysis of women's oppression.

The aim of most of the work in the 1980s was to explore the meaning and cultural construction of women's same-sex relationships. Writers sought to go beyond the psychological and biological explanations of earlier decades, arguing instead that women's relationships were embedded in and constituted wider social relations, of kinship (indigenous Australians), of exchange and trade networks (Azande cowives, mummies and babies, Chinese sisterhoods), and of ritual (native North Americans, indigenous Australians). In many cases these relationships coexisted with heterosexual marriage (Blackwood 1986; Gay 1986). Most authors presented rich, local studies of lesbian relations attuned to the nuances of the particular culture but not to larger colonial or postcolonial processes. Based on this evidence, Blackwood (1986) proposed a preliminary typology of women's relations. Contrary to masculinist typologies based on the type of sex partners, Blackwood based her typology on the level of integration of women's relations into larger social processes, distinguishing between relations that pertain only to the immediate social context (informal) and those that are part of a network or social structure extending beyond the relationship (formal) (1986:10). This typology underscored the idea that sexual relations are embedded within social systems and gain their meanings from the social context.

Work in lesbian studies in anthropology in the 1980s brought new material to the analysis of the relationship between gender and sexed bodies.

Shepherd (1987) argued that Mombasa lesbians did not change their gender, concluding that biological sex is a much more important determinant of gender than behavior in the Swahili sex/gender system.[13] Men are men and women are women; engaging in same-sex practices does not change that designation. Other work on transgender practices by female-bodied persons, however, helped to unsettle a model that linked sex with gender. Evidence from studies of two-spirit people suggests that, since a person can inhabit the gender not usually assigned to his or her particular body, gender and sex are separable (Blackwood 1984b; Midnight Sun 1988).

This work also helped to illuminate the social construction of categories that were frequently asserted to be "natural," such as the family, the domestic domain, and sexuality. The diversity in forms of women's sexuality underscored the bias of the Euro-American folk model that claimed only one form of "normal" sexuality. More importantly, the cases of long-term same-sex relations in other cultures, such as that noted by Evans-Pritchard for Azande women, problematized the privileging of heterosexuality as the model and basic grid for family, kinship, and sexuality. Where theories of kinship and family tended to emphasize women's roles as reproducers and mothers, this evidence broadened the view of women's lives to include a range of social relations not defined by domestic caretaking (for example, mummies and babies, Chinese sisterhoods). It even disputed the "naturalness" of male-female domestic coupling and marriage by revealing the fact that female-bodied persons (to use Cromwell's [1997] phrase) created families with women (for example, Native American female two-spirits) and took the father role (woman-marriage in some African societies).

Work in lesbian studies raised questions about the notion of compulsory heterosexuality, which has remained a central tenet in some feminist theories of sexuality. Rich (1980) argued that compulsory heterosexuality was a universal condition for womankind, asserting that all cultures require and, in many cases, force marriage. The debate that took place after publication of her article was not about her idea of compulsory heterosexuality but about her concept of the "lesbian continuum" and lesbianism as an act of resistance. Neither the historicity nor the validity of "compulsory heterosexuality" was adequately challenged. Ferguson criticized Rich for employing a transhistorical discourse but was more concerned that Rich had mistakenly portrayed compulsory heterosexuality as "the key mechanism underlying and perpetuating male dominance" (1981:170). As to Rich's suggestion of the universality of compulsory heterosexuality, Ferguson simply agreed that "lesbian and male-male attractions are indeed suppressed cross-culturally"

(1981:170), leaving in place a blanket of compulsory heterosexuality world-wide. Zita's (1981) analysis was more explicit in suggesting that compulsory heterosexuality is connected with patriarchy rather than with all cultures. Yet, more recently, Vicinus noted that "all societies that I know of have denied, controlled, or muted the public expression of active female sexuality," thus suggesting the general suppression of women's sexuality historically and reinforcing the idea of universal compulsory heterosexuality (1993:434).

Compulsory heterosexuality provided a limited vision of sexuality that was always already oppressive. Taken at its baldest, it assumes that women are forced through the dictates of male-imposed culture to be pawns in a sex and marriage system not of their own making and not for their benefit. Having misunderstood the historical production of compulsory heterosexuality, its proponents implied that women were not agents but passive victims or property in the cultural drama of patriarchy. Although little attention was paid to sexuality in societies outside of Europe and North America, a feminist view of Third World women primarily as victims (see critique by Mohanty 1984) had as subtext the idea that these women were shackled to their marriage beds, the objects of men's marriage and alliance schemes. Compulsory heterosexuality assumed that because women's sexuality was under men's control women were not participating in the active creation or production of culturally legitimated sexual practices. This view effectively denied any pleasure in heterosexual relations and meant that other forms of sexuality could be seen only as resistance to patriarchy.

In response to the feminist theory of compulsory heterosexuality, work on lesbian or same-sex sexualities in other cultures provided solid evidence of women's sexual agency. Blackwood (1986) challenged the notion of "compulsory heterosexuality" by showing that women did engage in legitimate forms of nonheterosexual practice. These practices were not simply resistant or "deviant" expressions of desire (outside the bounds of proper culture), but within the context of women's social lives and relations. Anthropological accounts of adolescent girls' same-sex play, sex practice in girls' initiation schools, same-sex relations between heterosexually married women, and intimate friendships between older and younger women and cowives in a number of cultures were evidence that women engaged in non-compulsory and nonoppressive forms of sexual practices.[14] The fact that women engaged in sex practices without men underscored women's agency in sexuality, showing that women actively created cultural practices and had the ability to construct and rework sexual meanings and desires of their own making.

This evidence exposed the inaccuracy of the concept of compulsory heterosexuality. Heterosexual marriage may be the norm in all societies, and often constitutes the only avenue to adulthood, but sexuality does not equal marriage nor does marriage deny women's creation of or participation in other sexual practices, heterosexual and otherwise. It was not *marriage* or *heterosexuality* that oppressed women or constrained their sexuality. The oppression of women's sexuality was located in particular systems in which masculinity and masculine desire were constructed as more valuable and powerful, while women's sexuality was seen as limited or necessarily confined.

The corollary to the concept of compulsory heterosexuality was the idea that lesbianism, where it existed, constituted a form of resistance to heterosexuality, the "breaking of a taboo" (Rich 1980; see also Clarke 1981). In Rich's romantic and eloquent view of lesbian resistance, she argued that

> women in every culture and throughout history *have* undertaken the task of independent, non-heterosexual, woman-connected existence, to the extent made possible by their context. . . . They have undertaken it even though few women have been in an economic position to resist marriage altogether; and even though attacks against unmarried women have ranged from aspersion and mockery to deliberate gynocide.   (1980:635, italics in original)

Like many others of the time, Rich was unaware of the range of women's sexualities and so was unable to imagine women's same-sex erotic practices except as resistance to compulsory heterosexuality. She was quite right, however, that many societies are characterized by a system of compulsory heterosexuality.

Several scholars in lesbian studies echoed the theme of resistance, arguing that in certain cases "lesbianism" was a resistant act. The Chinese women who joined sisterhoods declared publicly their refusal to be exchanged in marriage, rejecting a life dependent on and obligated to husbands and fathers. Their actions were seen as a rejection of men and heterosexuality in favor of strong friendships and erotic bonds with other women (Sankar 1986). Some scholars interpreted the efforts of passing "women" (females who passed as men) to live with women they loved as rejection of their assigned gender and usurpation of men's privileges (Crompton 1981; Katz 1976; Wheelwright 1989). To Shepherd, lesbian relations for wealthy Mombasa women made sense if understood as "the desire to escape the economic conventions of [heterosexual] marriage" (1987:268). Because these women lived in a patriarchal society, she argued that "being a lesbian brings freedom from the extreme constraint normally placed upon high-ranking women in

Muslim societies" (1987:257). All these studies foregrounded resistance as a way to understand women's same-sex relations.

The concept of resistance had the value of attributing agency to women as well as consciousness of the oppressive conditions under which they lived, but it was a negative agency, a reaction to, not a power for. Other lesbian studies in anthropology showed that not all same-sex relations between women were acts of resistance. For adolescent girls in Lesotho who became mummies and babies to each other, it was part of the romantic drama of growing up and learning the pleasures and responsibilities of relationships. Gay argued that "these relationships point to the normality of adolescent homosexuality" (1986:111). For Azande cowives, who solemnized their emotional and erotic relationships through the *bagburu* ritual, those relationships broadened their social and trade networks (Blackwood 1984a, 1986). For many two-spirit females, their lives as social men were understood as legitimate responses to spiritual visions or dreams (Blackwood 1984b; Medicine 1983). These studies suggested that women construct meaningful same-sex liaisons and forms of nonheterosexual pleasure in societies where women's sexuality is not closely tied to reproduction and inheritance. For some, however, the question remains why certain societies have legitimate female same-sex practices and others do not.

In sum, the anthropological evidence from cross-cultural studies of female transgender and same-sex practices has much to offer in understanding sexuality in general and lesbian relations in particular. The evidence bespeaks the plurality of women's sexual practices as well as the constraints of oppressive gender ideologies. "Lesbianism" is not only resistance, deviance, or a means to overthrow the patriarchy, it is also deeply embedded in the social relations of many cultures, expressed in sexual play as well as in intimate friendships. Research on female same-sex practices in the 1980s helped to pinpoint the meaning of sexuality by highlighting the relationship of gender to sexuality. It also underscored women's agency in the construction of sexual meaning. By highlighting women's, as distinct from men's, practices, this work demanded attention to and analysis of gender systems and female bodies, while making visible for the first time the extent of female same-sex and transgender practices.

The present volume builds on the insights of these earlier studies. It also contributes to a number of hotly contested issues arising across fields that are imbricated in diverse and contradictory ways: lesbian studies, studies of homosexuality, lesbian and gay studies, and queer theory.

NOTES

1. As in the introduction (chapter 1), we use the term "female" in reference to anatomical or physical sex of bodies and the term "woman" in reference to the gendered social characteristics and attributes thought to be associated with female bodies in many cultures. Although it is far from a catchy phrase, we use the term "female same-sex relations" rather than the term "lesbian," which is more familiar to a Western audience, because it is more inclusive of the range of female sexual relations across cultures (see discussion in chapter 1). Female same-sex relations, then, refers to sexual relations between individuals with female bodies and includes, among others, lesbians, butches, femmes, and transgendered females as well as women who have sex with other women but who do not identify as lesbians.

2. Interestingly enough, publication in 1967 of Malinowski's field diaries covering his research among the Trobrianders in the 1920s enabled a more open discussion of sexuality in the field than was hitherto common (Kulick 1995).

3. Murray (1997) noted that well-known anthropologists who wrote about homosexual behavior, such as Devereux and Landes, never got academic jobs. The French philosopher Foucault, one of the major theorists on male homosexuality, tried to hide his homosexuality from the larger public. For some time after his death in 1984, it was not revealed that he had died of AIDS. As he explained to a friend, the reason for being silent about his homosexuality was that "if he had been labeled a 'gay intellectual' he would not have had the audience that was his here and in the United States" (Miller 1994:25).

4. Their adversaries, not used to fighting against women, were confronted with this dance. The women displayed both their masculine fighting power and weapons and their femininity, swaying their hips and baring their breasts. It was precisely this combination of female bodies and power in an all-male game that scared their enemies most. They associated this with frightening spirits, as the founder of the army, King Gezo (1818–1858) had wisely figured out.

5. An infamous example is the tour through Europe of a south African woman, the so-called Hottentot Venus, to demonstrate aspects of her anatomy and genitalia that were deemed different from European women's (Fausto-Sterling 1995). The so-called difference in genitalia was probably the result of a common initiation practice among girls of lengthening their labia. This practice was thought to enhance their feminine beauty (see Karsch-Haack 1911:455–461 and 471–473).

6. See Nina Kammerer (1997) for an account of such a process among the Thai hill tribes.

7. We use the term "masculinist" to identify the theories and perspectives on homosexuality developed by men social scientists, who generally paid little attention to gender issues.

8. Evidence of female cross-gender behavior was available, in particular the

Mohave *hwame* (Devereux 1937) and the Philippines *lakin-on* (Hart 1968), but neither of these cases were cited.

9. The focus on sexuality and desire served to distance their theories from other possible cultural interpretations. See Elliston's (1995) critique of the concept of "ritualized homosexuality."

10. Karsch-Haack (1911) was an important German-language source of cross-cultural studies on lesbian practices, but his work was not consulted by American researchers, who based most of their observations on data from the Human Relations Area Files.

11. We are not including here the substantial writings by lesbians of color in the U.S. because we focus on countries outside of Europe and the U.S. This division is becoming increasingly arbitrary, however. As Grewal and Kaplan (1994) have noted, divisions between indigenous and diasporic, local and global, are rapidly breaking down in a transnational context. Important early works on lesbians of color in the U.S. include Hull et al. (1981), Moraga and Anzaldúa (1981), and Smith (1983).

12. See Topley (1975) and Sankar (1986) for a more detailed description of the wide range of social relations included under the term "sisterhood." These earlier works use the older orthography for Chinese. What is now spelled "Guangdon" was previously "Kwangtung."

13. Porter (1995) questioned Shepherd's assertion of the "utter clarity" of gender in Mombasa, arguing that "some homosexual men and women do transgress gender categories and thus pose a threat to elite male hegemony (:1357)."

14. Sources include Blackwood (1984a), Gay (1986), Gregor (1977), Mead (1928), Roheim (1933), and Shostak (1981).

REFERENCES

Adam, Barry. 1986. "Age, Structure, and Sexuality: Reflections on the Anthropological Evidence on Homosexual Relations." In Evelyn Blackwood, ed., *The Many Faces of Homosexuality: Anthropological Approaches to Homosexual Behavior*, pp. 19–33. New York: Harrington Park Press.

Allen, Paula Gunn. 1981. "Beloved Women: Lesbian in American Indian Cultures." *Conditions* 7:67–87.

Arguelles, Lourdes and B. Ruby Rich. 1985. "Homosexuality, Homophobia, and Revolution: Notes toward an Understanding of the Cuban Lesbian and Gay Male Experience," parts 1 & 2. *Signs: Journal of Women in Culture and Society* 9 (4): 683–699, 11 (1): 120–136.

Bateson, Mary Catherine. 1984. *With a Daughter's Eye: A Memoir of Margaret Mead and Gregory Bateson*. New York: Morrow.

Belo, Jane. 1949. *Bali: Rangda and Barong*. Seattle: University of Washington Press.

Blackwood, Beatrice. 1935. *Both Sides of Buka Passage*. Oxford: Clarendon Press.

Blackwood, Evelyn. 1984a. "Cross-Cultural Dimensions of Lesbian Relations." Master's Thesis, San Francisco State University.

____. 1984b. "Sexuality and Gender in Certain Native American Tribes: The Case of Cross-gender Females." *Signs: Journal of Women in Culture and Society* 10:27–42.

____. 1986. "Breaking the Mirror: The Construction of Lesbianism and the Anthropological Discourse on Homosexuality." In Evelyn Blackwood, ed., *The Many Faces of Homosexuality: Anthropological Approaches to Homosexual Behavior*, pp. 1–17. New York: Harrington Park Press.

____. In press. "Harems." In Bonnie Zimmerman, ed., *The Encyclopedia of Homosexuality*. Vol. 1, 2d ed. *Lesbian Histories and Cultures*. New York: Garland.

Caplan, Pat, ed. 1987. *The Cultural Construction of Sexuality*. London: Tavistock.

Carey, Peter and Vincent Houben. 1987. "Spirited Srikandhis and Sly Sumbadras: The Social, Political and Economic Roles of Women at the Central Javanese Courts in the 18th and Early 19th Centuries." In Elsbeth Locher-Scholten and Anke Niehof, eds., *Indonesian Women in Focus*, pp. 12–43. Dordrecht: Foris.

Carrier, Joseph M. 1980. "Homosexual Behavior in Cross-cultural Perspective." In Judd Marmor, ed., *Homosexual Behavior: A Modern Reappraisal*, pp. 100–122. New York: Basic Books.

Clarke, Cheryl. 1981. "Lesbianism: An Act of Resistance." In Cherríe Moraga and Gloria Anzaldúa, eds., *This Bridge Called my Back: Writings by Radical Women of Color*, pp. 128–137. Watertown, MA: Persephone Press.

Crompton, Louis. 1981. "The Myth of Lesbian Impunity: Capital Laws from 1270 to 1791." *Journal of Homosexuality* 6 (1/2): 11–25.

Cromwell, Jason. 1997. "Traditions of Gender Diversity and Sexualities: A Female-to-Male Transgendered Perspective." In Sue-Ellen Jacobs, Wesley Thomas, and Sabine Lang, eds., *Two-Spirit People: Native American Gender Identity, Sexuality, and Spirituality*, pp. 119–142. Urbana: University of Illinois Press.

Deacon, A. Bernard. 1934. *Malekula: A Vanishing People in the New Hebrides*, ed. Camilla Wedgewood. London: Routledge.

Devereux, George. 1937. "Institutionalized Homosexuality of the Mohave Indians." *Human Biology* 9 (4): 498–527.

Dover, Kenneth James. 1978. *Greek Homosexuality*. Cambridge: Harvard University Press.

Duberman, Martin, Martha Vicinus, and George Chauncey, Jr., eds. 1989. *Hidden from History: Reclaiming the Gay and Lesbian Past*. New York: Penguin.

Elliston, Deborah. 1995. "Erotic Anthropology: 'Ritualized Homosexuality' in Melanesia and Beyond." *American Ethnologist* 22 (4): 848–867.

Evans-Pritchard, E. E. 1970. "Sexual Inversion among the Azande." *American Anthropologist* 72 (6): 1428–1434.

Fausto-Sterling, Anne. 1995. "Gender, Race, and Nation: The Comparative Anatomy of 'Hottentot' Women in Europe, 1815–1817." In Jennifer Terry and

Jacqueline Urla, eds., *Deviant Bodies: Critical Perspectives on Difference in Science and Popular Culture*, pp. 19–48. Bloomington: Indiana University Press.

Ferguson, Ann. 1981. "Patriarchy, Sexual Identity, and the Sexual Revolution." *Signs: Journal of Women in Culture and Society* 7 (1): 158–172.

Firth, Raymond. 1936. *We, the Tikopia*. New York: American Book.

Ford, Clellan S. and Frank Beach. 1951. *Patterns of Sexual Behavior*. New York: Harper.

Foster, Jeannette. 1958. *Sex Variant Women in Literature*. London: Frederick Muller.

Garcia, Luc. 1988. *Le Royaume du Dahome: Face a la Penetration Coloniale (1875–1894)*. Paris: Karthala.

Gay, Judith. 1986. "'Mummies and Babies' and Friends and Lovers in Lesotho." In Evelyn Blackwood, ed., *The Many Faces of Homosexuality: Anthropological Approaches to Homosexual Behavior*, pp. 97–116. New York: Harrington Park Press.

Gayatri, BJD. 1997. *[Come] Outed but Remaining Invisible: A Portrait of Lesbian in Jakarta*. Unpublished manuscript. Jakarta.

Gebhard, Paul. 1971. "Human Sexual Behavior: A Summary Statement." In Donald S. Marshall and Robert C. Suggs, eds., *Human Sexual Behavior: Variations in the Ethnographic Spectrum*, pp. 206–217. New York: Basic Books.

Grahn, Judy. 1986. "Strange Country This: Lesbianism and North American Indian Tribes." *Journal of Homosexuality* 12 (3/4): 43–57.

Greenberg, David F. 1988. *The Construction of Homosexuality*. Chicago: University of Chicago Press.

Gregor, Thomas. 1977. *Mehinaku: The Drama of Daily Life in a Brazilian Indian Village*. Chicago: University of Chicago Press.

Grewal, Inderpal and Caren Kaplan, eds. 1994. *Scattered Hegemonies: Postmodernity and Transnational Feminist Practices*. Minneapolis: University of Minnesota Press.

Hart, Donn V. 1968. "Homosexuality and Transvestism in the Philippines." *Behavior Science Notes* 3:211–248.

Herdt, Gilbert. 1981. *Guardians of the Flute*. New York: McGraw-Hill.

_____. 1988. "Cross-Cultural Forms of Homosexuality and the Concept 'Gay.'" *Psychiatric Annals* 18 (1): 37–39.

Herskovits, Melville J. 1937. "A Note on 'Woman Marriage' in Dahomey." *Africa* 10 (3): 335–341.

Honig, Emily. 1985. "Burning Incense, Pledging Sisterhood: Communities of Women Workers in the Shanghai Cotton Mills, 1919–1949." *Signs: Journal of Women in Culture and Society* 10 (4): 700–714.

Hull, Gloria, Patricia Bell Scott, and Barbara Smith, eds. 1981. *All the Women are White, All the Blacks are Men, But Some of Us are Brave: Black Women's Studies*. New York: Feminist Press.

Kaberry, Phyllis. 1939. *Aboriginal Woman, Sacred and Profane*. London: Routledge.

Kammerer, Nina. 1997. "Hypersexuality: The Power of Sexual Stereotypes in Cross-Cultural Relations." Paper presented at "Beyond Boundaries: Sexuality Across Culture," Amsterdam.

Karlen, Arno. 1980. "Homosexuality in History." In Judd Marmor, ed., *Homosexual Behavior: A Modern Reappraisal*, pp. 75–99. New York: Basic Books.

Karsch-Haack, Ferdinand. 1911. *Das Gleichgeschlechtliche Leben der Naturvölker*. Munich: Reinhardt.

Katz, Jonathan Ned. 1976. *Gay American History: Lesbians and Gay Men in the U.S.A.* New York: Crowell.

Kerkhof, Gosse. 1992. "Het Indiesche Zedenschandaal: een koloniaal incident." In Raymond Feddema, ed., *Wat beweegt de Bamboe? Geschiedenissen uit Zuidoost Azie*, pp. 92–111. Amsterdam: Het Spinhios.

Kulick, Don. 1995. "Introduction." In Don Kulick and Margaret Willson, eds., *Taboo: Sex, Identity, and Erotic Subjectivity in Anthropological Fieldwork*, pp. 1–29. London: Routledge.

Lier, Rudolf van. 1986. *Tropische Tribaden: Een Verhandeling over Homoseksualiteit en Homoseksuele Vrouwen in Suriname*. Dordrecht: Foris.

Lorde, Audre. 1984. "Scratching the Surface: Some Notes on Barriers to Women and Loving." In *Sister/Outsider: Essays and Speeches by Audre Lorde*, pp. 45–52. Freedom, CA: The Crossing Press.

McIntosh, Mary. 1981. "The Homosexual Role Revisited." In Kenneth Plummer, ed., *The Making of the Modern Homosexual*, pp. 30–49. Totowa, NJ: Barnes and Noble.

Mead, Margaret. 1928. *Coming of Age in Samoa*. New York: William Morrow.

_____. 1959. *An Anthropologist at Work: Writings of Ruth Benedict*. Boston: Houghton Mifflin.

_____. 1972. *Blackberry Winter: My Earlier Years*. New York: Touchstone.

_____. 1974. *Ruth Benedict*. New York: Columbia University Press.

Medicine, Beatrice. 1983. "'Warrior Women': Sex Role Alternatives for Plains Indian Women." In Patricia Albers and Beatrice Medicine, eds., *The Hidden Half: Studies of Plains Indian Women*, pp. 267–280. New York: University Press of America.

Midnight Sun. 1988. "Sex/gender Systems in Native North America." In Gay American Indians and Will Roscoe, eds., *Living the Spirit: A Gay American Indian Anthology*, pp. 32–47. New York: St. Martin's Press.

Miller, James. 1994. *The Passion of Michel Foucault*. London: Flamingo.

Mohanty, Chandra. 1984. "Under Western Eyes: Feminist Scholarship and Colonial Discourse." *Boundary* 2/3:333–358.

Moraga, Cherríe and Gloria Anzaldúa, eds. 1981. *This Bridge Called my Back: Writings by Radical Women of Color*. Watertown, MA: Persephone Press.

Murray, Stephen O. 1992. *Oceanic Homosexualities*. New York: Garland.

_____. 1997. "Explaining Away Same-Sex Sexualities When They Obtrude on An-
thropologists' Notice At All." *Anthropology Today* 13 (3): 2–5.

Murray, Stephen O. and Will Roscoe, ed. 1997. *Islamic Homosexualities: Culture,
History, and Literature.* New York and London: New York University Press.

Porter, Mary. 1995. "Talking at the Margins: Kenyan Discourses on Homosexuality." In William Leap, ed., *Beyond the Lavender Lexicon: Authenticity, Imagination, and Appropriation in Lesbian and Gay Languages,* pp. 133–153. Amsterdam: Gordon and Breach.

Povinelli, Elizabeth A. 1994. "Sexual Savages/Sexual Sovereignty: Australian
Colonial Texts and the Postcolonial Politics of Nationalism." *Diacritics* 24
(2–3): 122–150.

Rich, Adrienne. 1980. "Compulsory Heterosexuality and Lesbian Existence."
Signs 5 (4): 631–660.

Roheim, Geza. 1933. "Women and their Life in Central Australia." *Journal of the
Royal Anthropological Institute of Great Britain and Ireland* 63:207–265.

Rubin, Gayle. 1975. "The Traffic in Women: Notes on the ('Political Economy') of
Sex." In Rayna R. Reiter, ed., *Toward an Anthropology of Women,* pp. 157–210.
New York: Monthly Review Press.

Sankar, Andrea. 1986. "Sisters and Brothers, Lovers and Enemies: Marriage Resistance in Southern Kwangtung." In Evelyn Blackwood, ed., *The Many Faces
of Homosexuality: Anthropological Approaches to Homosexual Behavior,* pp.
69–81. New York: Harrington Park Press.

Schaeffer, Claude E. 1965. "The Kutenai Female Berdache: Courier, Guide,
Prophetess, and Warrior." *Ethnohistory* 12 (3): 193–236.

Shepherd, Gill. 1987. "Rank, Gender, and Homosexuality: Mombasa as a Key to
Understanding Sexual Options." In Pat Caplan, ed., *The Cultural Construction
of Sexuality,* pp. 240–270. New York: Tavistock.

Shostak, Marjorie. 1981. *Nisa: the Life and Words of a !Kung Woman.* Cambridge:
Harvard University Press.

Smedley, Agnes. 1976. *Portraits of Chinese Women in Revolution.* Westbury: The
Feminist Press.

Smith, Barbara, ed. 1983. *Home Girls: A Black Feminist Anthology.* New York:
Kitchen Table Women of Color Press.

Topley, Marjorie. 1975. "Marriage Resistance in Rural Kwangtung." In Margery
Wolf and Roxane Witke, eds., *Women in Chinese Society,* pp. 57–88. Stanford:
Stanford University Press.

Vance, Carole S. 1991. "Anthropology Rediscovers Sexuality: A Theoretical Comment." *Social Science and Medicine* 33 (8): 875–885.

Vicinus, Martha. 1993. "They Wonder to Which Sex I Belong: The Historical
Roots of the Modern Lesbian Identity." In Henry Abelove, Michèle Barale,
and David M. Halperin, eds., *The Lesbian and Gay Studies Reader,* pp. 432–
452. New York: Routledge.

Wheelwright, Julie. 1989. *Amazons and Military Maids: Women who Dressed as Men in Pursuit of Life, Liberty, and Happiness*. London: Pandora.

Wieringa, Saskia. 1987. *Uw Toegenegen Dora D*. Amsterdam: Furie.

____. 1990. "Een Omgekeerde Parthenogenese: Antropologie en Vrouwelijke Homoseksualiteit." *Antropologische Verkenningen* 9 (1): 1–10.

____. 1993. "Feminist Anthropology since the Mid-Seventies: From Monocausality to Diversity, A Personal View." In M. Krueger, ed., *Was Heisst Hier Eigentlich Feministisch?* Bremen: Donat.

Winter, J. W. 1902. "Beknopte Beschrijving van het Hof van Soerakarta in 1824." *Bijdragen tot de Taal-, Land-, en Volkenkunde* 54:15–172.

Zita, Jacqueline. 1981. "Historical Amnesia and the Lesbian Continuum." *Signs: Journal of Women in Culture and Society* 7 (1): 172–187.

Indigenous Histories, Colonial Legacies

3

Giti Thadani

The Politics of Identities and Languages: Lesbian Desire in Ancient and Modern India

This essay[1] is an analysis of the historical shifts in "lesbian" nominations[2] within different contexts from Sanskrit scriptures to contemporary Indian sources. I use the word "lesbian" in a generic sense to connote various levels of interfeminine fusion and play that may be situated not only on sexual planes but also on cosmogonic, psychic, erotic, and kinship levels. Although the use of the word "lesbian" may seem somewhat essentialist, I choose to employ this concept because it raises the problematic of lesbian invisibility in non-Western histories. My use of the concept "lesbian" is a political choice meant to foreground erotic and sexual desire between women and to break the isolation that is imposed through compulsory heterosexuality.

In the nineteenth century a new perception of India's past was constructed in the interplay between nationalism and colonialism. A "Hindu" identity came into being based on a glorious "Aryan heritage" that privileged the patriarchal Vedic, brahmanic, and *kshatriya* traditions.[3] The management of women's sexuality was essential to both ideologies. The term "Aryan" was used to imbue "Hindu" civilization with racial superiority and signify a return to heroic warrior manhood (*virya*). Prepatriarchal and Shaktic[4] traditions were simply ignored. Women were seen mainly as the biological progenitors of a heroic male race. They could only move out of their domestic realm to fight against the alien nation provided they remained under male tutelage.[5]

In this essay I analyze texts, mainly in the *Rig Veda*,[6] that illustrate the gynefocal tradition of prepatriarchy prior to 1500 B.C.—a tradition that consisted of feminine genealogies and unconsorted dual and multiple feminine divinities—and its later destruction. Then I investigate the shifts taking place during the Vedic-Puranic period up to the Islamic invasions of the Indian subcontinent between 500 B.C. and A.D. 1200. This period shows a twofold development. On the one hand, women and their sexualities are rigidly circumscribed. On the other hand, there is a tradition of Shaktism and the unconsorted goddess. This latter current goes back to earlier pre-Vedic gynefocal traditions. In the last part of this chapter I briefly refer to the present situation of lesbian invisibility.

Rig Veda

The Vedic hymns are the earliest Hindu scriptures. The most important of these is the Rig Veda, a composite text of ten volumes of hymns, written over several centuries. Some of these hymns are clearly pre-Vedic, whereas other sections outline the beginnings of the patriarchal Vedic ideology. The Rig Veda has generally been interpreted as a homogeneous block, representing various forms of patriarchal cosmology and mythology in which the goddesses are mere consorts, mothers of sons, or sexual objects. However, the Rig Veda is neither a unified block of texts nor a completely authentic record of its epoch, having been written down many centuries later and containing certain sections that are older than others. Many parts of the Rig Veda have been derived and appropriated from the earlier feminine cosmogonies and function as a palimpsest. What makes the ten volumes of the Rig Veda fascinating is that in their present form they are testimony to a period marking the shift from the earlier feminine cosmo-social matrices to the establishment of what was perhaps the first patriarchy.

In the pre-Vedic period powerful interfeminine cosmogonies comprise an entire social order, which I call gynefocal. The Vedic period witnessed the development of patriarchy along with ideologies that normalized gender and heterosexuality. These ideologies continued into the Puranic period. The Puranas (Ancient Lore) are a set of Sanskrit hymns that date from approximately A.D. 350 through the thirteenth century. This period also witnessed very powerful women's traditions existing at the periphery of patriarchy and leading to a renewal of the independent feminine cosmogonies. The Puranas also contain references to pre-Aryan accounts of powerful goddesses. The contemporary period is a collection of many different entangled histories. The knowledge of earlier interfeminine cosmogonies is lost and lesbianism has come to be associated not with early pre-Vedic and Shaktic scriptures but with the corrupting influence of the West.[7]

Gynefocal Signals

In the prepatriarchal period there are multiple representations of interfeminine fusion and feminine deities. The most powerful images center around different forms of *jami* (twin) cosmogonies and triadic constellations.

The following fragments are from various sections of the Rig Veda:

> maidens moving together, with adjacent boundaries, sisters
> [*svasara*], twins [*jami*] in the expansiveness of the manes;
> they kiss—united, of the [universe's] focal point; may *dyava* [dual
> feminine deities] protect us and earth not be so immense.
>
> (*Rig Veda* 1.85.5)

> agile, dwelling, arriving at the nodal point of the immortal elixir
> [*amrit*];
> endless expansive, without limit, the circumambulating paths of
> *dyava prithvi* [dual earth goddesses].
>
> (*Rig Veda* 5.47.2)

One of the earliest cosmogonies recorded in the Rig Veda is that of the dual feminine deities, *dyava*. *Dyava* emerges from the word *dyavau*, which is the dualized feminine of the root *dyu*, light. The phonetic movement from "au" to "a" is the expression of the dual as one unit that is nevertheless retaining its dual identity. This dual cosmogony represented a holistic feminine union whereby the feminine twins could be seen as lovers, as mothers, and as sisters. In fact, in these early feminine cosmogonies one does not find consorted deities of the opposite sex but dual deities of the same sex, often referred to as twins (*jami*). *Jami* also connotes sisterhood as well as the sharing of the same archetypal womb space. This same archetypal womb space does not necessarily refer to a biological womb since the twins are said to originate in different spaces yet be *jami*.

The union that is symbolized is neither static nor a complete merger but instead a coming together, a meeting out of movement; it symbolizes the generation of a third space. In many instances the various points are in movement, in connection with another feminine deity, creating a triadic constellation.

In the first citation the kiss symbolizes the meeting or the pivotal focal point of the universe, which comes about through a moving together but with adjacent boundaries.

The second citation contextualizes *dyava* as dual mothers implicated in a feminine kinship genealogy with *prithvi* (earth) and as a continuing chain of dual mothers. *Dyava* here are a single unit and also a pair at the same time.

A triadic constellation is generated that is also a pair, as *dyava* (one unit) combines with earth (*prithvi*) to form a pair of mothers composed of a unity of two.

Another triadic form is found in *ushasa*[8] (dawn and dusk unit), which may be in conjunction with night (*nakta*) or day (*akta*). This moving triadic constellation was represented by the two *yonis* (wombs), dual sisters, dual mothers, or the double triangle. In this way a complex cosmological philosophy is created that consists of movements combining and meeting and in the process creating interchangeable feminine links, constellations, and patterns, and this philosophy is the driving principle of a generic feminine kinship system.

The double triangles symbolize harmony between the different kinds of fertility that are in circulation. Thus when the twin-lover energy is below, the light energy is below, representing psychoerotic fertility. Likewise when the earth energy is below, there is material fertility. No level is seen as separate from the other, neither is there any binary opposition between polarities but rather a passage, an in-between third space. Likewise, instead of the logic of separation, there is alternation between the elements composing the triangles, hence the ecology and alternation of the visible light and the dark, hidden spaces.

> The still one holding the six, the cows enclosing the *rit* [essential fluid], the three [f.] in movement, two hidden [*guhya*] and one manifest.
>
> (*Rig Veda* 3.56.2)
>
> that which contains the three *dyava* [dual goddesses] above which are the three earths, the six fold.
>
> (*Rig Veda* 7.87.5)
>
> this, the arrival of the best of lights, the birth of brilliant luminosity, thus fertility, generativeness as *ratri-usha* [night-dawn], one spoke of the wheel.
> the shining calf, resplendent, the arrival of the white, the one spoke-cow, the dark one of her other abode; akin, immortal, successive, of the genre of *dyava* [dual feminine deities] alternately moving.
> similar pathways of the two sisters, treading alternately, not opposing, not trying, of one form resplendent [are] *nakta-ushasa* [night-dawn], fused yet diverse.
>
> (*Rig Veda* 1.113.1–3)

Fertility is not severed from its psychic generative process nor is the luminous from the dark. The motif of the dual sisters-mothers-lovers in its association to the *jami* form of eros is based on the idea of the same cosmic self. This is also expressed in the etymology of the word sister, *sva-sri*, from *sv*, self, *sr*, to flow, and *sri*, blood.

> The dual *dyava-prithvi* [dual earth mothers], the two mothers of which are the dual mothers.
>
> > (*Rig Veda* 3.55.6)

> Twin sisters of various transforming forms, of the two one glowing, the other dark; *shyavi* and *arusi*, the two sisters[9] . . .
> bestowing lights, the two maidens of different forms, circumambulating the earth through their own self-desires;
> through the dark and the splendid shining spoke-wheel of the *nakta-usha* [night-dawn] alternately wandering.
>
> > (*Rig Veda* 3.55.6)

The state of fusion in movement not only intensifies "the same" but as it is in a constant state of transformation it also makes the movement from one pole to the other possible. The flows are not one-directional but multidirectional from *dyava* (dual feminine deities) to *prithvi* (earth) and vice versa. In this way dual elements can coexist as a single unit.

Thus the dual elements of *dyava-prithvi* (dual earth mother goddesses) and *nakta-ushasa* (night-dawn) can be seen as being composed of two units yet forming a triadic formation with *nakta* (night) and *prithvi* (earth) being the apex of the triangle of the dual forms of *ushasa* (dawn) and *dyava* (dual goddesses).

In the feminine triangle neither the single unit nor the dual forms are absent. Each exists in its own right and may be constellated within itself or within the triadic. The third point does not subsume the other points but only permits a different expression of the energy states. In addition, the apex of the triangle may at any point be changed. Thus one may have the following multiple flows in the configuration of *ushasa-nakta* (dawn-night): the singular *usha* (dawn) moving through *nakta* (night) to reach her twin *usha* (dawn), the singular *usha* (dawn) intensifying herself in the dual form being mirrored through her other diverse form *nakta* (night), or *nakta* (night) at the apex differentiating the two singular same *ushasa* (dawn). These flows effect a play between the same and the different through the triadic constellation. The same conception is apparent in *dyava-prithvi* (dual earth goddesses), where earth becomes the differentiating and earthing factor in the celestial light fusion.

The triadic may also be composed of the same elements. One may have three *ushas* (dawn), *dyaus* (light, f.), or earths. Here the triadic principle represents different levels. The flows are not between differentiated points but between the same points that exist at different levels in a spatial relationship. For instance, light may not be consigned only to the skies but may also exist within the interior underground, or the earth principle may also exist at the level of the atmospheric.

Various forms of the triad may exist because the triadic does not have an absolute value. That is, it may be composed of only three particular elements in one particular way. The triadic is only a principle, a frame of perception, as in the following line "three pathways (f) of the beyond (*paravat*), essence of the wind, you the dual sisters go" (*Rig Veda* 1.34.7).

Here the three pathways are composed of the two moving sisters and their driving force, the wind. The movement of the two sisters is not earthbound but is given another form through the wind creating the three atmospheric divinities of pathways (*nasatnya*).

Thus the major elements of this philosophy are embodied in dual feminine divinities. The most prevalent form is that of the *usha* (dawn) and *nakta* (night), which frequently are found in the triadic formation of *ushasa-nakta* (*ushasa* = dual dawns).

> One departs, one arrives, of diverse forms, moving together circumambulating successively from the dark hidden-cave [*guhya*] to the light with the chariot.
>
> (*Rig Veda* 1.123.7).

> knowing the first name of the day, she the white being born from the dark.
>
> (*Rig Veda* 1.123.9)

Here the notion of birth is a cyclic transformation of the dual diverse *jami*-sisters generating and renewing each other. Light and dark are not opposing forces but transforming and revolving halves.

> Diverse in form are the two daughters of the red, one bedecked with stars, the other of the realm of [sunlight].
>
> (*Rig Veda* 6.49.3)

The twins are elsewhere said to be generated by the great goddess through the vibration of the cosmic tongue. Through the two twin forms of *vapushi* (*vap*, weaving, and *ushi*, light) and *tapushi* (*tap*, steam, boil, and *ushi*, light), seen as a combination of light and dark, emerge the fusion, the couple (*mithuna*) and consciousness (*budhn*) (*Rig Veda* 3.39 3).

Vapu (*vap*, weave), which is often associated with *usha* (dawn), is described in the following hymn:

> Worthy of homage is this wondrous weaving [*vapu*], the unsaid,
>   through which the streams flow while the waters are still.
> emerging from the two mothers, the holders [of the universe] are
>   the twin sisters, closely linked though from different places
>   [literally, here and there].
>
> (*Rig Veda* 5.47.5)

The same hymn also refers to the mother-daughter relationship as one in which the mother renders the daughter conscious:

> the great mother awakens, renders conscious her daughter, en-
>   lightening the *yuvati-manisha*.[10]
>
> (*Rig Veda* 5.47.1).

The hidden, the dark, are not separate from the light realms but form one pathway of the dual.

> The wonderful pair [*dasme*, f.], placing the foot in the in-between,
>   one hidden, one revealed;
> she, the common pathway though differentiated. (*Rig Veda*
>   3.55.15). This hymn has various dual feminine motifs associ-
>   ated with parthenogenesis and the great indivisible eternal
>   feminine or the Goddess, Mahi.
> At the first of the first dawns, in the cow's home was born the
>   great eternal [*mahi*, f.].
>
> (*Rig Veda* 3.55.15)

Another motif concerns the first male mortal being generated through the woman who is fertile without being impregnated (*Rig Veda* 3.55.1 and 5):

> He, sleeping in the *parastat* [beyond], the two mothers and the
>   calf wander without limitation.
>
> (*Rig Veda* 3.55)

This motif also refers to concrete gynefocal kinship practices in which there is no concept of the rights of the father:

> In the former times the bonding of two mothers and one calf
>   [*vats*] was prevalent.
>
> (*Rig Veda* 3.55)

The kinship structure was not based on the concept of children and women as property, but on the nurturing aspect of collective motherhood. The choice of the word *vats* (calf) suggests that the child, much like its animal counterpart, upon becoming an adult would assume an independence while retaining a cosmic link. This may be seen as expressive of an archetypal identity vis-à-vis the great eternal feminine (*mahi*).

The hymn goes on to constellate the dual feminine in various ways:

> Twin sisters of various alternating forms, of the two, one glowing,
>   the other dark.
>
> (Rig Veda 3.55.11)

> lowing, licking, caressing and kissing the other's calf, where is the
>   source of her milk;
> she the goddess of the *rit* (essential fluid), sprinkled with fluid . . .
> invoked are the two cows, without progeny, may they give milk,
>   thus becoming the abundant unsuckled eternally renewed
>   pair of young evergreen women lovers [*yuvatyo*].
>
> (Rig Veda 3.55.15 and 16)

In the above hymns the dual feminine motifs are associated with fusion and fertility and are autogenerative and eternally renewable. The mother and daughter are compared to the image of the cow, giving of milk and suckling together. They are the pair residing in the *rit* (essential fluid). This is in accordance with the overall philosophy of the dual creating the third space or being implicated in a dynamic triadic constellation where there are different kinds of fertility outside the construction of progeny. Kinship is complex and does not stem only from a biological source but also from the movement and stillness associated with these cosmologies of the dual feminine.

The epithet of Usha, *duhita*, (*duh*, to milk, be milked), connoting the mother-daughter bond, is indicative too of the dual feminine mosaic, the source of which is the archetypal womb space of the *sayoni-sayona* (of the same womb), the etymological root of which is *sah*, to fuse, join together, and *yoni* (womb).

> The pair [f.] of *mayins*[11] mapping the luminous *jami sayoni* [twins
>   of the same womb] coming together the newly woven body
>   of light [*divi*, f.] beyond the oceanic boundaries [seen by]
>   the visionary poets.
>
> (Rig Veda 1.159.4)

> Worthy of homage is this wondrous weaving, the unsaid, through
>   which the streams flow while the waters are still.
> emerging from the two mothers, the holders [of the universe] are

the twin sisters, closely linked though from different places
[literally, here and there].

(*Rig Veda* 5.47.5)

This wondrous weaving is in other words a transforming mosaic of dual feminine motifs, some of which are as follows:

the pair [f.] through beauty are fulfilled
you two [f.] *dyava-prithvi* [dual earth goddesses], filled with *rit*
[essential fluid], the red, bearing the poets, of beautiful
birth between the two bowls [*dhishane*, f.] the sun in the
heat of the goddess.

(*Rig Veda* 1.160.1)

from the bosom of the mountain, desirous and content, two
mares, like two bright cows as mothers licking, caressing
and kissing.

(*Rig Veda* 3.33.1)

equivalent to the calf, the two mothers mutually licking, caressing,
kissing each other, flowing together to their common home
[*samanam yoni*].

(*Rig Veda* 3.33.3)

eternally moving, dwelling, arriving at the nodal point of the
elixir,
endless, expansive, without limit, the circumambulating paths of
dyava-prithvi [dual earth-goddesses].

(*Rig Veda* 5.47.2).

Partners, though separate, with distant limits, standing firm on
one place, watchful
the sisters becoming *yuvati* [young women lovers], speak to each
other twin [*mithunani*] names.

(*Rig Veda* 3.54.7)

with transforming hues, she shines in twofold splendor, revealing
her body in the east.

(*Rig Veda* 5.80.4)

rivers send forth, that which Indra[12] drank, the wave which makes
the two [f.] move
the well that springs from the cloud, desirous, wandering, the triadic mosaic
these winding streams with their twofold flows like cattle raiders
seek the lower levels, waters residing together, the mothers

> of beings, the protectors [f]. of the waters, swelling the *say-oni* [of the same womb] worshipped by the sages.
>
> (*Rig Veda* 10.30.9 and 10)

Thus, in the gynefocal tradition the following spectrum of dual feminine motifs occurs: mothers, daughters, sisters, lover-maidens, twins, flows, paths, bowls, cows, mares. They are associated with ideas of fusion, togetherness, erotic intimacy, equivalence, diversity in unity, congruence, complementarity, processes of moving together, circulation, suckling one child, containing, and grazing. Instead of identities being fixed, there is a flow creating movement from one to the other. Instead of binary oppositions, the guiding principle is cyclic and transformative.

The Rise of Patriarchal Vedic Civilization

The above cosmogonies of the twins, multiple mothers, and triadic constellations give way in the Vedic period to that of heterosexual consortship imposed through a complex technology of language practices creating a certain kind of gender schizophrenia. The establishment of the patriarchal Vedic civilization is based on the act of rape and the killing of the feminine. Compulsory heterosexuality is based on a universal masculine identity. Whereas the global feminine included all forms, the universal masculine has no place for the integration of the feminine.

The dual feminine *dyava* (dual goddesses) is converted into *Dyaus* (sky), a masculine and singular form that represents the father. Light is no longer the other side of darkness or the emergence from the primal waters but a light that kills, that conquers, that possesses, that becomes the normative law as a principle of truth. The cyclic generative principle is converted into a law that glorifies killing and the rape of Usha by the male god Indra. The plurality of the triadic principle is destroyed and replaced by universality. Diversity is no longer a reverberation of self-desire but is subsumed in a universal "truth."

In kinship terms this transformation means the construction of male genealogies and the first male sacrificers. The art of weaving infinite mosaics is replaced by the art of the sacrifice. Form is no longer organic but based upon the sacrifice of the split-off other. Within this genealogy women are objectified as biological mothers, the womb appropriated by the impregnating male.

> *dyaus* [sky] as the father, the overseer of the generative node and
>   the mother as *prithvi* [earth]
> the end of the unnamed *utanyo yoni* [expansive womb], thus the
>   father establishes himself in the womb of the daughter.

(*Rig Veda* 1.164.33)

This technology of breaking the twins (same sex) to create a pair (heterosexual) also marks the beginning of a medicalization of the body, a binary construction of gender, a shift of kinship, and a normatizing of heterosexuality. The kinship focus is no longer on Usha as the daughter of light but on the sons, who originate from Usha, as sacrificers. Usha is replaced as the point of origin by the penetrative act of splitting. The central factor becomes the production of male progeny. Representative of these shifts are the following sacrificial texts:

> There is uniformity [*jami*] in the sacrifice, in that there are two
>   sacrificial cakes [offered] in order.
> Between them he offers the silent sacrifice, to break the uniformity
>   [*atamitvaya*] and to make a pair.
>   (*Taittiriya Samhita* 2.6.6.4 in Gonda 1974:64)[13]

> When [there is] the non-penetrative act [*a-maithunam*], then
>   [there is] no progeny [*a-praja*] and thus it is *jami*;
> two men or women sleeping [*shayatam*] together [*sah*].
>   (*Jaiminiya Brahman* 1.300)

Penetration is necessary to induce procreation (*praja*), ensure malehood and thereby make the penis the transcendent sexually active organ. Sexual activity is defined by the penetrative action of the penis. Twinness, because it is based on togetherness, is thereby not accorded the sexual status of *ajamita* (penetration), which is determined through procreation, the result of heterosexual pairing. Within this ideology even the elements are genderized and thus paired.

> Voice [f.] and breath [m.] are a pair so that a productive union
>   [*mithunam prajanam*] of the *samidhenis* is therefore effect-
>   ed at the outset.
>   (*Taittiriya Samhita* 2.6.6.4 in Gonda 1974:64)[14]

The concept of *mithunam prajanam* (productive union) is very different from some of the earlier usages of *mithun*, couple, twin from the root *mith*, to join. The following hymn indicates that in the earlier usage the concept of *mithun* (join) referred to interfeminine pairs.

> Partners [f.], though separate, with distant limits, standing firm
>   on one place, watchful the sisters becoming youthful, speak
>   to each other twin [*mithunani*] names.
>   (*Rig Veda* 3.54.7)

Within the sacrificial Vedic traditions any *jami* (twin) intermingling results in the breakdown of the above binary categorization, giving rise to another taxonomy: the third gender, possession of the dark goddess Nirrti, and loss of malehood, a result of the free development of the embryo in the two *yonis* (wombs) (for instance referring to *dyava*, dual goddesses, or *ushasa*, dawn-dusk unit).

The goddess Nirrti is associated with both womb and death, the begetting only of girl children, female barrenness, and sexual "deviance." Death, instead of being the end of life, becomes that which is placed in-between: the space between one life and the next rebirth. However, from the patriarchal position this zone is the most dangerous and vulnerable for the virile male, a space that cannot be split but dissolves instead. Hence it must be concealed and kept out of sight.

The cosmography of Nirrti is a complex semantic spectrum arising from the cleaving of the life and death womb, the antithesis to normative heterosexuality, while progenic sexuality is associated with virility and fixed gender categories.

> That woman having a male form and that male having a woman's
> form are possessed by Nirrti.
>
> (*Maitrayani Samhita* 2.5.5.6)

The text, which is also an invocation to be freed from Nirrti, goes on to elaborate this state of possession by Nirrti as lessening the virile bull force of the male warrior god Indra, which is equivalent to the sin of *nipumsak* (without malehood, neuter).

In the Vedic cycle of hymns Kathak Samhita, there is the same formulation except for the rendering of the word *nipumsak* as *vi-pumsak* (*vi*, contrary) or contrary to malehood. This state is likened to darkness, the dark color, and above all death.

In the patriarchal period sexuality is to be solely reproductive and transmit the father's semen, as in the following example:

> He who does not drink the semen of the fathers; rather that desire
> weakens and halves virility. Further this produces the quali-
> ty of animalness instead of progeny. And this form of inter-
> course is without malehood [*ni-pumsak*].
>
> (*Kathak Samhita* 2.5.5.6)

In addition, the form of fire and its elements should be *ajam* (nontwin, not of the same sex) and not equivalent to the fire of Nirrti-Ahuti (autoerotic feminine fire). Any form of autosexuality is relegated to the sin of Nirrti. Deities of the dark genre like Nirrti are to be kept away so they do not destroy the sacrifice. For it is not the denial of the sexual energy or its diverse manifestations that is the crux of the sacrificial ideology but its appropriation for the use of procreative heterosexuality, which is accorded the status of "socially cultivated" sexuality. Expansive, ecstatic sexuality is seen as animal-like, belonging to the untamed forests.

In contrast to the binary system of opposites contained in patriarchal compulsory heterosexuality, the cosmography of Nirrti and the motif of *jami* (twin) as a state of togetherness within the same sex operate in a triadic mode, which is holistic. Nirrti becomes the universal goddess with infinite forms. She is the self-sister-mother, satisfying and drinking of her own *irane* (female fluid), emphasizing the nonprogenic erotic aspect of water, rivulet, and well, which is contrasted to semen:

> The self-enacted *irane-yoni* [female fluid-womb] [is] satisfied
> upon being eaten/attained by Nirrti.
> *(Kathak Samhita 2.55)*.

The *Kathak Samhita* has a further elaboration of practices related to Nirrti. The zone of Nirrti includes an associative spectrum of motifs connected with ardent desire. Her desire is dwarflike, crooked, and thus dangerous, but also expansive. It is linked to animal sexuality, which is associated with the pleasure and revelation of the cave waters. It is this energy that must be sequestered, restrained, cooked, and purified in order for it to be progenic instead of expansive. Only the fertile cow is to be used for the sacrifice and not the "expansive cow." Further, any form of "pulsating sexuality" is to be expelled or else possession by Nirrti is the consequence.

> When the mark of the day that is the form of the dark night
> possessing both genres, then must be expelled from the
> senses the vibrating and pulsating sexuality of the "de-
> moness" and wandering *asur* [alter ego of the male god]
> otherwise the male will become like the qualities of
> "womanhood": like a woman and will be possessed by
> Nirrti. The senses of whom will be akin to Nirrti and
> contrary to malehood [*vipumsak*].
> *(Kathak Samhita 13.5)*

Ayurvedic Texts

Sushrat and Charak are considered the fathers of the Ayurvedic medical tradition. Their texts, written around the first century A.D., contain several references to homosexuality. These medical texts identify homosexuality as *shanda*, that which is neither male nor female. One may have the male *shand* or the female *shanda*, which would be equivalent to the effeminate male homosexual or the masculine lesbian. The Sushrat Samhita (6.38.8) and the Charak Samhita (6.30.33–34) are still regarded as basic texts in the traditional Indian Ayurvedic practice of healing. In these texts, lesbians (*nari-shanda, shandha, shandhi*) are said to be suffering from a disease of the feminine generative organ (*yoniroga*). According to the Charak, this disease is caused by "inverted" intercourse or embryonic damage during conception due to a faulty sperm cell or ovum.

In the Sushrat (3.2.45) the etiology of lesbianism lies in the mother having played the male role in conceptive coition (the same origin as the anally receptive male), leading to the stereotypically male gender role behavior of the lesbian. In his comment on this passage Dalhan explains such behavior: "Although feminine in form she mounts the woman like a man and rubs her own *yoni* against that of the other" (cited in Sweet and Zwilling 1993:597). Such behavior would be equivalent to possession by Nirrti in the embryo.

> He, who not knowing the wheel upon perceiving the
> concealed/out of sight; engulfed in the mother's womb
> [*matur-yona*] gets possessed by Nirrti and progeny comes to
> an end.
>
> (*Rig Veda* 1.164.32)

The notion of embryonic damage is represented as an inability to split the dual *yonic*/triangle space of Nirrti and thereby failing to control the procreative *yoni*. This representation can be seen in the etymology of *shand*, which comes from the number six, the number of the double triangles or double *yonis*.

The following are the different epithets of the *shandhi* in the two *Samhitas* (Charak 6.30.34, Sushrat 6.38.18): man-hater, breastless, not fit for medical treatment, incapable of menstruation, possessing no ovum, hence sterile in the heterosexual sense.

The Reemergence of Independent Feminine Cosmogonies

Alongside the patriarchal Vedic tradition with its splitting of the dual feminine and its control of the realm of Nirrti and gender inversions, there occurred a return to pre-Vedic gynefocal traditions based on the concept of *shakti* (feminine energy). The two *yonis* are a major symbol of the reemergence of *shaktic* traditions.[15] The language practices of this tradition, as found in the Puranas and the Tantras, eroticize and celebrate the *yoni*.[16]

The *yoni* (womb) is seen as the creative space of the triangle, instead of a passive receptacle for the male phallus:

> in the triangle, of the vibrating state, she, creating reflections, the
> ever renewable.
>
> (*Yogini Hridayam*:263)

> the three-cornered *mandala* of which the women are the cities and
> three lines.
>
> (*Kalika Purana* 63.55)[17]

> three lines, three dwelling places on the earth, woman as the three
> summits illuminating the three *gunas*.
>
> (*Tripura Upanishad*:5)[18]

> worship the principle of attraction in the middle (of the tri-
> angle) thus worship the three *yoginis*[19] in the three
> women, in the corners

> the fusion or circulation of which gives the *yoginis bhagasya, bhag-*
> *malini, bhagodri, bhagaroha, bhagjihva, bhaga*.
>
> (*Kalika Purana* 63.102 and 103)

These texts refer to the *mandala* of Kamakhya (the goddess of eros and sexuality) and the double triangle, whose six points are named. *Bhaga* is the entirety of the woman's sexual organ. The above six appelations translate as: *bhaga*, belonging to *bhaga*, chain-garland of *bhagas*, tongue of *bhaga*, mounted on *bhaga*, *bhaga*, play. The two triangles are also allusive of the eros between the two *yonis*, women. This is recounted in the myth of the birth of Bhagirath, born from the union of two women.

> the name Bhagirath emerges when the *bhagas* are the mothers.
>
> (*Padma Purana* 16.16a)

One of the names of the goddess is Bhagirathi, a name that still exists today as the name of a river. In the more patriarchal version, however, the above myth is recounted somewhat differently. The dead king Dilip has left no male heir. In order to procreate a son to the dead king, the younger queen takes the male role (*purush bhaven*) and unites sexually with the older queen.

> the son however that is born is without bone structure as there has
> been no exchange of semen.
>
> (*Padma Purana* 16:15:16)

The transaction between two women is represented by the principle of fluidity, that of the male by structure and system. In another version of the myth, found only in manuscript form in Krittivas's Ramayana, the verb used to describe the sexual union of the two *bhagas* is *sambhog*. In this version, the two queens, *chandra* (moon) and *mala* unite. *Mal* is a feminine fluid, which is often the cause of parthenogenesis. The elephant god, Ganesh, is born through Parvati's *mal*.

The prefix *bhaga* is used in various texts as names of the goddess:

bhaga-anga (limb, part)*bhaga-lila* (play)
bhaga-rupa (form) *bhaga-alya* (dwelling place)
bhaga-eshwari (goddess) *bhaga-utsaha* (animation, energy)
bhaga-aradhya (splendor) *bhaga-utsava* (festival)
bhaga-bimba (reflection) *bhaga-vidya* (knowledge)
bhaga-klina (wet) *bhaga-sneha* (love)
bhaga-vati (possessor) *bhaga-sneha-vardhini* (to fill with love)
bhaga-yoni (womb) *bhaga-pushpa* (flower)
bhaga-prada (river) *bhaga-pushp-nivasini* (residing in the flower)
bhaga-guhya (cave) *bhaga-adhara* (on the base of, flowing from)
bhaga-avha (ride, marry)
bhaga-ananda (ecstasy)
bhaga-shalini (possessing)

Nominations like *bhagini* constitute certain aspects of the feminine genealogy, connoting feminine kinship and feminine linkage as well as sexual and erotic bonding. *Bhagini* symbolizes the autonomous woman. Sexuality between the *bhaginis* is seen as a fusion between two women. In the list above the concept of *bhaga* (women's sexual organ) is linked with concepts and images of play, flowers, love, wetness, flow, going into, residing within, ecstasy, festivity, and energy. These associations are also borne out by the following myth narrated in the *Mahabhagvat Purana*: The river Ganga wants to visit Kamakhya in Assam (Kamakhya is the goddess of eros and is also the name of a site). Understanding her intentions, the brahmin sage leads her astray while her guide Bhagirath in collusion with the sage stops blowing the conch. Padma (lotus) who is desirous to see her *bhagini*, Ganga, starts to blow the conch. When Bhagirath tries to stop the now speeding Ganga, Padma transforms herself into a fast flowing river and merges with Ganga into the ocean.

Sexual, erotic energy (*shakti*) is part of the feminine cosmo-social topography; it is therefore neither separated nor fetishized into the procreative act. Instead, erotic constellations comprise much more the idea of play, love, enjoying, eating and drinking from. *Maithun* (sexual union) in this context is seen as plural with each constellation, each divinity having its own particular form.

> equivalent to the nine *shakti* [female power] are the nine *maithun*
> [couplings] the enactment of the *sam* [perfect meeting,
> fusion] thus the arrival of the goddess again and again.
>
> *(Mahabhagvat Purana 4.63)*

> The nine *shakti* [feminine energy] emerge from the generative
> fusion of the primal three which is the fusion of the two
> triangles.
>
> *(Mahabhagvat Purana 8)*

This feminine eros is also described as *samriiv* (*sam*, same, fusion, perfect meeting)—the vanishing into the same, the fusional dissolution into water. As in the idea of *jami* (twin), in the *sam* pair there is no conception of a gender hierarchy or of active and passive but instead a mirroring, play, and fusion. The form that desire takes is transformation and the creation of a dwelling, a "secret" space. Some of the key motifs of dwelling spaces that emerge from the texts are cave and hiding place, residence.

The enclosed pentagon of the dual triangles is named the cave of eros (f.) *manobhavam-guham* in the Kalika Purana. This symbol is earlier referred to as the *trikutam* (three caves, cells) of the *devi* (goddess) of the great lightening, of the genre of the dark.

> the sixty-four *yoginis* each to be worshipped,
> the pleasurable cave [f.] and the great festival thus *sakhim*
> [woman-to-woman bonding].
>
> *(Kalika Purana)*

The principle of attraction is also to be found in the constellation of the double triangles and the *yoginis* as its embodiment.

Concealed Goddesses and Lesbian Invisibility

Although, given the plurality of the different sociocultural contexts, it is difficult to generalize, in present-day India there are no living languages that at their dominant level describe, nominate, accentuate, or emphasize woman-to-woman sexual and kinship relationships. In spite of the prevalence of sex-segregated areas of work and social life, these homosocial spaces are subordinate to the heterosexual family space, which constitutes an entire social nexus. Within the socioreligious spaces of various monotheistic religions, i.e., Islam, Christianity, or that of contemporary Hinduism and modern secularism, there exist no cosmological contexts for independent feminine goddesses or cosmogonies. Modern Hinduism is constructed on the principle of a transcendental all-important male gender identity similar to that of other monotheistic religions. In contemporary India the rich traditions of the feminine are either masculinized or subsumed under dominant male traditions. Secular historiography and writing about the present are no different in this respect, for they do not explore the shift from plural cosmogonic traditions to monotheistic or monoandrocentric religions. Instead, those kinds of writing simply become a liberal other to fundamentalist ideology and thereby subscribe to the absencing of the "cosmo-social-sexual" feminine.

This absence is carried out above all through language. Words such as *bhagini* (female erotic bonding), *sakhi* (female companion, lover), *jami* (twin) have lost their former sexual, cosmo-social meanings; they are translated today simply as "sister" or "woman friend." Most Hindi to Hindi dictionaries do not have any explicit word to connote lesbian sexuality. The words *shanda/shandali* are translated as follows:

a woman desiring like a man
a woman having the properties of a man
a biologically deficient woman
a woman having no breasts
a woman not menstruating
a wanton woman
a selfish woman
an autoerotic woman (as an epithet of Nirrti)

The above meanings come from either the Ayurvedic medical texts or the sacrificial ones and are seen as the sole existing and therefore visible histories.

Some recent English-Hindi dictionaries have the word *samlaingikta*, which is a literal translation of the English word "homosexuality" and not a derivation from older homoerotic histories. This phenomenon reflects the invisibility of "homosexual" identities in occidental contexts; earlier dictionaries do not have even the English word. Whereas the word *samlaingikta* emerges from a neutral position, the term "lesbian" is translated as pertaining to unnatural crime. In fact there has been a historical criminalization of lesbian acts. The earliest criminalization occurs in the law books of Manu:[20]

A *kanya* [young girl] who does it to another *kanya* must be fined 200 *panas* [coins], pay the double of the bride price and receive ten lashes of the rod.
But a *stri* [woman] who does it to a *kanya* shall instantly have her head

shaved or two fingers cut off and be made to ride through the town on a donkey. (*Manavdharamshastra* 8.369 and 370)

Lesbian sexuality is equated to male desire and thus invisibilized. Where there is visibility it is usually through reference to the "West" as either a neutral derivation of the English word or in a few cases as a return back to a homophobic historical context.

The only English-Hindi dictionary that has words from a more positive historical tradition is the Standard English-Hindi dictionary compiled by S. P. Mishra. In this dictionary the following words are given:

sam-ling-kami - desirous (*kami*) of the same sex
sam-ling-bhogi - enjoying, eating of (*bhogi*) of the same sex
sam-ling-rati - erotic pleasure (*rati*) of the same sex
sv-rati-shilta - auto erotic (*sv-rati*)

All the words are composed of feminine particles. Words such as *bhogi*, *rati*, and *kami* come from the shaktic traditions. Rati is also the goddess of eros. *Sv-rati* (autoerotic) is not simply representative of the experience of individualized autoeroticism but that of an entire gender. Rati embodies the pleasure of the feminine gender in and for itself.

Although I have looked only at language practices in Hindi, I suspect that the above generalizations hold for many of the other Indian languages. Within spoken languages, however, it is impossible to generalize, particularly because of the great difference between public and private speech. Many secret, coded language practices exist; yet because women do not share community spaces, unlike men of the *hijra* communities, expression of desire becomes extremely privatized and secret.[21] My own field work in Himanchal Pradesh showed that woman-to-woman desire was expressed either through silence, sublimation, or use of a male persona. Yet, when I showed historical images of the feminine, lesbian iconography and other women-centered images were by far the most popular and well-received. Despite this, the women I worked with never expressed any explicit sexual interest.

In effect, the space of desire was strictly private and nonverbal for women, contrary to the realm of the social in which duty was the visible mask that had to be maintained. In other words, identity arising out of desire is strictly taboo. For that matter any attempt to build a different gender identity confronts *dharma* (social and religious duty). For what is at stake is not opposing one identity to another but replacing the concept of duty with that of identity. Desire and duty lie at opposite poles, one occupying the secret, private space and the other the public.

Whereas the above describes the prevalent, dominant structures, within urban centers there are small beginnings of lesbian and gay visibility. The two most visible groups in India, Bombay Dost and Sakhi both use Hindi words but associate them with gay and lesbian, respectively. Some of the other gay and lesbian groups outside India have instinctively used words that go back to the shaktic traditions. That is, *shakti* (cosmic feminine energy), *samakami* (desirous of the same), *trikone* (triangle). These language strategies invert commonly voiced homophobic attitudes, such as the following: homosexual practices are Western phenomena; the words "gay" and "lesbian" have no meaning in an Indian context; there is no Indian term for homosexuality and therefore it does not exist in the Indian context.

The identification of *dost* (male friend) with gay and *sakhi* with lesbian creates another kind of sexual context and visibility. It also overturns both the colonial and indigenous homophobic representations of the other as the source of decadence and perversion. Whereas the colonial gaze constructed the Indian Other as perverse, in the official Indian tradition it is the West that is the embodiment of perversion and decadence.[22] Both the colonial and Indian traditions use the same tools of sexual repression.

The law on unnatural sexuality created by the British is still being used. Acts classified as such are not bailable and are punishable by life imprisonment. The following case was reported in the magazine *India Today*, April 15, 1990:

> Tarulata changed her sex to marry her girlfriend, Lila Chavda. Muljibhai Chavda, Lila's father, went to the Gujurat High Court, saying that as it was a lesbian relationship, the marriage must be annulled. Criminal action was called for under the above law. The writ of petition contended that "Tarunkumar (Tarulata) possesses neither the male organ nor any natural mechanism of cohabitation, sexual intercourse and procreation of children. Adoption of any unnatural mechanism does not create manhood and as such Tarunkumar is not a male."

The petition was accepted by the court. No further information is known. Despite the occidental origin of the law, its source has never been questioned in using it as a technique of coercion and repression. Instead it is linked to the indigenous traditional ideology of normal sexuality as procreation.

The bringing together of different geographic-sexual contexts through language is important in breaking the dichotomy set up by opposing ideologies. When a word like *sakhi* is associated with the word "lesbian," it creates a multiplicity of contexts. It grafts cosmological feminine traditions onto the sexual-political visibility generated by outside lesbian movements. Moreover, it questions the inherent bigotry of the compartmentalized "Western" and "traditional" beliefs of the modern urban Indian who would not question speaking in English but yet object to using the word "lesbian."

NOTES

1. To make this text accessible to lay readers I have omitted the diacritical marks that are so essential to understanding the original Sanskrit terms in the text. Instead I have used a simplified phonetic rendering of Sanskrit words and names. It is hoped that for readers versed in Sanskrit the complex phonetic subtleties are still apparent.

2. This concept refers to a process of naming in which the meaning of the original concept is replaced by a different meaning.

3. In the Indian caste system the *brahmans* (priests) and *kshatriyas* (warriors) are the highest castes.

4. *Shakti* is the immense power of the Great Goddess. This power can be experienced through a combination of ritual actions that often involve sexual acts and the recitation of *tantras*, texts that were elaborated during the latter part of the first millennium A.D. (see also Blurton 1992 and Rawson 1978).

5. See Chakravarti (1989) for a deconstruction of this process, focusing on its gendered implications.

6. The first known culture of the Indus valley was the Harappan culture, which was characterized by goddess worship. The Harappans are believed to be the ancestors of today's Dravidians. At about 2000 B.C. bands of nomadic Aryans swept down upon the Harappan people. The four Vedas give accounts of this invasion. The Rig Veda, the original Veda consisting of 1,017 hymns, contains references to the earlier Harappan culture. The Vedas were written between 1500–1000 B.C. (see also Dawson 1984 and Stone 1979).

7. For further elaboration of many of the elements of this essay, see Thadani 1996.

8. Usha is the auspicious goddess of dawn, who is associated with light and wealth. She is often likened to a cow. She is also associated with cosmic order, the foe of chaotic forces. In some parts of the Rig Veda she is called the mother of gods and the goddess of the earth (see also Kinsley 1988; O'Flaherty 1980; and Stone 1979).

9. *Shyavi* (dark) and *Arushi* (bright red) are the names of two *jami* sisters. Their bond is also likened to the mother-daughter relationship. The terms "mother" and "daughter" have diverse meanings not limited to biological kinship. In the dual form the mothers could also be seen as lovers, sisters, and twins.

10. *Yuvati-manisha* is a term for a feminine identity of youth that is constantly renewable through another feminine form.

11. *Mayins* refers to a group of people who derive their identity from the con-

cept of *maya*, which refers to the principle of personal desire, the power that enables a deity to act. It is often translated as illusion, but in Shaktic texts it is seen as the creative and desiring principle through which the material world manifests itself.

12. Indra is one of the most important male Hindu gods. His rape of Usha and his destruction of the dual earth goddesses mark the transition from the gynefocal cosmos and social order to that of patriarchy. In the process the mother figure is constructed as a singular biological form subordinate to the male who penetrates and impregnates her.

13. The Samhitas is a collection of hymns dating from 1400–1000 B.C.

14. These are sticks used for oblations in offering.

15. Shakti is often translated as cosmic energy, as the active power of a deity, and as, mythologically, the goddess-consort and queen. Shakti also refers to the female organ (Walker 1983:929). See also note 4.

16. Rawson defines Tantra in the following way: "It is a special manifestation of Indian feeling, art and religion. . . . Tantra is a cult of ecstasy focused on a vision of cosmic sexuality. Life-styles, ritual, magic, myth, philosophy and a complex of signs and emotive symbols converge upon that vision" (1978:1). Walker maintains that Tantrism is a "system of *yoni* worship, or female-centered sex-worship, allegedly founded thousands of years ago in India by women of a secret sect called Vratyas. . . . The basic principle of Tantrism was that women possess more spiritual energy than men and a man could achieve realization of the divinity only through sexual and emotional union with a woman" (1983:973).

17. A *mandala* is often used for meditation purposes; it is generally circular or has another regular shape, indicating the whole spectrum of earth and sky.

18. *Gunas* refer to the three threads of fate, colored white, red, and black. In Tantric symbolism these three colors stand for the three properties of the goddess Kali, *tamasic* (dangerous, destructive, also the fuel, the potential), *rajas* (the sensual, the material unfolding), and *sattvik* (the intellectual and artistic). See also Walker (1983:358).

19. Yogini are unconsorted feminine divinities related to the Kali spectrum of goddesses. Etymologically the term *yogini* is related to the root *yuj* (to fuse).

20. During the Vedic period patriarchal ideology was consolidated through a codification of, among other things, women's sexuality. One of the main techniques of its enforcement was the concept of *dharma*, patriarchal duty or "right mode of conduct." These scriptures emerged roughly between the fifth century B.C. and the second and third centuries A.D., when some of them were eventually recorded. The most important one is the Laws of Manu, or the *Manavdharamshastra*.

21. The best study to date of the *hijras* is the one produced by Serena Nanda. She defines *hijras* as follows: "The *hijras* are a religious community of men who dress and act like women and whose culture centers on the worship of Bahuchara

Mata, one of the many versions of the Mother Goddess worshiped throughout India. In connection with the worship of this goddess, the *hijras* undergo an operation in which their genitals are removed" (1990:xv). Being neither men nor women, they occupy what is often described as an institutionalized third gender role. Beside performing at certain ceremonies, such as weddings, or births, some of them also engage in prostitution.

22. See for instance the following letter, which appeared in the daily newspaper, the *Pioneer*, after an article on the first public lesbian and gay meeting in Delhi:

> "Call the cops!" Sir—It is surprising that your paper should publish a photograph of protesting gays (the *Pioneer* Nov 12th 93). This is a contemptible and immoral conduct. We don't have to ape all what goes on in the West. Today homosexuality is legal and acceptable there, and soon it will be accepted as normal conduct here as well. "Gays" is a fashionable word for an unnatural offence and [it] is punishable as a crime. Our police could have rounded up those appearing in the photograph as propagating unnatural acts. I hope the police gets moving now.
>
> (J. Mohan, New Delhi, *Pioneer*, Nov. 13, 1993)

REFERENCES

Sanskrit Texts

Rig Veda. Commentary Sayana, ed. Max Mueller. Varanasi 1983.
Charak Samhita. Delhi, 1963.
Kathak Samhita. Aundh, 1943.
Maitrayana Samhita. Paradi, 1983.
Jaiminiya Brahman. Sarasvati Vihar Series. Nagpur, 1954.
Kalika Purana, ed. B. N. Shastri. Chowkhamba, Varanasi, 1972.
Lakshmi Tantra. Adyar Library. Madras, 1959.
Shakti Sangam Tantra. Chinnamastakhand, ed. D. B. Bhattacharya and Pandit Dvicedi. Oriental Institute, Baroda, 1978.
Sushrat Samhita. Delhi, 1968.
Taittiriya Samhita. Calcutta, 1960.
Yogini Hridayam. Motital Banarsidas. Delhi, 1988.

Secondary Sources

Blurton, Richard T. 1992. *Hindu Art*. London: British Museum Press.
Chakravarti, Uma. 1989. "Whatever Happened to the Vedic *Dasi*? Orientalism, Nationalism, and a Script for the Past." In Kumkum Sangari and Sudesh Vaid, eds., *Recasting Women: Essays in Colonial History*, pp. 27–88. Delhi: Kali for Women.

Dawson, John. 1984. *A Classical Dictionary of Hindu Mythology and Religion.* Delhi: Rupa.

Gonda, J. 1974. *The Dual Deities in the Religion of the Vedas.* Amsterdam and London: North-Holland.

Kinsley, David. 1988. *Hindu Goddesses: Visions of the Divine Feminine in the Hindu Religious Tradition.* Berkeley: University of California Press.

Nanda, Serena. 1990. *Neither Man nor Woman: The Hijras of India.* Belmont: Wadsworth.

O'Flaherty, Wendy Doniger. 1980. *Women, Androgynes, and Other Mythical Beasts.* Chicago: University of Chicago Press.

Rawson, Philip. 1978. *The Art of Tantra.* New York: Oxford University Press.

Stone, Merlin. 1979. *Ancient Mirrors of Womanhood: A Treasury of Goddess and Heroine Lore from Around the World.* New York: New Sibylline Books.

Sweet, M. and L. Zwilling. 1993. "The First Medicalisation." *Journal of the History of Sexuality* 3 (4): 590–607.

Thadani, Giti. 1996. *Sakhiyani: Lesbian Desire in Ancient and Modern India.* London: Cassell.

Walker, Barbara G. 1983. *The Woman's Encyclopedia of Myths and Secrets.* New York: HarperCollins.

4

Sabine Lang

Lesbians, Men-Women and Two-Spirits: Homosexuality and Gender in Native American Cultures

In the following, I first set the stage for an understanding of how homosexual behavior is viewed and constructed in Native American cultures past and present by providing a general introduction to systems of multiple genders that traditionally existed and that, to some extent, still exist in those cultures. "Traditionally" here refers to the tribal cultures of prereservation time. Then I discuss the identities and life situations of contemporary Native American lesbians and gays with a special focus on lesbian women.[1]

People who belonged to special, "alternative" genders within the traditional systems of multiple genders often entered into sexual relationships with people of the same sex. Thus, quite a number of (especially) urban contemporary Native American lesbians and gays have come to view the "women-men" and "men-women" of the prereservation days as their immediate predecessors in the tribal cultures, and to refer to themselves as *two-spirit people* in order to express that continuum. For that reason, I explore both the traditional and contemporary identities and roles of people who had, and have, same-sex relationships. I suggest that the self-identity of present-day two-spirit people is shaped by a variety of factors, including the tribal traditions of gender variance, influences from the Western urban lesbian/gay communities, the experience of being Native American and homosexual as opposed to gay and lesbian from other ethnic groups, and homophobia within the Indian communities.[2]

Gender Variance and Homosexual Behavior in Native American Cultures: Women-Men and Men-Women

The so-called "berdache,"[3] a Native American male who partially or completely adopts the culturally defined role of a woman, often also donning women's garb, has been widely discussed in anthropological literature (e.g., Callender and Kochems 1983; Jacobs 1968; Jacobs and Cromwell 1992; Lang 1990, 1998; Roscoe 1987, 1991; Williams 1986a,b). Sources referring to females in Native American cultures who take up the ways of men, however, are comparatively rare, and they have mostly been touched on only peripherally in studies on the "berdache" traditions, with some exceptions (Blackwood 1984; Callender and Kochems 1983; Lang 1990, 1998; Roscoe 1988; Whitehead 1981; Williams 1986b).

Since women-men (males in Native American cultures who had partially or completely adopted the socially defined women's role) often entered into sexual relationships or even marriages with men, their roles, as well as the roles of men-women (females in a man's role), have long been viewed as examples of culturally institutionalized homosexuality, a homosexuality that was often considered innate or was categorized under Western culture's psychiatric concepts of deviance and perversion (e.g., Benedict 1934; Ford and Beach 1965; Katz 1985; Kiev 1964; Minturn et al. 1969; Stewart 1960; Werner 1979).[4] Within the past twenty years, however, the essentialist view that interpreted the "berdache" roles as a way to culturally integrate innately abnormal individuals has been replaced in anthropological literature by a view that takes into consideration the cultural and historical context (cf. Blackwood 1986:4f). Moreover, feminist approaches opened the path to a new understanding of the ways sex and gender are viewed and constructed differently in different societies. This view also made possible a reinterpretation of women-men's and men-women's roles and statuses in terms of gender rather than sexuality (cf. Callender and Kochems 1983; Jacobs and Cromwell 1992; Jacobs, Thomas, and Lang 1997; Kessler and McKenna 1977; Lang 1990, 1998; Martin and Voorhies 1975; Whitehead 1981; Williams 1986a,b). Martin and Voorhies to my knowledge were the first to refer to the North American male-bodied "berdaches" as a third gender and to their female-bodied counterparts as a fourth gender, implying that they constitute part of cultural constructions of gender that recognize additional genders apart from man and woman (Martin and Voorhies 1975:92ff.). Such "cultural expressions of multiple genders (i.e., more than two) and the opportunity for individuals to change gender roles and identities over the course of their lifetimes" (Jacobs and Cromwell 1992:63) are termed *gender variance* in recent anthropological literature.

Within their respective cultures women-men and men-women are classified as neither men nor women, but as genders of their own. This is also reflected in words used in Native American languages to refer to them. These words are different from the words for woman and man, and often indicate that women-men and men-women are seen, one way or another, as combining the masculine and the feminine (cf. Roscoe 1988; Lang 1990:299–302, 312–313; also Callender and Kochems 1983). The Cheyenne, for example, called women-men *heemaneh*, "half men, half women" (Grinnell 1962 2:39). Women-men in the Pueblo of Isleta were called *lhunide*, "man-woman" (Parsons 1932:246), the Subarctic Ingalik called them "woman pretenders" (Osgood 1958:261). A certain female at the Pueblo of Zuni who manifested masculine manners was called *katsotse*, "boy-girl" (Parsons 1939:38), and among the Shoshoni both males in a woman's role and females in a man's role were called *tainna wa'ippe*, "man-woman" (Clyde Hall, taped conversation; see also Steward 1941:353, where the spelling is *taϑgowaip*, the phonetic letter ϑ resembling the Greek *eta*). In Shoshoni, *tainkwa* or *tainna* means "man," *wa'ippe* "woman" (Miller 1972:136, 172).

Apart from gender constructions, the roles and statuses of individuals who are neither men nor women in Native American cultures are embedded within worldviews that emphasize and appreciate transformation and change. Due to the scope and subject of this contribution, such religious aspects cannot be discussed in detail here but have been elaborated upon elsewhere (Lang 1994, 1997b, forthcoming). Within such worldviews, an individual who changes her or his gender once or more often in the course of her or his life is not viewed as an abnormality but rather as part of the natural order of things. As Tafoya has observed, the emphasis on transformation and change in Native American cultures also includes the idea that an individual is expected to go through many changes in a lifetime (1992:257).

People who are familiar with their culture's traditions of gender variance emphasize elements of spirituality that were crucial to the roles of women-men and men-women and still are important where such roles continue to exist. This even holds true for contemporary "two-spirited" Native Americans who for that reason may feel restricted by categories like "gay" or "lesbian." These categories are defined in terms of sexual behavior instead of personhood, spirituality, and specific, complex identities deriving from the experience of being Native American (cf. Tafoya 1992:257), as opposed to being white or of any other ethnic heritage.

Gender variance at least traditionally was a widespread trait of Native American cultures in North America (see map 1). Its individual expressions, however, were very diverse, more diverse than can be elaborated upon here. Parents in quite a number of tribes would recognize a child that was to be-

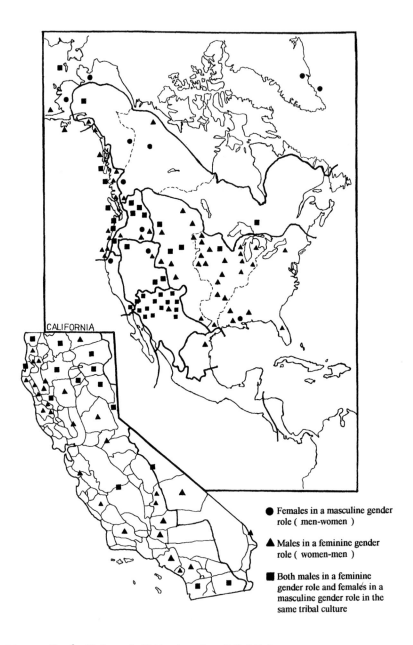

CALIFORNIA

● Females in a masculine gender
  role (men-women)

▲ Males in a feminine gender
  role (women-men)

■ Both males in a feminine
  gender role and females in a
  masculine gender role in the
  same tribal culture

MAP 1 Gender Variance in Native American Tribal Cultures

come a woman-man or man-woman by the way he or she acted while very young (cf. Lang 1990:256ff, 351f). In the Native American cultures of the Plains and the Prairies, and also in parts of California and the Northeast, women-men and men-women were/are seen as acting upon a vision or dream, which both explained and legitimized their choice to become a gender other than woman or man. Among the Canadian Dene-Tha, a phenomenon akin to gender variance occurs within a complex system of reincarnation beliefs, including the possibility of cross-sex reincarnation (Goulet 1982:9f.).

The statuses and roles of women-men and men-women also varied from tribe to tribe, even though some writers evoke the image of some timeless, universally present, and universally revered "berdache" role in Native American cultures, sometimes elevating especially women-men above everyone else.[5]

In a small number of cultures special supernatural powers were attributed to women-men, and therefore special ceremonial roles, because of their gender status and their vision, just as special religious roles were attributed to other people because of other kinds of supernatural powers and instructions they received in visions. In yet other cultures, women-men were healers or "shamans" apparently not because of their special gender status, but because of the gender role they had chosen. Thus, in tribes where predominantly the women were healers, women-men would choose that profession also; likewise, men-women might pick up the profession of a healer as part of their masculine gender role in cultures where healers were predominantly men. In still other Native American cultures, there is no predominance of either men or women in the healing profession, and women-men or men-women apparently picked up that profession if they were gifted for it, but did not—and did not have to—become healers if they did not possess that gift (cf. Lang 1990:173ff., 337).

In quite a number of Native American cultures, no supernatural impetus seems to have been needed for the members of a community to accept a child's choice to partially or completely adopt the role and manners of the opposite sex. Women-men and men-women were mixing, blending, and splitting gender roles to varying degrees, some of them taking up the role of the opposite sex completely, others only part of it. This mixing did not affect their classification as genders other than women and men. In some Native American cultures cross-dressing was an integral part of their role, in others it was not. In most cases people would take up the role and status of a gender that was neither man nor woman permanently; sometimes, however, they eventually might become a man or a woman again. Gender variance is as diverse as Native American cultures themselves. About the only common denominator is that in many Native American tribal cultures systems of multiple genders existed, classifying people of either sex according to their occupational preferences and expression of gender-specific personality traits and mannerisms as either men, women, women-men, or men-women.

Definitions of "Homosexuality" and "Heterosexuality" in Tribal Cultures

Often—but, as has been pointed out above, by no means always—women-men and men-women entered into sexual relationships with partners of the same sex. Since multiple genders were recognized in many Native American cultures, however, sexual relations between a woman-man or a man-woman and her/his same-sexed partner may be homosexual on the level of (physical) sex, but they are not so on the level of gender. If a man, for example, is having sex with a woman-man, he is not seen as having sex with another man, he is having sex with someone who belongs to a gender different from his own. The same holds true, of course, for a woman who has sex with either a woman-man or a man-woman. The partners in such relationships are never of the same gender, regardless whether they are of the same sex or not (cf. Tafoya in Levy et al. 1991). Thus, at least in the prereservation and early reservation Native American cultures where systems of multiple genders were still intact, a same-sex relationship was by no means identical with a same-gender relationship.

Little is known about homosexual relationships as defined by Western culture in Native American tribal societies, even though there are some scant references in the literature (Lang 1990:375ff.). Regarding the Yuma, for example, Forde notes that "casual secret homosexuality among both women and men is well known. The latter is probably more common. This is not considered objectionable but such persons would resent being called *elxa'* or *kwe'rhame*" (Forde 1931:157). *Elxa'* and *kwe'rhame* are the Yuma terms for women-men and men-women, respectively. Thus, among the Yuma there existed sexual relationships between women-men and men-women and partners of the same sex and also sexual contacts between two men and two women, and these two kinds of same-sex behavior were clearly distinguished from each other by the Yuma themselves. Among the Flathead there apparently existed words that referred to sexual relations between two women and two men (Turney-High 1937:85, 156f.). The word for lesbianism, which according to Turney-High contains the root "kiss," was *ntalá* (Turney-High 1937:156).

Within systems of multiple genders native definitions of homosexuality were based on the gender rather than the physical sex of the people involved, and also took into account such factors as visionary experiences. Among the Navajo, for example, there traditionally existed four genders—women, men, women-men and men-women, the two latter categories being called *nádleehé*, "someone who is in a constant process of change." An individual who is classified as nádleehé is usually already recognized in childhood because she/he shows a marked preference for occupations culturally assigned to the opposite sex. A homosexual relationship as defined by the Navajo is a sexual relationship between two individuals of the same gender (two men, two women, two female-bodied nádleehé, two male-bodied nádleehé), or of closely related genders (a woman and a male-bodied nádleehé, a man and a female-bodied nádleehé). While a homosexual relationship in Western culture is basically defined as a relationship between individuals of the same sex and the same gender, the Navajo definition of homosexuality is more subtle and based on gender rather than on characteristics of biological sex and anatomy. Thus it might more appropriately be termed a *homogender relationship* (cf. Tietz 1996). Quasi-heterosexual (or *heterogender*) relationships among the Navajo include relationships between a man and a woman, a man and a male-bodied nádleehé, and a woman and a female-bodied nádleehé. Such relationships are met with approval, whereas relationships between members of the same gender or closely related genders are considered to be culturally inappropriate, at least traditionally (Thomas 1993). The idea, for example, of two nádleehé of either sex having a sexual relationship with each other is unthinkable to traditionally raised Navajo (cf. Thomas 1993).

Among the Shoshoni, on the other hand, the difference between a "gay," or homosexual, individual and a woman-man and a man-woman is traditionally defined in terms of both occupational preferences and spirituality. *Tainna wa'ippe* (women-men and men-women who, as among the Navajo, are both subsumed under one term) act on a powerful vision that causes them to adopt and manifest the ways, occupations, and clothing of the other sex, but their tainna wa'ippe status does not limit their choices as far as sexual partners are concerned. Unlike nádleehé, male- and female-bodied tainna wa'ippe can have relationships with both men and women, the only kind of relationship considered inappropriate being a relationship between two tainna wa'ippe of either sex, which apparently is viewed as incestuous since, according to Clyde Hall (personal communication 1992), at least male-bodied tainna wa'ippe refer to each other as "sisters." A "gay" person as opposed to a tainna wa'ippe is largely defined as lacking the spiritual element, acting on personal preference instead of manifesting spiritual power. Homosexuality in this case is defined on the basis of the presence or absence of the spiritual element. A "gay" relationship, therefore, in Shoshoni culture is a relationship between two persons of the same sex and the same gender that does not involve a tainna wa'ippe. To my knowledge, such relationships were, and are, not considered inappropriate.

While constructions of homosexuality and heterosexuality, or rather of homogender and heterogender relationships, differed among the tribal and early reservation cultures, the general way of classifying relationships and the attitude toward these various kinds of relationships are summarized in the figure below (see Figure 1).

Native American Lesbians and Gays Today

The attitude toward sexuality in general and same-sex relationships in particular has changed dramatically on many reservations over the past century due to colonization and acculturation.[6] In many cases the traditions of gender variance have been forgotten or repressed; in other cases they have

Gender Status	Woman	Man	(female-bodied) Man-Woman	(male-bodied) Woman-Man
Woman	homo-gender	hetero-gender	hetero-gender	hetero-gender
Man	hetero-gender	homo-gender	hetero-gender	hetero-gender
(female-bodied) Man-Woman	hetero-gender	hetero-gender	homo-gender (?)	hetero-gender
(male-bodied) Woman-Man	hetero-gender	hetero-gender	hetero-gender	homo-gender*

Fig. 1: Classifications of Sexual Relationships in Native American Tribal Cultures (following Thomas, in print, and Tietz 1996, and based on the data compiled in Lang 1990)

▓   Relationships that are culturally acknowledged, accepted and sanctioned

☐   Relationships that may be tolerated, but not formally acknowledged

*   Relationships that are culturally tabooed universally in North America (Relationships between two women-men are the only kind of relationships that traditionally are considered inappropriate almost universally.)

(?)   No information obtainable about cultural acceptance or nonacceptance

FIGURE 1 Classifications of Sexual Relationships in Native American Tribal Cultures

gone underground and become invisible to white government officials, researchers, and others, sometimes even to other Native Americans. Today only very few individuals living on reservations adopt the role and manners of the "other" sex, or more importantly, are classified as women-men or men-women by the other members of their communities within a still functioning system of multiple genders (cf. Lang 1997a). There are exceptions, of course. On some reservations people were still familiar with the traditions of gender variance in the 1950s and 1960s. Even today in some cases an elder or relative, usually a grandmother, who recognizes that a child is manifesting personality and behavioral traits of a woman-man or man-woman, will see to it that that child is allowed to grow up to fulfill a gender role according to this special gender status.

Recognition of a potential woman-man or man-woman on the grounds of occupational preferences requires a sexual/gendered division of labor. But the sexual division of labor that existed in tribal cultures has disappeared just as the life of the prereservation days has disappeared. Life—especially economy—on Indian reservations has become integrated into twentieth-century capitalist society. In many areas, the differences between "man's work" and "woman's work" have become blurred. Still, there are areas of work that are cross-culturally considered more masculine or more feminine. People pick non-Native or at least not culturally specific occupations that best fit their gender identity. Contemporary men-women (as well as "butch" lesbians) become, for example, firefighters, road construction workers, crane operators, and the like; that is, they choose physically strenuous occupations dominated by men. In the rural areas, they may also choose to compete with men by participating in rodeos, riding bulls, and roping cows. Erna Pahe (Navajo) told me about such a woman whom she had witnessed in the late 1950s and 1960s. Among the Shoshoni on the reservation I visited, I was told that contemporary mannish females hunt deer and elk, as do the men, while most women do not. Present-day Native American women-men (as well as gays), on the other hand, have a tendency to choose occupations defined as feminine and "nurturing" in the Western sense, such as nurses and social workers.

The issue of identity has become complex over the past decades. Some people, usually raised in families that are oriented toward the traditions of their cultures, still identify themselves as women-men or men-women, and are viewed and labeled that way by the other members of their respective communities. Such individuals are to be found almost exclusively on the reservations. Often they do not have any role models, that is, women-men or men-women of the generations before them. In order to recreate a role for themselves, they turn to the elders (and sometimes to anthropological and other writings about Native American gender variance) and refashion their role to fit into the late twentieth century. Their identity and status is still, as in the old days, based on occupational preferences and/or spiritual experiences rather than on sexual preference. As a rule they do not identify themselves as gay or lesbian due to the cultural constructions of sexuality noted above.

Other people on and off the reservations set themselves apart from others of their community not by cross-gender occupational interests and personality traits, but by a sexual preference for partners of the same sex. They identify with Western concepts of lesbian and gay; they do not view themselves as women-men or men-women but as gay *men* or lesbian *women*. In defining their identity, they emphasize sexuality and deemphasize occupational aspects and spirituality.

Still other, usually urban, Native Americans manifest an identity that is a combination of the traditions of gender variance and of Western concepts of homosexuality. Their identity is, on the one hand, gay and lesbian, so they exclusively or predominantly enter into relationships with same-sex partners. On the other hand, they perceive themselves, as Native American homosexual individuals, as inherently combining elements of both the masculine and the feminine within themselves on a spiritual rather than an occupational level. For them a combination of the masculine and the feminine is tied to sexual orientation rather than to gender status. While two-spirit people may be "butches" or "queens," most of them unambiguously identify themselves as women or men, not as an intermediate gender that combines both.

There are also Native Americans who on some reservations basically live a contemporary version of the ways of women-men and men-women but do not necessarily label themselves as such. Many people in the respective communities remember that cross-gender behavior once was culturally acceptable, but they do not necessarily remember the details of women-men's and men-women's roles and statuses or the terminology used to refer to them. Masculine females in such cases may or may not identify themselves as belonging to a gender different from both man and woman, but they are perceived by others in their community as being masculine in their personal expressions and occupational choices, and thus as being different from other females.

Colonization and Homophobia

Due to the influences of white concepts and Christianity, gender variance and homosexual behavior have come to be met with strong disapproval on and off the reservations. People either adopted white attitudes and values or did not wish to see their cultures criticized by Whites for permitting expressions of "perversion."[7] On the other hand I have also heard stories about—and have witnessed this myself—contemporary women-men and men-women as well as lesbian or gay couples living on the reservation unharmed and quite comfortable. It is my impression that on a number of reservations it is possible for same-sex couples to live undisturbed unless they make their sex life a public issue the way urban lesbians and gays in the cities do. A common remark people made to me was that same-sex relationships "are not talked about" on the reservations, neither by those involved in them nor by other members of their communities. At first I took this as an indication of discrimination. At least in some cases it seems to be a matter of decorum, however.

People of whatever sexual inclination are expected to fit into the everyday life of their rural reservation community. It is considered inappropriate to set oneself apart on the grounds of sexuality. The inappropriateness here does not necessarily lie in the fact that sexuality is concerned, but that certain people try to set themselves apart on whatever grounds from the community at large. Erna Pahe (Navajo) for example, said that for one thing it is considered bad taste to hurl one's sex life or sexual preference into everyone's face. She also pointed out to me:

> [On the reservation] you wouldn't go out and advertise a gay barbecue, gay picnic, or something like that, because in their [the other Navajos'] eyes it would show that there is this group of people that are trying to be separate from the People, you know, all of our people on the reservation.

Thus lesbians and gays on the reservations will get together for informal private gatherings, barbecues, or parties, but it seems uncommon—or sometimes maybe even unnecessary—for them to formally organize themselves. Male-bodied nádleehé know each other but apparently do not feel any need to formally organize themselves on the grounds of their gender or sexuality because they are integrated within their families and local communities. A Nez Percé woman I talked to said that it is her impression that back on the reservation "everybody knows, but they just don't pay attention, they don't really care, you know, it's not a big deal. They tease you about it, [but] the only ones that really gave me any trouble were the ones that were Christian Indians."

But it is impossible to generalize about the presence or absence of homophobia in Indian communities. As Paula Gunn Allen (Laguna/Sioux) remarked, "there are people being raised even today in a number of tribal universes . . . in the rural areas, not the big cities, and they're raised with complete acceptance. . . . But it's a pretty mixed bag. There are a number of reservations that are throwing queers off and won't let them come back. . . . It's pretty horrifying in a lot of respects because we're still going through the agonies of colonization and the remnants of the colonial mind that has been imposed upon us" (quoted in Levy et al. 1991).

Two-Spirited People: Identity Issues

Many Native Americans who at some point in their lives have had a same-sex relationship have also had heterosexual relationships, a fact that confuses the more narrowly defined Western categories of "gay," "lesbian," "bisexual," and "straight." To identify themselves as lesbian to many Native American women means that for the time being they prefer women as partners, and maybe they will continue to do so, but it does not necessarily mean that they exclusively live or intend to live in relationships with women. Moreover, mannish women on and off the reservation will not seldom prefer the company of (heterosexual) men over that of women, because it is the men and not the women who share their way of life and personal manners. Still other Native American self-identified lesbians greatly enjoy the company of Native American gays.

The idea of being restricted to one kind of sexual choice for all of their lives or of even banning men from their lives altogether seems to be far-fetched to many Native American lesbians I talked to, even though some prefer a way of life centered entirely around women. Many of the lesbians I talked to had a history of relationships with men, which they did not seem to remember with repugnance. Amelia (pseudonym), an urban woman in her late thirties who is of mixed heritage and identifies herself as bisexual, recalled how she felt alienated by the codes of the white lesbian community in the 1970s:

> I think my first big romance was [with] a girl, another girl, when I was in junior high. I was thirteen, she was fifteen. She was an older woman. [Chuckles.] I think I fell in love with girls first, but I was also attracted to boys. I think that sometimes in trying to fit in with some of the lesbian stuff in the seventies—I wasn't really experimenting with men that much, but it's

like a lot of the lesbians just wouldn't *talk* about any attraction to men, although I think that there is probably lesbians who occasionally sleep with men, more than people want to talk about, but there's so much denial around it. So I mean to some extent I'm perfectly happy to sleep with women for the rest of my life, but if it turns into a real iron-clad thing like that, it kind of loses its appeal.

My data indicate that a high proportion of self-identified lesbian/two-spirited Native American women have given birth to children (who were not conceived by artificial insemination but by intercourse with men). The importance of children for Native American women was repeatedly emphasized to me by lesbian women. Erna Pahe said that in Navajo culture

> there is a special role that women play, too, I mean, as the bearers of the next generation. There's a distinct position that women play within the tribe, and so even though nádleehé women [in the sense of lesbian/two-spirited, S. L.] exist, it's of a different level. They're *mothers*. I mean, like myself, I'm a mother. The first thing is you're a child. And you become a young woman. And then you become a mother, so whether you're a nádleehé or not, the first, before anything else, is, you are a mother.... So when you speak about nádleehé women, the thing is that they're mothers first.

Another example of the connection of motherhood with sexual preferences that are not exclusively homosexual is a Shoshoni woman, Shirley (pseudonym), and her first partner. They decided they wanted to raise a child, so Shirley, who was many years younger than her partner, got pregnant by a relative of her partner's and gave birth to a daughter. The partner had guardianship of the girl from the time she was born, so they decided that the partner should adopt the child, which was finally arranged by a (two-spirited) tribal judge. When the two women separated, the girl stayed with the partner, but Shirley regularly spent time with the child.

While Shirley apparently has spent most of her adult life in relationships with older women, she did not exclude the possibility of entering into a long-term relationship with a man. She dreamt of having her own cattle and cultivating alfalfa, and an older, male, cowboy-type partner would have been just as welcome to her in that imaginary future as the kind of female partners she had. The possibility for a mannish female to choose either a woman or a man for her partner is consistent with the traditional pattern among the Shoshoni.

Within their Native American cultural frames of reference, conceiving and giving birth to children is an essential part of womanhood regardless of a woman's sexual preference. Thus, some of them label themselves bisexual rather than lesbian, which some women perceive to be a rigid Western category created by self-identified lesbian white women that runs contrary to lived life where sexual preferences may change.[8]

Urban Lesbians and Gay Men

Because of problems many encounter within their families and communities, but also to find better opportunities for work and education, a considerable number of lesbian and gay Native Americans leave their reservations to join Native American lesbian and gay communities in the cities. They may return to their reservations periodically to see their relatives, which often also means going back into the closet (Randy Burns, personal communication 1992). Even though the lesbian and gay subcultures in the cities might still not provide specific role models for Native American lesbians and gays, the latter at least find themselves in a position to express same-sex relationships in a noncloseted way. Erna Pahe recalls:

> On the [Navajo] reservation, you never see a lot of touching of lovers. Even in straight relationships, they don't do much touching, you know, holding hands is about the extent of any public showing that you're in a relationship, right? So it was nice, going down the Castro [Castro Street, the heart of the gay/lesbian neighborhood of San Francisco, S. L.], and you're actually able to put your arms around your lover, and, you know, *touching* women has always been exciting for me. I mean, it was just so different.

This example also illustrates the influence of the urban gay/lesbian context on urban Native American lesbians' and gays' lives. While the experience of being Native American is a strong part of their identity, they do incorporate behaviors that are available to them in the lesbian/gay subcultures in the cities but not on the reservations.

Many lesbian and gay Native Americans basically identify themselves as members of the lesbian/gay/bisexual communities (Tafoya 1992:257). Yet others do not quite feel at home there because of the racist discrimination they face. These individuals are searching for identities and lifestyles that are, in the broadest sense, specifically "Indian," as opposed to white gay and lesbian, and different from other gays and lesbians of color. Many turn to their native cultures in search of identities and role models and rediscover the tribal traditions of multiple genders, of women-men and men-women whose same-sex relationships were accepted and who, moreover, sometimes were very respected members of their communities.

Many Native American gays and lesbians in the cities see their contemporary roles as a continuation of the roles of women-men and men-women in tribal cultures. They view the women-men and men-women of the tribal cultures as their "gay" and "lesbian" predecessors. Consequently, they also see the "traditional" role as a "gay" role. "Gay" in this context assumes a meaning that in some respects differs from Western definitions, referring not only to sexual preferences but also to special roles and responsibilities (artists, providers, healers) that are linked to homosexual individuals in tribal cultures (cf. Burns 1988:1f.).

This perception is reflected in the term "two-spirit" that urban lesbian and gay Native Americans have coined for themselves. The term two-spirit/two-spirited refers to tribal traditions of gender variance, to the roles and statuses in Indian cultures of women-men and men-women who combined both masculine and feminine traits. Such a concept of two-spirit/two-spirited both helps Native American lesbians and gays to gain acceptance within the Indian communities and provides them with positive role models. While women-men and men-women in the tribal societies often were such in very tangible ways (e.g., by combining masculine and feminine work activities), contemporary urban two-spirited people view such a combination in a more abstract way. A combination of the masculine and the feminine is more often seen as a spiritual quality innately inherent in homosexual women and men. The choice of the term "two-*spirit*" (and not, for example, "two-gendered") also reflects an emphasis on spiritual gifts Native American gays and lesbians perceive to be innately bestowed on them.

Even though Native American lesbians, for example, who label themselves two-spirited draw on the tribal traditions of men-women, they do not usually view themselves as being of a gender different from "woman" and "man." The combination of abstract, spiritual masculine and feminine energies that they perceive to dwell within themselves does not affect their classification in terms of gender. As a rule, they view themselves as women-loving *women*, not as men-women.

The postulated historical continuum from the women-men and men-women of the tribal cultures to the urban Native American lesbians and gays of today is not entirely unproblematic, however. According to both the written sources and various people who are intimately familiar with the traditions of gender variance in their respective cultures, the last "old-time" women-men and men-women on many reservations were alive in the 1920s and 1930s, in a few cases up to the 1940s. Even by then, the institution had already dramatically declined due to acculturation, as has been outlined above. The contemporary two-spirit identity is strongly based on research done by urban lesbian and gay Native Americans since the mid-1970s into the written anthropological and historical sources. In many ways, this identity reflects the way white researchers up to the 1980s have interpreted women-men's and men-women's roles and statuses—as ways to culturally integrate innately homosexual individuals, who at the same time often held special, highly respected statuses.

In the old-time roles and statuses of women-men and men-women there is an emphasis on gender while in those of contemporary two-spirit people the emphasis is on sexuality, ethnicity, and a spirituality that is viewed as innate in Native American homosexual women and men. Thus, in many ways the concept of two-spirit reinterprets the old-time traditions of gender variance in a way to fit the needs of Native American lesbians and gays in the late twentieth century. As gender variance has ceased to exist on the reservations, urban Native American lesbians and gays have been reinventing a new tradition of two-spiritness that draws on tribal cultures, on the experience of being Native American in an urban multiethnic environment, and on urban gay and lesbian lifestyles.

Two-spirit can probably best be characterized as a largely pan-Indian gay/lesbian identity that emphasizes ethnicity and spirituality. During the past years, the term has sometimes come to encompass also the traditions of gender variance past and present, Native American bisexuals, transgendered people, butches and queens as well as gender variance in indigenous cultures outside North America (cf. Tietz 1996:205). The urban two-spirit communities are comprised of people of various tribal backgrounds and of a number of people who are of mixed heritage. Their knowledge of tribal culture varies widely, depending on how and where they were brought up. Interaction during intertribal two-spirit gatherings is facilitated by the use of pan-Indian symbols and actions, mostly of Plains origin, such as the use of sage (or other plants that are connected with special cleansing power) for smudging, sweat lodges, talking circles, powwows, and giveaways.

Not all Native American lesbians and gays consider themselves two-spirited in the sense outlined above. Two-spirited is a concept prevalent in the cities and at intertribal gatherings that are mostly attended by urban Indian gays and lesbians, and it has not yet spread to the reservations on a large scale. Moreover, a considerable number of lesbian and gay Native Americans still choose an identity and lifestyle closer to white homosexual identities, trying to merge into the gay and lesbian urban subcultures with their bars and other gathering places.

Native American Lesbians: A Sketch

As I talked to more and more people, very diverse life histories began to un-fold. It is impossible to go into many details here because of this diversity (the results of the project will be presented in detail in Lang forthcoming).[9] It may suffice, however, to offer a few glimpses of the lives of a few contemporary Native American lesbians.

One theme usually runs through each of these life histories like a red thread. With Amelia (pseudonym), the main theme was her mixed heritage and attempts to find an identity that harmoniously combines both sides of her heritage instead of denying one of them. With Joan (pseudonym), a Nez Percé woman, the main theme was the experience of having grown up as a tomboy, always different from other children. Joan was born around 1953 and lived in urban surroundings since her family relocated in the late 1950s, but she still has ties to her reservation.

> I was really a tomboy. By the time I came out it was more or less suspected already, you know? I just always was very different! So when I finally really came out and started bringing lovers home and stuff, then they started treating me more like I was just like a guy. As I was growing up some of these In-dian males on the reservation that are straight and that I visited growing up, they just treat me like a guy. I've always been the kind of person who hung out with the guys.

Another experience she elaborated on was being nonmonogamous. At the time we talked she had one main relationship and a number of more loose ones.

Michael Owlfeather told me about an earlier generation of women on the Shoshoni reservation, his grandmother and several of her women friends, who had husbands and children and who were nevertheless considered specially gendered:

> My grandmother was a two-spirited person herself, and it's known among the lesbian people there.... There's another woman that always hung around her ..., and people like that, that took pride in doing anything that a man could do, and doing it better. But these women also had children, got married, you know? But they had their women friends and were always respected for that and everything else. But it was nothing overt, they didn't hold it out to the community. But everybody knew what was going on.

Some Shoshoni women (about ten to twelve according to Michael Owl-feather) on the reservation today are contemporary examples of gender vari-

ance. They are quite "butch" in appearance and manners and seem to identify as mannish women rather than as a gender of their own. While they
enter into relationships with each other (and, interestingly, *not* with feminine women), it nevertheless appears to be not unusual for them to also have
sex with men and give birth to and raise children.

While one woman I talked to referred to herself and others like her on the
reservation as lesbian, it eventually became apparent that this was not identical with the Western concept of lesbian. She used the term to refer to the
masculine females on the reservation and their way of life, including sexual
relationships that are by no means exclusively homosexual. "Lesbian" to her
meant a contemporary "man-woman," although I am not sure how familiar
she was with her culture's traditions of gender variance. She told me about a
woman who lives a quite masculine life and, according to my consultant,
competed with men in boxing matches. She characterized her friend with
the words: "She's a lesbian, too."

I do not know what generic term is used among the other Shoshoni to
refer to those women or if any term is used. It is my impression that it is sufficient to drop one or two names of the women concerned, and everyone
knows what particular group of women is being talked about—the reservation is small (the Indian population there numbers a little over 3,000), and
everyone knows everyone else. Among the general population on the reservation, the way of life and relationships of these mannish women is apparently not disapproved of. Michael Owlfeather half jokingly described them
to me as a female version of "good old boys." Moreover, they seem to be ready
to pick a fight if someone insults them, so people who do not condone their
way of life usually leave them alone. They have a reputation of roughness
and toughness.

The lives of the Shoshoni mannish women on the reservation I visited (as
well as the life of the modern Shoshoni woman-man at whose home I stayed
for various periods of time) did not seem closeted. They are rural people
with interests centering around rural occupations and recreational activities.
Shoshoni mannish women take up male-dominated pursuits. At least two
women I met used to work as firefighters; they also hunt elk.

The mannish females on the reservation are integrated into the life of
their community and socialize with both straights and other two-spirits. Of
course there are people who try to discriminate against them, an action
sometimes prompted by the women's overall way of life rather than by their
sexual behavior. My consultant Shirley told me about an incident where one
of her brothers showed up drunk and started to insult her and her partner,

asking whether they thought they were men. "I'm more of a man than you are," Shirley replied, adding that she had regular work and led an orderly life, whereas he had lived on welfare all his life. One word led to another, until a fight ensued. Finally the brother was lying on the floor, Shirley and her partner pinning him down. They called the police and had him thrown into jail. While there may be discrimination on the reservations, Native American lesbians and gays are by no means always helpless victims but may very well take a stand against it.

There was another side to Shirley, her proneness to physical violence. People told me that the lesbians on the reservation resort to physical fights among each other when quarrels arise, especially when they have been drinking in bars in the nearby towns. People did not necessarily find this objectionable since physical fights under the influence of alcohol occur among straight women as well. Shirley was no exception. When drunk, she had a tendency toward violence, which she was herself very aware of. She told me that she once broke the jaw of a woman barkeeper who had somehow offended her and went to jail for it.[10]

In spite of the fact that many Native American lesbians cooperate and organize with gay men, they recognize that their own specific experiences and needs sometimes require women-only gatherings. Thus even though Native American lesbians often work closely with men in organizations like Gay American Indians, and attend the annual two-spirit gatherings with gay Native men, there are a few events that are restricted to Native American lesbians or to Native Americans and other lesbians of color and designed specifically to empower them. One example is the Women's Sun Dance, which is held annually. Only women of color may pledge to dance and be the actual performers of the Sun Dance, even though white women are welcome to attend, provided they show respect for the ceremony and its participants and help with the many things that have to be done (cooking, keeping the fire near the sweat lodge going, cutting firewood, hauling water).

Native American lesbians are acutely aware of the impacts of triple discrimination directed at them as women, lesbians, and Native Americans/women of color. An Ojibwa (Aniishnabe) woman summarized her experiences and those of other Native American lesbians as follows:

> As a two-spirited woman of the First Nations, you become aware of "triple oppression." You are lesbian, female and Native in a society dominated by a world that does not honor women or indigenous peoples and by a world that says your sexuality is non-existent, a phase, a threat or a sin against God. . . .

[You] find yourself in a city built on racism and fed on the oppression of everyone who is not heterosexual, white, and male (quoted in Tietz 1994:1).

There are some Native American lesbians who have become so disenchanted with white people, including white lesbian women, or who have come to reject white/Western society that they have established small communities restricted to Native American women or people of color. Two women I know live on women's land in the Midwest. Other women, mostly of mixed heritage, have recently purchased land in northern California where they plan to live self-sufficiently in the traditions of their tribal ancestors, turning their backs to the white culture, which they perceive as disrespectful toward nature and humans and as destructive.

The identities of contemporary Native American lesbians emerge at the intersection of traditional tribal models of multiple genders, ways of life that have emerged in the lesbian/gay subcultures in the cities, and an awareness of being Native American as opposed to being white or of any other ethnic heritage. In the tribal societies, there were no roles and identities that are strictly comparable to those of late twentieth-century lesbian women. In those societies systems of more than two genders led to the cultural acknowledgment and valuation of other genders in addition to the genders "woman" and "man." These additional genders accommodated males and females who markedly manifested personality traits and occupational preferences culturally attributed to the other sex. The roles of such women-men and men-women often included socially condoned sexual or marital relationships with partners of the same physical sex, but not of the same gender.

The women-men and men-women of tribal cultures have been presented as the predecessors of contemporary Native American lesbians and gays in numerous publications by white and Native writers alike. Urban lesbian and gay Native Americans view the traditions of gender variance as examples of how people who had same-sex relationships were traditionally accepted and valued in Native American cultures. As a result of this, during the last decade the term and concept of "two-spirit" has emerged at intertribal gatherings of mostly urban Native American lesbians and gays. Two-spirit, an identity that is largely pan-Indian, combines the experience of being Native American with that of being lesbian/gay.

On some reservations the once favorable attitude toward same-sex relationships and manifestations of cross-gender behavior gave way to a homophobia that condemns both gender variance and homosexuality. On other reservations, while the traditions of gender variance may be forgotten or repressed, masculine females and feminine males may still be treated with acceptance. The roles of lesbians on some reservations seem to reflect the tribal roles of men-women rather than urban lesbian identities, which are influenced by the white lesbian/gay subcultures. At the same time, their sexual relationships are usually not exclusively homosexual, which is a trait they share with many urban Native American lesbians. Motherhood is perceived as an essential component of Native American womanhood regardless of sexual preference. Thus, "lesbian" to many self-identified lesbian women on and off the reservation does not imply an exclusive preference for sexual relationships with women.

The lives of Native American lesbians are just as diverse as were the lives of men-women and women-men in the tribal societies. It is problematic to make any generalizations that may not do justice to individual life experiences. An oversimplified and misleading picture results if one reduces women-men's and men-women's lives to their sexuality. The same holds true for contemporary Native American lesbians and gays.

NOTES

1. This work is based on literature research and fifteen months of fieldwork conducted in 1992–1993.

2. Lesbian and gay Native Americans emphasize common ground and their common struggle as Native Americans for a specifically "Indian" lesbian/gay identity rather than differences in their experiences. In the mid-1980s when some lesbian members of Gay American Indians, an organization based in San Francisco, suggested a renaming of the organization to include the word "lesbian," the suggestion was rejected by women and men alike on the grounds that "gay" encompasses both men and women and it would be disruptive to the common cause if the women set themselves apart (Randy Burns and Erna Pahe, personal communication). Much of what is said here holds true for lesbians as well as gays, yet an effort has been made to highlight lesbian women's experiences.

3. The term "berdache" originally derived from an Arab term for male prostitutes or "kept boys" (Angelino and Shedd 1955). Even though in anthropological literature that term has never been used to imply that the individuals concerned were male prostitutes but only to refer to males in a woman's role in Native American cultures, the term has come to be rejected as inappropriate or even discriminating by quite a number of Native Americans and native and nonnative anthropologists alike. Thus, wherever it seemed necessary to use the word "berdache" in the present contribution, it is in quotation marks. I do not, however, follow the suggestion to replace "berdache" with "two-spirit." As becomes apparent from the present contribution, the term "two-spirit" originally

came into being under specific historical circumstances and with specific political intentions (the postulation of a historical continuum between the old-time women-men and men-women and present-day Native American gays and lesbians, in order to counteract homophobia in modern Native American communities). Instead of replacing one "loaded" term with another, I have decided to use the descriptive terms *women-men* (for males in a woman's role) and *men-women* (for females in a man's role).

4. It will be noted that the use of "man-woman" in this essay differs from the way the word is used both in Native American languages and in anthropological writings (e.g., Roscoe 1991; Fulton and Anderson 1992). There, "man-woman" usually refers to males in a woman's role. Yet, as will be pointed out in the section on the classification of sexual relationships, in Native American cultures a person's gender status in a sense overrides her or his (physical) sex. It therefore makes sense to refer to males in a woman's role by a term that puts the gender to which the chosen gender role belongs first and the physical sex second. This usage has already been recognized by Bleibtreu-Ehrenberg (1984), who titled her book on male gender variance in various cultures *Der Weibmann* (The woman-man). For the same reason, it seems appropriate to refer to females in a man's role as "men-women."

5. For a critique of such writings that do not take into account cultural variations and changes of Native American gender variance traditions and related phenomena within the historical context, therefore blurring diversities, see Blackwood's (1987) review of Williams (1986b).

6. Williams (1986a,b) provides a very optimistic view of the status especially male-bodied "berdaches" held in Native American tribal cultures. Trexler's book (1995) is the other extreme, stressing persecution faced by women-men in aboriginal North America. The historical truth lies probably somewhere in the middle (cf. Lang forthcoming).

7. The latter has already been pointed out by Lurie in the early 1950s where she observed that the Winnebago had become ashamed of the custom of *shiaðge* (woman-man) "because the white people thought it amusing or evil" (Lurie 1953:708). Even back then—Lurie did her fieldwork in 1945–47—the last woman-man among the Winnebago had died fifty years earlier.

8. The limitations of using Western categories such as gay, lesbian, or bisexual in trying to understand the lives of Native American two-spirited people are aptly pointed out by Tafoya (1992:257).

9. As a matter of fact, while there are quite a number of references to Native American female gender variance in the sources (see, for example, Blackwood 1984), hardly anything has ever been written about lesbians, with the exception of some contributions by Native Americans themselves to women-of-color anthologies (e.g., Brant 1984; Moraga and Anzaldúa 1981; Silvera 1991), the anthology *Living the Spirit* (Gay American Indians and Roscoe 1988), and other pieces

of prose and poetry contained in collections of writings of explicitly lesbian Native American writers (e.g., Chrystos 1988, 1991).

10. Some time after I last visited the reservation, friends from the reservation wrote me that Shirley started to "act crazier and crazier as time passed." She acted aggressively toward various people. One day early in 1994, she got drunk, got her rifle, and shot her partner to death.

REFERENCES

Allen, Paula Gunn. 1981. "Lesbians in American Indian Culture." *Conditions* 7:67–87.

Angelino, Henry and Charles L. Shedd. 1955. "A Note on Berdache." *American Anthropologist* 57 (1): 121–126.

Benedict, Ruth. "Anthropology and the Abnormal." *Journal of General Psychiatry* 10 (1934): 59–82.

Blackwood, Evelyn. 1984. "Sexuality and Gender in Certain Native American Tribes. The Case of Cross-Gender Females." *Signs: Journal of Women in Culture and Society* 10:1–42.

——. 1986. "Breaking the Mirror: The Construction of Lesbianism and the Anthropological Discourse on Homosexuality." In Evelyn Blackwood, ed., *The Many Faces of Homosexuality: Anthropological Approaches to Homosexual Behavior*, pp.1–18. New York: Harrington Park Press.

——. 1987. "Review of *The Spirit and the Flesh* by Walter L. Williams." *Journal of Homosexuality* 15 (3/4): 165–176.

Bleibtreu-Ehrenberg, Gisela. 1984. *Der Weibmann: Kultischer Geschlechtswechsel im Schamanismus*. Frankfurt: Fischer.

Brant, Beth, ed. 1984. *A Gathering of Spirit: A Collection by North American Indian Women*. Ithaca and New York: Firebrand Books.

Burns, Randy, 1988. "Preface." In Gay American Indians and Will Roscoe, eds., *Living the Spirit: A Gay American Indian Anthology*, pp. 1–5. New York: St. Martin's Press.

Callender, Charles and Lee Kochems. 1983. "The North American Berdache." *Current Anthropology* 24:443–470.

Chrystos. 1988. *Not Vanishing*. Vancouver: Press Gang Publishers.

——. 1991. *Dream On*. Vancouver: Press Gang Publishers.

Ford, Clellan S. and Frank Beach. 1965. *Formen der Sexualität*. Hamburg: Rowohlt.

Forde, C. Daryll. 1931. "Ethnography of the Yuma Indians." *University of California Publications in American Archaeology and Ethnology* 28 (4): 83–278.

Fulton, Robert and Steven W. Anderson. 1992. "The Amerindian 'Man-Woman': Gender, Liminality, and Cultural Continuity." *Current Anthropology* 33:603–610.

Gay American Indians and Will Roscoe, eds. 1988. *Living the Spirit: A Gay American Indian Anthology.* New York: St. Martin's Press.

Goulet, Jean-Guy. 1982. "Religious Dualism among Athapaskan Catholics." *Canadian Journal of Anthropology* 3 (1): 1–18.

Grinnell, George B. 1962. *The Cheyenne Indians.* 2 Vols. New York: Cooper Square.

Jacobs, Sue-Ellen. 1968. "Berdache: A Brief Review of the Literature." *Colorado Anthropologist* 1:25–40.

—— and Jason Cromwell. 1992. "Visions and Revisions of Reality: Reflections on Sex, Sexuality, Gender, and Gender Variance." *Journal of Homosexuality* 23 (4): 43–69.

——, Wesley Thomas, and Sabine Lang, eds. 1997. *Two-Spirit People: Native American Gender Identity, Sexuality, and Spirituality.* Urbana: University of Illinois Press.

Katz, Jonathan N. 1985. *Gay American History: Lesbians and Gay Men in the USA.* New York: Harper & Row.

Kessler, Suzanne and Wendy McKenna. 1977. *Gender: An Ethnomethodological Approach.* New York: Wiley.

Kiev, Ari. 1964. "The Study of Folk Psychiatry." In Ari Kiev, ed., *Magic, Faith, and Healing: Studies in Primitive Psychiatry,* pp. 3–35. New York: The Free Press of Glencoe.

Lang, Sabine. 1990. *Männer als Frauen—Frauen als Männer: Geschlechtsrollenwechsel bei den Indianern Nordamerikas.* Hamburg: Wayasbah.

——. 1994. "Hermaphrodite Twins, Androgynous Gods: Reflections of Gender Variance in Native American Religions." Paper presented at the 93d Annual Meeting of the American Anthropological Association, Atlanta, Ga.

——. 1997a. "Various Kinds of Two-Spirit People: Gender Variance and Homosexuality in Native American Communities." In Sue-Ellen Jacobs, Wesley Thomas, and Sabine Lang, eds., *Two-Spirit People: Native American Gender Identity, Sexuality, and Spirituality,* pp. 100–118. Urbana: University of Illinois Press.

——. 1997b. "Zwillingshermaphroditen und androgyne Götter: Geschlechtliche Ambivalenz in oralen Traditionen indianischer Kulturen." *kuckuck* 1 (1997): 29–34.

——. 1998. *Men as Women, Women as Men: Changing Gender in Native American Cultures.* Austin: University of Texas Press.

——. Forthcoming. *Visions and Choices: Glimpses of Native American Two-Spirited People's Lives.* Austin: University of Texas Press.

Levy, Lori, Michel Beauchemin, and Gretchen Vogel. 1991. *Two-Spirited People: The Berdache Tradition in Native American Cultures.* Videotape, Dept. of Anthropology, University of California, Berkeley.

Lurie, Nancy O. 1953. "Winnebago Berdache." *American Anthropologist* 55 (5): 708–712.

Martin, M. Kay and Barbara Voorhies. 1975. *Female of the Species*. New York: Columbia University Press.

Miller, Wick. 1972. "Newe Natekwinappeh: Shoshoni Stories and Dictionary." *University of Utah Anthropological Papers* 94:1–172.

Minnesota Indian AIDS Task Force. 1989. *Honored by the Moon*. Videotape, Minneapolis, Minn.

Minturn, Leigh, Martin Grosse, and Santoah Haider. 1969. "Cultural Patterning of Sexual Beliefs and Behavior." *Ethnology* 8:303–318.

Moraga, Cherríe and Gloria Anzaldúa, eds. 1981. *This Bridge Called my Back: Writings by Radical Women of Color*. New York: Kitchen Table Women of Color Press.

Osgood, Cornelius. 1958. "Ingalik Social Culture." *Yale University Publications in Anthropology* 53:1–289.

Owlfeather, Michael. 1988. "Children of Grandmother Moon." In Gay American Indians and Will Roscoe, eds., *Living the Spirit: A Gay American Indian Anthology*, pp. 97–105. New York: St. Martin's Press.

Parsons, Elsie C. 1932. "Isleta, New Mexico." *Annual Report, Bureau of American Ethnology* 47:193–466.

——. 1939. "The Last Zuni Transvestite." *American Anthropologist* 41 (2): 338–340.

Roscoe, Will. 1987. "Bibliography of Berdache and Alternative Gender Roles among North American Indians." *Journal of Homosexuality* 14 (3/4): 81–171.

——. 1988. "North American Tribes with Berdache and Alternative Gender Roles." In Gay American Indians and Will Roscoe, eds., *Living the Spirit: A Gay American Indian Anthology*, pp. 217–222. New York: St. Martin's Press.

——. 1991. *The Zuni Man-Woman*. Albuquerque: University of New Mexico Press.

Silvera, Makeda, ed. 1991. *Piece of my Heart: A Lesbian of Color Anthology*. Toronto: Sister Vision Press.

Steward, Julian H. 1941. "Culture Element Distributions 13: Nevada Shoshoni." *Anthropological Records* 4 (2): 209–359.

Stewart, Omer C. 1960. "Homosexuality among the American Indians and other Peoples of the World." *Mattachine Review* 6 (1): 9–15, (2): 13–19.

Tafoya, Terry. 1992. "Native Gay and Lesbian Issues: The Two-Spirited." In Betty Berzon, ed., *Positively Gay: New Approaches to Gay and Lesbian Life*, pp. 253–259. Berkeley: Celestial Arts Publishing.

Thomas, Wesley. 1993. "A Traditional Navajo's Perspectives on the Cultural Construction of Gender in the Navajo World." Paper presented at the University of Frankfurt, Germany.

——. 1997. "Navajo Cultural Constructions of Gender and Sexuality." In Sue-Ellen Jacobs, Wesley Thomas, and Sabine Lang, eds., *Two-Spirit People: Native American Gender Identity, Sexuality, and Spirituality*, pp. 156–173. Urbana: University of Illinois Press.

Tietz, Lüder. 1994. "Two-Spirited People in Canada: Between Triple Discrimination and Empowerment." Paper presented at the 93d Annual Meeting of the American Anthropological Association, Atlanta, Ga.

——. 1996. "Moderne Rückbezüge auf Geschlechtsrollen indianischer Kulturen." Master's thesis, University of Hamburg, Institut für Ethnologie.

Trexler, Richard T. 1995. *Sex and Conquest: Gendered Violence, Political Order, and the European Conquest of the Americas.* Ithaca: Cornell University Press.

Turney-High, Harry H. 1937. "The Flathead Indians of Montana." *Memoirs of the American Anthropological Association* 48:1–161.

Voegelin, Erminie W. 1942. "Culture Element Distributions 20: Northwest California." *Anthropological Records* 7 (2): 47–251.

Werner, Dennis. 1979. "A Cross-Cultural Perspective on Theory and Research on Male Homosexuality." *Journal of Homosexuality* 4:345–362.

Whitehead, Harriet. 1981. "The Bow and the Burden-Strap: A New Look at Institutionalized Homosexuality in Native North America." In Sherry Ortner and Harriet Whitehead, eds., *Sexual Meanings: The Cultural Construction of Gender and Sexuality,* pp. 80–115. London: Cambridge University Press.

Williams, Walter L. 1986a. "Persistence and Change in the Berdache Tradition among Contemporary Lakota Indians." In Evelyn Blackwood, ed., *The Many Faces of Homosexuality: Anthropological Approaches to Homosexual Behavior,* pp. 191–200. New York: Harrington Park Press.

——. 1986b. *The Spirit and the Flesh: Sexual Diversity in American Indian Culture.* Boston: Beacon Press.

PART II

Erotic Intimacies and Cultural Identities

5

Gloria Wekker

"What's Identity Got to Do with It?" Rethinking Identity in Light of the *Mati* Work in Suriname

At minimum, all social construction approaches adopt the view that physically identical sexual acts may have varying social significance and subjective meaning depending on how they are defined and understood in different cultures and historical periods. Because a sexual act does not carry with it a universal social meaning, it follows that the relationship between sexual acts and sexual identities is not a fixed one, *and it is projected from the observer's time and place to others at great peril.*

—Vance 1989:18, emphasis mine

The concept of "homosexual identity" plays a privileged and tenacious part in discussions about homosexual behavior (cf. D'Emilio 1984; Vance 1989; De Cecco and Elia 1993). The concept is used as a particularly powerful mediator of gay and lesbian behaviors. Sometimes these discussions are limited to the Western world, but the concept is also, apparently without much hesitation, used in cross-cultural contexts. Even though in constructionist approaches the relationship between sexual acts and sexual identities is thought to be variable, scholars often do not question the notion of homosexual (or homoerotic) identity in itself nor its ubiquitousness (cf. Vance's statement quoted above; Newton and Walton 1984; Lewin 1995). Whether "homosexual identity" is conceived of as an essentialist category, with biological and physiological influences preceding cultural ones and setting limits on the latter, or as a constructionist concept privileging social and cultural experiences, it is striking that a concept used with such frequency in the literature is not subjected to more reflection. However the concept is conceived, it apparently speaks to deeply ingrained, ethnopsychological notions in Western subjects that the core of our being, our essence, the privileged site in which the truth about ourselves and our social relationships is to be found, corresponds to something that we call (homo-)sexual identity (Foucault 1981; Kulick 1995). What has generally been lacking is an exploration of the implication and embeddedness of "identity" in hegemonic, Western thought, even if in feminist and "queer" versions. While it is not my intention here to give a thorough "reading" of the history of this concept in either Western folk wisdom or in various disciplinary domains, I think it generally will be agreed upon that "identity" carries heavy connotations of stasis, "core, unitary character," that which is immutable about a person, whether this core is ascribed to inborn or to learned characteristics (Geertz 1984; Weedon 1987; Kondo 1990). It will be my contention in this article that students of sexuality should problematize the notion of "identity" in order to avoid circuitous reasoning and premature closure.

By way of focusing on a widespread institution among Creole[1] working-class women in Paramaribo, Suriname, called the *mati* work, I want to present a differently conceived sexual configuration that does not posit a fixed notion of "sexual identity." Mati, although by no means a monolithic category, are women who engage in sexual relationships with men and with women, either simultaneously or consecutively, and who conceive of their sexual acts in terms of behavior. In focusing on female mati, I embark on a much overdue project in a Caribbean context: "to theorize from the point of view and contexts of marginalized women not in terms of victim status or an essentialized identity but in terms that push us to place women's agency, their subjectivities and collective consciousness, at the center of our understandings of power and resistance" (Alexander 1991:148).

First, I will describe the mati work within its historical and sociocultural setting, and I will consider how this "unruly sexuality" relates to dominant, heterosexual patterns in the same context. Second, I want to defend the claim that conceptualizing homosocial bonding and homoerotic behavior among women in this Third World context as "identity" inscribes and reproduces hegemonic Western analytical categories. Third, and more generally, I will address the question of how to proceed fruitfully in theorizing homoerotic behavior cross-culturally, without radically distorting emic realities. It is vital to put the genesis of "homosexual identity under capitalism" (D'Emilio 1984) into cultural and historical perspective as just one possible configuration among many, without universal validity. Thinking about homosexuality should start from the realization that "homosexualities"[2] cross-culturally have in common sexual acts between same-gendered people, but these acts are also and importantly different and contextually conceived in multiple ways.

The Mati Work

I was alerted to the mati work by the literature while doing research for my master's thesis in the early 1980s. The institution is first mentioned in 1912, when a high Dutch government official, Schimmelpenninck van der Oye, on a fact-finding mission concerning the health situation of the population in the colony of Suriname, deplores the widespread occurrence of the "sexual communion between women, the *mati play*" (Ambacht 1912). Another observer in the 1930s remarks upon the fact that "the unusual relationships among women in Suriname . . . were not dependent on social rank, intellectual development, race or country of origin" (Comvalius 1935). In the course of this century, several studies—mostly by men, occasionally by white women—have dealt with "the unusual relationships between women" (Herskovits 1936; Buschkens 1974; Janssens and van Wetering 1985; van Lier 1986). My curiosity about the phenomenon was piqued by these descriptions, and I decided to devote my doctoral research to the mati work.

From January 1990 through July 1991, I explored how working-class Creole women construct themselves sexually in Paramaribo, Suriname.[3] As a black sociocultural anthropologist, born in Suriname and trained in the Netherlands and the United States, my interest in local constructions of subjectivity, gender, and sexuality clearly bespeaks issues in my own situated life (Wekker 1992b). In the course of my sexually coming-of-age in Amsterdam, the Netherlands, during the seventies, I noticed that there were at least two models available to me on how to be a woman who loved other women. There was a dominant model, mostly engaged in by white, middle-class women, in which the rhetoric of "political choice," feminist chauvinism, conformity between partners along a number of dimensions, including socioeconomic status and age, and predominantly childlessness, played central parts. And there was a subjugated model, of which I discerned merely the contours at the time but which I later learned to identify as the mati work. The latter was lived by working-class Afro-Surinamese women, who often differed greatly in age from their women partners, typically had children, and apparently maintained their ties with men, either as husbands, lovers, friends, or sons. My awareness of these two models, which did not seem to come together on any shared ground, made me increasingly aware of the situatedness and sociocultural construction of my own (Eurocentric) sexuality and its axioms, which I had taken for granted. When at a later stage I chose to occupy various sexual sites that are distinguished within a Western universe, it became clear that significant amounts of mental, psychological, and social work were necessary, both within myself and within the predominantly middle-class (white and black) circles in which I moved to obtain any kind of credibility for those choices. My periodically returning structural malaise in applying Western sexual labels (hetero-, homo-, and bisexuality) to myself while failing to "identify" with them was a major impetus to engage in this particular research. As Reinharz, among others, has noted "in feminist research 'the problem' frequently is a blend of an intellectual question and a personal trouble" (1992:258).

Most of the authors, who have dealt with the mati work, locate its emergence at the beginning of this century, when men were frequently absent from the city due to migrant labor as gold diggers and balata bleeders in the interior of Suriname. Ironically, these authors explain the widespread occurrence of the mati work among women by the absence of men, either in a strict numerical sense or in a psychological or emotional sense. I have interpreted Creole working-class women's sexual behaviors by focusing on the accounts women themselves give of them, while locating them within an African-American diasporic framework. It should be clear that when talking about the mati work, I am not referring to a recent or a marginal phenomenon. In contradistinction to the periodization most students of the mati work give, I have argued that there is no good reason to assume that it was not already present from, possibly, the time of the Middle Passage and the beginning of the colony in the seventeenth century. Although it is, of course, impossible to obtain reliable quantitative data on the occurrence of the mati work in Paramaribo in the past or today, it is clear for those who have eyes to see (the symbolic behaviors) and ears to hear (the powerful, metaphorical language mati speak to each other) that it is widespread in the working class. I have suggested that three out of four working-class Creole women will be engaged in it at some point in their lives. There is no significant stigma attached to the mati work in a working-class environment. The longevity, tenacity, and vitality of the mati work are striking, given the fact that I first "saw" the mati work in Amsterdam—after large communities of Surinamese had migrated to the metropolis at the time of independence (1975)—without being fully cognizant of what it was I saw.

Although there is a comparable, yet less institutionalized, less visible, and less widely accepted, phenomenon also called mati work among Creole men, in this contribution I will focus exclusively on Creole, working-class women. While some mati, especially older women who have borne and raised their children, do not have sex with men anymore, other, younger mati have a variety of arrangements with men, such as marriage, concubinage, or a visiting relationship. Women's relationships with women mostly take the form of visiting relationships, although a minority of female partners with their children shares a household. These varied arrangements are made possible by the circumstance that most Creole working-class women own or rent their own houses and are single heads of households. Mati thus form part of and actually continually "cross over" in a dual sexual system, which comprises an opposite-gendered and a same-gendered arena. I will come back to this sexual system in more detail later.

I Am a Gold Coin

The most frequent response working-class women gave me when I asked them to name a proverb that most closely expressed how they saw themselves, was "I am a gold coin." Creole culture, like other Black cultures in the diaspora, abounds with verbal arts: *odo* (proverbs), riddles, stories, word games, and songs. Blacks formulated odo during slavery as a running commentary on their everyday experience, and many odo bespeak a woman's everyday reality (Wekker 1997). "I am a gold coin" is a clipped version of an odo, used by insiders who often only need the first three or four words to understand what is being referred to. The entire odo goes like this: *"Mi na gowt' monni, m'e waka na alasma anu, ma mi n'e las' mi waarde"* ("I am a gold coin, I pass through all hands, but I do not lose my value"). It expresses with precision, yet characteristic indirection, some important features of the (sexual) universe Creole working-class women inhabit. An analysis of the odo gives important insights into this universe, while it simultaneously contradicts some of the most frequent, hegemonic explanations of social and gender patterns in the Caribbean.

The entire odo points to working-class women's adherence to a value structure in which middle-class values like legal marriage, monogamy, the heterosexual contract, one man fathering all one's children are designated as irrelevant to their reality. In effect, working-class women (whether exclusively involved with men, women, or both) are saying: It does not matter how many relationships I have had, whether with men or with women. What counts is how I carry myself through life, as a mother, with dignity, (self-) respect, and savvy, all of which characterize a *dyaya uma* (a mature woman, who knows how to take care of business). This autonomous set of values, found in the working class, runs counter to such a concept as "the lower-class value stretch" (Rodman 1971), which implies that working-class black people stretch middle-class values like monogamy and marriage, until their own practices can be said to fall within middle-class parameters.

My (African-American) understanding of the mati work and the alternative value structure in which it is embedded also flies in the face of Wilson's "respectability and reputation" paradigm (1969). Wilson stipulates that Afro-Caribbean working-class women are the bearers and perpetuators of inegalitarian, Eurocentric "respectability" due to their closer association with the master class during slavery as concubines and domestic slaves. Afro-Caribbean men, on the other hand, are said to subscribe to the egalitarian value system of "reputation," an indigenous counterculture based on the ethos of equality and rooted in personal as opposed to social worth. As I have shown elsewhere, Creole women participate fully in the local reputation system through their leadership roles in Winti, spirit possession, prophecy and healing, the significance and desirability of motherhood, their oral skills, and their entrepreneurial, political, and organizational roles (Wekker 1992b, 1997). Creole women have been and are central to cultures rooted in the tradition of slave resistance, which emerged in response to colonialism and the plantation system and which continued later in opposition to hegemonic, middle-class value patterns. My understanding of the frequency and openness of the phenomenon builds on West African heritage, the "grammatical principles" (Mintz and Price 1992) surrounding selfhood, gender, and sexuality, which Surinamese slaves elaborated upon under a specific constellation of historical, demographic, and cultural-political circumstances (Wekker 1992b). In addition, there are strong reasons to believe that slave women in other parts of the Caribbean developed comparable forms of relating to each other (Lorde 1983; Silvera 1992), pointing to the resiliency of the West African cultural heritage.

On a final note, the odo flatly denies the heterosexist representations of Caribbean women, encapsulated in the concept most widely used (and abused) to explain Caribbean family patterns and gender relations: matrifocality. The gendered sexual images that can be culled from the prolific literature on matrifocality is that men are sexually hyperactive, high performers, while women wait around patiently and pitifully for the hunter to bestow his favors upon them. So far, it has apparently been extremely difficult for (mostly male, heterosexual?) anthropologists to conceive that women did not wait around but took responsibility for orchestrating their own sexual pleasures.

Multiplicitous Subjectivities

Analyzing the parts of the odo "I am a gold coin," we first find an identification with *gold*. By inserting this adjective, women indicate that they consider themselves inherently worthy and valuable, which is symbolized by the allusion to the most desirable, durable, and precious good available in Surinamese society. Furthermore, gold is wanted to adorn and placate instantiations of the multiplicitous self as it is envisioned within the framework of the Afro-Surinamese Winti folk religion. Unlike the Western version of the subject as "unitary, authentic, bounded, static, trans-situational" (Geertz 1984), the self in an Afro-Surinamese working-class universe is conceptualized as multiplicitous, malleable, dynamic, contextually salient. Winti builds deeply upon West African "grammatical principles" (Mintz and Price 1992) and pervades virtually all aspects of life, from before birth to beyond death. Within this framework there is a relatively egalitarian gender ideology, in which both men and women are thought to be composed of male and female *winti*, gods. Also, importantly, both men and women are deemed to be full sexual subjects, with their own desires and own possibilities to act on these desires. Sexual fulfillment per se is considered important, healthy, and joyous, while the gender of one's object choice is regarded as less important. The following quote comes from an eighty-four-year-old mati, Misi Juliette Cummings, a retired market woman, who has had a variety of relationships with men in her life. She bore twelve children, seven of whom are alive today. The "apples of her eye," throughout her long life, were definitely women:

> *"Mi, noit' mi ben wan' trow, ef' mek' verbontu nanga man*[4] [I never wanted to marry or "be in association with a man"]. *Mi yeye no ben wan' de ondro man* [My "soul"/"I" did not want to be under a man]. Some women are like that. I am somebody who was not *hebzuchtig* [greedy] on a man, *mi yeye ben wan' de nanga umasma* [my "soul," "I," wanted to be with women]. It is your "soul" that makes you so. It is more equal when you are with a woman; the same rights you have, I have too. (Wekker 1992b:284)

In this quote Misi Juliette demonstrates some of the different instantiations of "I": in referring to herself she talks about *mi* (I) and *mi yeye* (my "soul"/I) wanting to be with women. *Yeye* refers to a decisive component of "I," made up of a male and a female God, both of which accompany the individual from birth (Wekker 1992b). An emic explanation of the mati work takes into account that one of the Gods, making up the *yeye*, is a male God, an Apuku, who desires women. This God, who is strong and jealous, cannot bear to see his child, the woman, involved on a long-term basis with a real flesh-and-blood male. Thus a mati is conceptualized as a woman, part of whose "I" desires and is sexually active with other women. Since the "I" is conceived as multiple and open, it is not necessary to claim a "truest, most authentic kernel of the self," a fixed "identity" that is attracted to other women. Rather, mati work is seen as a particularly pleasing and joyous activity, not as an identity. Linguistically, this conceptualization of sex as behavior is apparent in the phrase mati use to describe themselves. When pressed about the issue, as I often did in my role of "outsider within" (Hill Collins 1990) asking most impertinent, direct questions, they would say: *M'e mati*, using a verb ("I mati"), instead of: *"Mi na wan mati"* ("I am a mati").

A Dual Sexual System

In a further analysis of the odo "I am a gold coin" the identification with a coin is striking. First, this elicits the obvious connotation of a coin, passing from hand to hand, with its counterpart of women going from one relationship to the next, "trying to find their happiness," as they themselves explain. The analogy between money and women having multiple relationships is made without attaching negative value to it, as the third part of the odo—"but I do not lose my value"—shows.

But there is a second, relatively hidden, meaning to the allusion to money. Far from sovereignly imagining oneself above money, it is the standard by which women measure the seriousness of intent of their male partners: women envision a relatively straightforward exchange relationship between sex and money in their connections with men. As one woman told me, when she was describing an imaginary but, in her eyes, most undesirable and ludicrous outcome of such a cross-gender connection: *"A kon sidon na mi tapu, dan e n'e tya mi sensi kon . . . dan m'e law"* ("Then he comes, sits down in my house and doesn't bring me my money, then I must be crazy") (Wekker 1992b:178).

The transactional nature of opposite-gender relationships is by no means an exclusively Afro-Surinamese phenomenon. It is a connection found in divergent urban working-class settings, such as nineteenth- and early twentieth-century white New York (Peiss 1984, 1986), contemporary white American (Rubin 1976), African-American (Liebow 1967; Stack 1974), Nairobian (Nelson 1979), and Jamaican working-class cultures (Harrison 1988). It has, furthermore, been found in white middle-class settings that women tend to make more "pragmatic" choices regarding their mates, "knowing . . . that economic security is more important than passion" (Peplau and Gordon 1985:264). Working-class women, both mati and women who are exclusively involved with men, by their own accounts, need men to make them children in a system where the epitome of womanhood is motherhood, and they need men's financial contributions to keep their households afloat (Wekker 1992b). Demonstrating one's fertility, by having a large *bere* (literally, belly: children and grandchildren) used to be important to both men and women in a working-class culture that leaves few other avenues for distinguishing oneself. Younger women, in general, do not want to raise large families anymore, but motherhood remains vital. In accounting for their relationships with men, some women, who are embedded in the Afro-Surinamese Winti religion, argue that it is unhealthy for your "insides" not to have sexual communion with men at least once in a while. This argument, again, needs to be understood in the framework of an outlook on subjectivity, embedded within Winti, that stresses the importance of balancing the multiple aspects of the self; male and female "instantiations" of the person need to be satisfied and kept in harmony.

In their relationships with women, mati deploy money in a much less direct way. Although female lovers do exchange money and help each other cope financially, this aspect of the relationship is embedded in a rich flow of reciprocal obligations, which include the sharing of everyday concerns, the raising of children, nurturing, emotional support, and sexual pleasure. Money, as an exchange object for sex, thus plays an independent and outspoken role in relationships with men, but it is part of a more elaborate, a "thicker" stream of exchanges and reciprocal obligations in relationships with women. In fact, the term *work* in mati work implies that there are mutual obligations involved between two female partners. Mati contrast mati work with another modality they call *didon gewoon*, i.e., "just lying down"/"sleeping around," a sexual connection that does not imply rights and obligations toward another woman. *Didon gewoon* is not part of an ongoing relationship but marks an unencumbered, incidental sexual encounter. The rights and obligations in mati work generally involve the (social, psychological, economic) activities that are needed to help one's partner weather life. This may be by going to the doctor with her when she is ill, helping her finance a "crown" year celebration (when she reaches an important, five-yearly birthday), or, as the younger partner in the relationship, by showing one's mati the appropriate, respectful behavior. Most important, mati have sexual obligations toward each other: when one partner feels sexual desire, the other is obliged to satisfy her. It is generally agreed by mati that when a woman's desire is consistently denied by her partner, she may go and seek sexual pleasures with someone else. This may very well spell the demise of the relationship, since few women will tolerate it when their partner openly engages in sex with another woman.

During my research period, I asked several women to reflect on what some of the differences were between being in a sexual relationship with a man or with a woman. My landlady Misi Juliette, the eighty-four-year-old market woman, often explained to me that, "I really did not mind much, when that man [Dorus, the man she had five children with] went to visit other women. Frankly, I often thought: Well, it is better that he goes and harasses them instead of me. I also didn't mind when Coba, her mati, lay down with a man. If she could find a little money with him, why not? But if she slept with another woman, now that was different business!! I did not tolerate it."

In this and other conversations we had, it was abundantly clear that the intensity of Juliette's feelings was entirely focused on Coba, not Dorus, and that jealousy was channeled toward Coba's encounters with other women, not men. It made the socially constructed nature of such "natural" feelings as jealousy vividly clear to me.

The following quote from Lydia de Vrede, a thirty-seven-year-old nurse's aide, mother of five, who is currently married to the father of her last two children, helps to further illustrate these differences:

> I see it like this: love between two women is stronger than between a man and a woman. Maybe emancipated women will tell a man what they like in the bedroom, or tell him: do this or do that! But to satisfy that man, most women will pretend that they have come. But with a woman, you know what you like sexually and so does she, *dus a san' kan law yu ede zodanig, a kan tya' yu go na Kolera* [so the thing can make you so crazy, it may carry you into a mental hospital]. (Wekker, 1992b:283)

Before she was married, Lydia had several relationships with women, but given the jealous nature of her husband, she presently misses having a female lover but finds it impossible to accommodate a woman in her situation.[5] The quote reveals the existence of a dual sexual system, in which different power dynamics between partners obtain. There is an opposite-gendered arena in which masculine values and men are hegemonic. This arena within the working class is fed by an array of societal forces and influences, including inegalitarian middle-class gender arrangements and values, government regulations producing inequalities between men and women in the area of, among others, income,[6] and media and educational institutions transmitting homogenizing, normative, nuclear family contents. Men, because of their stronger economic positions and because they mostly do not carry the exclusive or main financial burden of having to bring up children, have more free-floating capital. As elsewhere in the Caribbean, we find in Suriname an overall picture of a dually segmented labor market, where men are found in the heavier and more profitable sectors of the formal and informal economy, working under better conditions and with higher salaries; women, on the other hand, work in the softer sectors of the economy, for the government, where wages are notoriously low, and in the informal sector (Tjoa 1990; Wekker 1992b). It is through their economically stronger position, however tenuous it may in itself be at times, that men get the upper hand in defining the proceedings of opposite-gender sexual encounters. Within this opposite-gender exchange system, women have less room to maneuver, and even less so within a steadily declining economy and following the adoption of Structural Adjustment Programs. The following account by forty-three-year-old Mildred Jozefzoon, a hairdresser and mother of four children, illustrates some features of her visiting relationship with Johnny Samuel, who is the father of three of her children and who lives with another woman:

> I get 100 or 125 Surinamese guilders from him, a week.[7] Mostly he comes around 11:30 A.M. and needs to be out of my house by 1:00 P.M. He wants it to be quick-quick. The way I feel about it is that somebody has come to take something away from me and then he leaves. I feel misused, taken in, even though he gives me the money. It goes like this: he takes off his shirt and his trousers, lies down on my bed. Then he wants me to come lie down beside him. Sometimes I sabotage the whole business by being agonizingly slow in taking off my clothes. Sometimes I say I don't feel like it. Then he says: I will make you feel like it. What can I do? He wants it so often and I need the money. (Wekker 1992b:224)

Pertinent in this segment of the sexual system is also that women tend to see each other as competitors for men's favors, and they do not exchange sexual information. Women consistently report an unfavorably skewed sex ratio, i.e., that the number of women far exceeds the number of men, yet what seems more likely to be the case is that the number of men whom women consider *eligible*—i.e., economically viable partners—is rather limited. Yet women still refuse, to varying degrees, to give up their subject status and agency. By elaborating on the concept of *kamraprekti*, chamber (i.e., sexual) obligations, women, whether they are in a permanent or in a more incidental relationship with a man, assert their own standards of fairness concerning the exchange of sexual favors for money; from unfavorable positions women try to adjust and manage the unequal balance of economic power with men (Wekker 1992b).

In the other domain of the dual sexual system, the same-gendered one, women are able to define what their sexual and emotional pleasures are. Life in society as a whole, but most markedly in the working class, is constituted along distinctly homosocial lines; men spend most of their time with other men, while women, whether they mati or not, are more likely to share time, work, attention, nurturing and, possibly, sexual encounters with other women. Since most women spend the greater part of their time in the company of other women, this means that there is no marked difference in the daily, social environments of mati and women who are sexually active only with men. On the contrary, working-class women, regardless of the gender of their sexual partners, frequently mingle and share the same environments. Among older mati we find relationships that have sometimes lasted thirty, forty, or more years. They raise their children together, share everyday concerns and ritual obligations and celebrations: "*Let' anu e was' krukt' anu*" ("the right hand washes the left"), is how older women typically conceive of their bonds with their mati. Traditionally, older women who were in a mati relationship used to wear dresses made out of the same material, *parweri*, but nowadays that is seen less often. Among younger mati there is a lively, sexual culture enacted at parties at people's homes and at *Winti Prey*, outdoor ritual gatherings in the framework of the Winti religion. Flirting and seeking each other out by linguistic, symbolic, and behavioral means have been made into an art form in this universe. By all accounts, sex with women is an important feature of women's lives, and they talk about it, often indirectly and metaphorically, but with obvious gusto (Wekker 1992a,b). One such narrative, which illustrates the joy inherent in sex with women, is told by Milly Pinas, a fifty-six-year-old street sweeper, mother of three children:

> I had this lady that I was really infatuated with, Ingrid. She had a steady relationship with Lucia and I was living with a man at the time. One Saturday afternoon, I took the bus to her place, bringing a bag of groceries and some ice-cold beers. She was expecting her lover that afternoon, too, however, so she told me to lock the door from the outside and climb through a window. Pretty soon we were upstairs in bed. We were "stealing," so it had to be fast work. We were almost hitting, when *pam-pam-pam*, who comes knocking at the door? I was not afraid, I wanted to go on, but Ingrid was shaking. She jumped from the bedroom window unto her neighbor's roof. It turns out that Lucia had a spare key to the house, so she came upstairs. I was sitting on the bed, wearing only a black slip. She said: "Good afternoon." I said: "good afternoon to you, too." Ingrid stayed outside, did not dare to come in. Lucia had been after me for a long time, so we hit on each other right away. (Wekker 1992b:275)

Women friends actively exchange sexual information and young girls are often initiated into the mati world by older women, sometimes explicitly in the form of an apprentice relationship (Wekker 1992a,b). Women often structure their relationships erotically into a "male" and a "female" role, with the male role having more prerogatives, just as in the world out there. These sexual roles are not carved in stone, however, and many women can and do change roles, either in the same relationship or in another one. Economically, mati relationships are more egalitarian than those between men and women. I have also concluded that sexually and emotionally they are more satisfying to many women than their cross-gendered relationships.

If the foregoing analysis of a dual sexual system in the Afro-Surinamese working-class, namely an opposite-gendered and a same-gendered arena, holds any validity, it is to be expected that there will be "leakage" between these two domains. There is considerable overlap in the personnel moving from one part of the system to the other, notably in the persons of mati, and it thus should not be surprising that several features of sexual culture, in the form of shared practices, are held in common in both parts of the system. The importance of motherhood; the polarization of roles within relationships, in a "male" and a "female" counterpart with accompanying role expectations; the existence of patterns of jealousy and violence between partners; the existence of sometimes wide age gaps between partners; and the underlying cosmology as it pertains to personhood and sexual being are all part of mati culture as well as of opposite-gender sexual arrangements. Thus the notion that the same-gendered arena proceeds according to a specific set of ideas, rules, and practices, which is totally distinct and insulated from what takes place in the opposite-gendered domain, cannot be held up.

While it is true that in many Western gay and lesbian sexual arrangements elements of dominant heterosexual culture are evoked, the point I am making here is a different one. From an emic point of view, mati and women exclusively involved with men have more in common with each other than is different between them. Being sexually active and fulfilled is more important than the object of one's passion. Mati are not singled out or stigmatized in a working-class environment nor do they feel the necessity to fight for their liberation or to "come out." Thus to the extent that I have stressed the differences between mati and women relating to men only, I may paradoxically and involuntarily have been highlighting the pernicious tendency of Western, bounded, fixed categories to insert and reproduce themselves in radically different constructions of being a (sexual) person.

What's Identity Got to Do with It?

It is clear that within this Afro-Surinamese working-class setting, there is a radically different conceptualization of personhood and same-gender desire than is customarily the case within a Western frame of reference. I will first briefly address the latter configuration. The troubled Western relationship with homosexuality, naturalized, compartmentalized, medicalized, consecutively made into sin and into the "deepest, truest" expression of the self, of one's identity, is historically and culturally embedded (Foucault 1981; De Cecco and Elia 1993). Whether a homosexual identity is understood as the pure sediment of biological or physiological processes, or whether some kind of interaction between the biological and the cultural is envisioned, or whether primacy is given to sociocultural experiences, the notion of a sexual identity in itself carries deep strands of permanency, stability, fixity, and near-impermeability to change. Furthermore, the mere existence of a sexual identity is usually taken for granted. The static nature of sexual identity is in line with the ways personhood in general is envisioned within a Western universe. Despite much evidence to the contrary, this culture stubbornly persists in the fictive notion that a person has a stable "core" character (Shweder and Bourne 1984): "a bounded, unique, more or less integrated motivational and cognitive universe . . . organized in a distinctive whole and set contrastively . . . against other such wholes" (Geertz 1984:126).

It is noteworthy that in most Indo-European languages there is only one way to make statements about the self: the personal pronoun "I." This particular understanding of a person as a bounded, fixed, rational, and self-determining agent is produced and reproduced in and by modern political, legal, social, and aesthetic discourses. Subjectivity has, until recently, implicitly been envisaged along masculine lines, thus leaving femininity no conceptual space but the nonmasculine; femininity is not just different, but in a hierarchically subordinate position to the masculine (Weedon 1987; Haraway 1991). While male sexuality is seen as aggressive and potent, female sexuality is conceptualized as passive and weak, needing to be awakened by a stronger force. Furthermore, one is either heterosexual or homosexual, with bisexuality muddying these clear waters. Dichotomous, either/or, hierarchical thinking characterizes this system.

A Creole universe is characterized by additive, inclusive, both/and thinking (cf. Hill Collins 1990). A person is conceived of as multiple, malleable, dynamic, and possessing male and female elements. Furthermore, all persons are inherently conceived of as sexual beings. A linguistic reflection and construction of this multiple, dynamic conceptualization of personhood is that in Sranantongo, the local creole, there are infinite possibilities to refer to "I" (Wekker 1992b). It is possible to talk about the self in masculine and in feminine terms, in singular and in plural forms, and in terms of third person constructions, regardless of the gender of the speaker. All of these different terms refer to different instantiations of "I."

A human being in this universe is understood to be made up of human and "godly" elements. From conception until death, a person is "carried" and protected by winti, gods. These gods are very near to a person's experience, and they are conceptualized like human beings, possessing the same virtues and vices. A person who is carried by Mama Aisa, the Uppergoddess of the Earth, for example, likes beautiful clothes and jewelry and is caring and nurturing. Both men and women can be carried by Aisa. Some characteristics of a person, such as those that she gets from the gods who accompany her throughout her life, or traits inherited from a biological parent, are seen as permanent, while others are temporary and contextually realized.

Women who engage in the mati work are, as we have seen, thought to be carried by a strong, male god, an Apuku, who is jealous of his "child," the woman, engaging in permanent sexual relationships with flesh-and-blood males. The Apuku is believed to be so strong and demanding that his child will have difficulty relating to men and will be more attracted to other women. An emic explanation of the mati work does not claim a core homosexual identity; rather, the behavior is conceived of as engagement in a pleasant activity, desired and instigated by one particular instantiation of the "I." It is the Apuku who is sexually attracted to women, and there is no emic reason to privilege this instantiation of the "I" above others by making him the decisive, "truest" element of the self. Likewise, when women state that it is good for your "insides" to have sex with men at least once in a while, they are building on an understanding of multiplicitous personhood that temporarily privileges a female instantiation of "I," which desires a man.

It is in keeping with the multiplicity of the "I" that a multiplicitous sexual repertoire was realized in the Creole working-class. There is no significant stigma attached to parts of this repertoire. Girls growing up in Creole working-class neighborhoods are confronted with different sexual choices and engaging in one variety—e.g., the same-gendered one—does not expose the girl to disapproval nor does it predispose her to stay in that part of the sexual system forever. Thus we see women who are alternately or simultaneously active in either part of the system. There are clear economic coordinates associated with their behavior (Wekker 1992b). Conceiving of same-gender sexual behavior embodied in the mati work in terms of "identity" inscribes and reproduces Western thought categories with their legacy of dichotomy, hierarchy, and permanency, thus distorting a phenomenon that is emically experienced in quite different terms.

Theorizing Same-Gender Sexual Behavior Cross-Culturally

Finally, what does all of this mean in light of our ongoing efforts to theorize same-gender sexual behavior cross-culturally? First of all, I hope to have made a case for the critical investigation and bracketing of the concept "homosexual identity." The deeply essentialist strand it often unwittingly introduces hampers rather than facilitates our understanding of the behavior we are trying to understand cross-culturally.

In the second place, emic constructions and explanations of same-gender sexual behavior need to be taken seriously. There is no reason to assume that the Western folk knowledge about sex, which has been elevated into academic knowledge (cf. Lutz 1985), should have any more validity than folk knowledge anywhere else. Feminist anthropology has proven not to be immune against problems that have haunted the discipline from its inception: the exclusion, erasure, or negation of the subjectivity and the critical agency of the colonized, especially women (cf. Mohanty 1991; Harrison 1993).

Third, the cross-cultural study of same-gender sexual behavior should proceed from the realization that "homosexualities" are multiple and manifold, realized in different contexts and charged with different meanings. Clearly, there are some institutional domains within every society that seem crucial in understanding the local constructions of the phenomenon—such as notions of personhood, gender systems—in their ideological and practical dimensions and their crosscutting ties with other domains, such as the economy and religion. It is misleading and self-defeating to talk of same-gender sexual behavior as one single, cross-cultural institution. The use of seemingly innocuous concepts, such as "homosexual identity," contributes to the export of Western categories of thought.

Finally, if in participant observation it is the person of the researcher that serves as the most central and sensitive instrument of research, it behooves those of us who do (cross-cultural) sex research to be transparent, accountable, and reflective about our own sexualities (cf. Kulick and Willson 1995). Awareness of the situatedness and sociocultural construction of our own sexuality and about the different modalities in which we engage with others are only some of the minimal requirements we ought to place on ourselves.

NOTES

1. Creoles, the second largest population group in Suriname, are the descendants of slaves and are a mainly urban group. I will alternately call them Creoles, the local designation, and Afro-Surinamese. They distinguish themselves cultur-

ally, psychologically, and ethnically and are recognized by others to be distinct from other blacks, Maroons. The latter are the descendants of fugitive slaves who fled the plantations starting in the beginning of the seventeenth century.

2. In the rest of this article I will, sometimes at great and laborious length, avoid speaking of hetero-, homo-, and bisexuality. Because of their embeddedness within radically specific theological, medical, and social discourses, these concepts cast a distorted light on the phenomena I want to analyze here. As I have argued elsewhere (Wekker 1993), the mati work differs from bisexuality in sociohistorical background and embeddedness and in emic understanding.

3. This fieldwork was made possible through grants of the Inter-American Foundation (Washington, D.C.) and the Institute of American Cultures (UCLA).

4. *Mek' verbontu nanga man*, to make an association with a man, can be used in two ways: (1) It refers to a ritual oath a man and a woman may take not to have other sexual partners. If people do not keep this oath, it is believed that punishment, in the form of sickness or death, will follow. Women also can take this oath together. (2) It refers to the institution, initiated by the Evangelical Brethren Society during slavery when slaves were not allowed to marry, that men and women state publicly in church that they will be faithful to each other.

5. This particular husband's reaction is not the only imaginable one, nor, I would say, the most typical. Working-class men, who are also embedded within Winti and share its weltanschauung, display a variety of reactions toward their wives or lovers engaging in relationships with women. If they, too, understand the need of the woman's "I" to be with other women, many men know and accept it.

6. Functioning as an economic safety net, the government is the largest employer in Suriname, employing about 45% of the total labor force. Of the female labor force (an estimated 40% of the total), 67% work for the government, mostly as cleaners, streetsweepers, and lower office personnel, thus in the lowest salary scales (Tjoa 1990). Furthermore, due to the flagrantly invalid, patriarchal notion that men are heads of households and that women earn merely additional income and have a breadwinner at home, women earn consistently less than men for the same labor.

7. Price index middle of 1991. Since then, inflation has risen rapidly.

REFERENCES

Alexander, Jacqui. 1991. "Redrafting Morality: The Postcolonial State and the Sexual Offences Bill of Trinidad and Tobago." In Chandra Mohanty, Ann Russo, and Lourdes Torres, eds., *Third World Women and the Politics of Feminism*, pp. 133–152. Bloomington: Indiana University Press.

Ambacht. 1912. *Het Ambacht in Suriname*. Rapport van de Commissie Benoemd bij Goevernementsresolutie van 13 januarie 1910, No. 13. Paramaribo.

Buschkens, Willem. 1974. *The Family System of the Paramaribo Creoles.* Verhandelingen van het Koninklijk Instituut voor Taal-, Land-, en Volkenkunde, no. 71. Gravenhage: Martinus Nijhoff.

Comvalius, Th. 1935. Het Surinaamsch Negerlied: De Banja en de Doe. In *West-Indische Gids* 17:213–220.

De Cecco, John and John Elia. 1993. "A Critique and Synthesis of Biological Essentialism and Social Constructionist Views of Sexuality and Gender." In John De Cecco and John Elia, eds., *If You Seduce a Straight Person, Can You make them Gay? Issues in Biological Essentialism and Social Constructionism in Gay and Lesbian Identities*, pp. 1–26. New York: The Haworth Press.

D' Emilio, John. 1984. "Capitalism and Gay Identity." In Anne Snitow, Christine Stansell, and Sharon Thompson, eds., *Powers of Desire: The Politics of Sexuality*, pp. 100–113. London: Virago.

Foucault, Michel. 1981. *The History of Sexuality.* Vol. 1, *An Introduction.* Harmondsworth: Pelican.

Geertz, Clifford. 1984. "From the Native's Point of View: On the Nature of Anthropological Understanding." In Richard A. Shweder and Robert A. LeVine, eds., *Culture Theory: Essays on Mind, Self, and Emotion*, pp. 123–136. Cambridge: Cambridge University Press.

Haraway, Donna J. 1991. *Simians, Cyborgs, and Women: The Reinvention of Nature.* London: Free Association Books.

Harrison, Faye. 1988. "Women in Jamaica's Informal Economy: Insights from a Kingston Slum." *Nieuwe West-Indische Gids* 62 (3 & 4): 103–128.

——. 1993. "Writing against the Grain: Cultural Politics of Difference in the Work of Alice Walker." *Critique of Anthropology* 13 (4): 401–427.

Herskovits, Melville J. and Frances Herskovits. 1936. *Suriname Folk-Lore.* New York: Columbia University Press.

Hill Collins, Patricia. 1990. *Black Feminist Thought: Knowledge, Consciousness, and the Politics of Empowerment.* London: Harper Collins Academic.

Janssens, Mari-José and Wilhelmina van Wetering. 1985. "Mati en Lesbiennes, Homoseksualiteit, en Etnische Identiteit bij Creools-Surinaamse Vrouwen in Nederland." *Sociologische Gids* 54 (6):394–415.

Kondo, Dorinne. 1990. *Crafting Selves: Power, Gender, and Discourses of Identity in a Japanese Workplace.* Chicago: University of Chicago Press.

Kulick, Don. 1995. "Introduction: The Sexual Life of Anthropologists: Erotic Subjectivity and Ethnographic Work." In Don Kulick and Margaret Willson, eds., *Taboo: Sex, Identity, and Erotic Subjectivity in Anthropological Fieldwork*, pp. 1–28. London: Routledge.

—— and Margaret Willson, eds. 1995. *Taboo: Sex, Identity, and Erotic Subjectivity in Anthropological Fieldwork.* London: Routledge.

Lewin, Ellen. 1995. "Writing Lesbian Ethnography." In Ruth Behar and Deborah

Gordon eds., *Women Writing Culture*, pp. 322–335. Berkeley: University of California Press.

Liebow, Elliot. 1967. *Tally's Corner: A Study of Negro Streetcorner Men.* Boston: Little, Brown.

Lorde, Audre. 1983. *Zami: A New Spelling of My Name.* New York: The Crossing Press.

Lutz, Catherine. 1985. "Ethnopsychology Compared to What? Explaining Behavior and Consciousness among the Ifaluk." In Geoffrey White and John Kirkpatrick eds., *Person, Self and Experience: Exploring Pacific Ethnopsychologies,* pp. 35–79. Berkeley: University of California Press.

Mintz, Sidney and Richard Price. 1992. *The Birth of African-American Culture: An Anthropological Perspective.* Boston: Beacon Press.

Mohanty, Chandra Talpade. 1991. "Under Western Eyes: Feminist Scholarship and Colonial Discourses." In Chandra Mohanty, Ann Russo, and Lourdes Torres, eds., *Third World Women and the Politics of Feminism,* pp. 51–80. Chicago: University of Chicago Press.

Nelson, N. 1979. "How Women and Men Get By: The Sexual Division of Labour in the Informal Sector of a Nairobi Squatter Settlement." In R. Bromley and C. Gerry, eds., *Casual Work and Poverty in Third World Cities,* pp. 283–302. Chichester, NY: John Wiley.

Newton, Esther and Shirley Walton. 1984. "The Misunderstanding: Toward a More Precise Sexual Vocabulary." In Carol Vance, ed., *Pleasure and Danger: Exploring Female Sexuality,* pp. 242–250. Boston: Routledge and Kegan Paul.

Peiss, Kathy. 1984. "'Charity Girls' and City Pleasures: Historical Notes on Working-Class Sexuality, 1880–1920." In Ann Snitow, Christine Stansell, and Sharon Thompson, eds., *Powers of Desire: The Politics of Sexuality,* pp. 74–87. London: Virago.

———. 1986. *Cheap Amusements: Working Women and Leisure in Turn-of-the-Century New York.* Philadelphia: Temple University Press.

Peplau, Letitia and Stephen Gordon. 1985. "Women and Men in Love: Gender Differences in Close Heterosexual Relationships." In Virginia E. O'Leary, et al., ed., *Women, Gender, and Social Psychology.* Hillsdale: Lawrence Erlbaum Associates.

Reinharz, Shulamit. 1992. *Feminist Methods in Social Research.* Oxford: Oxford University Press.

Rodman, Hyman. 1971. *Lower-Class Families: The Culture of Poverty in Negro Trinidad.* London: Oxford University Press.

Rubin, Lillian. 1976. *Worlds of Pain: Life in the Working-Class Family.* New York: Basic Books.

Shweder, Richard and Edmund Bourne. 1984. "Does the Concept of the Person Vary Cross-Culturally?" In Richard A. Shweder and Robert A. LeVine, eds.,

Culture Theory: Essays on Mind, Self, and Emotion. Cambridge: Cambridge University Press.

Silvera, Makeda. 1992. "Man Royals and Sodomites: Some Thoughts on the Invisibility of Afro-Caribbean Lesbians." *Feminist Studies* 18 (3): 521–532.

Stack, Carol. 1974. *All our Kin.* New York: Harper and Row.

Tjoa, Twie. 1990. *Vrouw Zijn in Suriname: Inleiding in het Kader van de Vierde Lustrumviering van de Vereniging van Medici in Suriname.* Paramaribo: ms.

Vance, Carole. 1989. "Social Construction Theory: Problems in the History of Sexuality." In Dennis Altman et al., eds., *Homosexuality, Which Homosexuality?*, pp. 13–34. Amsterdam: An Dekker/Schorer.

Van Lier, Rudolf. 1986. *Tropische Tribaden: Een Verhandeling over Homoseksualiteit en Homoseksuele Vrouwen in Suriname.* Dordrecht: Foris Publications.

Weedon, Chris. 1987. *Feminist Practice and Poststructuralist Theory.* Oxford: Basil Blackwell.

Wekker, Gloria. 1992a. "'Girl, It's Boobies You're Getting, No?' Creole Women in Suriname and Erotic Relationships with Children and Adolescents: Some Impressions." *Paidika: The Journal of Paedophilia* 2 (4): 43–48.

——. 1992b. "I Am Gold Money (I Pass Through All Hands, But I Do Not Lose My Value): The Construction of Selves, Gender, and Sexualities in a Female, Working-Class, Afro-Surinamese Setting." Ph.D. diss., University of California, Los Angeles.

——. 1993. "Mati-ism and Black Lesbianism: Two Idealtypical Expressions of Female Homosexuality in Black Communities of the Diaspora." *Journal of Homosexuality* 24 (3/4): 145–158.

——. 1997. "One Finger Does not Drink Okra Soup: Afro-Surinamese Women and Critical Agency." In M. Jacqui Alexander and Chandra Mohanty, eds., *Feminist Genealogies, Colonial Legacies, Democratic Futures*, pp. 330–352. London: Routledge.

Wilson, Peter. 1969. "Reputation and Respectability: A Suggestion for Caribbean Ethnology." *Man* (n.s.) 4 (1): 70–84.

6

Alison J. Murray

Let Them Take Ecstasy:
Class and Jakarta Lesbians

Through visiting and living in Jakarta since 1983 I have witnessed a basic so-cial division, reproduced by propaganda, myth, and mutual incomprehen-sion and the barbed wire that physically separates elite houses from their al-leyside neighbors. Gated communities, guarded shopping malls, and the "beautification" of sections of central Jakarta increasingly distinguish the land of the "haves" from that of the "have-nots" crushed in between and around them: a dichotomy based on class.

Indonesia's vast wealth is highly concentrated in the hands of the upper class: "upper class" here is shorthand for the royal Javanese, the government, the bureaucratic and army elites, and the expanding business classes to whom they are financially linked. The lower classes are formed of the origi-nal Betawi people, ex-slaves brought from around the archipelago, and later immigrants, mostly from Central and West Java, who have formed spatially identified, urban *kampung* communities. The upper class looking outward to an internationalized consumer culture has little connection with the lower class looking inward to the neighborhood (cf. Murray 1991a). Ostenta-tious displays of wealth and developments like toll roads and gated com-plexes displacing the old *kampung* are increasing the alienation and dispos-session of lower-class youth growing up to unemployment.

I want to show that class is also a major division between Jakarta lesbians. A discussion of the dominant ideology of women's sexuality that invisibi-lizes and stigmatizes homosexuality and scenes from everyday urban life will illustrate how lesbian experiences vary according to context. Jakarta's domi-nance creates contradictions in that it is both the pinnacle of the ideology of

"Indonesian culture" (seen as essential to unite the country), and the gateway to Western ideas such as lesbian/gay culture (seen as deviant and destabilizing). While Western decadence should be withheld from the masses, the segregation of the elite allows the latter to play in private. At the same time, Indonesia has its own traditions of homosexuality outside of the state's *Pancasila* dogma, which are now overlaid with a globalizing culture creating various hybrid local scenes.

The relation of the elite to urban subcultures is more complex than "class conflict," but I am using class as a starting point and lesbian as a signifier of nonconforming sexuality. There is no lesbian "community" in Jakarta since class overdetermines both gender and sexuality, but there can be strategic communities and identities in specific times and spaces (cf. Wieringa's contribution to this volume). For the lower class without privileges to lose, overt signifiers of "deviance" within a subcultural street milieu suggest a source of resistance to power. However, in order to avoid entrenching individual women in any specific context, I prefer the concept of multiple and shifting identities.[1]

Thus my aim is not only to add to the small amount of work describing and acknowledging Asian lesbians but to develop an understanding of the context of sexual practice and the effects of class differences. While the work of Western women in Asia has been criticized by some postcolonial feminists (e.g., Spivak 1987), I feel that it can be useful as long as the author's position is clearly stated. Academic studies from outside and inside Indonesia have tended to reproduce the elite-based view of women and sexuality, or they have only addressed representations of this view (e.g., Parker 1995; Sen 1993; Suryakusuma 1987). Due to the mutually suspicious relationship between classes, which an outsider can sometimes circumvent, I think it is valid to discuss my experiences of Jakarta's subcultures. The author's sexuality and sexual experiences significantly affect the research, and this should no longer be a taboo subject (see Kulick and Wilson 1995).

Sex, Class, and Discourse

Now that there is more openness about what really happens in "the field," I should say that while I may identify myself, depending on the occasion, as a lesbian or a sex worker or an academic, in Jakarta I have had male and female lovers and clients, both Indonesians and non-Indonesians. These experiences often had nothing to do with my research at the time, but they have helped to inform the present analysis of sexuality and class. The people I knew during the 1980s were part of Jakarta's lower-class subcultural milieu, where lesbian sex is more common than the lesbian identity confined to women with short hair and other prescribed "lesbian" signifiers. Meanwhile closeted networks of upper-class lesbians are linked to the growing global lesbian and gay movement, but these women usually maintain a "straight" appearance in Jakarta. Again, Wieringa's essay (this volume) shows that rigid distinctions should be avoided since the importance of class and/or butch/femme signifiers varies in time and between groups of women. Because of the separation of social worlds, it was only through the international circulation of gays and lesbians through Sydney that I met people who later introduced me to their friends in Jakarta in 1993; without personal introductions it would have been difficult to find these women.

Indonesia's all-pervasive state ideology attempts to create an "imaginary community" (Anderson 1987) based on Javanese elite and Dutch petit-bourgeois values combined with the requirements of capitalist expansion. The ideology of the "happy and healthy" nuclear family indoctrinates people with the idea that marriage to a man is essential to make a woman complete; sexuality and sexual practices are thereby controlled by being subsumed within correct gender roles. Suryakusuma (1987) describes the systematic social pressure on (elite) women to fulfill their "destiny" as housewives and mothers, which is constantly reinforced through the education system, the family welfare program, and official women's organizations. Predominant among these is the civil service wives' organization, in which the husband's rank determines the wife's position.

The model of the faithful housewife is clearly inappropriate for lower-class women, to whom it is extended through family welfare organizations. To some extent the elite construct of the ideal woman aims to protect upper-class women from the uncivilized and promiscuous tendencies of the lower classes, who are constructed en masse as "deviant bodies" (cf. Foucault 1978; Groneman 1995). The danger represented by the overwhelming numbers of the "Other" encourages the appearance of elite conformity to the construct of the ideal woman, while a concept of the masses as uneducated and dependent justifies unequal status and privilege.[2]

The dominant discourse distinguishes regulated sexuality in the public arena from hidden sexuality. Upper-class women who can afford to employ maids to do the housework have a choice of occupations and amusements within their enclaves. Since appearances are all-important, extramarital sex is acceptable, even expected, as long as it stays in the hidden realm: it does not really matter who the sex is with or if money is exchanged. Behind closed doors there are model housewives with spare time and rising disposable incomes running escort services, distributing pornography, and having gay affairs. They make arrangements by phone, and if they leave their gated sanctums, their cars have human or electronic devices to ensure that the gates open and close without their having to set foot on the street (cf. Krisna 1978). In contrast, the street life and high-density housing of the lower classes does not give them the option of hiding, but their behavior and sexuality have been mostly ignored by the authorities.

Western Labels and Jakartan Juices

While lesbianism is not officially illegal, the minister for women's affairs has stated that lesbianism is not part of Indonesian culture or state ideology (*Suara Karya*, June 6, 1994); this is an example of the common technique of blaming anything undesirable on the decadent West while simultaneously embracing all kinds of clearly inappropriate Western technologies and consumer goods. The minister's statement is ridiculous since "Indonesian culture" is an imposed construct and Indonesia has deeply rooted homosocial traditions. Islam is influential in the construction of "Indonesian culture." Given that 90 percent of Indonesians list Islam as their religion, my impression is that there exists a disproportionate number of Indonesian lesbians from Christian, Chinese, or other backgrounds. Interpretations of Islam are used to repress sex in general, even extending to pre-Islamic traditions. For instance, an artist friend had a painting depicting a *lingga* and *yoni* (Hindu male and female symbols of fertility) removed from her exhibition without notice. Research shows the presence of homosexual and homosocial activities in the Hindu-Buddhist pantheon, Javanese legends, and in other parts of the archipelago (Oetomo 1991, 1995; Gayatri 1995).

Covert lesbian activities are thus an adaptation to the ideological context. The distinction between hidden and exposed sexual behavior allows for fluidity in sexual relations ("everyone could be said to be bisexual," according to Oetomo 1995) as long as the primary presentation is heterosexual/monogamous. It is not lesbian activity that has been imported from the West, but the word *lesbi* used to label the Western concept of individual identity based on a fixed sexuality. I have found that Indonesian women do not like to use the label to describe themselves since it is connected with unpleasant stereotypes and the pathological view of deviance derived from Freudian psychology (cf. Foucault 1978).

The concept of butch-femme also has a different meaning in Indonesia from its current Western use and implies a subversion of norms and playful use of roles and styles (cf. Nestle 1992; Wieringa in this volume). In Indonesia (and other parts of Southeast Asia like the Philippines, or Thailand's tom-and-dee [Chetame 1995]) the roles are quite strictly, or restrictively, defined and related to popular, pseudopsychological explanations of the "real" lesbian. In the simple terms of popular magazines, the butch (*sentul*) is more than 50 percent lesbian, or incurably *lesbi,* while the femme (*kantil*) is less than 50 percent lesbian, or potentially normal. Blackwood's (1995) description of her secretive relationship with a butch-identified woman in Sumatra brings up some cross-cultural differences and difficulties they experienced and could not speak about publicly. The Sumatran woman adopted masculine signifiers and did not allow herself to be touched sexually; she wanted to be called "pa" by Blackwood, whom she expected to behave as a "good wife." Meanwhile Blackwood's own beliefs, as well as her higher status due to class and ethnicity, made it hard to take on the passive female role.

I want to emphasize here that behavior needs to be conceptually separated from identity, as both are contextually specific and constrained by opportunity. It is common for young women socialized into a rigid heterosexual regime, whether in Asia or the West, to experience their sexual feelings in terms of gender confusion: "if I am attracted to women then I must be a man trapped in a woman's body." Women are not socialized to seek out a sexual partner (of any gender), or to be sexual at all, so an internal "feeling" may never be expressed unless there are role models or opportunities available. If the butch-femme stereotype as presented in the Indonesian popular media is the only image of lesbians available outside the metropolis (e.g., in Sumatra), then this may affect how women express their feelings. However, urban lower-class lesbians engage in a range of styles and practices: some use the butch style consciously to earn peer respect, while others reject the butch as outdated. The stereotype of all lower-class lesbians following butch-femme roles or conforming to one subcultural pattern is far from the reality, reflecting the media and elite's lack of real knowledge about street life.

The media have an important role in influencing public opinion to accept the ideological construct of heterosexism (cf. Oetomo in *Jakarta Jakarta,* June 22, 1993; Gayatri 1995; and the clippings collection, *Gays in Indonesia*) through the persistent portrayal of any sexual behavior outside marriage as sick and deviant. Articles are reinforced by "expert" psychologists and advice columns, even though Indonesia's official medical guidelines finally stopped classifying homosexuality as abnormal in 1983. On the rare occasions that lesbians have been mentioned, typical reports cover suicides, women forced to go to psychiatrists to be "cured" and forced into marriage, and lesbian pseudomarriages where one woman takes the "man's role." I think the report from the Beijing women's conference that Indonesian lesbians are "declared mad and locked up" (*Sydney Morning Herald*, September 11, 1995) is an example of a lesbian rights group pushing their case a bit too far, however.

The imagery of sickness creates powerful stigmatization and internalized homophobia: women may refer to themselves as *sakit* (sick). An ex-lover of mine in Jakarta is quite happy to state a preference for women while at the same time expressing disgust at the word *lesbi* and at the sight of a butch dyke. However, I have generally found that the stigma connected with lesbian labels and symbols is not translated into discrimination against individuals based on their sexual activities. I have been surprised to discover how many women in Jakarta either admit to having sex with women or to being interested in it, but again, this is only rarely accompanied by an open lesbian (or bisexual) identity. I have found it hard to avoid the word "lesbian" to refer to female-to-female sexual relations, but it should not be taken to imply a permanent self-identity. It is very important to understand the social contexts of behavior in order to avoid drawing conclusions based on inappropriate Western notions of lesbian identity, community, or "queer" culture.

Where are the Lesbians in Gay Jakarta?

As Altman has pointed out, while there is a relationship between copied Western models and hybrid responses to local conditions, we should "interrogate the assumptions of the international lesbian/gay movement about a common global identity which is the basis for a new sort of global political movement" (1995:1). It seems that Indonesians, particularly gay men, are finding a place in the international movement and its political agenda as well as in its cosmopolitan bar scene—probably more so than Indonesian gays and lesbians are finding a common identity among themselves.

The growing strength of gay and lesbian voices internationally has helped the rapid expansion of Indonesia's gay movement and the magazine *Gaya Nusantara* headed by Dede Oetomo. Oetomo noted the absence of lesbians in the movement in an article, "Indonesian Lesbians: Where are you?" (*Gaya Nusantara*, no. 10, 1989), followed by Rosawita's "Where are the Indonesian Lesbians?" ("*Di mana para lesbian Indonesia?*" *Gaya Nusantara*, no. 18, 1992). Rosawita points out that the ideological suppression of women in all spheres makes lesbians more silent than gay men and gives them little basis for a coalition with gay men. At the *Gaya Nusantara* national conference of 1995 held in Bandung only one woman attended. She was from Ujung Pandang and had only just "come out" as a lesbian. If sexuality is perceived as male, and people are defined in relation to men, then it follows that gay men are hypervisible and lesbians are invisible (cf. Murray 1994).

I suggest that the form of this invisibility varies with class: higher-class lesbians choose to hide to retain their power, while the regime chooses not to see the lower-class subculture at all. To acknowledge lesbians would allow women an active sexuality that is not part of "women's destiny." Blackwood argues that, "in male-dominant cultures ... it is impossible for women to assume a cross-gender role because such a behaviour poses a threat to the gender system and the very definitions of maleness and femaleness" (1986:14), but this seems to apply specifically to the upper class in Indonesia, and perhaps more so than in other Southeast Asian societies (for instance, in Thailand there are a number of butch *toms* in senior business positions).

Various authors have commented on the relatively strong position of lower-class Javanese and Balinese women (e.g., Stoler 1977). Women in Jakarta can identify themselves strategically with the subversive potential of the street milieu, which is not specifically focused on "gay and lesbian solidarity." The lower-class male equivalent of the gender-crossing butch dyke, the *banci/waria* (transvestite or transgender), has been popularized and given a "traditional" place in Indonesian culture with organizations enjoying government patronage (Oetomo 1995; Murray 1991b). The overt *banci* are only a small percentage of men who have sex with men without necessarily identifying themselves as gay. Gay male style in Jakarta has become more open and trendy since at least the mid-1980s (Murray 1991b; *"Gay makin gaya," Jakarta Jakarta*, May 22, 1993), but its focus on socializing in a bar scene at night is not considered appropriate for unmarried women and is unaffordable for lower-class women unless they are bar girls.

In Bali the long history of Western gay male presence is now being revived. With the growth of gay tourism and the power of pink dollars, it is even being encouraged and advertised in Sydney's gay press (*Sydney Star Observer, Capital Q*). Hinduism and tourism have influenced the state to allow greater sexual freedom, but it should be emphasized that Bali's cruising spots and bars are oriented to the tourist. Some bars do not allow entrance to locals unless they are accompanying tourists. Western lesbians have also started going to Bali, usually in pairs, although there is no equivalent cruising scene. A resident wrote to Sydney's *Lesbians on the Loose* that "Bali is hell for lesbians," although she subsequently "came out" in America and then met a Western woman back in Bali.

Indonesia can appear to Westerners as a very tolerant culture. Segregation of the sexes is accompanied by very physical public homosocial behavior.

However, in discussions with lesbians, they repeat how confusing it is to feel sexually attracted to women without feeling deviant, how difficult it is to meet other lesbians, and how hard it is even to recognize them. As an outsider, it is easier for me to ask people straight questions about their sex lives. Many Indonesian lesbians seem to be much more open in the company of non-Indonesians and away from the rules of conventional behavior. Women from rural areas often move to the nearest city and then to Jakarta to find other lesbians and greater anonymity.

I met an upper-class woman from Semarang (a town on the east coast of Java), who had just arrived in Jakarta hoping to meet lesbians. She said she was not brave enough to venture out at night and then asked whether a woman with short hair must seek a partner with long hair, whether lesbians are sick or sinful, and what they do in bed. She wanted to know the signs to identify lesbians, but there are no definite signs or "secret handshakes" that I am aware of, except for slang expressions for lesbian like "*Lisa Bonet/Lisbon*." In the next sections I will discuss first the world of upper-class lesbians, closeted at home but "out" overseas, and second the hybrid milieu of lower-class lesbians, and the gulf of mutual incomprehension between the two.

Global Gay Style and Mutual Incomprehension

The international lesbian/gay movement is an urban phenomenon only accessible to the wealthier classes in Jakarta, who have more opportunities to meet lesbians from overseas, are aware of role models such as kd lang, and have access to gossip about the sex lives of Indonesian film stars and ministers. Thus, in spite of being hidden inside Indonesia, in the early 1990s upper-middle-class lesbians have come out overseas and enjoyed the international gay lifestyle with its meccas in Amsterdam, San Francisco, and Sydney. Conferences and festivals are increasingly interested in assisting representatives from the "Third World"; Indonesian lesbians are also involved in the Asian Lesbian Network (ALN).

ALN was formed in 1986 and holds regular conferences around the region, promoting networking and human rights and exploring "sources of pleasure as well as oppression" in an Asian identity (Fung 1995:128). ALN has lately been split by controversy such as the problem of differentiating lesbians living in Asia and those living in the diaspora. The ALN network can offer interesting comparisons around the region. For instance, the upper-middle-class networks in Singapore and Kuala Lumpur are as secretive as those in Jakarta, and only in the Philippines did I find women debating class issues (from a Marxist perspective). Women living in the West have been more explicit in aiming to strengthen Asian lesbian visibility—for instance, Sydney Asian Lesbians won a best float award for the Sydney Gay and Lesbian Mardi Gras parade in 1995.

Occasionally, educated Indonesian women have tried to form lesbian organizations informed by feminist ideas (feminism is also un-Indonesian, according to the women's minister). The link with feminism is another barrier to a coalition with gay men. Some feminist lesbians have stated they are reacting against "patriarchy" rather than claiming a definite primary attraction to women. There is little consensus over whether homosexuals are born, made, or curable, although essentialism ("I was born like this, so I can't help it") may be used strategically in the pursuit of particular agendas (see also Wieringa's critique of constructionism [1989]). My perspective of multiple and shifting identities attempts to avoid any simplistic binary division of the population (cf. Valentine 1993).

Feminist critiques of butch-femme roles as reproductions of the patriarchy alienate some women, while feminist nongovernmental organizations that do not openly support lesbian rights often have lesbians among the staff who feel unable to be open about their sexuality. The prevailing ideology of the real or butch lesbian means that women who are prepared to organize and identify themselves as lesbians are expected to be butch and therefore are stigmatized (cf. Gayatri 1995, who founded the lesbian network *Chandra Kirana*). Gayatri has described the "sort of upper class network in Jakarta, with its 'active rumor and gossip circuit'" (1995:6), consisting of cosmopolitan, well-read, and well-traveled women. These women often "came out" or had their first lesbian experience overseas and tend to compare Indonesia unfavorably with the "freedom" of the West. They come out to each other through private dinner parties and so on, but not to their families or wider society because of family pressure: according to Gayatri, strategies like sham marriages and silence are a form of resistance.

I would argue that rather than being a form of resistance, this silence is a conservative response because these women have a stake in the status quo and a primary identification with the immediate family as part of the ruling elite. Maintaining the hierarchies of power means making sure the family does not "lose face." For these women, ostracism from the family would mean losing their position; crossing the class divide by associating with lower-class women would also be a path to "social exile." Probably only those who have grown up in Indonesia can appreciate the difficulty of taking such a step, not least because of the distrust and suspicion with which the poor treat the elite. No one is likely to come out of the closet if it offers no advantage or if it is possible to live a "double life" with one foot in the busy lesbian scenes of the West.

Lower-class lesbians are excluded from the global movement by the lack of two essentials: money and the English language (cf. Altman 1995). There are other ways in which class divides Jakarta lesbians. The hidden elite networks are closed to lower-class women and upper-class women with "good" reputations and "good" jobs have little desire and less opportunity to understand or try to meet lower-class women. The gulf of mutual incomprehension is reinforced by spatial segregation and assumptions that associate lower-class lesbians with butch-femme roles, promiscuity, and an insalubrious nightlife. Elite women are at pains to avoid these associations and to sanitize the image of lesbians.

When I took an upper-class woman to a bar in the nightlife area of Blok M, Jakarta, she called her girlfriend to come down and join us. When that woman arrived, she called her friend by mobile phone from her car outside to check that it was really safe to come into such a place. Similarly, when I was in Bali, I talked to a lesbian from Jakarta about favorite places to check out women (*cuci mata*). She responded that she would never go to places like Blok M at night as she liked only educated girls, not bar girls. When I have taken lower-class friends to upper-class women's houses, they have said later that they were made to feel uncomfortable. One woman said, "I felt like a servant," but I felt she had also slipped into deferential behavior. These examples illustrate that while divisive attitudes may be unintentional, they are certainly entrenched.

Style and Subculture: Sex, Drugs, and HIV

The lived subcultures of the urban poor reclaim the spaces between power and powerlessness by constructing an alternative style (Hebdige 1978). Subcultural styles tend to be dismissed by both intellectuals and the authoritarian state, however, unless they can be commercialized and appropriated (for instance, the *banci* or transgender style, Murray 1991b). Jakarta's subcultural styles are not coherent or easily categorized but are rather a bricolage of local elements, reinterpretations of imported concepts, transient subgroups and spaces. Visible lesbian style such as a butch-femme aesthetic is part of a range of sexualities and sex-for-trade.

State control in Jakarta reaches down to the household level with intrusive family planning programs regulating sexuality and identity cards essential for people to claim citizenship and for their right to move around. Laws are unclear and applied inconsistently; security forces have seemingly unlimited powers of extortion and violence. In order to adapt and survive, the lower class exploits the contradictions between what is said and what is done. People of the lower class are inclined to take risks, live for the moment, and worry about consequences when they happen. For instance, the neighborhood in Manggarai where I lived in 1984–85 has been threatened with demolition for more than ten years, but when I visited in 1995, the people were still there making the most of their everyday lives, having nowhere else to go.

With limited access to communications technology or long-distance travel, people still rely on face-to-face interaction and their own networks identified with a small location in regard to which they have no sense of ownership or permanence. Discrete local scenes exist away from the main thoroughfares of urban life. As central Jakarta is incrementally "tidied up" and street life forcibly discouraged, I have found that many subcultural elements have relocated to the outskirts. For instance, a number of my friends now live in Depok, south of the city, which has rapidly grown into a heterogeneous urban sprawl. A particular street stall that provides cheap beer and food until the early hours and is run by a strong and extroverted woman has been adopted as an informal meeting place. In my experience this kind of highly localized arrangement, depending on personal acquaintance, is typical of the lower-class scene.

In addition to informal or temporary night stalls, subcultural or "queer" spaces include bars, prostitution locations, shopping malls, and alienated land. As none of the people within the milieu are able to conform to elite social norms anyway, they prefer to reject them altogether and to establish status among their immediate peers. While different groups may have conflicting or competing interests, this does not amount to discrimination. Women who choose to identify themselves as butch are able to take pride in creating a good "act" (similar to other adopted styles, such as *banci*/transvestites, *perek*/"experimental girls" and *jago*/street toughs). Butches have been characterized as baboons, fighting over femmes for supremacy, but this is far from the reality. It is true, however, as in other subcultures, that there is a loose hierarchy of small groups and local leaders, who are generally butch women.

Street butch style with its signifiers, including short, slick hair, men's clothes, smoking, drinking, sharp pool playing, and pimping of girlfriends, can be compared with the demimonde of American bars in the 1950s: "It was here in this sexual and social underworld that lesbians developed distinctive styles of dress, forms of romantic interaction and character types, all of which were rooted in working class subculture" (Murray 1994:351, cf.

Kennedy and Davis [1993] on lesbians and class). These bars were places where lesbians were accepted rather than specifically lesbian spaces. Similarly in Jakarta, a typical subcultural scene such as a *jaipongan* (popular lower-class dancing) venue under an expressway overpass is popular with lesbians but also attracts transvestites, underage prostitutes, local godfathers in safari suits, street toughs, and so on.

While taking pride in the butch style is some women's choice, it is not the only option. Contemporary Jakarta is a world away from 1950s America and has a hybrid urban subculture that draws on and parodies the discourse of 1990s technology and official jargon as well as images, such as Madonna and lipstick lesbians, that sometimes appear on the nonsatellite TV channels. While the butch-femme style exists, I don't think it is as evident, numerically large, or stylistically marked as in the Philippines, for instance. Further, because the butch lesbian is considered the "real" lesbian, women who do sex work or otherwise sleep with men, or who are in relationships where neither they nor their girlfriend is butch, do not need to equate sexual behavior with a sexual identity; they have the freedom to play without closing off their options.

I first met lower-class lesbians in the Blok M bar scene. In fact, my first experience of lesbian sex was when a Western man paid to watch me with an Indonesian woman. While some of the bar workers are emphatically not interested in women, many of them are; there is a strong link between lesbian and prostitute bar and street genres. Bar workers who are living in a "contract wife" situation with an expatriate (living together for the period of a work contract) are relatively well off. When their boyfriends are out of town, they may pay for sex with women. Australian workers call these "boyfriends" regular clients, while the Jakarta women claim a level of emotional attachment linked to long-term aspirations of marriage and/or emigration, as is common in expatriate bar scenes throughout Southeast Asia. Greater sexual freedom and notions of romantic love are integrated with economic pragmatism and necessity.

It is common knowledge in Jakarta that "ladies nights" at various discos giving free admission to women are frequented by "women-loving women." Some other places, such as a bar in Menteng (Sunindyo and Sabaroedin 1989), may become known as a place to meet or pick up lesbian prostitutes, but they are usually very transient. At "ladies nights" there are butch-femme couples, where the femme may also be a sex worker, and a range of other women whose sexuality is too fluid to pin down with a label. They have no strategic use for "lesbian" but also no need to appear "straight." Those who have moved to Jakarta to avoid family pressure as well as lower-class "families" and households are also less likely to conform to the bourgeois norm. Their households include a variety of disparate people, individuals renting rooms for themselves, transient and nonmonogamous relationships. Early marriage is often rapidly followed by divorce, thereby avoiding the taboo against premarital sex; two women living together are not usually considered worth talking about.

Western organizations may influence some upper class lesbian groups to construct their situation in terms of "human rights," but their lesbian practice is not the source of oppression for most lower-class women. Although the *Perlesin* group organized itself around a butch-femme subculture and its sense of "difference" (see Wieringa 1989), I have not found that overt lesbians experience discrimination in the poor urban *kampung*. Indonesian opposition groups have tended to dismiss issues of sexuality as upper-class concerns tangential to the main political struggle for social justice. Recently the potential of HIV/AIDS to decimate the urban poor has suggested the need to prioritize sexuality. However, AIDS needs to be seen in the context of Indonesia's preexisting urban health problems, such as high levels of infant mortality, which remain unaddressed.

This overview of lower class lesbian life in Jakarta suggests the dangers of the long-standing assumption that lesbians are at low risk for HIV/AIDS. While women may prefer women, they also have sex with men, commercially and for pleasure, and are involved in intravenous drug use (IDU), which has recently increased in preference to previous methods of slashing the skin or smoking drugs. (IDU is another taboo subject in Indonesia; I have found that the stigma is still too great to be able to write about it.) This has serious implications for HIV and shows the urgent need for more research on female-to-female transmission. The reasons leading to avoidance of a lesbian identity also mean that an HIV/AIDS campaign targeting lesbians is unlikely to succeed. The best practical strategy would need to cover women's sexuality in a range of scenarios appropriate for lower-class women.

New Emerging Sexualities and the Islamic Backlash

Apparently conflicting but probably related trends in 1990s Jakarta are the subversion of dominant discourse by the "new emerging sexualities" (see Murray forthcoming) flaunted by upper-class youth and the increasing repression based on Islamic morality and conservatism. Neither offers anything for the urban lower classes, who continue to be seen as disposable and getting in the way of development. On the other hand, gays and lesbians seem to be more accepted as a result of the new openness about sexuality that has come with the era of AIDS and the government's inability to control people's awareness of overseas trends, such as the international gay and lesbian movement, due to overseas travel and information superhighways. Young urban women are aware of more options than the butch-femme stereotype. I have heard of a female-to-male sex change in Jakarta (described as a "teapot with a permanent erection").

Increasing commodification of everything, including the body, and rising disposable incomes have also been linked to the phenomenon of upper-class *perek* ("experimental girls") selling sex to businessmen in shopping malls. While these experimental girls were exposed as a scandal in the late 1980s (e.g., *Tempo*, September 3, 1988 "*Oh Remaja, Oh Jakarta*" (Oh Youth, Oh Jakarta), and *Jakarta Jakarta's* "*Pelajar? Pelacur?*" (Schoolgirl? Prostitute?), the term *perek* is now commonly used to infer promiscuity and bisexuality. If alternative sexualities are seen as trendy and cosmopolitan by the upper classes, perhaps the hypocrisy associated with the distinction between regulated and hidden sex will start to decrease. There has also been a great proliferation in the types and availability of drugs, including designer drugs such as ecstasy, and an explosion in their use among the upper classes, including "scandals" involving pop stars (Suryakusuma 1994, "*Hobi Baru: Ecstasy*" [New hobby: Ecstasy], *Forum Keadilan*, December 4, 1995).

The countertrend of Islamic conservatism has lead to a backlash against sex, drugs, and prostitution. A clampdown on nightlife has reduced the nightclub trade without affecting the distribution of ecstasy throughout "young executive" society (*Review Indonesia*, July 24, 1996); the eradication of discos has also spread to Bali (*Bali Post*, September 6, 7, and 20, 1996). Legal forms of oppression are being strengthened. AIDS education efforts have met with stiff opposition from religious leaders demanding that people wanting to buy condoms should have to produce a marriage certificate. Suryakusuma's analysis points to an authoritarian regime under threat: "In the midst of the spate of social, economic and political crises, the clampdown on the sex industry is the easiest, the most sensational and the most hypocritical as it does not touch the fundamental root of social unrest: violence, manipulation and injustice, all of which are condoned, even carried out, by the state" (1994:18).

The clampdown is not only hypocritical but has class-differentiated effects. Rich people whose behavior seems to have gone beyond current limits are observed by the cynical to avoid censure by embarking on a *haj* pilgrimage to Mecca. The sex industry is a big money-spinner for the government, army, and businessmen; most moves of the government against the sex industry are symbolic and ineffective. It is mainly street and bar prostitutes who are arrested, causing a disruption in the survival strategies of the street milieu in which they work. Commercial sex is an important economic support for alternative subcultures, for lesbians more than any others, since they have fewer economic opportunities or options for male support.

The crackdown on drugs and alcohol has led to the crushing of late-night informal drinking stalls and street entertainment places. Cheap alcohol known as AO, and backyard production pills such as "BK" are denigrated as gutter rubbish and increasingly hard to find, at the same time as $100 pills of ecstasy, well beyond the means of the urban poor, are flooding Jakarta. The new consumers are the children of the elite, whose own pockets are lined with the profits of drugs and corruption (*Forum Keadilan*, ibid.). Even if they knew about it, they would not see a problem in the disappearance of local street drugs ("let them take ecstasy").

Power and Multiple Identities

Sydney University's conference on emerging Asian lesbian and gay communities in September 1995 acknowledged the rapid development of alternative sexual discourses, influenced by the strength of the Western lesbian and gay movement, in countries like Indonesia. However, when thinking about Jakarta's lesbians, I see the Western-Indonesian dualism as too simplistic, as is the homo-heterosexual distinction, which is impossible to quantify or apply in a fixed way to either behavior or identity in Indonesia. I have argued that class is the central divisive factor preventing the development of an Indonesian lesbian community, but the general distinctions I have made between lower- and upper-class women should not be taken as setting up another binary opposition.

In the hybrid urban lower-class milieu, people marginalized in various ways develop survival strategies and subcultures, in which a range of sexual behaviors are accepted; sex work is an important source of earnings. Lesbians, even if they identify with this imported label, are unlikely to want to segregate themselves from this supportive milieu. The performance of identity and experience of the body varies with time and place—an obvious example being the lesbian sex worker—therefore it is more appropriate to use a concept of multiple and shifting identities in the context of local specificities of power.

Lower-class women's relative powerlessness due to lack of money, education, and connections ironically leaves them freer to create their own subcultures; in order to retain its power the upper class has had to hide behind a wall of "socially correct roles." A lack of understanding of "how the other half lives" has made it more likely that people believe the government propaganda and media stereotypes. The ideological basis of power would be undermined if people from different backgrounds in Jakarta were more willing to communicate with each other straightforwardly. Despite this problem, I have found that many Jakartans are quite accepting of a range of sexual behaviors in people they know; even more so, some women manage to have a wild time and get away with it.

The struggles of feminist lesbians and butch-femme street scenes are largely unknown to urban women under the age of twenty and growing up with a barrage of global signifiers no more or less meaningful than the repressive ideology of Javanese elitism. They have the general impression that with money one can do anything. Sex work offers quick money, but it is also changing. The butch pimp/femme worker is in decline: younger women are more likely to play with butch signifiers than aim to "do" butch best among their peers. Despite, or because of, the government's efforts, sexuality in Jakarta is becoming "postmodern"—multiple, fluid, and experimental.

I have described diverse sexual practices and identities to show how women may adapt or perform according to local structures of power, arguing that power in Jakarta is experienced and strategically deployed through class. I have glossed the range of urban social constructions into a dialectical pairing of "upper" and "lower" class as a snapshot, taken through the lens of lesbian sexuality, of a rapidly developing and complex picture. The inherent contradictions in Jakarta's superculture, which allows the elite to spend its wealth in the global supermarket while imposing a national moral standard on a poor, largely agricultural country of nearly 200 million, have succeeded in dividing and silencing lesbian voices, probably more so than for most marginalized Indonesian groups. However, hypocrisy cannot grow indefinitely. Challenges to the existing hierarchy and its barbed-wire walls come from the possibilities of communication in virtual space and the overt sexuality of both elite youth and lower-class subcultures that bring people together in the same physical space of the street.

NOTES

1. I develop the concept of multiple and shifting sexual identities further in Murray (forthcoming). The ideas about lesbians and class in this chapter have been presented at the forum on Alternative Sexualities at the Asia-Pacific Congress on HIV/AIDS at Chiang Mai, September 17–21, 1995, and at the conference

Emerging Asian/Australian Lesbian and Gay Communities, Sydney University, September 29–30. Finally I am grateful to the International Institute for Asian Studies, Leiden, for a visiting exchange fellowship, which allowed me to complete writing this essay.

2. *Wong cilik*, or little people, a term used to refer to the lower classes, infers that people have lower requirements for space and resources; scaling-down reduces individual characteristics and thus also the claims to individual human rights. Indonesian political cartoons generally depict lower-class people as very small, while the elite and security forces are so big that often only a hand or foot fits in the frame of the picture.

REFERENCES

Altman, Dennis. 1995. "The Globalisation of Gay Identities." Paper presented at the conference "Emerging Lesbian and Gay Communities," Sydney University, September 29–30.

Anderson, Benedict. 1987. *Imagined Communities: Reflections on the Origins and Spread of Nationalism*. London: Verso.

Blackwood, Evelyn. 1986. "Breaking the Mirror: The Construction of Lesbianism and the Anthropological Discourse on Homosexuality." *Journal of Homosexuality* 11 (3/4): 1–18.

——. 1995. "Falling in Love with An-Other Lesbian: Reflections on Identity in Fieldwork." In Don Kulick and Margaret Wilson, eds., *Taboo: Sex, Identity, and Erotic Subjectivity in Anthropological Fieldwork*, pp. 51–75. New York: Routledge.

Chetame, Matthana. 1995. "Lesbian Lifestyles and Concepts of the Family." Paper presented at the conference "Thai Sexuality," The Australian National University, July 11–12.

Foucault, Michel. 1978. *The History of Sexuality*. Vol. 1, *An Introduction*. London: Penguin.

Fung, R. 1995. "The Trouble With Asians." In Monica Dorenkamp and Richard Henke, eds., *Negotiating Lesbian and Gay Subjects*, pp. 123–130. New York: Routledge.

Gays in Indonesia: Selected Articles from the Print Media. 1984. Fitzroy: Sybylla Press.

Gayatri, BJD. 1995. "Coming Out but Remaining Oppressed: Lesbians in Indonesia, a Report for Human Rights." Paper for International Gay and Lesbian Human Rights Commission, Global Lesbian Rights Report. San Francisco.

Groneman, Carol. 1995. "Nymphomania: The Historical Construction of Female Sexuality." In Jennifer Terry and Jaqueline Urla, eds., *Deviant Bodies: Critical Perspectives on Difference in Science and Popular Culture*, pp. 219–250. Bloomington: Indiana University Press.

Hebdige, Dick. 1978. *Subculture: The Meaning of Style.* London: Methuen.

Kennedy, Elizabeth and Madeline Davis. 1993. *Boots of Leather, Slippers of Gold: The History of a Lesbian Community.* New York: Routledge.

Krisna, Y. 1978. *Remang-remang Jakarta.* Jakarta.

Kulick, Don and Margaret Willson, eds. 1995. *Taboo: Sex, Identity, and Erotic Subjectivity in Anthropological Fieldwork.* New York: Routledge.

Murray, Alison. 1991a. *No Money No Honey: A Study of Street Traders and Prostitutes in Jakarta.* Singapore: OUP.

——. 1991b. "Kampung Culture and Radical Chic." *Review of Indonesian and Malayan Affairs* 25 (1): 1–16.

——. Forthcoming. *On Bondage, Peers, and Queers: Sexual Subculture, Sex Work, and AIDS Discourses in the Asia-Pacific.*

Murray, Sarah E. 1994. "Dragon Ladies, Draggin' Men: Some Reflections on Gender, Drag, and Homosexual Communities." *Public Culture* 6:343–363.

Nestle, Joan. 1992. *The Persistent Desire: A Femme-Butch Reader.* Boston: Alyson.

Oetomo, Dede. 1991. "Homosksualitas di Indonesia." *Prisma* 7:84–96.

——. 1995. "The Dynamics of Transgendered and Gay Identities in Indonesian Societies." Paper presented at the conference "Emerging Lesbian and Gay Communities," Sydney University.

Parker, L. 1995. "Conceptions of Femininity in Bali." Paper presented at the Third International Bali Studies Workshop, Sydney University, July 3–7.

Sen, Krishna. 1993. "Repression and Resistance: Interpretations of the Feminine in New Order Cinema." In V. Hooker, ed., *Culture and Society in New Order Indonesia*, pp. 116–133. Singapore: OUP.

Spivak, Gayatri. 1987. *In Other Worlds.* New York: Routledge.

Stoler, Ann. 1977. "Class Structure and Female Autonomy in Rural Java." *Signs: Journal of Women in Culture and Society* 3 (1): 74–89.

Sunindyo, Saranoati and Syarifah Sabaroedin. 1989. "Notes on Prostitution in Indonesia." In Gail Pheterson, ed., *A Vindication of the Rights of Whores.* Seattle: Seal Press.

Suryakusuma, Julia. 1987. "State Ibuism: The Social Construction of Womanhood in the Indonesian New Order." Master's thesis, Institute of Social Studies, The Hague.

——. 1994. "The Clampdown on Indonesia's Sex Industry." *Indonesia Business Weekly*, September 16, p. 18.

Valentine, Gill. 1993. "Negotiating and Managing Multiple Sexual Identities: Lesbian Time-Space Strategies." *Transactions of the Institute of British Geographers*, n.s. 18:237–248.

Wieringa, Saskia. 1989. "An Anthropological Critique of Constructionism: Berdaches and Butches." In Dennis Altman et al., eds., *Homosexuality, Which Homosexuality?*, pp. 215–238. London: GMP Publishers.

7

Kendall

Women in Lesotho and the (Western) Construction
of Homophobia

My search for lesbians in Lesotho began in 1992, when I arrived in that small, impoverished southern African country and went looking for my own kind. That was before the president of nearby Zimbabwe, Robert Mugabe, himself mission-educated, declared moral war on homosexuality and insisted that homosexuality was a "Western" phenomenon imported into Africa by the colonists.[1] When I left Lesotho two and a half years later, I had not found a single Mosotho[2] who identified herself as a lesbian. However, I had found widespread, apparently normative erotic relationships among the Basotho women I knew, in conjunction with the absence of a concept of this behavior as "sexual" or as something that might have a name. I learned not to look for unconventionality or visible performance of sex role rejection as indicators of "queerness." Most Basotho women grow up in environments where it is impossible for them to learn about, purchase, or display symbols of gay visibility, where passionate relationships between women are as conventional as (heterosexual) marriage, and where women who love women usually perform also the roles of conventional wives and mothers. I have had to look again at how female sexualities express themselves, how privilege and lesbianism intersect (or do not), and whether what women have together—in Lesotho or anywhere else—should be called "sex" at all. I have concluded that love between women is as native to southern Africa as the soil itself, but that homophobia, like Mugabe's Christianity, is a Western import.

Background: Lesotho and its History

Surrounded on all sides by South Africa, Lesotho, with no natural resources except population, squirms in an ever-tightening vise. Only 10 percent of the land in Lesotho is arable, but 82 percent of its population of over two million is engaged in subsistence agriculture (Internet World Factbook 1995). Most Basotho have no source of cash income at all, while a few are wealthy even by U.S. standards. Under these circumstances "mean national income per household member" means little, but in 1994 it was M56.57 per month (about $13) (Gay and Hall 1994:20).[3] The conclusion of international experts is that Lesotho is experiencing a "permanent crisis" (Gay and Hall 1994:9) exacerbated by unemployment, population growth, decline in arable land, reduction in soil fertility, desertification, and hopelessness.

Lesotho acquired independence from British "protection" in 1966, but it is still mostly "rural," meaning that the population is scattered throughout mountainous areas with no roads, no electricity or telephone lines, few commercial outlets, few towns, and relatively little contact with the so-called "global village." Although information about Lesotho is available on the internet, most Basotho have never even seen a computer, and net-surfing is restricted to a few computers at the National University (where even the telephone lines fail to function more often than not, and where e-mail works only a few months in the year) and in the capital city, Maseru. Urban sprawl is confined to the lowlands near Maseru, where there are a few good-sized towns that have been impacted by "modernization" in the form of Kentucky Fried Chicken stands, South African fashions, newspapers, and TV.

There is a national radio station that broadcasts most of every day and a national television station that operates a few hours a day. Lesotho contains all the "contrasts" that have long been clichés of ministries of tourism in Africa, but it is mostly a nation of villages full of destitute people. Most men are jobless and illiterate. Although in 1976, up to 48 percent of the men worked as laborers in South African mines, now only 25 percent have mine employment; by 2001 it is estimated that only about 17 percent will be so employed (Gay et al. 1995:170). Home beer-brewing keeps the little cash there is in circulation in the villages, but it also contributes to the problem of alcoholism. Some studies show that as many as 50 percent of the families experience problems resulting from alcoholism (Gay et al. 1995:75). Some young men till small gardens or fields; some guard diminishing herds of sheep on overgrazed open land. First World pastimes are not available; only two percent of households have electricity (Gill 1992:2). There is precious little for men to do in Lesotho, except drink, develop social and sexual relationships, and hang out.

The situation for girls and women is different from that for men. Owing to social customs reinforced by Christian missionaries, girls and women have plenty to do. They haul water, often from distances as far as an hour away (Gill 1992:13), gather firewood from increasingly deforested hillsides, wash and mend clothing (though often there is no soap, no thread for mending), tend children, gather "wild vegetables" (known in other countries as weeds), cook, clean, sweep, and decorate their houses. Lesotho is unlike most of Africa in that Basotho women are more likely to be literate than Basotho men, though because census figures are old, outdated, and questionable at best, no reliable literacy figures exist.

Women's legal status is nil. All women are legally "minors" in Lesotho under customary law. Under common law women are minors until the age of twenty-one, but they revert to minor status if they marry, attaining majority status only if single or widowed (Gill 1992:5). Women cannot hold property; they have no custody rights in the case of divorce; they cannot inherit property if they have sons; they cannot borrow money, own or manage property or businesses, sign contracts, buy and sell livestock, land, or "unnecessary" goods. Nor can a woman obtain a passport without a husband's or father's consent (Gill 1992:5). Although women do now vote, the franchise is one of the few areas in which women have gained legal rights since independence in 1966. A few well-educated middle-class women are fighting for greater equity. The Federation of Women Lawyers has "mounted an awareness campaign on the rights of women" and is trying to secure legal rights for women, but with three legal codes operative in Lesotho (customary law based on tradition and the chieftaincy, common law based on the Roman-Dutch system of South Africa, and constitutional law) the going is difficult, to say the least, for Basotho feminists (Thai 1996:17).

Social stratification by education, religion, income, occupation, and mobility in Lesotho means that there is no social hegemony; it also means that it is difficult to define class in this African nation by the standard denominators used in Western countries. The Lesotho of a bilingual woman who is a government or university administrator educated abroad is very different from the Lesotho of a woman in a mud-and-thatch dwelling on a dirt track in the rural mountains, educated for a few years in a mission school, who has perhaps twice been to the capital city by bus. Their Lesothos are different from that of a woman in the Roma Valley who cleans house for a succession of expatriates whose clothes, books, and memories speak of distant and more prosperous ways of life. None of them, not even the white-collar government worker, enjoys enough income or other privileges to qualify as "middle class" by American standards. The government worker may have electricity in her home (or she may not); she probably has no telephone and no car, but she may have a domestic servant who regards her as privileged.

This is not to say that Lesotho is merely destitute and cultureless. While the majority of people do struggle to stay alive, there is also a culture of community life, of ritual (and the Saturday funerals are among the most significant rituals I observed there), and of celebration. In the Roma Valley where I lived, most of the community celebrations are variants on Roman Catholic festivals, not only funerals and weddings, but first Holy Communions, new-home blessings, and a number of pre-Christian rituals having to do with pregnancy and childbirth. Home beer-brewing not only contributes to alcoholism but has a positive aspect, in that it leads to song and dance to express the joviality that arises when five to fifteen people gather around a homestead to drink beer together. These beer-drinking occasions help to preserve songs and dances that might otherwise be lost, and indeed beer-drinking is one of the few activities that may involve men and women together. Most Basotho cultural events are gender-segregated. Men socialize with men and women with women.

A final but important aspect of the background of this study is that women in Lesotho endure physical abuse almost universally. Marriage is compulsory by custom, and divorce is very expensive; the divorce rate is only 1 percent for this reason (Gill 1992:5). However, women manage up to 60 percent of the households on their own, in small part because of male migrant labor, but in larger part because of de facto separation and divorce occasioned by couples never having been married and then separating, by male abandonment, or by women leaving abusive mates (Gill 1992:21).

In the two years I lived in Lesotho, I met only one woman who said she had never been beaten by a husband or boyfriend, and she said she was the only woman she knew who had been so fortunate. According to precolonial tradition, a man claimed a woman as a wife by raping her, and this custom is still common in the mountain areas. One scholar notes the "apparent tolerance of a man's unbridled right to exploit women sexually" (Epprecht 1995:48). Men are conditioned to abuse women; women are conditioned to accept abuse. In this context, women often seek comfort, understanding, and support from other women. In addition, the homosocial nature of Basotho society, both before and after colonization, separates boys and girls from early childhood and conditions members of one gender group to regard members of the other gender group as a distinct "other." Thus, whatever her sexual desires and impulses may be, a Mosotho woman is likely to establish significant emotional bonds only with other women and with children and to become accustomed to expressing affection toward members of her own sex. Indeed, it is common all over Lesotho to see people of the same sex walking hand-in-hand or arm-in-arm, but it is so rare as to be remarkable to see public displays of affection between males and females. In this context, it is not surprising that some women who experience sexual desire for other women find it easy to express that desire, and it is also not surprising that the lines between what is affection and what is sex or desire blur.

Problematizing the Author

I cannot claim to have conducted an objective scientific study of Basotho women and sexuality, nor would I want to make such a claim. In every respect, what I see or understand of Basotho women's experience is filtered through my own range of perceptions and beliefs and is colored by my own experience of what is sexual, what is affectional, and what is possible between women. My experience as a lesbian shapes my interpretation of behavior I perceive as being "erotic" or "lesbianlike."[4] My experience as a white working-class woman, who has made it into academe and thereby lost her class connections and identity, shapes my understanding of privilege and its relationship to "lesbianism" as a lifestyle. I have now been "out" for twenty-one years, but I prefer not to share a household with my partner and resent definitions of lesbianism that reify the tidy domestic arrangement that features two middle-class women under one roof, so popular in lesbian communities in the U.S. My personal experience strongly influences my perception of the intersections of class privilege (or the lack of it) and sexual choices in Lesotho. My informants were all black women, Basotho friends, neighbors, and acquaintances, mostly residents of the Roma Valley, an area of Lesotho steeped in and named for the Roman Catholic religion.[5] Although many of the women with whom I discussed women's sexuality had migrated to the Roma Valley from the mountains and can tell about rural women's lives firsthand, nonetheless there is a distance and separation of their experiences from those of the mountain women who have not migrated. The very fact that they were talking to a white woman about bodily functions set them apart from women in the mountains who have never done so. Their lenses, like mine, are unique, and not ideally representative, if indeed such a thing as ideal representativity exists. I speak Sesotho, but not fluently, and I am not an anthropologist. Much of what I have learned about women, class, and sexuality in Lesotho has come to me through lucky coincidences.

In fact, I got to Lesotho by accident. I had been chosen as a Senior Fulbright Scholar in Performance Studies on the strength of my application to do research and teaching in Nigeria. When I found I was allergic to malaria preventives, I was hastily reassigned to Lesotho, and within two weeks I found myself living in a country about which I knew virtually nothing. My search for information on Lesotho during those two weeks turned up little more than its being one of the fifteen poorest countries in the world. I found it on a map: a tiny island of basaltic mountains surrounded on all sides by South Africa. I stumbled across a line in a guidebook averring that the "mountain kingdom in the sky" is "a nation of women and children," because most able-bodied Basotho men work in the mines and factories of South Africa. Although I was soon to learn that the myth of the absent miner was outdated and had never been accurate, it piqued my interest, because as a theater historian specializing in lesbian dramatic literature in Queen Anne's England, I had come to the conclusion that women in homosocial environments are likely to explore homosexual expression (Kendall 1986, 1990, 1993). This notion is reinforced by others who have studied homosocial societies (cf. Shepherd 1987:249–50). I imagined that a "nation of women and children" might be very attractive from my point of view, and I looked forward to further discoveries with considerable hope and enthusiasm.

Women in Lesotho

Probably the most important accident in my quest for lesbians in Lesotho was that on my arrival at the university I was housed at the guest house, where I befriended 'M'e Mpho Nthunya, the cleaning woman.[6] I learned before long that 'M'e Mpho had actually, in a sense, married another woman (more about that later). When I asked her if she knew of any women-loving women in Lesotho, she was puzzled. "Many of us love each other," she said, laughing. Thinking she had misunderstood me, I said I meant not just affectionate loving, but, well, I stammered, "Women who share the blankets with each other," that being the euphemism in Lesotho for having sex.

'M'e Mpho found that uproariously funny. "It's *impossible* for two women to share the blankets," she said. "You can't have sex unless somebody has a *koai* (penis)." This concise, simple observation led me to two different but related trains of thought.

First, 'M'e Mpho's "impossible" brought to mind one of Greenberg's remarks in *The Construction of Homosexuality*, to wit, "the kinds of sexual acts *it is thought possible to perform,* and the social identities that come to be at-

tached to those who perform them, vary from one society to another"
(1988:3, italics mine). Greenberg continues:

> Homosexuality is not a conceptual category everywhere. To us, it connotes a
> symmetry between male-male and female-female relationships. . . . When
> used to characterize individuals, it implies that erotic attraction originates in
> a relatively stable, more or less exclusive attribute of the individual. Usually it
> connotes an exclusive orientation: the homosexual is not also heterosexual;
> the heterosexual is not also homosexual.
>
> Most non-Western societies make few of these assumptions. Distinctions
> of age, gender, and social status loom larger. The sexes are not necessarily
> conceived symmetrically. (1988:484)

Lesotho is one such non-Western society, and Basotho society has not constructed a social category "lesbian." Obviously in Lesotho the sexes are not
conceived symmetrically. Nor is "exclusive orientation" economically feasi-
ble for most Basotho women. There is no tradition in Lesotho that permits
or condones women or men remaining single; single persons are regarded as
anomalous and tragic. Thus women have no identity apart from that of the
men to whom they are related; only comparatively wealthy divorced or widowed women could set up housekeeping alone or with each other. As in
many other African societies, including that of Swahili-speaking people in
Mombasa, Kenya, "a respectable adult is a married adult" (Shepherd
1987:243). However, there is much less wealth in Lesotho than in Mombasa.
The lesbian unions Shepherd describes as common and "open" among married and formerly married Swahili-speaking women are based, as she notes,
on the constructions of rank and gender in that society, as well as upon the
existence of a considerable number of women with sufficient economic
power to support other women (1987:262–265). Even more important,
Swahili-speaking women, according to Shepherd, do have a concept of the
possibility of sexual activity between women. In Swahili the word for lesbian
is *msagaji*, which means "a grinder" and has obvious descriptive meanings
for at least one variety of lesbian sexual activity. Although I found no evidence of any comparable use of words in the Sesotho language, what is more
significant is that Basotho women define sexual activity in a way that makes
lesbianism linguistically inconceivable; it is not that "grinding" does not take
place, but it is not considered "sexual."

The second train of thought 'M'e Mpho Nthunya's "impossible" led me
to is the great mass of scientific sex studies. From Kraft-Ebbing through Kinsey and Hite and on up to the present, these studies repeatedly show that lesbians "have sex" less frequently than heterosexuals or gay men. Marilyn Frye

(1992) cites one study by Blumstein and Schwartz that shows that "47% of lesbians in long-term relationships 'had sex' once a month or less, while among heterosexual married couples only 15% had sex once a month or less" (110). Frye is amused by how the sexperts count how many times people have sex. She notes that the question "how many times" they "had sex" is a source of merriment for lesbians. For what constitutes "a time"? Frye continues, "what 85% of long-term heterosexual married couples do more than once a month takes on the average eight minutes to do" (1992:110). In contrast, what lesbians do so much less frequently takes anything from half an hour to half a day to do and can take even longer if circumstances allow. Frye concludes: "My own view is that lesbian couples. . . don't "have sex" at all. By the criteria that I'm betting most of the heterosexual people used in reporting the frequency with which they have sex, lesbians don't have sex. There is no male partner whose orgasm and ejaculation can be the criterion for counting 'times'" (1992:113).

Or as 'M'e Mpho Nthunya put it: no *koai*, no sex. Diane Richardson writes on a similar tack,

> How do you know you've had sex with a woman? Is it sex only if you have an orgasm? What if she comes and you don't? . . . What if what you did wasn't genital, say you stroked each other and kissed and caressed, would you later say you'd had sex with that woman? And would she say the same? The answer, of course, is that it depends; it would depend on how you and she interpreted what happened. (1992:188)

Since among liberated Western lesbians it is difficult to determine when one has had "sex" with a woman, it is not at all surprising that in Roman Catholic circles in Lesotho, "sex" is impossible without a *koai*. Among Basotho people, as among those surveyed in numerous studies in the U.S. and the U.K., sex is what men have—with women or with each other. The notion of "sex" or the "sex act" is so clearly defined by male sexual function that 'M'e Mpho Nthunya's view of it should not surprise any of us. However, women in Lesotho do, as 'M'e Mpho said, love each other. And in expressing that love, they have *something*.

Judith Gay (1985) documents the custom among boarding school girls in Lesotho of forming same-sex couples composed of a slightly more "dominant" partner, called a "mummy," and a slightly more "passive" partner called a "baby." The girls do not describe these relationships as sexual, although they include kissing, body rubbing, possessiveness and monogamy, the exchange of gifts and promises, and sometimes genital contact (112).[7] Gay also describes the custom among Basotho girls of lengthening the labia minora, which is done "alone or in small groups" and "appears to provide opportunities for auto-eroticism and mutual stimulation among girls" (1985:101). Certainly there are ample opportunities for Basotho women of various ages to touch each other, fondle each other, and enjoy each other physically. The fact that these activities are not considered to be "sexual" grants Basotho women the freedom to enjoy them without restraint, embarrassment, or the "identity crises" experienced by women in homophobic cultures like those of the U.S. and Europe. Margaret Jackson writes convincingly that the valorization of heterosexuality and the "increasing sexualization of western women [by sexologists] which has taken place since the nineteenth century should not be seen as 'liberating' but rather as an attempt to eroticize women's oppression" (1987:58).

I have observed Basotho women—domestic workers, university students, and secretaries (but not university lecturers)—kissing each other on the mouth with great tenderness, exploring each other's mouths with tongues—and this for periods of time of more than sixty seconds—as a "normal," even daily expression of affection. The longest kisses usually take place out of view of men and children, so I presume that Basotho women are aware of the eroticism of these kisses and are protective of their intimacy, yet never have I heard any Mosotho woman describe these encounters as "sexual." When I called attention to this activity by naming it in speaking with a Mosotho professional researcher who was educated abroad, she told me, "Yes, in Lesotho, women like to kiss each other. And it's nothing except—." She seemed at a loss for words and did not finish the sentence but skipped, with some obvious nervousness, to "Sometimes—I—I—I—don't like it myself, but sometimes I just do it."

It is difficult to discuss women's sexuality in Lesotho because of the social taboos (both precolonial and postcolonial) against talking about it. Even now, it is socially taboo in Lesotho for a woman who has borne children to discuss sex with girls or women who have not. (Fortunately for my research, I have borne children; a childless American colleague also doing research in Lesotho found it difficult to have discussions about sexuality with adult Basotho women.) My Basotho women friends would not dream of explaining menstruation to their daughters; rather, they expect girls to learn the mysteries of their developing bodies and of sexual practices from other girls, perhaps a year or two older than themselves. Like everything else in Lesotho, this is changing—very slowly in more remote rural areas and rather quickly in the towns. Sex education two or three generations ago took place in "initiation schools" for boys and girls, but these traditional schools were a major target of missionary disapproval and have now just about disappeared in all but the most remote areas. The taboo on talking about sex certainly hampered the efforts of family planning advocates to institute sex education during the 1970s. The Roman Catholic Church did little to change that, but as a result of concerted efforts of a number of nongovernmental agencies and of the Lesotho government itself, birth control information, drugs, and other pregnancy-prevention techniques are now widely available in health clinics. For the most part, the Church now seems to look the other way when women line up at the clinics for pills, IUDs, and injections to prevent pregnancy. More recently, government-sponsored AIDS education workers have been at pains to dispel dangerous myths kept alive by groups of prepubescent teenagers, to popularize the use of condoms, and to encourage young people to learn about and talk about "safe sex." Over time this may have profound and lasting affects on sexual behavior in Lesotho.

A number of difficulties remain. The Sesotho language was first written down by missionaries, who compiled the first Sesotho-English and Sesotho-French dictionaries; not surprisingly, these dictionaries include few words to describe sexuality or sex acts. If there ever were words for "cunnilingus," "g-spot," or "Do you prefer clitoral or vaginal orgasm?" in Sesotho, they certainly did not make it into the written records of the language nor do translations of these terms appear in phrase books or dictionaries.

My attempts to "come out" to rural women and domestic workers were laughable; they could not understand what I was talking about, and if I persisted, they only shook their heads in puzzlement. Despite this, I had some long conversations with Basotho women, especially older university students and domestic workers, who formed my social cohort in Lesotho and who trusted me enough to describe their encounters in as much detail as I requested. From these I learned of fairly common instances of tribadism or rubbing, fondling, and cunnilingus between Basotho women, with and without digital penetration. This they initially described as "loving each other," "staying together nicely," "holding each other," or "having a nice time together." But not as having sex. No *koai*, no sex.

Lillian Faderman's observation that "A narrower interpretation of what constitutes eroticism permitted a broader expression of erotic behavior [in the eighteenth century], since it was not considered inconsistent with virtue" (1981:191) makes sense here. If these long, sweet Basotho women's kisses or incidences of genital contact were defined as "sexual" in Lesotho, they could be subject to censure both by outside observers who seem to disapprove of sex generally (nuns, visiting teachers, traveling social workers) or by the very women who so enjoy them but seek to be morally upright and to do the right thing.[8] If the mummy/baby relationships between boarding-school girls were defined as "sexual," they would no doubt be subject to the kind of repression "particular friendships" have suffered among nuns.

Since "sex" outside of marriage in Roman Catholic terms is a sin, then it is fortunate for women in this mostly Catholic country that what women do in Lesotho cannot possibly be sexual. No *koai*, no sex means that women's ways of expressing love, lust, passion, or joy in each other are neither immoral nor suspect. This may have been the point of view of the nineteenth-century missionaries who so energetically penetrated Lesotho and who must have found women-loving women there when they arrived. Judith Lorber writes, "Nineteenth-century women were supposed to be passionless but arousable by love of a man; therefore, two women together could not possibly be sexual" (1994:61).

'M'e Mpho Nthunya dictated her entire autobiography to me over the two years I lived in Lesotho, a book called *Singing Away the Hunger: The Autobiography of an African Woman* (1997). In it she describes, in addition to a loving and affectionate (though compulsory) heterosexual marriage, a kind of marriage to a woman that included an erotic dimension. According to Judith Gay (1985), these female marriages were common among women of Nthunya's generation. Gay writes, "elderly informants told me that special affective and gift exchange partnerships among girls and women existed 'in the old days' of their youth" (1985:101).

Nthunya describes how the woman she calls 'M'alineo chose her as her *motsoalle* (special friend) with a kiss. Nthunya writes:"It's like when a man chooses you for a wife, except when a man chooses, it's because he wants to share the blankets with you. The woman chooses you the same way, but she wants love only. When a woman loves another woman, you see, she can love with her whole heart" (1997:69).

Nthunya describes the process of their relationship, the desire that characterized it, the kisses they shared, their hand-holding in church, their meetings at the local cafe. And she describes the two ritual feasts observed by themselves and their husbands, recognizing their relationship. These feasts, held one year apart, involved ritual presentation and slaughter of sheep as well as eating, drinking, dancing, singing, exchanges of gifts, and general merriment and validation of the commitment they made to each other by all the people they knew. "It was like a wedding," Nthunya writes (1997:70). This ritual, which she describes as taking place around 1958, was widespread and

Mpho Nthunya and her motsoalle

well-known in the mountains where she lived. She describes the aftermath of her feast this way:

> So in the morning there were still some people drinking outside and inside, jiving and dancing and having a good time.
>
> Alexis [my husband] says to them, "Oh, you must go to your houses now. The *joala* [home-made beer] is finished."
>
> They said, "We want meat."
>
> He gave them the empty pot to show them the meat is all gone. But the ladies who were drinking didn't care. They said, "We are not here to see you; we are coming to see [your wife]."
>
> They sleep, they sing, they dance. Some of them are motsoalle of each other. (1997:71)

It would appear from Nthunya's story that long-term loving, intimate, and erotic relationships between women were normative in rural Lesotho at that time and were publicly acknowledged and honored. Gay (1985) describes an occasion when she was discussing women's relationships with three older women when a twenty-four-year-old daughter-in-law interrupted the discussion by clapping her hands. "Why are you clapping so?" asked the straightforward ninety-seven-year-old woman. "Haven't you ever fallen in love with another girl?" (1985:102). Both Nthunya's and Gay's accounts emphasize the fact that while such relationships were common and culturally respected up to the 1950s, they no longer seem to exist, or at least young women of the 1980s and 1990s are unaware of this cultural activity so central to their grandmothers' lives. What remains are the affectionate relationships among girls and women, the public kissing and hand-holding, and the normativity of homosocial and homoerotic relationships among working-class or poor women.

The celebration of motsoalle relationships with gift-giving and feasting bears a striking similarity to the celebration of *bagburu* relationships among the Azande women of the Sudan as described to Evans-Pritchard (1970) by male Azande informants in 1962 and 1963. However, since Evans-Pritchard was unable to talk with Azande women involved in such relationships, one can only speculate about what the Azande women's relationships really involved and whether or not they were similar to motsoalle relationships. Evans-Pritchard's secondhand information is full of the same sort of male fantasies about lesbian lovemaking that European males indulge in (see John Cleland's *Fanny Hill* [1749] for example, for the assumption that women need to acquire and indeed strap on penis substitutes in order to give each other sexual pleasure).

What is most interesting to me about Evans-Pritchard's work is that one of his informants, who clearly believed that the Azande *bagburu* relationships included sexual activities resembling male-female intercourse, reported, "once a woman has started homosexual intercourse she is likely to continue it because *she is then her own master* and may have gratification when she pleases and not just when a man cares to give it to her" (1970:1432, italics mine). This may be merely male conjecture about what women feel, but it does unself-consciously spell out a man's perception of connections between lesbianism and personal agency and between heterosexuality and the domination of women. Jackson develops this line of thought very provocatively as follows:

> Although individual women, and different groups and classes of women, will experience heterosexuality as more or less coercive according to their specific circumstances, in terms of the production and reproduction of male supremacy it is absolutely crucial that the vast majority [of women] be structured into the system of hetero-relations which lies at the very base of that supremacy. (1987:77)

There is no indication in Nthunya's account, however, that she viewed her relationship with her motsoalle as an alternative or a threat to her marriage. She says that her husband and her motsoalle's husband were both supportive of the relationship; that she and her motsoalle enjoyed kissing and touching (but she says nothing about genital touching), and that in her own case, the heterosexual marriages outlasted the motsoalle relationship. Whether Evans-Pritchard's informants were right or not about what Azande women did in bed, it is clear that Nthunya's husband would have had no justification for sharing Azande men's fears about women in acknowledged special relationships with each other.

The Sexuality Debates

After 'M'e Mpho Nthunya told me her story, I tried several times to get more detailed information from her about her motsoalle relationship. I asked her to describe what she and 'M'e Malineo did in detail, and on these occasions she avoided making eye contact with me and said that kisses and hand-holding were the extent of it. As I stumbled over words on these occasions, trying to translate her answers into English and my questions into Sesotho, I felt the same kind of embarrassment I would have felt had I asked such questions of my own grandmother. Why, I wondered, do I think I need to know her answers to these questions? Why does it matter to me what 'M'e Mpho and 'M'e

Malineo did in 1958? Why does it feel important to me to know whether there are or were women in Lesotho who might be called lesbian? Why do I care what women did in bed in Queen Anne's England or in Lesotho at any time and how they thought about or named what they did?

After all, constructing or recovering lesbian history is, in a way, an act of legitimation that presumes illegitimacy. If, in Lesotho, love between women was (and still is) perfectly legitimate, and not limited to "sexual" behavior but rather viewed as an activity or a feeling as ubiquitous as air, my prying questions become irrelevant, and the laughter which most often greeted those questions becomes understandable. Judith Roof explains that legitimation is not about "power or authorization, but anxiety and emptiness" (1994:64). The need for legitimacy would then only arise in cultures (like my own) in which love between women had been pathologized or made illegitimate. Instead of lesbian history, I might examine the history of heterosexist social institutions. I might ask, as Shane Phelan suggests, "Why is homophobia virulent in some societies and mild or nonexistent in others?" (1993:771). Phelan suggests that lesbian scholars avoid "constructions of lesbianism that trap us" into prying into our foremothers' bedrooms, because these constructions reify the notion that there is a "natural, or an authentic lesbian identity, by which we can measure and justify our existence" (1993:771).[9]

It is partly because I identify myself as something that has been socially constructed (in Western cultures) as monstrous that I go looking for others like me. It is also partly because I have been targeted for abuse in my own culture that I feel this "anxiety or emptiness" Roof describes and that I seek support and recognition from others who might be like me. It is also, of course, because I enjoy the company of other women who find women emotionally and physically attractive that I seek out other lesbians. Among them I don't have to pretend to be what I am not or to have interests or attractions I do not have. Among lesbians I am not presumed to be heterosexual; I do not have to explain myself or my personal life, and that, for me is a great relief.

My discovery of lesbian or lesbianlike behavior among Basotho women, and my perception of its similarity to behavior among privileged women in Queen Anne's England, has clarified my own thinking about homophobia and women's ways of loving each other. In addition, it may offer a way out of the realist/essentialist versus nominalist/social constructionist controversy in queer and lesbian studies. The classical exchange in this debate pits a realist/essentialist, who believes that lesbians have existed in most cultures and throughout history, against a nominalist/social constructionist, who believes that lesbians only appear where and when there is the socially constructed concept, "lesbian."[10] What the situation in Lesotho suggests is that women can and do develop strong affectional and erotic ties with other women in a culture where there is no concept or social construction "lesbian" and where there is no concept of erotic exchanges among women being "sexual" at all. And yet, partly because of the "no concept" issue and in part because women have difficulty supporting themselves without men in Lesotho, there has been no lesbian lifestyle option available to Basotho women. Lesbian or lesbianlike behavior has been commonplace, conventional, but it has not been viewed as "sexual" or as an alternative to heterosexual marriage, which is both a sexual and an economic part of the culture.

The situation in Lesotho might be evidence that the realist/essentialists are right (or one step closer to being right) in supposing that women will love women anywhere and in any culture and will express that love erotically when it occurs to them to do so, even if there are no words to describe it.[11] The social constructionists are also right that the idea of having a sexual identity, the possibility that what women do together could be called "sex," and the notion that "lesbian" is an identity that one might claim and celebrate are culturally specific.

Homophobia

It should not be surprising that Nigerian scholar Ifi Amadiume finds "shocking and offensive" the assertions made by some African-American lesbians that some of their ancestors in the motherland were lesbian (1987:7). Amadiume, through the lenses of her own virulent homophobia, sees African-American lesbians as legitimizing themselves at the expense of African women's reputations. She claims, "These priorities of the West are of course totally removed from, and alien to the concerns of the mass of African women" (1987:9). If by "priorities of the West" Amadiume means cultural expressions, such as self-conscious and defiant lesbian costuming, lesbian literature, and lesbian families, she is probably justified in claiming they are removed from the concerns of the mass of African women. However, it would be insulting and essentializing in the extreme to suggest that the bonds of love and loyalty among Basotho women are in any way "Western" or that the erotic expression of those bonds is "alien" to the women who enjoy them. The evidence seems to me to lead to the conclusion that *homophobia* is a priority of the West that is removed from and alien to the concerns of the mass of African women.

If there has been a tendency on the part of Black heterosexist cultural observers like Amadiume and Zimbabwe's President Mugabe to insist that lesbianism is a "white" or a "Western" thing, there has also been a tendency on the part of white Western lesbians to attribute their own cultural issues to lesbians or women who express lesbianlike behavior in other parts of the world. Queer theory, based on queer people's performances of themselves as nonconformists in gendered societies, privileges both nonconformity and the visible.[12]

The Basotho domestic workers I met who love each other do not perform themselves as "queer." They marry men and conform, or appear to conform, to gender expectations. Most will bear and tend the culture's children, carry those children on their backs, fetch firewood and water, which they will then carry on their heads, cook, work for wages if they can find wagework, manage their households, and cater to the physical needs of their husbands or boyfriends. I found no models of other ways to be, and despite close and sometimes erotic relationships occurring between many of the women I knew, the fact remains that I found no women in Lesotho performing themselves as gay, lesbian, or queer.[13]

After an earlier version of this article was published in Lesotho, I received a letter from a young professional woman with whom I had worked closely in writing workshops. She had read my article, came out to me in the letter, observed that she had not deduced that I was a lesbian either, and confirmed, "Life goes on in this place and like you said, we conform, smile and flirt with the male *homo sapiens* that we desperately wish to do without" (Anonymous 1997). She concluded her letter, "You cannot imagine the confusion and loneliness that drove me deeper into myself just wishing all the time I was raised in a different, freer society" (ibid.). This young Mosotho woman found the information about motsoalle relationships an interesting bit of history, and yet clearly, homophobia has now intervened in the lives of professional women to such an extent that she feels she has no permission to express her own sexuality.

In examining the question of options or choices it may be useful to clarify to what extent women in Lesotho have social or sexual options. Five years before Judith Gay wrote her article "Mummies and Babies," she wrote a Ph.D. dissertation at Cambridge called "Basotho Women's Options: A Study of Marital Careers in Rural Lesotho" (1980). In that paper she examined the lives of married women whose husbands are migrant workers and those whose husbands remain at home, of widows, and of separated or divorced women. Gay does not even mention the possibility of single, independent women living alone, or of lesbianism as an option for Basotho women. Instead she states, "marriage is the principal means whereby these women attain adult status and gain access to the productive resources and cash flows which are essential to them and their dependents" (1980:299). She predicts with accuracy the likelihood of growing unemployment among men in Lesotho and conjectures, "It is possible also that the resulting marital conflict and economic difficulties will lead to increasing numbers of independent women who become both heads of matrifocal families and links in matrilateral chains of women and children" (1980:312). That is certainly happening, and perhaps in another decade the lesbian option, as it is experienced in the northern hemisphere (or the "West"), will have come to Lesotho. But its shadow, homophobia, has already preceded it.

'M'e Mpho Nthunya concludes the story of her "marriage" to 'M'e Malineo as follows: "In the old days [note that here she refers to a period up to the late 1950s] celebrations of friendship were very beautiful—men friends and women friends. Now this custom is gone. People now don't love like they did long ago" (1995:7). As Nthunya and I were preparing her autobiography for publication, I asked her if she could add something to the conclusion of that chapter, to perhaps explain why people do not love like they did long ago. She added the following: "Today the young girls only want men friends; they don't know how to choose women friends. Maybe these girls just want money. Women never have money, so young girls, who want money more than love, get AIDS from these men at the same time they get the money" (1996:72). Perhaps that is all there is to it, though I would have thought that women in the "old days" needed money too. And the young professional woman who came out to me via the mail, who does not need money as desperately as the girls in Nthunya's experience, experiences homophobia in what she describes as a "soul-destroying" way (Anonymous 1997).

I believe that one pressure leading toward the demise of the celebration of *batsoalle*[14] is the increasing westernization of Lesotho and the arrival, at least in urban or semiurban areas and in the middle class, of the social construction "homophobia" with and without its name. Gay noted in her study of lesbianlike relationships in Lesotho that women who live "near the main road and the South African border" were "no longer involved in intimate female friendships" (1985:102). Living near a "main road" or a South African border would expose a woman to imported ("Western") ideas and values, as would formal education. Women in rural areas would be less likely to suffer the pollution of homophobia.

By scrutinizing homophobia as the "queer" thing it is, given examples of healthy lesbian activity in indigenous cultures in Lesotho and elsewhere, we might conclude that homophobia is an "unnatural" vice, that homophobia is far more likely to qualify as "un-African" (if it were not essentialist to use such a word) than homosexuality, that homophobia is the product of peculiar (Western or northern-hemisphere) cultures.

As Michel Foucault writes in his groundbreaking *History of Sexuality*, it is useful to view sexuality not as a drive, but "as an especially dense transfer point for relations of power" (1981:103). No *koai*, no sex. In that case the loving and egalitarian erotic friendships of Basotho women would not be "sexual" at all, which is exactly what Basotho women have been saying whenever anyone asked them. The freedom, enjoyment, and mutual respect of Basotho women's ways of loving each other, occurring in a context in which what women do together is not defined as "sexual" suggests a need to look freshly at the way Western constructions of sexuality and of homophobia are used to limit and oppress women. Having a (sexualized) "lesbian option" may not be as liberating as many of us have thought.

NOTES

An earlier version of this paper appeared in *NUL Journal of Research* 6 (1996): 1–24. Research was funded in part by the Fulbright Foundation of the USA and in part by research funds from the University of Natal in South Africa.

1. Mugabe was quoted in the South African newspaper *Mail and Guardian*, declaring homosexuality "immoral," "repulsive," "an 'abhorrent' Western import" (p. 15, August 4–10, 1995).

2. Lesotho is the country; Sesotho is the language; one person from Lesotho is a Mosotho; two or more are Basotho.

3. M stands for the unit of currency in Lesotho called the Maloti; it is pegged to and therefore equal in value to the South African rand, which fluctuated in 1996 at around 4.5 rand to the dollar.

4. If by "lesbian" we mean an identity that emerged in the twentieth century in certain Western cultures, then by definition the word cannot be applied to the Basotho situation. Some scholars are using the term "lesbianlike" to describe erotic and deeply affectional relationships among women who do not have the option of identifying themselves as lesbian. See, among others, Vicinus (1994) and Jenness (1992).

5. The particular form of Roman Catholicism that prospers in Lesotho is strongly influenced by Basotho customary beliefs and has incorporated much of the African religion, which was well developed when the missionaries arrived.

6. *'M'e* is the honorific or Sesotho term of address for a mature woman. It literally means "mother" and is used with the woman's first name. It is an insult to speak of her without the honorific or to speak of her by her surname only. In

submission to Western academic custom, I sometimes refer to *'M'e* Mpho as "Nthunya" in this paper, but I would never address her in that form. One Mosotho woman said to me, "to speak of a grown woman without using *'M'e* is the same as stripping off all her clothes."

7. Interestingly, John Blacking (1978) reports an almost identical custom among school girls in Venda and Zulu schools in South Africa.

8. There are two words for "pervert" in the *English-Sotho Vocabulary* (Casalis, ed., 11th ed. rev. 1989), one is *mokhelohi,* which literally means "one who goes the wrong way" and the other is *mokoenihi,* "one who changes his mind." These words are apparently not in common use. When I asked people if they had ever known a *mokhelohi* or a *mokoenihi,* I got only puzzled stares and incomprehension.

9. Also see Sheila Jeffreys (1992) and Martha Vicinus (1994). It is unfortunate that we are, as Vicinus notes, "excessively concerned with knowing-for-sure" (1994:57).

10. For summarizing discussions of this debate see the introduction to *Hidden From History: Reclaiming the Gay and Lesbian Past* (Chauncey et al. 1989); see also Boswell (1992), Foucault (1983), and Greenberg (1988).

11. One might argue that the existence of motsoalle relationships and the visibility of women expressing affection for each other in erotic ways constitutes the construction of a "lesbian" way of being in Lesotho, but to do that, one would have to construct a nonsexual definition of "lesbian," which, in my opinion, begs the question.

12. See Phelan (1993) and Butler (1990) for enunciation of "Queer Theory" in lesbian contexts; see Vicinus (1994) for a criticism of privileging the visible.

13. On this issue I would be glad to be proved wrong. No doubt there are exceptions. I heard but was unable to confirm that some prostitutes in the capital city live in same-sex couples, some of which are "lesbian." In mountain villages there are bound to be widows or single women who have established long-term unions that may also feature erotic expression; it would be astonishing if there were not. There may even have been lesbian relationships flourishing in Roma, where I lived and studied, among women to whom I had no social access. My point does not rest on the presence or absence of some defiant or closeted lesbians, but on the absence of exclusive unions among the women I did know who openly expressed physical affection and attraction for each other and among whom erotic exchanges were commonplace.

14. Plural of motsoalle, special friend.

REFERENCES

Amadiume, Ifi. 1987. *Male Daughters, Female Husbands: Gender and Sex in an African Society.* London: Zed Books.
Anonymous. Letter to Kendall, July 10, 1997.

Blacking, John. 1978. "Uses of the Kinship Idiom in Friendships at Some Venda and Zulu Schools." In John Argyle and Elinor Preston-Whyte, eds., *Social System and Tradition in Southern Africa*, pp. 101–117. Cape Town: Oxford University Press.

Boswell, John. 1992. "Categories, Experience, and Sexuality." In Edward Stein, ed., *Forms of Desire: Sexual Orientation and the Social Constructionist Controversy*, pp. 133–173. New York: Routledge.

——. 1983. "Revolutions, Universals, and Sexual Categories." *Salmagundi* 58–59:89–113.

Butler, Judith. 1990. *Gender Trouble: Feminism and the Subversion of Identity.* New York and London: Routledge.

Chauncey, George Jr., Martin Duberman, and Martha Vicinus. 1989. "Introduction." In Martin Duberman, Martha Vicinus and George Chauncey, Jr., eds., *Hidden from History: Reclaiming the Gay and Lesbian Past*, pp. 1–13. New York: Penguin.

Cleland, John. 1749. *Fanny Hill.* London: Fenton.

Epprecht, Marc. 1995. "'Women's Conservatism' and the Politics of Gender in Late Colonial Lesotho." *Journal of African History* 36:29–56.

Evans-Pritchard, E. E. 1970. "Sexual Inversion among the Azande." *American Anthropologist*: 1428–1434.

Faderman, Lillian. 1981. *Surpassing the Love of Men: Romantic Friendship and Love Between Women from the Renaissance to the Present.* New York: William Morrow.

Foucault, Michel. 1981. *The History of Sexuality.* Harmondsworth: Penguin.

——. 1983. "Sexual Choice, Sexual Act: An Interview with Michel Foucault." Transl. James O'Higgins. *Salmagundi* 58–59:10–24.

Frye, Marilyn. 1992. *Willful Virgin: Essays in Feminism, 1976–1992.* Freedom, CA: The Crossing Press.

Gay, John et al., eds. 1995. *Lesotho's Long Journey: Hard Choices at the Crossroads.* Maseru, Lesotho: Sechaba Consultants.

Gay, John and David Hall. 1994. *Poverty in Lesotho, 1994: A Mapping Exercise.* Lesotho: Sechaba Consultants.

Gay, Judith. 1980. "Basotho Women's Options: A Study of Marital Careers in Rural Lesotho." Ph.D. diss., University of Cambridge.

——. 1985. "'Mummies and Babies' and Friends and Lovers in Lesotho." *Journal of Homosexuality* 2 (3–4): 97–116.

Gill, Debby. 1992. *Lesotho, a Gender Analysis: A Report Prepared for the Swedish International Development Authority.* Lesotho: Sechaba Consultants.

Greenberg, David F. 1988. *The Construction of Homosexuality.* Chicago: University of Chicago Press.

Internet World Factbook. 1996.: http\www\world.

Jackson, Margaret. 1987. "'Facts of Life' or the Eroticization of Women's Oppression? Sexology and the Social Construction of Heterosexuality." In Pat Caplan, ed., *The Cultural Construction of Sexuality*, pp. 52–81. London: Tavistock.

Jeffreys, Sheila. 1989. "Does It Matter If They Did It?" In Lesbian History Group, eds., *Not a Passing Phase: Reclaiming Lesbians in History, 1840–1985*, pp. 19–28. London: The Woman's Press.

Jenness, Valerie. 1992. "Coming Out: Lesbian Identities and the Categorization Problem." In Ken Plummer, ed., *Modern Homosexualities: Fragments of Lesbian and Gay Experience*, pp. 65–74. London: Routledge.

Kendall [Kathryn]. 1993. "Ways of Looking at *Agnes de Castro*." In Ellen Donkin and Susan Clement, eds., *Upstaging Big Daddy: Directing Theatre as if Race and Gender Matter*, pp. 107–120. Ann Arbor: University of Michigan Press.

———. 1990. "Finding the Good Parts: Sexuality in Women's Tragedies in the Time of Queen Anne." In Mary Ann Schofield and Cecilia Macheski, eds., *Curtain Calls: An Anthology of Essays on Eighteenth-Century Women in Theatre*, pp. 165–176. Columbus: Ohio University Press.

———. 1986. "From Lesbian Heroine to Devoted Wife: Or, What the Stage Would Allow." *Journal of Homosexuality* 12 (3/4): 9–22.

Lorber, Judith. 1994. *Paradoxes of Gender*. New Haven: Yale University Press.

Nthunya, Mpho 'M'atsepo. 1995. " 'M'alineo Chooses Me." In K. Limakatso Kendall, ed., *Basali! Stories by and about Basotho Women*, pp. 4–7. Pietermaritzburg: University of Natal Press.

———. 1997. *Singing Away the Hunger: Stories of a Life in Lesotho*. Ed. K. Limakatso Kendall. Pietermaritzburg: University of Natal Press, 1996. Reprint, Bloomington: Indiana University Press.

Phelan, Shane. 1993. "(Be)Coming Out: Lesbian Identity and Politics." *Signs: Journal of Women in Culture and Society*, 18:765–790.

Richardson, Diane. 1992. "Constructing Lesbian Sexualities." In Ken Plummer, ed., *Modern Homosexualities*, pp. 187–199. London: Routledge.

Roof, Judith. 1994. "Lesbians and Lyotard: Legitimation and the Politics of the Name." In Laura Doan, ed., *The Lesbian Postmodern*, pp. 46–67. New York: Columbia University Press.

Shepherd, Gill. 1987. "Rank, Gender, and Homosexuality: Mombasa as a Key to Understanding Sexual Options." In Pat Caplan, ed., *The Cultural Construction of Sexuality*, pp.240–270. London: Tavistock.

Stein, Edward. 1992. *Forms of Desire: Sexual Orientation and the Social Constructionist Controversy*. New York: Routledge.

Thai, Bethuel. 1996. "Laws Tough on Basotho Women." *Sowetan* 17.

Vicinus, Martha. 1994. "Lesbian History: All Theory and No Facts or All Facts and No Theory?" *Radical History Review* 60:57–75.

Wetherell, Iden. 1995. "Mugabe Cracks Down on Gay Rights." *Mail & Guardian*, August 4–10:15.

PART III

Doing Masculinity:

Butches, Female Bodies, and Transgendered Identities

8

Evelyn Blackwood

Tombois in West Sumatra:
Constructing Masculinity and Erotic Desire

During anthropological fieldwork on gender and agricultural development in West Sumatra, Indonesia, in 1989–90, I pursued a secondary research goal of investigating the situation of "lesbians" in the area. I met a small number of "women" who seemed butch in the way that term was used in the U.S. at that time (masculine-acting women who are erotically attracted to other women).[1] In West Sumatra these individuals are called *lesbi* or *tomboi* (derived from the English words "lesbian" and "tomboy"), terms that have been used and popularized by the Indonesian media since the early 1980s (Gayatri 1997). Although there are similarities, a tomboi in West Sumatra is different from a butch in the U.S., not surprisingly since social constructionists have shown that sexual practices reflect particular historical and cultural contexts (Elliston 1995; Weston 1993). The term *tomboi* is used for a female acting in the manner of men (*gaya laki-laki*). Through my relationship with a tomboi in West Sumatra, I learned some of the ways in which my concept of "lesbian" was not the same as my partner's, even though we were both, I thought, women-loving women.

This article explores how tombois[2] in West Sumatra both resist and shape their identities from local, national, and transnational narratives of gender and sexuality. By focusing on West Sumatra, I provide an in-depth analysis of the complexities of tomboi identity for individuals from one ethnic group in Indonesia, the Minangkabau. Although the lives of lesbis and tombois in Jakarta bear certain similarities to the individuals I describe here (see Wieringa this volume), I do not attempt to draw out those connections in this article. Much excellent work on postcolonial states explores the interplay of national and transnational narratives in the production of genders and sexualities. This article provides a cultural location for tombois oriented to Minangkabau culture as well as national and transnational discourses.

Theories concerning the intersection of genders and sexualities provide considerable insights into, and a variety of labels for, gendered practices cross-culturally (see, for example, Bullough, Bullough, and Elias 1997; Epstein and Straub 1991; Herdt 1994; Jacobs, Thomas and Lang 1997; Ramet 1996). In opposition to biological determinism, social constructionists argue that gender is not an essence preceding social expression but an identity that is constructed and fluid. The multiplication of gender categories in cross-cultural studies, however, suggests that gender remains a problematic concept. Part of the problem, I would argue, comes from the conflation of two distinct but interacting processes, gender as subjective experience and gender as cultural category.

Viewing gender as a cultural category foregrounds the social structural and ideological processes that make it seem bounded—all the more so in a "scientific" age replete with minute diagnostics of human experience. Studying gender as a cultural category highlights normative representations of gender and the ways they are legitimated, privileged, and hegemonic. It allows us to identify so-called traditional gender systems, or "everyday categories of gender" (used by Poole 1996), as ideological discourses and to establish which gender representations are dominant or acceptable and thereby which ones are transgressive. By highlighting gender as a cultural category, I can delineate normative gender through an analysis of dominant ideological discourses at the local and state levels.

Viewing gender as subjective experience exposes all the processes of negotiation, resistance, manipulation, and displacement possible by human subjects. Gender in this sense constitutes a set of social identities multiply shaped from and through cultural contexts and representations (see also Bourdieu 1977; Poole 1996; Yanagisako and Collier 1987). Viewing gender as a subset of possible social identities allows us to do two things, first, to remove gender as a fundamental aspect of sexed bodies and, second, to investigate the way culturally constituted categories shape, inflect, and infuse gender identities. Learning, piecing together, adopting, or shaping identities (such as race, class, gender, or sexuality) is an ongoing social process through which individuals negotiate, produce, and stabilize a sense of who they are. These identities are shaped and redefined in relation to dominant gender ideologies that claim constancy and immutability.

In this essay I argue that because tombois are enmeshed in several discursive domains of gender and sexual identity, they produce a complex identity not reducible to a single model. I show how the gender and kinship ideologies of the Minangkabau, the dominant ethnic group in West Sumatra, construct a system of oppositional genders ("man-woman" as polar opposites) that persuades tombois to see themselves as masculine. The discourses of a modernizing Minangkabau society, the Indonesian state, and Islam reinforce this system through their representations of femininity and "female" nature. At another level, the tomboi identity incorporates new models of sexuality and gender made available by the transnational flow of lesbian and gay discourse from Europe and North America.

This essay also explores the relation between gender ideology and the production of gender transgression. I use the term gender transgression here to provide a new angle on a wide range of cultural practices not usually included under that term. The Random House Webster's College Dictionary (1991) defines transgression as a violation of a law, command, or moral code; an offense or sin; or more neutrally, passing over or going beyond (a limit, boundary, etc.). I use the term gender transgression to refer to any gender identities (transgendered, reversed, mixed, crossed, cross-dressed, two-spirited, liminal, etc.) that go beyond, or violate, gender-"appropriate" norms enshrined in the dominant cultural ideology. By defining gender transgression in this way, I want to highlight the way various social structures and cultural ideologies interconnect to produce gender transgression.

Central to this analysis is the concept of hegemony (as developed and used by Gramsci 1971; Williams 1977; and Ortner 1989). Hegemonic or dominant gender ideologies define what is permissible, even thinkable; they serve as the standard against which actions are measured, producing codes, regulations, and laws that perpetuate their definition of a particular ideology. Dominant ideologies generate discourses that further stabilize, normalize, and naturalize gender (Yanagisako and Delaney 1995), although within any dominant ideology there are emergent meanings, processes, and identities vying for legitimacy, authority, and recognition (Williams 1977).

Work on gender transgression has prompted some preliminary, and in most cases, implicit, formulations about the conditions that produce it. The growing literature on female-bodied[3] gender transgressors tends to cast the transgression as resistance to an oppressive gender ideology (male dominance or patriarchy). For instance, American gender ideology has produced at various junctures butch-femme (Kennedy and Davis 1993), camp and drag (Newton 1972, 1993), and transgendered people (Bolin 1994; Stone 1991).

These gender identities are interpreted to be the result of a hierarchical system with a rigid insistence on heterosexuality and oppositional genders.

The Minangkabau tomboi identity poses an interesting challenge concerning the cultural production of gender transgression. The Minangkabau are a hierarchical, kin-based society in which both women and men lineage elders have access to power. The presence of tombois in West Sumatra raises questions about the relation of male dominance and oppositional genders to the production of gender transgression. Whether a dominant ideology produces gender transgressors, and in what form, depends, I argue, on a number of processes, only one of which may be an oppressive gender hierarchy. A closer reading of cultural processes in West Sumatra suggests the interrelation of kinship, capitalism, and the state in producing gender transgressions.

Misreading Identities

In the following I provide a brief description of West Sumatra to set the stage for the story of my introduction to tomboi identity. I use this narrative of misreadings and negotiation to show the moments that moved me beyond my own culture-bound interpretations and led me to realize that different identities were in operation.

West Sumatra is the home of the Minangkabau people, one of the many ethnic groups that have been incorporated into the state of Indonesia. The Minangkabau, with a population over 4 million, are rural agriculturalists, urban merchants, traders, migrants, wage laborers, Muslim, and matrilineal. Their matrilineality means that even though they are devout Muslims, inheritance and property pass from mother to daughter. I conducted research in the province of Lima Puluh Kota near the district capital of Payakumbuh, which had a population of 86,000 in 1990.

Far from being an isolated region, the area is well integrated into global trade networks. Many Minangkabau men and women are itinerant travelers, who live for long years in the major cities of Indonesia, making West Sumatra well connected to the larger national and international scene. Despite out-migration, many villages continue a rich cultural life based on kinship ties; most social and economic activities are centered in and organized by the matrilineages in each village. Other villages are more urban-oriented, particularly where migration has led to reliance on outside sources of income.

After several months of living in West Sumatra, I was introduced through mutual friends to a woman who was said to be a lesbian, Dayan.[4] I was given the impression that such women were very coarse and tough, more like men than women. Dayan, however, did not fit the stereotype. In hir mid-twenties, s/he appeared to me to be boyish-looking in hir t-shirt and shorts and short hair, but s/he did not seem masculine or tough in any way that I could perceive.[5] I consequently felt quite confident that I had met another "lesbian." In my mind s/he was a "woman-loving woman." The term lesbi that my friends used offered familiar footing to an outsider from the United States.

Negotiating our relationship proved to be a perplexing process in which we both tried to position the other within our different cultural categories of butch-femme and *cowok-cewek*. "Butch-femme" is an American term for a masculine-acting woman and her feminine partner; butch and femme identities originated in the early part of the twentieth century (see Nestle 1992).[6] Cowok-cewek are Indonesian words that mean "man" and "woman" but in the more informal sense of "guy" and "girl." They are also used to refer to a tomboi and hir feminine partner (this usage is only among insiders and not known to most Indonesians). Whereas butches consider themselves women (although this distinction is getting blurred, compare Nestle [1992] to Halberstam [1994]), tombois see themselves as men. Yet, in both the U.S. and West Sumatra female couples rely on and draw from dominant cultural images of masculinity and femininity to make sense of their relationships. These similarities were enough to cause both my partner and me to assume that we fit into each other's cultural models, an assumption I was forced to give up.

Dayan operated under the assumption that I was cewek, despite the inconsistencies of my behavior, since that fit with hir understanding of hirself in relation to hir lovers, who had all been cewek. My failure to cook for hir or organize hir birthday party were quite disappointing to Dayan. When I visited an American friend of mine at his hotel, s/he accused me of sleeping with him. In hir experience, ceweks are attracted to men and also like sex better with men. As the one with the cash in the relationship, however, I was allowed to pay for things despite it not being proper cewek behavior. In rural Minangkabau households men are expected to give their wives their cash earnings, while among middle-class Indonesians, men are considered the breadwinners who earn all the income for the family. Perhaps s/he justified my actions on the grounds that I was an American with considerably more income than s/he. Certainly s/he was willing to entertain the possibility of my difference from hir understanding of cewek.

One day I overheard the following exchange between Dayan and a tomboi friend. Dayan's friend asked if I was cewek, to which Dayan replied, "Of course."

"Can she cook?"

"Well, not really."

Then the friend exclaimed, "How can that be, a woman who can't cook? What are you going to do?"

Clearly, I was being slotted into a gender identity rather than the sexual identity I thought I occupied. Because I was Dayan's partner, hir friend assumed that I was a particular gender, in this case the feminine "domestic wife." The fact that I had a relationship with Dayan said nothing to me about what kind of woman I was. I interpreted my relationship with Dayan, whom I positioned at that time as a butch woman, as reflective of my sexual identity (a desire for other women).

For my part, I assumed that Dayan was butch, more or less in congruence with that category in the U.S. in the 1980s, a masculine-acting woman who desired feminine partners. S/he always dressed in jeans or shorts and t-shirts or polo shirts, a style that was not at odds with the casual wear of many lesbians in the U.S. Then I heard a friend of hirs call hir *co*, short for cowok. I knew what cowok meant in that context; it meant s/he was seen as a "guy" by hir close friends, which did not fit my notion of butch. I heard another female couple use the terms *mami* and *papi* for each other, so I started calling Dayan *papi* in private, which pleased hir very much. But when I told Dayan s/he was pretty, s/he looked hurt. Then I realized my mistake: "pretty" (*cantik*) is what a woman is called but not a man. Dayan wanted to be called "handsome" (*gagah*), as befit a masculine self.

Dayan's personal history underscored hir feelings that s/he was a man. S/he said s/he had felt extremely isolated and "deviant" when s/he was growing up, being more like other boys and having desires for girls. As a teenager, s/he bound hir breasts because s/he did not want them to be noticeable. When s/he was young, s/he was called *bujang gadis*, or boy-girl, a term used to refer to an effeminate male or a masculine female (although not much in use currently). As an adult, s/he felt hir behavior was masculine. Dayan said s/he often gets mistaken for a man if someone only sees hir walking from behind. Sometimes in public, particularly in urban areas, s/he is called *mas*, an Indonesian term of address for a man. S/he said s/he felt like a man and wanted to be one. I finally had to admit to myself that tombois were not the Indonesian version of butch. They were men.

Cowok-Cewek

During the time I was in West Sumatra, I met two other tombois, both friends of Dayan. The first time I met Agus, s/he was wearing a big khaki shirt and jeans; even I couldn't mistake the masculine attitude s/he project-ed. S/he wore short hair that was swept back on the sides. S/he carried her-self like a "man," smoked cigarettes all the time, played cards, and made crude jokes, an attitude that struck me as coarse and like cowok were said to be. For hir part, Dayan seemed to admire but at the same time compete with Agus and thought Agus was the more handsome of the two.

Dayan told me that Agus, who was approximately thirty years old, had only been with women, never with a man, and had several lovers, all beauti-ful, all feminine. One former lover is now married with two children, but Dayan thought Agus probably still sees her occasionally. Agus spends much of the time now at hir current lover Yul's house, a large residence only a few minutes outside of Payakumbuh. Yul, who is in her early fifties and has grown children, wanted her children to call Agus *papi.* She would get angry and refuse to give her children money if they did not act respectfully toward Agus. She said she didn't care if her children disapproved of her relationship. But one of her daughters argued that since Agus is not married to her moth-er, why should s/he be part of the family and be treated better than her own father had been? The constant squabbling and lack of privacy were too much for Agus, who spent less and less time with Yul and finally moved back to hir sister's house nearby.

The other tomboi I met, who was at that time living at hir mother's house in a rural village, seemed quiet and somber. Boyish features and oversized clothes that hid hir breasts made it impossible for me to tell if s/he was male or female. The mother had forced hir to marry; s/he had had a son, but did not remain with hir husband. S/he lived with a lover (who, Dayan said, was feminine) for several years in Jakarta, trying to avoid the prying eyes of rel-atives, but under pressure from hir family had returned home with hir son, hoping to find some way to support both of them. Hir lover, however, even-tually left and married a man.[7]

Where tombois are clearly marked linguistically in West Sumatra, their sexual partners or lovers have no distinct designation or identity but belong to the category woman. Like an earlier generation of femmes in the U.S. (Nestle 1992), the partner is nearly invisible in rural areas. These women maintain a "feminine" gender, that is, they adhere to the hegemonic stan-dards of femininity in their appearance and behavior. Dayan said hir part-ners have always been feminine (proper women) and are really bisexual. "Unfortunately, they will leave you for a man if one comes along they like," s/he said. "It's our fate that we love women who leave us." Agus's former lovers are now married with children, and some of Dayan's now have boyfriends. These women who maintain a "feminine" gender identity and have sexual relationships with tombois are not marked as different by their sexual behavior.

For the feminine partner of a tomboi her gender is unproblematic. Although the fact that these women sleep with tombois makes them "bad" women in the eyes of local people, since premarital sex and adultery are not acceptable for women, they are still women. For example, Yul had never been with a tomboi before she met Agus and said she had never even thought about sleeping with one before. Yul is feminine in appearance. She has shoulder-length, permed hair, wears makeup and lipstick and has long fingernails. Although she sometimes wears slacks and smokes, even hangs out at the local coffeeshop with Agus and plays the card game *koa*, she is called *ibu* (mother) by the men and *mami* by Agus. No one would think she is a tomboi, just because she is the partner of one; she is cewek.

Performing Masculinity

Tombois pride themselves on doing things like a man. They know how to play *koa*, a card game like poker, which is thought to be a men's game. They smoke like men do; rural women rarely take up smoking. They go out alone, especially at night, which is men's prerogative. Like men, they drive motorcycles while women ride behind (except when women drive alone to work). Like Minangkabau husbands, they move into and out of their partners' houses. Because s/he is a man, a tomboi considers marrying or bearing a child like women unconscionable. Of the tomboi who was forced to marry Dayan said, "This person is cowok! How could s/he have done that, especially having a baby. That's wrong."

It is through taunts, joking and swapping stories of their relationships, I argue, that tombois create, confirm, and naturalize their identities as masculine females. Agus and Dayan teased each other about their behavior and their relationships. The teasing helped to consolidate the boundaries of tomboi masculinity. Agus's questioning of my femininity was one example. Another incident occurred when we were hanging out at a coffeeshop one evening with Agus while s/he was playing cards (*koa*) with some men. It was getting late and Dayan told Agus s/he wanted to leave. S/he wanted to get back to the privacy of hir own place, which was a forty-five minute drive by motorcycle.

Agus said tauntingly, "You're a guy (*laki-laki*)! How come you're afraid of the night?" S/he implied that Dayan was acting like a woman since only women have to be indoors at night.

Another time Agus overheard me call Dayan by hir first name instead of *papi*. S/he gave Dayan a disparaging look, letting Dayan know that s/he was not demanding enough respect from me as hir cewek.

Tombois model masculinity in their behavior, attitudes, interests, and desires. Dayan often spoke of being brave (*berani*) as an important part of who s/he was. S/he attributed the ability to be a tomboi to being *berani*; it meant one could withstand family pressures to get married. S/he said the ones that are *berani* become butch. In talking about Agus, Dayan commented that Agus wasn't brave enough to sleep at Yul's house anymore. The comment implied that Agus wasn't being much of a tomboi. Dayan thought Agus shouldn't let Yul's children force hir to move out. In this context bravery is something that one must maintain in order to live up to the cowok identity.

The sparring and comparing of masculine selves reinforces and interrogates the masculine code of behavior. The two friends' behavior suggests that being cowok is an identity one can be better or worse at, more or less of, something that is practiced and claimed (which is not to say it is inauthentic, as no gender identity is more or less authentic than the other, but more or less approximating the hegemonic ideological domain accorded to that gender). As any man does, they are negotiating the ideology of masculinity in their culture.

The dominance of the normative model of gender and heterosexuality persuades tombois to construct their actions and desire for women on the model of masculinity. The oft-repeated statement that their lovers were all feminine underscored their position as masculine females who attract the "opposite sex." Their use of gendered terms of endearment, *mami* and *papi*, or the terms of reference, cowok and cewek, reflects the tombois' understanding of themselves as situated within the category "man" (*laki-laki*). Tombois' adherence to the model of masculinity and their insistence on replicating the heterosexuality of a man/woman couple point to the dominance of the normative model of gender and heterosexuality.

Gender Ideology and Gender Transgression

In constructing themselves as masculine and their relationships as heterosexual, tombois are gender transgressors who nevertheless reflect the dominant ideology. Tombois' transgression raises the issue of the relation between gender ideology and the production of gender transgression. What social conditions produce transgression of the dominant ideology? As I noted in the introduction some preliminary attempts have been made to identify the conditions that produce gender transgression. Several scholars argue that oppressive gender ideologies (male dominance) force gender transgression.[8] According to Kennedy and Davis, butch-femme identities in the U.S. developed in a period in which "elaborate hierarchical distinctions were made between the sexes" (1992:63). Because men and women were culturally constructed as polar opposites ("the opposite sex" being a typical folk designation for the two genders in the U.S.), behaviors and privileges associated with men, including erotic attraction to women, were restricted to those with male genitalia. Male dominance and an ideology of oppositional genders created resistance to and subversion of the dominant paradigm by butches and femmes.

Some gender theorists argue that "women" become "men" (including "berdaches," female soldiers, passing "women," and cross-dressers) because of sexual desire for other women (Newton 1984; Rich 1980; Rubin 1975; Raymond 1979; Trumbach 1994; Wieringa 1989). In this view, because "women" are not allowed "freedom of sexual expression," they are forced to pass as men (with great caution, however) in order to be with women. Thus, the constraints on their sexual desire, which arise from an ideology of male dominance and men's control of sexuality, force women to transgress. Although this interpretation may work in some cultural locations, it is implausible for the tomboi. Dayan said s/he was called *bujang gadis* since s/he was small; thus s/he had already established a masculine identity before s/he was aware of hir sexual desires. Yet since puberty, s/he said s/he had always been attracted to women and never had any sexual desire for men. This story suggests that it was not sexual desire for women that "drove" hir to produce a masculine identity. I argue that having already established a masculine gender (s/he was called *bujang gadis*), s/he also laid claim to a sexual desire for women, a move that accords with the hegemonic cultural ideology, in which sexuality is thought to follow naturally from one's sex/gender.

Minangkabau Ideology and Oppositional Genders

What social conditions produce the tomboi identity? Are tombois forced into a transgendered role by an oppressive, male dominant society? To answer this question I turn now to social processes (cultural ideologies) in West Sumatra and the Indonesian state, looking first at the interrelations of Minangkabau kinship, gender, and economics in the production of gender transgression.

The construction of gender in West Sumatra is complex; Minangkabau women draw from and constantly rework several models of womanhood based on the ideologies of *adat*, Islam, and the state (Blackwood 1993, 1995b).

Despite the various models available, there are marked gender differences attached to male and female bodies. Gender markers signify differences in rights and privileges without, however, encoding a hegemonic male superiority.

I base my description of the structures and practices of gender on information from one village near Payakumbuh, West Sumatra. Although there are many Minangkabau's, many "fantasies" of Minangkabau ethnic identity (to borrow Sears's [1996] term), which differ even from one village to the next, the Minangkabau gender ideology I describe has its basis in rural village life.

Through its very commonness something as simple as the gender segregation of girls and boys enculturates and reinforces ideas about difference between the sexes. Typical of many Islamic cultures, there is lifelong physical segregation of the sexes in most public spaces and events. Young girls and boys socialize in predominantly single-sex groups. Teenage girls and women are expected to stay in at night; going out alone after dark is frowned upon. In contrast, adolescent boys and men can be outside at night, and often hang out in predominantly male-only spaces, such as coffee shops. These gender differences reflect the Minangkabau (and Islamic) view that men and women have different natures.[9] Men are said to be more aggressive and brave than women. Boys are admonished not to cry—crying is what girls do. Women are expected to be modest, respectful, and humble (all contained in the word *malu*), especially young, unmarried women.

These gendered notions encode difference and men's privilege, yet they coexist with practices and discourses that encode women's privilege and power (Blackwood 1993, n.d.). Women as elders in their lineages are powerful figures who, if they are wealthy, may control land, labor, and kin. Among elite men and women, kinship affairs are conducted in democratic fashion, with neither women nor men able to enforce or carry out decisions without the agreement of the other side. Economically, women control the distribution of land and its produce. Men figure peripherally in their wives' houses, but they maintain important relations with both natal and affinal houses. Husbands are treated with respect and even deference by their wives (in certain matters); some elite men hold important family titles and are considered the protectors of lineage property.

The structure of Minangkabau kinship and marriage may have the greatest relevance for understanding the construction of sexuality. Individuals, whether male or female, are not considered adult until they have married heterosexually. Everyone is expected and strongly encouraged (in some cases forced) to marry, an expectation generally true throughout Indonesia and Southeast Asia as a whole. While this imperative is one of the commonplaces of culture, its significance goes beyond the mere requirement to reproduce. Marriage constructs an extended network of kin and affines that forms the basis of social life in the village. For Minangkabau women the continuation of this matrilineal kinship network through marriage and children is critical to their own standing and influence both in the kin group and in the community.

An unmarried daughter denies the lineage any offspring through her and risks the future of the lineage.[10] Her behavior is a threat to the integrity and status of the lineage and to the community's understanding of family. A woman's marriage to a husband of lower or higher rank can effectively change the standing of their lineage in future generations. A son's marriage does not produce lineage heirs, making men peripheral to lineage reproduction. Consequently, lineage elders exert greater control over young women than over men to avoid the risk of a bad marriage or no marriage at all. Senior elite women are invested in controlling young women through their desires to maintain and strengthen their own lineage standing (Blackwood 1993). In this matrilineal system, men are not the primary ones controlling women through marriage; it is women heads of lineages who desire their daughters (and their sons) to marry and have children.

In the context of a rural agricultural society, kinship ideology requires heterosexual marriage. Within the terms of the kinship ideology, women are producers and reproducers of the lineage. There are no acceptable fantasies of femininity or female bodies in rural villages that do not include marriage and motherhood. This ideology remains hegemonic at the same time that emerging discourses of modernity and capitalism have opened up possibilities of resistance to marriage restrictions (see Blackwood 1993).

Minangkabau culture produces gender transgression, I argue, because of restrictive definitions and expectations of masculinity and femininity attached to male and female bodies. In this case male dominance is not an adequate reason for gender transgression because the Minangkabau do not fit any standard criteria for male dominance. It is not "men" (or patriarchy) and their oppressive gender hierarchy that creates transgressions, but a gender and kinship ideology that privileges women and men, yet insists on oppositional genders.

How does this sex/gender system induce the tomboi to claim a masculine identity? Why is (or was) this the form transgression took? I am assuming here the precedence of gender-based identities (cowok-cewek) to more recent identities available through the lesbian and gay movement internationally (to be discussed later). Tombois imagine themselves masculine and as such are tolerated to a certain extent,[11] but there is a contradiction between the way tombois define themselves and the way the larger culture defines them. Even for a tomboi there is great pressure to carry out family obligations, to marry a man and be reproductive, according to hir sex. Dayan said every time s/he sees hir mother or sister, they ask when s/he is getting married. Hir mother argues that a woman can't support herself alone; she needs a husband. She worries that no one will take care of Dayan after she is gone.

The constant pressure to get married and the threat of forcible marriage reveal the way one's body in this culture determines one's gender. Within the hegemonic sex/gender system denying the female body is impermissible. The refusal by others to allow the tomboi to participate in family and community life as a man attests to the fact that hir gender identity is conceptualized as deviant, as a transgression that is illegitimate and unauthorized. Although tombois insist on being treated as men by their partners, their masculinity lacks cultural validation. Society insists on the priority of the body in determining gender.

The Promotion of Heterosexuality

At the state level the tomboi can easily be seen as rejecting an oppressive gender ideology. As other authors have noted, the Indonesian state, particularly since the inception of the New Order in 1965,[12] has avidly pursued a policy promoting nuclear families and motherhood (called *ibuism* by some Indonesian scholars).[13] State ideology emphasizes the importance of women's role as mothers and consciously purveys the idea that women are primarily responsible for their children and their family's health, care, and education (Suryakusuma 1996; Manderson 1980; Sullivan 1983). All state family policies are oriented toward a nuclear family defined as a husband, wife, and children, in disregard of the many forms of family found within the nation of Indonesia.

The state argues that motherhood has been the traditional role for women in Indonesia since before Dutch colonization. According to Gayatri (1995), this line of argument has been used to discourage homosexuality. The minister of women's affairs asserted that female homosexuality is not in accord with Indonesian culture and is a denial of women's natural destiny to become mothers (Gayatri 1995). One cannot be a lesbian and be a proper Indonesian woman at the same time.

Other representations of motherhood and sexuality come from fundamentalist Islam, which claims that motherhood is the natural role for women, the one they were born to (Blackwood 1995b). Rejection of same-sex sexuality is taught in some Islamic sects, and that was Dayan's understanding of hir faith. Not being "true" to one's own sex by acting like a man is considered a sin and offensive to Allah since it is a rejection of the way one was made (underscoring the belief that biology and gender are the same).

TV and magazines are replete with images of soft, pretty, domestic women. Advertisements bombard women with the most fashionable clothes and skin care and health care products necessary to make them successful women. (Avon, Revlon, and Pond's are some of the leading non-Indonesian companies promoting this vision of femininity.) Women characters on the *Sinetron* television series are primarily domestic, irrational, emotional, obedient creatures incapable of solving their own problems (Aripurnami 1996). This emphasis on hyperfemininity and the importance of motherhood reinforces restrictive gender boundaries. The message for women is that it is a national and religious duty to marry heterosexually and be feminine.

Minangkabau newspapers serving readers in West Sumatra reflect the state propaganda on femininity. One local newspaper has a women's section devoted to health and beauty tips. A columnist advised women not to worry if they are not beautiful; there are other characteristics they can develop that will still be attractive to men. Another column claimed that men and women need each other; each sex is really incomplete without the other. "Although it's not impossible for a woman to find meaning without a man," advised Fadlillah, "it gives women's lives new meaning when a man is there" (1996:3, author's translation). Other articles admonish women to be modest (*malu*) and warn against too modern an attitude, "modern" here referring to the "loosened" values and attitudes of those in the cities.

As Indonesia moves further in line with the imperatives of the global market and its own created traditions, it is clear that the state and Islam are becoming more dominant, even at the local level, in the creation of a particular form of heterosexuality. The emphasis on heterosexual marriage and the nuclear family suggests that heterosexuality is actively being produced at the national level by the state, the media, and multinational corporations. It is not only the heterosexual family that is being promoted but a heterosexual imperative that reproduces a limiting and ultimately coercive form of gender, marriage, and sexuality predicated on male control and desire. Dominant state ideology offers no options to females other than marriage and motherhood, which in this case is a male dominated vision of gender, further substantiating the dictates of sex/gender congruence enunciated by Minangkabau gender and kinship ideology. For those who do not fit the normative model of gender, or find it limiting and oppressive, such a model persuades them of their masculinity, producing gender transgression.

Transnational Lesbian and Gay Discourse

In addition to local and state discourses tomboi identity is situated within a transnational lesbian and gay discourse circulating in Indonesia primarily through national gay organizations and their newsletters. Organized in the early 80s, these groups have nurtured a small but growing nationwide community of gays and lesbians (Boellstorff 1995), in the process developing a consciously new gay identity for Indonesians. *Gaya Nusantara* (*GN*), a national magazine for gay men and lesbians that began publication in 1987, has been the leading edge of the movement. *GN* is produced by a working group of gay men; their chief editor is Dede Oetomo, a Cornell-educated Indonesian gay man. Magazine articles range from discussions of gay and lesbian identity and events on the international scene to issues of local concern. *GN* also carries stories about and advice on relationships and how to make them work as well as personal ads for those seeking to get in touch with others within and beyond Indonesia. *GN* articles assume a readership "out there" who, once they understand what being gay really is, will become part of the community and identify themselves as gay. Contributors to the magazine often urge readers to be out as much as possible, while recognizing that such a position is extremely difficult in Indonesia.

Oetomo is one of the most visible members of the *GN* group. He has published several of his own articles in the newsletter as well as in national magazines and international journals. Oetomo himself uses the terms *gay* and *lesbi* "more or less as they are in the contemporary West; they refer to people who identify themselves as homosexuals, belong to delineated communities, and lead distinct subcultural lifestyles" (Oetomo 1996:259, fn. 1). His work has been influential in constructing an Indonesian lesbian and gay identity, which although not the same as that of the "West" (see also Boellstorff 1995), shares with it the idea of a sexual identity distinct from a gender identity.

Because *GN* reaches primarily a male audience, a few politically active lesbians have made efforts to build a nationwide network of lesbians. These efforts were spearheaded by Gayatri, a well-traveled activist with a college education. In an anonymous article for *Gaya Lestari*, the lesbian addition to *GN*, one author admonished lesbians to come out, bemoaning their invisibility and their preference for *GTM* (*Gerakan Tutup Mulut*, the close-mouthed movement) (See Boellstorff 1995). References to "our lesbians" and "the lesbian world" in the article suggest that the author imagines the existence of a group of women who hold a common identity. This new lesbian identity she envisions demands outward resistance to the heterosexual paradigm.

The new lesbian and gay movement in Indonesia is creating a gay and lesbian identity distinct from the gender-marked banci/tomboi identities. Much as the post-Stonewall (post-1969) American gay and lesbian movement separated itself from the butches, femmes, and drag queens (Kennedy and Davis 1993), some gay and lesbian activists in Indonesia distinguish themselves from both bancis and tombois. Gay and lesbian identity is associated with a "modern," educated middle class, while banci is a "lower-class construction" (Oetomo 1996:263). Similarly, cowok-cewek are thought to be predominantly from the working class and not like the lesbians of the middle and upper-middle classes (Gayatri 1994). In the emerging lesbian movement tombois are perceived as imitating men, and hence in need of modernization and education (see also Murray; Wieringa in this volume). In actuality sexualities and gender identities in Indonesia surpass binary oppositions of tomboi/lesbi, banci/gay, or heterosexual/homosexual, as Murray's evocation of Jakarta's working class sexualities suggests, providing a proliferation of models and plays on established and emerging identities.

Since the early 1980s print media in Indonesia have also been a source of alternative images of gays and lesbians through stories about gay liberation and Euro-American gay lifestyles. Although perpetuating the image that "real" lesbi are masculine women whose partners are feminine (Gayatri 1997), stories about Indonesian lesbians who either tried to marry or live together made visible for the first time a lesbi desire to live together. Such stories broadcast the possibility of an alternative lifestyle for same-sex couples.

The circulation of transnational gay discourse among tombois and their partners has presented new cultural models of sexuality. In discussing gay culture in Indonesia's urban centers, Oetomo suggests that "whoever joins the metropolitan superculture adopts the going construction there, although traces of a local construction still may color the way s/he . . . construes gender and sexual orientation" (1996:260). Movement between urban and rural areas means that local and urban identities confront each other and must be negotiated and claimed in hybrid ways. "The going construction" is brought back "home" to be remarked on with others, reworked, and then updated with each new trip to the metropole. (Oetomo's gay subjects are most likely permanent residents of the metropole.) Tombois and their partners have heard of Western lesbian and gay couples living together. From their urban cohort they have been told of a "lesbian" identity that is an unchanging part of oneself and have been urged to claim that identity. These new models are being incorporated into older gender-based models (cowok-cewek) in contradictory ways.

Plural Identities

I want to pull together all the various threads of this argument to reveal how one particular tomboi is situated within these narratives of gender, sexuality, and culture. Extrapolating from Sears's (1996) discussion of Indonesian femininities, I argue that many representations of lesbi and tomboi circulate in Indonesia. There are many different ways in which female subjects who are masculine or erotically attracted to women are constituted and constitute themselves. They are seen as "deviants" from the model of mother and wife so central to state ideology, as the stereotypically masculine lesbian portrayed by the media, as women who love each other (the model favored by some activists), and as men (the identity claimed by tombois).

Dayan is positioned within all these possibilities. A product of the post-colonial Indonesian school system, s/he graduated from a technical high school with ambitions for a career job, not farming. But like many others in the working class, s/he struggles to find work. S/he is a member of hir mother's lineage, but is living with an older sister on their deceased father's land in a village about thirty minutes from the mother's. The brothers have jobs or own small businesses in the nearby town. This village is a migrant community only fifteen minutes from the district capital. Members of most households migrate between local and other urban areas. Not a vibrant *adat* community, this village is moving into the margins of urban life in Indonesia.

Dayan's location on the fringes of urban culture helps to explain hir rejection of Minangkabau womanhood. Raised in a family with little matrilineal money or land, and thus dependent on the father's family to provide land and house, s/he, mother, and sister have lost some of the crucial connections that authorize women's power. Further, since not all daughters benefit equally or are treated favorably by their mothers, some, like Dayan, may never attain the power of a senior woman. Beyond that, the family's marginal position between rural and urban means that their desires are directed toward urban opportunities, not village and matrilineal relations. The Minangkabau experience Dayan knows is that of a struggling, urban-oriented family.

Like many young people, Dayan has been influenced by divergent ideologies of womanhood. Educated in the "modern" school system, this generation has received little state validation for the importance of Minangkabau women in their lineages. Recent local efforts to provide greater education about Minangkabau culture have only highlighted the role of men as "traditional" leaders (see Blackwood 1995b). School girls learn "proper" gender roles and are indoctrinated in the importance of becoming wives and serving their husband's needs. They are inundated through media with representations of urban middle-class, docile womanhood. Many young women grow up believing that they are better off today under the patriarchal New Order because they can seek their own jobs and choose their own husbands. In these young women's minds the Minangkabau of powerful elite women, wrapped up in the esoteric *adat* of ritual ceremonies and hard work in the rice fields, seems distant and old-fashioned. Thus, the images of womanhood that Dayan is familiar with underscore the burden of privilege—of marriage, children, and lineage priorities—and the fear of dependence—of being a wife under a husband's control.

The masculinities that tombois construct reflect their different locations in the local/global market as well. Hegemonic masculinity is represented and enacted differently in the village, in urban areas, and on movie screens. It too is a hybrid of local, national, and transnational representations. In rural villages a young man may smoke, drink, gamble, and use coarse language, but he is also admonished to be industrious, respectful of his elders, and responsible to his lineage and his wife's family. The bravado and coarseness of young urban (poor, working-class) men in Indonesia is far from the polite, respectful demeanor of men in rural villages. While Dayan's masculinity reflects more of the village, Agus's interpretation reflects a combination of the coarse masculinity and male privilege of urban areas. Dayan told me that when Agus is at Yul's house, "s/he expects to be served and won't do anything for hir wife except give her money." This interpretation of a man's role could be drawn from middle-class images of manhood, but also seems to selectively draw on older representations of high-ranking Minangkabau husbands who, as guests in their wives' houses (male duolocal residence), were served by their wives. Agus's "macho" behavior presents an extreme style of masculinity, one that is easily read as masculine by others.

Dayan's experience of lesbian and gay discourse creates another distinction between himself and Agus. Dayan described Agus as an old-fashioned tomboi, one who "is like a man and won't be any other way." Hir statement implies that s/he sees Agus as holding onto certain normative ideas of gender that contemporary Indonesian lesbians no longer find satisfying. S/he said further that "Agus has never been out of the *kampung* [village]" (although s/he had been at least as far as Payakumbuh), implying that if s/he had been, Agus might have seen other models of lesbian relations and quit trying to be so much like a man.

Dayan has lived in Jakarta several times for one to two years at a time, living predominantly among women and men of the working class. Both at home and in Jakarta the friends s/he mainly associated with inhabit the cowok-cewek style, but they also know about Euro-American lesbian and gay identities. Depending on the context, Dayan claimed a masculine identity while at other times s/he invoked a lesbi identity. S/he told me s/he has always been the way s/he is, but s/he also called herself a lesbi. Hir statements imply that despite feeling like a man, the availability of other models makes it possible to interpolate the tomboi identity with a lesbian identity. As with the proliferation of transgender identities in the U.S. (Bolin 1994; Cromwell forthcoming), tomboi identity is constantly being negotiated and redefined in response to local, national, and transnational processes.

Identity for tombois in West Sumatra at this point in time is a bricolage, a mix of local, national, and transnational identities. If their identity growing up was shaped by local cultural forces that emphasized oppositional genders, their movement between cities and rural areas means they have been exposed to other models of sexuality and gender identity that they have used to construct a new sense of themselves. The complexities of their gender identity make it pointless to align tombois with any one category, whether woman, lesbian, or transgendered person.

Tomboi identity refracts and transgresses normative gender constructs. While some theorists identify gender transgression as resistance to male-dominated hegemonic order, tombois in West Sumatra cannot be read simply as the product of male dominance. The Minangkabau kinship ideology that requires daughter's obedience can be read as oppressive but only in the context of recent transformations that have weakened lineage priorities and promoted other images of family and happiness. What this story reveals is that gender transgression is produced within the processes of postcoloniality, capitalism, and modernity, suggesting a more complicated cultural production of gender transgression.

At the national level the tomboi can be read as resisting the constraints of state *ibuism* in much the same manner as European and American lesbians, gay men, and transgendered people are said to resist dominant gender ideology. At the same time, although there is state enforcement of heterosexuality, wage labor and capitalism create a space for the tomboi to live as a single female. The discourse of modernity—education, careers, achieving a middle-class status—legitimates other models than motherhood and femininity for females. So though the tomboi remains a deviant, s/he is finding more room to negotiate a future.

The tomboi identity in Minangkabau culture speaks to the significance of a hegemonic sex/gender system in producing particular forms of gender transgression. With each gender rigidly distinct and based on two sexes, some masculine females produce a masculine gender because it is the most persuasive model available. At the same time other sexual and gender models are becoming visible in a globalized world, so that a multiplication of social identities is taking place. Where sexuality was embedded in the ideology of oppositional genders (man-woman, cowok-cewek, banci-laki asli [real man]), sexual identities and the possibility of sexuality between two women or two men are emergent cultural practices. Erotic desire is being rewritten for some as a product of the variability of human sexuality rather than the "natural" urge of the male body and the prerogative of men.

NOTES

Material for this paper was collected during fieldwork in West Sumatra in 1989-1990 and 1996. A longer version of this paper was published in *Cultural Anthropology* 13 (4), 1998. I am grateful to Mildred (Jeff) Dickemann, Deborah Elliston, Saskia Wieringa, Carolyn Martin Shaw, Jason Cromwell, and Daniel Segal for their invaluable comments at different stages in the development of this work.

1. By putting "women" in quotes, I immediately want to problematize the use of "woman" for individuals who are female-bodied but do not identify themselves as women. As I use it, "female" refers to physical sex characteristics, and "woman" refers to a set of social behaviors and characteristics that are culturally constructed and attributed to female bodies. I use "women" in this instance because at the time of first meeting, I assumed these individuals were women.

2. In Indonesian the plural is formed by doubling the noun. I choose to use a hybrid form to represent the plural, attaching the English "s" to the Indonesian term.

3. The term "female-bodied" is Cromwell's (1997) and refers to physiological sex.

4. I use fictitious names for the individuals mentioned in this article. Dayan (pronounced Dai-yon) lived with an older married sister in a small town about an hour from where I lived. I visited Dayan mostly on weekends at the sister's house.

5. Although I have used the pronoun "she" in the past to refer to a tomboi (Blackwood 1995a), at this point in my thinking "she" seems inadequate to represent the complexity of the tomboi identity, particularly because of the conno-

tations an English-speaking reader brings to it. The Indonesian language provides no guidance in this matter because its pronouns are gender-neutral. The third-person pronoun for both women and men is *dia*. I have decided to use the pronominal constructions "s/he" (for "she/he") and "hir" (for "her/his" and "her/him"), pronouns that are gaining currency in the transgender movement in the U.S. (see Wilchins 1997). This usage should not, however, be taken as a sign that tombois are transgendered people.

6. As Nestle says more eloquently, "a butch lesbian wearing men's clothes in the 1950s was not a man wearing men's clothes; she was a woman creating an original style to signal to other women what she was capable of doing—taking erotic responsibility" (1992:141).

7. I heard this news when I was in West Sumatra in 1996, but whether she was forced to marry or not, I do not know.

8. The relevant literature includes Dickemann 1997; Katz 1976; Kennedy and Davis 1993; Newton 1984; Rubin 1992; Shapiro 1991; Wikan 1977.

9. Islam in West Sumatra is part of the everyday life of the Minangkabau, who generally see no conflict between *adat* (local customs, beliefs, and laws) and Islam. The two have come to be mutually constructed (see Blackwood 1993).

10. This is not an insignificant concern since prestige, status, and property are all at risk. One young married woman of a wealthy lineage I knew was in turmoil over whether to have another child. Although she has a daughter and son, her only daughter is not a strong child. So although she already has two children, a number that the Indonesian state says is sufficient for a family, she worries that she should try to have another daughter to ensure the perpetuation of her lineage.

11. One young *bencong* (effeminate male homosexual) in West Sumatra, however, was forced to go to a *dukun* (shaman) by hir sister in an effort to "cure" hir.

12. The New Order refers to the postwar regime of General Suharto, who became acting head of state in 1966 and remains as president up to the present (1997).

13. Some of the relevant literature on women and the state includes Alexander and Mohanty (1997), Kandiyoti (1991), Williams (1996), Parker et al. (1992), Ong and Peletz (1995), Suryakusuma (1996).

REFERENCES

Alexander, M. Jacqui and Chandra Mohanty, eds. 1997. *Feminist Genealogies, Colonial Legacies, Democratic Futures.* New York: Routledge.

Aripurnami, Sita. 1996. "A Feminist Comment on the Sinetron Presentation of Indonesian Women." In Laurie Sears, ed., *Fantasizing the Feminine in Indonesia*, pp. 249–258. Durham: Duke University Press.

Blackwood, Evelyn. 1993. "The Politics of Daily Life: Gender, Kinship, and Identity in a Minangkabau Village, West Sumatra, Indonesia." Ph.D. diss., Stanford University.

———. 1995a. "Falling in Love with An-Other Lesbian: Reflections on Identity in Fieldwork." In Don Kulick and Margaret Willson, eds., *Taboo: Sex, Identity, and Erotic Subjectivity in Anthropological Fieldwork*, pp. 51–75. London: Routledge.

———. 1995b. "Senior Women, Model Mothers, and Dutiful Wives: Managing Gender Contradictions in a Minangkabau Village." In Aihwa Ong and Michael Peletz, eds., *Bewitching Women, Pious Men: Gender and Body Politics in Southeast Asia*, pp. 124–158. Berkeley: University of California Press.

———. N.d. "Subverting Subordination: Gender and Peasant Households in West Sumatra."

Boellstorff, Thomas. 1995. "The Gay Archipelago." Unpublished manuscript, Stanford University.

Bolin, Anne. 1994. "Transcending and Transgendering: Male-to-female Transsexuals, Dichotomy, and Diversity." In Gilbert Herdt, ed., *Third Sex, Third Gender: Beyond Sexual Dimorphism in Culture and History*, pp. 447–485. New York: Zone Books.

Bourdieu, Pierre. 1977. *Outline of a Theory of Practice*. Cambridge: Cambridge University Press.

Bullough, Bonnie, Vern Bullough, and John Elias, eds. 1997. *Gender Blending*. Amherst, NY: Prometheus.

Cromwell, Jason. 1997. "Traditions of Gender Diversity and Sexualities: A Female-to-male Transgendered Perspective." In Sue-Ellen Jacobs, Wesley Thomas, and Sabine Lang, eds., *Two-Spirit People: Native American Gender Identity, Sexuality, and Spirituality*, pp. 119–142. Urbana: University of Illinois Press.

———. Forthcoming. *Making the Visible Invisible: Transmen and Transmasculinities*. Urbana: University of Illinois Press.

Dickemann, Mildred. 1997. "The Balkan Sworn Virgin: A Traditional European Transperson." In Bonnie Bullough, Vern Bullough, and John Elias, eds., *Gender Blending*, pp. 248–255. Amherst, NY: Prometheus.

Elliston, Deborah. 1995. "Erotic Anthropology: 'Ritualized Homosexuality' in Melanesia and Beyond." *American Ethnologist* 22 (4): 848–867.

Epstein, Julia and Kristina Straub, eds. 1991. *Body/Guards: The Cultural Politics of Gender Ambiguity*. New York: Routledge.

Fadlillah. 1996. Wanita, Malin Kundang, dan Feminisme. *Singgalang*, June 30, p. 3.

Gayatri, BJD. 1993. "Coming Out but Remaining Hidden: A Portrait of Lesbians in Java." Paper presented at the International Congress of Anthropological and Ethnological Sciences, Mexico City, Mexico.

———. 1994. "Sentul-kantil, Not Just Another Term." Unpublished manuscript, Jakarta.

———. 1995. "Indonesian Lesbians Writing Their Own Script: Issues of Feminism and Sexuality." In Monika Reinfelder, ed., *From Amazon to Zami: Towards a Global Lesbian Feminism*, pp. 86–98. London: Cassell.

———. 1997. *[Come] Outed but Remaining Invisible: A Portrait of Lesbian in Java.* Unpublished ms. Jakarta.

Gramsci, Antonio. 1971. *Selections from the Prison Notebooks of Antonio Gramsci.* Transl. Q. Hoare and G. Smith. New York: International Publishers.

Halberstam, Judith. 1994. "F2M: The Making of Female Masculinity." In Laura Doan, ed., *The Lesbian Postmodern*, pp. 210–228. New York: Columbia University Press.

Herdt, Gilbert, ed. 1994. *Third Sex, Third Gender: Beyond Sexual Dimorphism in Culture and History.* New York: Zone Books.

Jacobs, Sue-Ellen, Wesley Thomas, and Sabine Lang, eds. 1997. *Two-Spirit People: Native American Gender Identity, Sexuality, and Spirituality.* Urbana: University of Illinois Press.

Kandiyoti, Deniz, ed. 1991. *Women, Islam, and the State.* Philadelphia: Temple University Press.

Katz, Jonathan Ned. 1976. *Gay American History: Lesbians and Gay Men in the U.S.A.* New York: Crowell.

Kennedy, Elizabeth and Madeline Davis. 1992 "'They Was No One to Mess With': The Construction of the Butch Role in the Lesbian Community of the 1940s and 1950s." In Joan Nestle, ed., *The Persistent Desire: A Femme-Butch Reader*, pp. 62–79. Boston: Alyson Publications.

———. 1993. *Boots of Leather, Slippers of Gold: The History of a Lesbian Community.* New York: Penguin Books.

Manderson, Lenore. 1980. "Rights and Responsibilities, Power and Privilege: Women's Role in Contemporary Indonesia." In *Kartini Centenary: Indonesian Women Then and Now*, pp. 69–92. Melbourne: Monash University.

Nestle, Joan. 1992. "The Femme Question." In Joan Nestle, ed., *The Persistent Desire: A Femme-Butch Reader*, pp. 138–146. Boston: Alyson Publications.

Newton, Esther. 1972. *Mother Camp: Female Impersonators in America.* Chicago: University of Chicago Press.

———. 1984. "The Mythic Mannish Lesbian: Radclyffe Hall and the New Woman." *Signs: Journal of Women in Culture and Society* 9 (4): 557–575.

———. 1993. *Cherry Grove, Fire Island: Sixty Years in America's First Gay and Lesbian Town.* Boston: Beacon.

Oetomo, Dede. 1996. "Gender and Sexual Orientation in Indonesia." In Laurie Sears, ed., *Fantasizing the Feminine in Indonesia*, pp. 259–269. Durham: Duke University Press.

Ong, Aihwa and Michael Peletz, eds. 1995. *Bewitching Women, Pious Men: Gender and Body Politics in Southeast Asia.* Berkeley: University of California Press.

Ortner, Sherry. 1989. "Gender Hegemonies." *Cultural Critique* 14:35–80.

Parker, Andrew, Mary Russo, Doris Sommer, and Patricia Yaeger, eds. 1992. *Nationalisms and Sexualities.* New York: Routledge.

Poole, John Fitz Porter. 1996. "The Procreative and Ritual Constitution of Female, Male, and Other: Androgynous Beings in the Cultural Imagination of the Bimin-Kuskusmin of Papua New Guinea." In Sabrina Ramet, ed., *Gender Reversals and Gender Cultures: Anthropological and Historical Perspectives*, pp. 197–218. London: Routledge.

Ramet, Sabrina Petra, ed. 1996. *Gender Reversals and Gender Cultures: Anthropological and Historical Perspectives*. London: Routledge.

Raymond, Janice. 1979. *The Transsexual Empire: The Making of the She-Male*. Boston: Beacon Press.

Rich, Adrienne. 1980. "Compulsory Heterosexuality and Lesbian Existence." *Signs: Journal of Women in Culture and Society* 5 (4): 631–660.

Rubin, Gayle. 1975. "The Traffic in Women: Notes on the 'Political Economy' of Sex." In Rayna R. Reiter, ed., *Towards an Anthropology of Women*, pp. 157–210. New York: Monthly Review Press.

——. 1992. "Of Catamites and Kings: Reflections on Butch, Gender, and Boundaries." In Joan Nestle, ed., *The Persistent Desire: A Femme-Butch Reader*, pp. 466–482. Boston: Alyson Publications.

Sears, Laurie J. 1996. "Fragile Identities: Deconstructing Women and Indonesia." In Laurie Sears, ed., *Fantasizing the Feminine in Indonesia*, pp. 1–44. Durham: Duke University Press.

Shapiro, Judith. 1991. "Transsexualism: Reflections on the Persistence of Gender and the Mutability of Sex." In Julia Epstein and Kristina Straub, eds., *Body/Guards: The Cultural Politics of Gender Ambiguity*, pp. 248–279. New York: Routledge.

Stone, Sandy. 1991. "The 'Empire' Strikes Back: A Posttranssexual Manifesto." In Julia Epstein and Kristina Straub, eds., *Body/Guards: The Cultural Politics of Gender Ambiguity*, pp. 280–304. New York: Routledge.

Sullivan, Norma. 1983. "Indonesian Women in Development: State Theory and Urban Kampung Practice." In Lenore Manderson, ed., *Women's Work and Women's Roles: Economics and Everyday Life in Indonesia, Malaysia, and Singapore*, pp. 147–171. Canberra: Australian National University.

Suryakusuma, Julia. 1996. "The State and Sexuality in New Order Indonesia." In Laurie Sears, ed., *Fantasizing the Feminine in Indonesia*, pp. 92–119. Durham: Duke University Press.

Trumbach, Randolph. 1994. "London's Sapphists: From Three Sexes to Four Genders in the Making of Modern Culture." In Gilbert Herdt, ed., *Third Sex, Third Gender: Beyond Sexual Dimorphism in Culture and History*, pp. 111–136. New York: Zone Books.

Weston, Kath. 1993. "Lesbian/gay Studies in the House of Anthropology." *Annual Review of Anthropology* 22:339–367.

Wieringa, Saskia. 1989. "An Anthropological Critique of Constructionism: Berdaches and Butches." In Dennis Altman et al., eds., *Homosexuality, Which Homosexuality?*, pp. 215–238. London: GMP.

Wikan, Unni. 1977. "Man Becomes Woman: Transsexualism in Oman as a Key to Gender Roles." *Man* 12 (n.s.): 304–319.

Wilchins, Riki Anne. 1997. *Read My Lips: Sexual Subversion and the End of Gender*. Ithaca: Firebrand Books.

Williams, Brackette, ed. 1996. *Women Out of Place: The Gender of Agency and the Race of Nationality*. New York: Routledge.

Williams, Raymond. 1977. *Marxism and Literature*. Oxford: Oxford University Press.

Yanagisako, Sylvia and Jane F. Collier. 1987. "Toward a Unified Analysis of Gender and Kinship." In Jane Collier and Sylvia Yanagisako, eds., *Gender and Kinship: Toward a Unified Analysis*, pp. 14–50. Stanford: Stanford University Press.

—— and Carol Delaney. 1995. "Naturalizing Power." In Sylvia Yanagisako and Carol Delaney, eds., *Naturalizing Power: Essays in Feminist Cultural Analysis*, pp. 1–22. New York: Routledge.

9

Saskia E. Wieringa

Desiring Bodies or Defiant Cultures:
Butch-Femme Lesbians in Jakarta and Lima

In the early 1980s I coordinated a research project on women's movements and organizations in several countries.[1] My own fieldwork within that project took place mainly in Indonesia and Peru. In the margins of my work I came into contact with butch-femme (b/f) groups in both Jakarta and Lima. Being socialized in the Dutch women's movement where the earlier b/f[2] cultures had been rejected as "old" lesbian, I was fascinated by these women.[3] I was also happy to meet them as by that time the general opinion in both the Northern and the Southern women's movements was that lesbianism was a Western phenomenon.

My involvement with their lives made me rethink lesbian desire and, more broadly, sexual desire. So far I had embraced most tenets of the constructivist paradigm, especially where it questions the "naturalness" of heteropatriarchy and biological determinism. Studies by Foucault and Weeks particularly had made me realize the technologies of domination (Foucault 1978) that have regulated sexuality over the ages. I had come to reject transhistorical and transcultural sexual essentialism and thus the search for the causes of sexual desire in the workings of hormones, genes, or the individual psyche. Weeks (1981) especially had documented convincingly that homosexual identity as we know it is actually a relatively modern institutional complex. In The Netherlands, too, several studies analyzed the different and changing meanings of sexual and social practices (such as cross-dressing) over the ages (Dekker and Van de Pol 1981; Hekma 1987; Everard 1994).

I had come to accept that desires are not prediscursive biological or psychological entities arising out of invariate drives. However, my encounters with the f/b cultures in Jakarta and Lima and my subsequent readings of many more forms of defiant desires and marginal sexualities in different historical and cultural settings made me question the persistence of such desires. If bodies are as passive and docile as constructivist theories would have it, whence the origins of sexual rebellion? Most accounts of nonheterosexual encounters of women come to us from specific sociocultural niches, such as that of the African woman-marriages, the American Indian two-spirit people (formerly called "berdaches") or the Chinese sisterhoods.[4] Thus it seems legitimate to analyze these marginal sexualities first of all as social constructions, as Whitehead (1981) does in her analysis of North American "berdaches." Yet these stories also tell tales of great individual perseverance in an effort to be accepted as belonging to those niches (Wieringa 1989).

"Strong" constructivist authors tend to ignore aspects of embodiment in their analyses of sexuality.[5] This may have the consequence, as Holland and others (1994) also pointed out, that an opposition is perceived between essentialism and poststructuralism. The material body is seen as fixed and stable, while the socially constructed, the gendered body is regarded as plural and shifting. There are two questions that "strong" constructivism finds it difficult to address. The first question deals with individual desire—is it a product of social conditioning, of innate propensity, or of some combination, in which both sex and gender, the body and the social, are seen to interact and shape each other? And more specifically, how is it that individual women exhibit such levels of rebellion that they prefer to face physical maltreatment, prison, or social ostracism rather than not live their desires? Second, what forces lead to the initial setting up of deviant sexual institutions? How do individual women who form those communities decide that these are the ones they have been looking for all along?

Kennedy and Davis (1993), for instance, maintain a constructivist position in their landmark study of lesbian bar cultures in Buffalo, New York, focusing on the b/f communities of the 1940s, 50s, and 60s. As they beautifully and meticulously analyze the growth and development of these communities, they also note the hostility, isolation, loneliness, and social ostracism of lesbian life before the women found each other and carved out a community. Life in the community only lifted part of their isolation, for the outside world remained hostile. Some of the women who flocked to these communities had refused to conform to the sociosexual dictates of their society at a very early age, and some were even sent to reform schools. Although Kennedy and Davis emphasize the "learning" of f/b roles, their narrators also tell them how much, even before learning the ropes of the trade, these roles appealed to them. As "Toni" remembers upon entering a lesbian bar for the first time in her life "there were all women and immediately I saw the roles, the butches and the fems. And that's what I wanted" (1993:78). And another narrator, "Marla," exclaims in the same situation: "Oh, I'm home" (ibid.).

In this essay I make use of Foucault's analysis of the "techniques of subjectification" to analyze some aspects of the b/f cultures of Jakarta and Lima. I investigate how both femmes and butches construct their own identities in these cultures. I will explore how far Foucault's theory of the "practices of the self" allows us to understand the women living in and constructing these f/b cultures, both their defiant desires and their sexual rebellion, and the cultural niche they have carved out for themselves, their deviant cultures. In so doing I will avoid the Scylla of essentializing their identities and the Charybdis of only looking at their socially constructed behavior. I will point at the interplay of the environment, with its strong elements of peer group pressure, and embodied desires.

Subjectivity and Fieldwork

First I stake my own claims in this inquiry and sketch the contours of my position as researcher. The current emphasis on self-reflexivity in anthropology (Myerhoff and Ruby 1992) has highlighted the critical importance of positioning oneself as a fieldworker. The recent collections of Kulick and Wilson (1995) and Lewin and Leap (1996) have stressed the critical link between epistemology, politics, and the sexual identity of the anthropologist. Before the publication of Malinowski's fieldwork diary in 1989 scant attention was paid to the issue of sexuality in fieldwork. Like other anthropologists in the early 1980s, I too felt that sex in the field was not done. This was one of the reasons why I felt such reluctance to see my encounters with the members of the b/f cultures and other lesbians I met as worthy of academic attention. They were my friends and occasional lovers, how could I have enough distance to write about them with the gaze[6] of the anthropologist?

Anthropology is always in some way or other a reflection on the relation between "self" and other/s. In my case I was both insider and outsider in the f/b groups that are the topic of the present essay. I not only observed their ways of relating with each other but also actively took part in their lives, while they actively tried to socialize me. In their view my behavior did not always fulfill their expectations, and they set out to correct me. If I wanted to go out with them, I had to behave in ways that they felt conformed to my role, that is, I had to learn to be butch. Their exasperation when I fell short of their expectations taught me about the internal dynamics in these f/b cultures and about the techniques individuals employ to shape their identities. The butches tried to teach me to be one of them and the femmes made clear what they expected from me in the way of chivalry and lovemaking. At the same time it was a process of mutual learning, for I tried to explain to them how the lesbians I knew in The Netherlands sought to shape their lives. This was a topic that aroused much interest and debate ("so there are other women just as we are?").

At first I just sought the company of other lesbians after exhausting days of interviews and meetings. I was both curious to see how they lived and happy to finally meet some like-minded women. Although I didn't consider the b/f groups I eventually came in contact with as "my field," I never gave up my professional habit of noting down anything that I felt was interesting. In between my field trips I told some of my stories to my friends back home. I had never considered writing about these experiences, but when I realized there was a great interest in these "overseas sisters," I started to entertain the idea of writing about them. As I felt at the time that producing academic work, complete with footnotes and all other scientific paraphernalia, would not do justice to what we had gone through together, I decided to write it as fiction.

I invented an alter ego, Dora D., and let her write a travelogue, a fictionalized documentary of lesbian life based on Dora's adventures (Wieringa 1987).[7] I chose the pseudonym Dora D. for various reasons, first, because it allowed me to create distance between me and the protagonist of the story, and second, because of the lesbophobia in my institute and my work at large. I lecture in a postgraduate program of women's studies that mainly caters to women from the South. In the mid-1980s when the first stories of Dora D. began to appear in a lesbian periodical, the Southern and the Northern women's movements were strongly divided on the issue of lesbianism. I didn't want to taint the program or the project I coordinated with the stigma of lesbianism. At the same time the name Dora D. provided sufficient markers of lesbianism to the initiated. It referred both to Freud's Dora[8] and to Doris Day, a film star and sex symbol of the 1950s and 1960s, who played the tomboy Calamity Jane in the film of that name, a film that gained cult status as a lesbian western.[9] I later attached less importance to the homophobia surrounding my work and my life and published the novel under my own name.[10]

During my field trips, I felt that my identity shifted between the two poles of native or outsider.[11] I was an outsider because I differed in culture, class, and, to a certain extent, language from these women, yet we shared our sexual preferences, however we defined and lived them. And for them, too, their sexual identity was among the most important aspects of their lives. This commonality at times overruled our differences. Yet my position was always ambiguous; I could shift from being "in" and "out" of their lives and thus occupied a privileged position. The self should be seen as a "politically situated discursive arrangement" characterized by open boundaries and fluidity rather than by closure and separation (Probyn 1991, cited in Kulick 1995:16). For this reason I take the socialization process I underwent as one of the more enlightening instances of fieldwork itself. I not only observed "the others" but also myself as an anthropological object, blurring the distinction between the subject and object of inquiry.

Practices of the Self

At least since de Beauvoir feminists have been wary of biological determinism based on essentialized notions of identity and the self. In the process of rejecting essentialism Foucault's writings on sexuality have been a major source of inspiration for constructivist authors. In his well-known *Introduction to the History of Sexuality* (1978) he focuses on the sociohistorical mechanisms in which sexuality is regulated in societies at large. He has been criticized for ignoring individual agency, for rendering bodies "passive" (McNay 1992; see also Braidotti 1991). In his two later volumes of this history, *The Use of Pleasure* (1985) and *The Care of the Self* (1986), he pays more attention to the agency of individuals and investigates how subjects are capable of intervening in or transforming their social environment. So, as McNay (1992) points out, he complements his analysis of the technologies of domination with the analysis of the technologies of subjectification, the practices and techniques through which individuals actively fashion their own identities. His focus shifts from an almost exclusive attention to social determinants to a "genealogy" of "desiring man" (*sic*) (1985:5). He attempts to "investigate how individuals were led to practice, on themselves and on others, a hermeneutics of desire" (ibid.), or the "aesthetics of existence" (McNay 1992:49). In this effort he maintains his antiessentialist stance for, in spite of his insistence on human agency, these practices of the self are always in the final analysis at least suggested, if not imposed, by the broader social context in which the individual is located.

Foucault derived his insights from his study of Greek antiquity and the rise of Christianity. Since he insisted that this theory would provide a suitable analytical category to investigate human desire in modern society (McNay 1992), I will apply this approach to my reading of femme-butch societies.

Foucault distinguishes four practices of the self. First is the "determination of ethical substance," which is the way the individual chooses to focus on a part of the self or mode of behavior as the core of his ethical conduct.[12] Second is the "mode of subjection," the way in which an individual relates his ethical behavior to a given rule and sees himself as obliged to put it into practice. The third principle Foucault distinguishes is related to the "forms of elaboration of ethical work," how certain codes of conduct are internalized as practices. In the last instance Foucault insists on the "telos of the ethical subject," the underlying moral code of conduct to which the individual subscribes (Foucault 1985:25–28; see also McNay 1992:52).

In the following pages I first outline some major dilemmas around the theme of b/f relations and then present my own fieldwork data. In the last section I relate these accounts to Foucault's four practices of self. A major question I address is whether these techniques of subjectification are sufficient to understand the processes by which individuals exhibit a code of conduct that poses great potential dangers to them.

The Butch-Femme Controversy

The most well-known f/b cultures were those in major cities in Europe and the U.S. in the 1940s, 1950s, and 1960s. In those days most women saw their belonging to this b/f culture as arising out of an innate desire. With the coming of feminism a major controversy arose: role-playing came to be seen as copying the most conventional aspects of both masculinity and femininity. Butch women were stereotyped as "derelict and pathetic imitators of men," while the feminine lesbians were seen as the "dupes of their butches" (Kennedy and Davis 1996). One of the earliest feminist lesbian groups in the U.S., the Daughters of Bilitis, actively tried to discourage b/f behavior with its dress codes and lifestyle (Case 1993).

In contrast, Nestle emphasizes that "femme flamboyance" and "butch fortitude" should not be seen as poses or stereotypes but "a dance between two different kinds of women, one beckoning the other into a full blaze of colour, the other strengthening the fragility behind the exuberance" (Nestle 1992:14). Others too reject the influence of what they perceived to be the "thought police" of the feminist movement.[13] Nestle points to the longevity of this "persistent desire" to argue for seeing b/f self-expression as "a lesbian-specific way of deconstructing gender that radically reclaims women's erotic energy," rather than as reflecting "the pernicious strength of heterosexual gender polarization" (ibid.).

Ideologues of the second wave of the feminist movement blamed b/f women for not being subversive enough, for playing the game of heteropa-triarchy. In this argument two crucial points are missed. In the first place, as Creed (1995) points out, all sexual practices actually function within the con-straints of heterosexism and phallocentrism. That is, the only insurgence possible is one of degree: roles can be reversed, boundaries stretched, certain elements ignored or stressed, but there is no escape possible from the tenets of heteropatriarchy. Second, a major reversal is actually taking place in f/b cultures: the fact that it is an all-women's game radically dislocates the pat-terns. The focus of sexuality is no longer the satisfaction of male desire, but rather sexuality has become the expression of the autonomous sexual desire of women for each other. Women proclaimed themselves as overtly sexual beings, with desires that escaped male control.

Precisely because b/f role-playing, even if it taunts heterosexual patterns by subverting them, "is" never heterosexuality, f/b lesbians are most obvious as women-loving women and are the object of much ridicule and aggres-sion. Hatred against b/f lesbians and other openly out lesbians is recorded everywhere, by Nestle (1992) and Kennedy and Davis (1993) for the U.S. in the 1950s and by Chan Sam (1995) in South Africa; it may take the form of battering, rape, social ostracism, psychiatric treatment, or treatment by priests.[14] Lesbians and gay men are especially persecuted in totalitarian regimes, both from the left and the right, as is borne out by the cases of China, Indonesia, Chile, and Argentina under military rule.[15] From the 1970s on the b/f culture was not only despised by heteropatriarchy but by "politically correct" feminist and lesbian-feminist groups, such as the Daughters of Bilitis, as well. Nowadays it has become more chic to play with gender roles and a new, more playful form of f/b behavior has become bon ton. The difference to the older b/f culture is that some of these younger women see it as a game, one of many sexual and erotic expressions with which one might choose to divert oneself, and no longer as an identity (Healey 1996; Wilton 1995).

The "older" b/f women in the North and the members of the non-West-ern groups I came in contact with, however, never described their lifestyle as a matter of choice. The "mannish" lesbian of the 1950s lived her life of defi-ance and marginality more or less as Radclyffe Hall created Stephen Gordon: she considered her forbidden desires innate.[16] Both Nestle (1992) and Grahn (1984) indicate that b/f lifestyles are perceived by those who adopt them as based on natural drives. As Grahn asserts, butches are not copying males, they imitate dykes, not men. At least they present powerful erotic images for their femme women:

What butch is though, I don't know. I think it's a gender position which is not masculinity and is not femininity, and it's not particularly bound to hetero-sexual paradigms, although it's obviously influenced by them. I think it's something that is genuinely and specifically erotic to lesbian culture, and it's very much an erotic identification for me, I mean I get a thrill out of it.

(Munt in Ainley 1995:161)

As notorious a butch as the South African gangster Gertie Williams saw her love life as something she was born with. When a preacher told her "Gertie, my girl, it is a sin to play man when you are woman," she is recorded as re-plying: "if it was a sin, then God would have shown me the sick-bed" (in Gevisser and Cameron 1995:131).

Femme desire has been more enigmatic to observers. On the one hand, femmes have been seen as unthreatening to the heterosexual order, as they might be "cured," one reason why sexologists at the beginning of the centu-ry hardly paid any attention to them. They were much more interested in the butch lesbians whom Havelock Ellis classified as "inverts." In their eyes femmes were the victims of butch seductive power. On the other hand, femme flamboyance could easily be mistaken for heterosexual femininity, and it therefore signified that "normal" women could become lesbians, ex-cluding males from a world of all-female desire. Femme women stress their erotic power over their butches. Nestle, one of the most powerful femmes I know, talks of "femme hunger" and femme receptiveness as an active art (1992:15–6). The sexual codes, the dress styles, and the mannerisms of b/f cultures are described as a highly stylized "erotic dance" by Loulan (1990), one in which both players have active parts and more often than not femmes initiate the games of seduction.

If Nestle and Grahn focus on "innate drives" as the origin of b/f desire and the development of f/b cultures, other authors focus on sociohistorical fac-tors. Foucault (1978), Weeks (1981), and Hekma (1987) focus on the "med-icalization" of the homosexual. Faderman (1991) points to the Second World War (in which apparently many women had learnt about love between women), the growth of big cities, and the medical and political leaders who declared that those who love others of the same sex "were" homosexuals as causes leading to the development of gay and lesbian identities and the b/f culture of the 1950s. Kennedy and Davis (1993) in their analysis of the Buffa-lo b/f community point out that the most important effect of the war was that more women than butches were drawn into the industrial sector, there-by making lesbians more like other women and less easy to identify (1993:38). The continuation of the b/f culture in the 1960s, Faderman writes, must be attributed to the "essentially conservative nature of a minority group as it attempts to create legitimacy for itself by fabricating traditions and rules" (1991:169). She cannot completely maintain her constructivist position, though, for she has to concede that some also chose the role because it "felt sexually most natural to them" (1991:172).

B/f cultures, according to Faderman, developed out of a desire for conformity and security and so paralleled the categories of the parent culture. It even emulated a certain kinship structure, a sense of membership, of belonging. It gave the subculture "a comforting illusion of structure and propriety that was meaningful and important to the group" (1991:174). However, this illusion led to severe police harassment, ostracism, rape, violence, and enormous problems in finding a place in the labor market. The question thus arises, if these women just wanted a comfortable niche to belong to, couldn't they have selected a less troublesome spot?

The rich and subtle history of the Buffalo b/f community provided by Kennedy and Davis stresses, as I indicated above, the construction of this community. But it also provides evidence of the existence of butch-fem sexuality without women having had contact with a lesbian community (1993:203). They write about fem desire: "A fem wants the feeling that the butch's most sought after goal is to reach her femininity, *the core of who she is*" (emphasis added) (1993:211). That is, the b/f community is embedded in a sexuality that is not always sufficiently captured by the canons of constructivism.

Havelock Ellis and other sexologists have been perceived by Faderman and others as providing a role model upon which b/f lesbians structured their identities.[17] The "medicalization" of homosexuality is said to sexualize the "innocent" nineteenth-century female friendships. Before creating Stephen Gordon, Radclyffe Hall indeed had consulted Havelock Ellis and other sexologists, who all emphasized the congenital origins of sexual orientation. Ellis even wrote a preface to the book. But shouldn't we reverse the picture? Instead of ascribing to the sexologists the "creation" of inverts, or the category third gender, credit them for simply describing what they saw around them? Possibly romantic friendships existed side by side with lesbians who signalled their desire for each other in a more stylized bipolar form. Tomboys or tribades or mannish lesbians and their femmes existed alongside the more conventional form in which women of those days cast their longing to live with each other, the female friendships.

Newton points out that in the nineteenth century "sex was seen as phallic . . . and could only occur in the presence of the imperial and imperious penis" (1984:561). Therefore women endowed with active lust for other women signalled their desire in the style deemed most appropriate to express such desire. She maintains that the "mannish lesbian" existed side by side with the "romantic friends." The cross-cultural persistence of tomboys or whatever name is given to virile women who actively signal their desire for other women and their erotic partners makes the issue of the character of such desires (innate, social, or some combination?) even more pertinent. The answers given by the sexologists, gender inversion for the butch lesbian and puzzled neglect in relation to the desire of the femme lesbian, have been sufficiently refuted by constructivist theorists. Yet they too cannot avoid recourse to essentialist formulations. In their concluding chapter, Kennedy and Davis write: "Working-class lesbians of the 1930s, 1940s and 1950s acted upon an *irrepressible urge* to be with others of their kind, to pursue sexual liaisons, and to have a good time" (1993:373–374, emphasis added).

In the following sections I take a closer look at the b/f cultures I came to know in Jakarta and Lima. I focus on those aspects of their cultures in which I noted a certain complementarity, disregarding the obvious ways in which they differed from each other and which demonstrate their cultural embeddedness. Studying the ways in which they differed might yield important insights into their respective dominant gender regimes; analyzing where they overlap may reveal certain aspects of the embodiedness of the individuals who make up these groups.

Femmes and Butches in Jakarta and Lima

Although b/f lesbians were not the only lesbians in Jakarta and Lima in the early 1980s, they had visible communities. In Indonesia the existence of lesbians was officially denied. In Jakarta I met a small group of determined lesbians, who in codes of dress and behavior publicly demonstrated their alternative lifestyles. The butches among them were the most manifest lesbians. Most of them had already resisted the dress codes for teenage girls, running home after school hours to replace their school uniform, in which skirts for girls are obligatory, with a pair of pants. Some of them had refused to attend university for this reason. They usually demonstrated this behavior before they associated themselves with the f/b group. So the first technique of subjectification Foucault proposes, the "determination of ethical substance," actually had taken place outside of any kind of social setting that could have provoked this behavior although the form their rebellion took was clearly inspired by the prevalent codes of heteropatriarchy, as is also documented in some cases by Kennedy and Davis (1993).

Although the butches I met were not aware of it, there is a history of women assuming the male role, cross-dressing, and possibly making love to other women in Indonesia. Cases of gender inversion are known for the royal courts of Surakarta and Yogyakarta in Central Java. Lady soldiers, "Javanese Amazons" as Carey and Houben (1987) call them, were dressed in male attire. These soldiers were admired for their military prowess and were also trained in dancing, singing, and making music (Kumar 1980).[18] Another indication of female-to-male gender inversion is found in the concept of *ardhnariswari*, originally a Sanskrit term meaning "mistress or queen who is half male." This term was used for Kèn Dhedhes, a queen of Singasari in the thirteenth century. She is seen as an incarnation of the Hindu goddess Durga, whose destructive powers, if tamed by a potent husband, "could be transmuted to fertile and beneficent influence crucial to the cosmic harmony of the realm" (Carey and Houben 1987:15, quoting Lind).

Karsch-Haack (1911) summarized some of the most important sources of same-sex relations among both men and women in the "Malay archipelago" prior to the first decade of this century. In his section on male homosexuality he devoted over thirty pages to what is now called Indonesia, in which he gives numerous examples of transvestism (called *banci* in Java), hermaphroditism,[19] pederasty, and sodomy. He devotes considerably fewer pages to women (only three), and in those he dwells on the dildos (some of) the women used: in Aceh the women made them of wax, as did the women in Bali, while Dayak women used a combination of wood and wax. He remarks that in East Java one can find transgendered women who dressed and behaved like men from an early age. They were referred to by the same name used for the men, *wandu*, which is Javanese for *banci* (1911:488–491). Gayatri (1997) also provides some examples that indicate that cross-dressing and transgender behavior historically have been part of the cognitive domain in Indonesia.

For the butches I met in the 1980s finding a decent job was a major concern, not only to survive but to provide for their girlfriends, as the butch code prescribed (or at least to pay for their consumption in the bars and discos they sometimes visited). Their subjection to a butch dress code, a certain corporeal style (a little swagger, heads held up defiantly, cigarette in hand), and gendered structures of language was so important to them that it overruled other concerns, such as financial security.

Dede told me on the first day we met that she had just been fired at the technical bureau where she worked. She was not taken seriously by the clients of her office. Koes, a butch with limited education, found it so hard to keep a job as driver that she was finally forced to accept the charity of a shady lawyer, who refused to pay her a wage.

Femmes had less problems in this regard. They could always pass as "normal" women. Their apparently greater conformity to the dominant form of heteropatriarchy was an eternal source of mistrust on the part of the butches. The butches were constantly afraid their femmes would return to a "normal" life. As some butches liked to court women who were in heterosexual relations or in between two boyfriends, their fears were at times confirmed. As husbands and male lovers often didn't take the butch lovers of their wives or girlfriends seriously, women who didn't want to risk giving up the relative safety of their male partner found it easier to sleep with a woman than with a male lover. This insecurity made some butches feel that they were the only "real" lesbians.

The dress code was strict (the androgynous look that had become popular in the West had not gained any ground in Indonesia yet). Femmes dressed in an exaggeratedly feminine fashion, in dresses with ribbons and frills. They always wore heavy makeup and high heels. Some of them had jobs as secretaries or were selling cosmetics. Others did sex work. The butches were dressed in male attire; their pants, shirts, and underwear were bought in men's dress shops. They would put bandages around their breasts to appear flat-chested. Deviations were hardly tolerated, and in fact Foucault's third principle, the "elaboration of ethical work," could be seen in operation constantly. Dress and body style were important topics of debate. In one of the earliest conversations we had on the topic, the butches criticized my way of dressing: my wristwatch was too small, my trousers were not tailored in a masculine style, and I was even wearing a bra! They confessed themselves puzzled by my appearance. Why didn't I just conform to what they felt I should look like?

I was indeed confused. I had never been confronted with lesbians who so clearly and unquestioningly proclaimed themselves to belong to what was called in the Dutch lesbian movement of the 1970s the "old-style" lesbian way. Having been socialized in that movement, I had never doubted androgyny as the major characteristic of the "new-style" lesbians with whom I mixed. We were feminists, we had decreed; we were doing away with patriarchy and therefore also with the role modeling that characterized most of the visible lesbians up to that time. Roles, we announced, were derived from heteropatriarchy. We were proud to be liberated women and we would shape the world according to a model based on equality. Our model of equality was not complicated yet by the ensuing debates on differences and multiple identities.[20]

So I was at first rather taken aback when I was confronted with women who were lesbians like myself but who claimed completely different identities. I asked the butches why they were not proud of their women's bodies. They answered that to them their bodies did not matter that much. They wanted to love women, and they had noticed that persons with male bodies had much less trouble in finding women partners than they had. When I protested and told one of them, Ade, that I wondered why she was not proud of her body, as she was "such a beautiful woman," Ade only knitted her brow. Later she told me I had actually offended her by not calling her "handsome" (Wieringa 1987:16).

The division of acts during lovemaking was similarly strict. During one of our discussions on the topic, the Jakarta butches voiced their astonishment at my preference for reciprocity:

> "How is that possible?" they asked, "Isn't that confusing, for in that case you would have to play two roles at the same time."
>
> "What do you mean?"
>
> "Well, both active and passive." With them that is strictly separated. The butches take the initiative in chatting up, which is what their girlfriends expect from them. On the other hand they assume that their lovers take on the expecting and caring roles. (Wieringa 1987:16)

Yet the above statement reflects more the norms as the butches wanted me to believe them than reality. For the ones who made the first passes, as I soon found out, were often the femmes. While the butches were busy making me conform to the role they expected of me, I met a woman who in *Dora D.* is referred to as "the film star." She was high femme and courted me by explaining in detail what she expected of me as her butch lover. That is, the femme controlled the scene and the butch could play her part, the active part, according to the specifications of her femme lover. Indeed, the film star explained to me that this was exactly what made butches such good lovers. Male lovers would hardly pay so much attention to their women. In the end it was not so much the butches who socialized me into roles and taught me the ropes of the game, but the "film star."

When I visited Lima, I also encountered a group of femmes and butches there. Their lives centered on a bar called the "Ferretería." The following fragment from *Dora D.* reveals similar techniques of subjection to the reigning b/f code as in Jakarta:

We picked up some beers and sat down at an empty table. When I looked up I saw a woman approaching me from the other side of the room. . . . For a Latin woman she was rather tall and dark. She was very slim, her face was expressive. Swinging her hips she crossed straight to our table, ignoring the dancing couples. After the usual introductions she asked me "what I was."

"*Soy una mujer*" (I'm a woman).

She kept me at arm's length and looked me up and down with a quick glance.

"No" she said decisively. "You're a *chita*"[21] OK, a butch then.

"As you wish," I said courteously.

But that promise had consequences. Up till now she had taken the initiative, now I was supposed to do that. So I had to lead the dance.

(Wieringa 1987:27–28)

In both b/f communities the distinction between butches and femmes was rigorously maintained. When I danced with a feminist lesbian friend of mine in one of Jakarta's discos, our friends greeted us with a "Hi *hemong*!" They explained to me that we were called *hemong* because as two butches we danced together. The term means "homoguy"; we were considered to be two homosexual lesbians. It didn't help that we tried to explain that we didn't quite feel that classification fit us.

The distinction between femmes and butches is maintained not only in dress and in sexual codes. In general the behavioral codes are strictly dichotomized. Sem, for instance, a trained karate fighter, was very proud that she had never hit one of her femme girlfriends, however much they might have provoked her. She once broke a bone in her hand because she hit the doorpost next to a femme she was quarreling with. She told that story with pride, as it indicated both her butch prowess and the level of her butch courtesy toward women. She had no such qualms with her butch friends.

In other ways, too, certain gendered stereotypes were upheld. The film star, for instance, adopted a very motherly and caring attitude toward me as far as food was concerned (women's domain), while I was supposed to open taxi doors, escort her through Jakarta's busy traffic, and carry her bags. Or, Dede, who had been rather badly bruised in a motor accident, would rather bite her lip than cry in front of me when she told me the story the following morning. A real butch does not cry.

One of the most revealing events I participated in was the meeting in which the first organization of Indonesian lesbians was to be founded, PER-LESIN, Persatuan Lesbian Indonesia. This concerned a group of lower- and lower-middle-class lesbians, mainly butches. They were encouraged by a shady lawyer, called Pak Abram (Father Abraham).

I went to the meeting at the invitation of the only feminist lesbian I knew at the time in Jakarta, Sigit. She was very worried because she didn't trust this Father Abraham in the least. He had drawn up statutes and suggested that everybody should fill in a form and supply a photograph. In that way, Sigit feared, the military, the police, or whoever wanted to crack down on lesbians would have no trouble whatsoever finding them. Or, alternately, the lawyer might use the files to inform their employers and blackmail the members. I wholeheartedly agreed with her. After all, President Suharto had founded his military power on a campaign fueled by absurd accusations of sexual perversions.[22] It was not unlikely that if ever the dictator would feel threatened, he would again resort to these kinds of methods. What better scapegoats than an organization of lesbians?

At the meeting Sigit proposed that instead of a formally registered organization a more informal structure should be built based on trust and friendship. But before that proposal was more or less accepted, discussions flared up that yielded critical insights into the self-perception of the assembled women and the social pressure under which they lived.

In the first place, it soon became clear that only the butches were supposed to register. As Father Abraham had explained, they were the ones who bore the brunt of the discrimination. They would always be visible as lesbians; they were fired again and again. The femmes didn't run those risks, he said, they could pass as "normal" women. All those present, some fifteen butches and five femmes, agreed to this. The following passage from *Dora D.* reveals the technologies of subjectification involved.

> [Ari] picked up her pile of admission forms and went on to explain how they had to be filled in.
> "Can we all become members?" Sigit asked innocently.
> "Of course."
> So they can join as well?" Sigit pointed to the three femmes and Roekmi who had ensconced themselves behind the typing machine. Two of them giggled nervously when all the attention was turned to them. The third one smiled defiantly. Roekmi ruffled her hair with her hand and pretended that she was not involved.
> "No, of course not!" Ari said decidedly "It is only for us."
> "Why not?" I asked. "After all we're all lesbians, aren't we?" Now everybody stepped in.
> "Look, Dora," Sem explained above all the noise "there are positive and

negative lesbians. We are positive lesbians. We are pure, 100% lesbian. With them you can never know. Before you know it, they are seeing a man again, and we are given the good-bye."

Father Abraham, who had entered during her last words, took over. "Let me explain. . . . Take Koes. Again and again her girlfriends leave her. Soon she'll be old and lonely. Who will help her then? For these girls it is just an adventure, while for butches like Koes it is their whole life."

"Yes, well, Abraham, . . . my experience is limited, of course, but it seems to me that the femmes flee the same problems that make life so hard for the butches. So they'd rather support each other."

"In any case," Sigit added, "they have become active now, that's why they're here, isn't that so?" And she looked questioningly at the three dolls behind the typing machine, Roekmi and my neighbour. The most brazen femme had been nodding in a mocking manner while Sigit and I were talking.

"So we're only supposed to be wives? We're not suited for something serious, are we? Maybe we should set up a wives' organization, Dharma Wanita,[23] the Dharma Wanita PERLESIN? Just like all those other organizations of the wives of civil servants and lawyers?" . . .

"Come on, Ari," Sigit insisted, "why don't you just ask them? You could at least ask them whether they want to join?" Ari found it extremely hard. Helplessly she looked at the other butches.

"Do you really mean that I should ask whether our wives would like to join *our* organization?" One of the butches nodded.

"Ok, fine." She directed herself to the dolls.

"Well, what do you want? Do you want to join us? But in that case you shouldn't just say yes, then you should also be involved with your whole heart."

"You never asked that of the others," the brazen femme pointed out, "but yes, I will definitely dedicate myself to the organization." Roekmi and the two femmes at her side also nodded. (Wieringa 1987: 89–91)

The above example is indicative of the social marginalization of the b/f community. It also captures it in one of its moments of transformation. The defiance of the femmes of the code that prescribes the division of butches and femmes into "positive" and "negative" lesbians respectively indicates a more active appropriation of lesbianism as a core element of their subjectivity. At the same time it illustrates the hegemony of the dominant heterosexual culture with its gendered principles of organization.

Yet, however much the butches conformed to male gender behavior they didn't define themselves as male; their relation to their bodies was rather ambiguous. At times they defined themselves as a third sex, which is nonfemale, as the following poem demonstrates. It was read by one of the prospective members of PERLESIN, and is a cry for recognition.

The Fate of Lesbians

I greet you my beloved friends who share my fate
We are getting old and we spent so much time together
Is there still a road ahead for us friends?
Or do we have to wait until we are old?
Uselessly waiting with our chin in our hands?
Friends, our soul and our feelings are not those of a woman
We don't belong to our sex.
Friends, think of our future
Let's move on undauntedly in spite of the many obstacles
We face, let us chase away the voices in minor key which
Don't agree with our feelings and let's turn our notes into
    a melody.
Together we are strong, divided we will be destroyed,
Friends, let us remind each other of this saying,
Friends, this determination must be in our hearts and souls
Let's confront all this, friends, without fear
For we are humans who have already been created.
Greetings to PERLESIN

                                                Ari

For all its call for action this poem rather reminds one of Radclyffe Hall's *Well of Loneliness* than of present-day feminist calls for gender bending (Butler 1993). Yet this novel was not known to them. Their call for organization was not linked to a feminist protest against rigid gender norms. Rather they felt that nature had played a trick on them and that they had to devise ways to confront the dangers to which this situation gave rise. Jakarta's b/f lesbians when I met them in the early eighties were not in the least interested in feminism. In fact, the butches among them were more concerned with the case of a friend of them who was undergoing a sex change operation. They clearly considered it an option, but none of them decided to follow this example. When I asked them why, all of them mentioned the health risks involved and the costs. None of them stated that they rather preferred their own bodies. Their bodies, although the source of sexual pleasure and as such the object of constant attention, didn't make it any too easy for them to get the satisfaction they sought or, at least, to attract the partners they desired.

In Lima in the early eighties the femme-butch community resisted the dictums of the feminist critique of role-playing. With a more vigorous feminist movement in Lima, the reaction of the bar lesbians to feminism was much stronger than in Jakarta, where feminism was so insignificant that it could more easily be ignored. During the Second Encounter of Latin American and Caribbean feminists, which was held in Lima in 1983, the first meeting of lesbians was held. It was a very emotional setting in which several women openly came out. I had just come back from that session when I went to the lesbian bar "Ferretería" mentioned above. The following conversation with the tall, dark femme who had made me lead the salsa, an activity I was clearly totally unfit for, gives an indication of the atmosphere of the time:

"What are you doing here anyway, *gringa* [f., foreigner]," my dance partner suddenly asked while I was thinking that I was beginning to understand the basic steps.

"I attended a feminist meeting."

"A feminist meeting? Does that mean you are a feminist?"

She looked at me with such incredulity, that I was rather taken aback.

"Eh, well, . . . yes."

"Women, look, a feminist!" she called mockingly to the group she had left when she went after me, some five frightful looking butches, two timid femmes. Some of them laughed, others looked rather suspiciously.

"So you're a feminist?" she repeated, "and you're also like us? How's that possible? What are you doing?"

I told her that to me feminism and lesbianism were not two totally distinct issues, but that they had much in common.

She interrupted me impatiently: "Now you listen to me. I am a Cuban refugee. Not because I am opposed to socialism as such, but because what they make it look like in Cuba is far removed from socialism. Likewise I don't trust all those feminists. Have they ever done anything for us? Have they ever cared about us?" (Wieringa 1987:28–29)

Actually, she was right. One of the issues discussed during the lesbian session of the encounter had been the case of a lesbian teacher who had been fired. She had asked in vain for support from the feminist movement.

In 1984 the lesbian-feminist group GALF was founded, the Grupo de Autoconsciencia de Lesbianas Feministas (Self-Awareness Group of Lesbian Feminists), one of several lesbian groups of that name in Latin America (see Mogrovejo in this volume). One of the issues in their struggle against heterosexual values was role-playing. As everywhere else in the feminist movement of those days, it was considered a heterosexual relic. The existence of

GALF led to a greater visibility of lesbianism in society (which incidentally may have been one of the factors leading to increased police harassment, such as the raid on a lesbian bar a few years later). GALF has been very active in promoting the discussion of sexuality within the feminist movement. A result of the greater awareness of the connection between patriarchal oppression in general and the oppression of women's sexual expression in general has been the downplaying of the sexual autonomy and courage of the b/f lesbian community. As elsewhere, they were at best seen as old-fashioned lesbians, at worst as traitors of the feminist cause.

Women who decided to join the f/b communities in Jakarta and Lima conformed to certain "technologies of subjectification," as put forth by Foucault (1985). The major part of their identity, the "ethical substance," is determined by their sexual object choice. The mode of subjection to the b/f codes they aspire to is rather rigid; there is little leeway for variation within the established norms, although the foundation of PERLESIN demonstrates that transformation is possible. The forms in which their adherence to the b/f codes is "lived" are subject to a constant process of surveillance and socialization. This may have the effect that identities become more fixed than under conditions of lesser surveillance. In this regard Foucault's first three principles are useful tools for the analysis of the inner workings of marginalized sociosexual groups. As far as his fourth practice is concerned, the telos of the subject, this points in my view to a code of behavior that is built on the conviction that subjects have the right to live according to the dictates of their bodies, as the women perceive them.

In spite of the usefulness of Foucault's theory of the "aesthetics of the self" in analyzing the way women conform to certain codes and transform them and themselves in the process, there are also certain limitations. The project of analyzing the construction of the self as a desiring body within a marginalized and beleaguered sexual community such as the b/f cultures runs into great difficulties. A major problem is that Foucault's analysis of the practices of self is actually based on a model of reactive forms of subjectification. In this view human agency is always analyzed in relation to an overdetermining and already existing social context. In Foucault's opinion this social background at least suggests, if not imposes, the options the individual has. His analysis does point to certain technologies individuals employ in a process of becoming-subject within a certain community. However his "aesthetics of existence" shed no light on the factors that propel individuals to select certain groups as their social surroundings or to feel they have "come home." Thus this model makes it difficult to analyze defiant desire, a desire that has no place in dominant models of sexuality and is actively persecuted. Why do certain people make choices that make life so hard on them? And why are these choices made so persistently in such widely diverging cultures as Jakarta and Lima?

Foucault's analysis allows us to study the characteristics and the transformation of b/f cultures and the conduct of the members of these cultures, but not the mechanisms that drive individuals to become part of them. He cannot explain forms of conduct individuals exhibit even before they have decided to join these marginalized groups.

A second, related problem with Foucault's theories is that they are built on his rejection of the notion of a "sovereign, founding subject" as the origin of social action, which is understood as universal (McNay 1992:61). Foucault excludes the possibility of multiple founding subjects able to establish different forms of sociosexual communities in interaction with a prior social context and with each other. It is clear that individuals cannot be separated from the sites in which their selves are constructed; in the process of becoming-subject they change both themselves and their surroundings. Individuals are also embodied beings; although the materiality of the body can only be "known" through its discursive context, it cannot be ignored. I am not suggesting here that bodies and desires are stable and fixed entities that of necessity lead to the assumption of certain identities. I see bodily processes rather as interacting with social processes in ways in which both phenomena reshape themselves.

I suggest that to study the genealogy of b/f desire, different theoretical models must be devised that allow for the integration of the analysis of multiple levels of desires. This theory need not revive the model of a singular founding subject or a one-dimensional essentialism based on the workings of invariate drives, but will allow for the analysis of the multiple modes of subjectification arising from the analysis of complex and plural individual properties, as they are acted out in relation to other individuals and social communities. After all, even if the sexologists' hypothesis of sexual inversion was wrong, it does not mean that questions about "irrepressible urges" and feelings of "homecoming" have lost their relevance. I suggest that individuals are endowed with sexualities of varying intensities that may, depending on the specific sociohistorical contexts in which they live, lead to various identities.

The study of the micropolitics of physical desires in their sociohistorical contexts and especially the study of the defiant desires and deviant cultures that question the hegemony of dominant sociosexual discourses may shed light both on the interaction of social and bodily processes and on the technologies in which male dominance is organized. In this sense the study of f/b cultures should not be driven by a will to police the women demonstrating these lifestyles but by the realization that b/f behavior demonstrates a form of sexual rebellion and erotic self-determination.

NOTES

1. These countries were India, Indonesia, Peru, Somalia, the Sudan, and three countries in the Caribbean region, Jamaica, Trinidad, and St. Vincent. See Wieringa 1995a.

2. I use butch-femme(b/f) interchangeably with femme-butch (f/b) to indicate that the word order does not imply any form of hierarchy between the partners.

3. According to Morgan (1993), in present day New York many still perceive women who identify as b/f as "dinosaurs," however much playing with b/f styles has become chic and stylish.

4. For literature on the two-spirits ("berdaches") see Blackwood (1984, 1986), Lang in this volume, Roscoe (1991), Whitehead (1981), and Williams (1986); for literature on the Chinese sisterhoods see Sankar (1986), Topley (1975); and for woman marriages Amadiume (1987), Herskovits (1937), and Krige (1974).

5. For a discussion on the degrees of constructivism, see Vance (1989).

6. Feminist epistemologists, such as Haraway (1988), Harding (1991), and Hartsock (1989), have blown up the myth of the all-knowing scientific gaze and have pointed out the importance of positionality and the essential subjectivity (i.e., related to the "standpoint" of the viewer) of knowledge claims.

7. *Dora D.* is written in Dutch. All translations in this chapter are done by the author. It is at present being translated into English, but I have no access to this translation at the moment of finalizing this text. It is thus possible that when the translated *Dora D.* will be published, there will be slight differences.

8. See Gallop (1982) and Brennan (1989) for feminist analyses of Freud's case-history of his homosexual patient Dora. In 1983 the Dutch translation appeared of Cixous's (1983) *Portrait of Dora*. It was widely read and discussed in the Dutch women's movement.

9. Although Calamity Jane is "tamed" in the end in a heterosexual marriage and even has to hand over her gun when she leaves in her wedding dress, the most moving love scenes are between her and the femme singer from Chicago.

10. See Wieringa (1990) for this process.

11. See Narayan (1993) for a discussion of the dynamics of "native" anthropology.

12. Foucault wrote so consistently about men and from a male perspective

that I decided to adhere to his habit of using the masculine pronoun when referring to his work.

13. See the interview that Ainley (1995) had with Janet Green.

14. See Rosenbloom (1996) for an overview of the human rights situation in relation to lesbians. Records of psychiatric treatment I heard both in Latin America and Indonesia, while in the U.S. it is only recently that homosexuality is no longer classified as a psychiatric disorder. For Jamaica, Silvera writes, "if a woman was found out to be a sodomite or man royal, men would organize and gang rape whichever woman was suspect" (1992:524). See for instance Chan Sam (1995) for a priest being brought to pray for the "recovery" of lesbian women in South Africa.

15. For Chile see for instance Borren in *Sek*, 10 (1987), for Argentina Csörnyei in Reinfelder (1996). The Chinese fear of lesbianism was particularly apparent during the forum in Huairou that accompanied the Fourth World Conference on Women held in Beijing 1995.

16. *The Well of Loneliness* (Hall 1982) has become such an important lesbian role model that in Johannesburg a building that was almost exclusively occupied by lesbians and gay men was renamed "Radclyffe Hall" (Gevisser 1995:20).

17. Jeffreys (1985) analyzed the historical background in which Havelock Ellis worked and documented his denunciation of the feminist movement, especially female friendships. His wife also had relations with women.

18. One of the most feared cavalry commanders of the Javanese prince Diponegoro who led the Java war (1825–30) was Radèn Ayu Yudokusuma, who shaved off her hair like many male commanders (Carey and Houben 1987:20).

19. The fascination of Karsch-Haack and his sources with hermaphroditism, elongated clitorises, etc., must be seen in the light of the premodern one-sex model as analyzed by Laqueur (1990). In this view "mannish women," either with a dildo or by means of an enlarged clitoris, penetrated their partners.

20. See for instance Braidotti (1991) or Butler (1993).

21. Diminutive (f.) of "macho."

22. See Wieringa (1995b, 1998). After the putsch of leftist military men supported by some communist leaders, Suharto organized a campaign in which he accused members of the communist women's organization *Gerwani* of castrating and killing the right-wing generals who had become the victims of the putschists. This campaign fueled the massacre of probably a million leftist people that followed.

23. *Dharma Wanita*, literally Duty of Women, is the name given to the organizations of wives of male civil servants or other male employees. After Suharto took over the presidency from Sukarno, these organizations have had to abandon any feminist leaning they might have had in the "Old Order" of Indonesia's first president. They have now become instruments of government control over

women in an effort to "resubordinate" women after the Old Order, when women's organizations were much more independent (Wieringa 1985).

REFERENCES

Agar, Michael H. 1980. *The Professional Stranger: An Informal Introduction to Anthropology.* New York: Academic Press.

Ainley, Rosa. 1995. *What Is She Like? Lesbian Identities from the 1950s to the 1990s.* London: Cassell.

Amadiume, Ifi. 1987. *Male Daughters, Female Husbands: Gender and Sex in an African Society.* London: Zed Books.

Blackwood, Evelyn. 1984. "Sexuality and Gender in Certain Native American Tribes: The Case of Cross-Gender Females." *Signs: Journal of Women in Culture and Society* 10:24–42.

——, ed. 1986. *The Many Faces of Homosexuality: Anthropological Approaches to Homosexual Behavior.* New York: Harrington Park Press.

Braidotti, Rosi. 1991. *Patterns of Dissonance.* Cambridge: Polity Press.

Butler, Judith. 1993. *Bodies That Matter: On the Discursive Limits of Sex.* New York: Routledge.

Brennan, Teresa, ed. 1989. *Between Feminism and Psychoanalysis.* London: Routledge.

Carey, Peter and Vincent Houben. 1987. "Spirited Srikandhis and Sly Sumbadras: The Social, Political, and Economic Roles of Women at the Central Javanese Courts in the 18th and early 19th Centuries." In Elsbeth Locher-Scholten and Anke Niehof, eds., *Indonesian Women in Focus,* pp. 12–43. Dordrecht: Foris.

Case, Sue-Ellen. 1993. "Toward a Butch-Femme Aesthetic." In Henry Abelove, Michele Aina Barale, and David N. Halperin, eds., *The Lesbian and Gay Studies Reader,* pp. 294–307. New York: Routledge.

Chan Sam, Tanya. 1995. "Five Women: Black Lesbian Life on the Reef." In Mark Gevisser and Edwin Cameron, eds., *Defiant Desire, Gay and Lesbian Lives in South Africa,* pp. 186–193. New York: Routledge.

Cixous, Hélène. 1983. *Portret van Dora.* Amsterdam: SUA.

Creed, Barbara. 1995. "Lesbian Bodies: Tribades, Tomboys, and Tarts." In Elizabeth Grosz and Elspeth Probyn, eds., *Sexy Bodies: The Strange Carnalities of Feminism,* pp. 86–104. London: Routledge.

Dekker, Rudolf and Lotte van de Pol. 1981. *Daar was laatst een meisje loos: Nederlandse vrouwen als matrozen en soldaten—een historisch onderzoek.* Baarn: Ambo.

Everard, Myriam. 1994. *Ziel en Zinnen: Over lust en liefde tussen vrouwen in de tweede helft van de achttiende eeuw.* Groningen: Historische Uitgeverij.

Faderman, Lillian. 1991. *Odd Girls and Twilight Lovers: A History of Lesbian Life in Twentieth-Century America.* New York: Penguin.

Foucault, Michel. 1978. *The History of Sexuality.* Vol. 1. *An Introduction.* New York: Vintage Books.

——. 1985. *The History of Sexuality.* Vol. 2, *The Use of Pleasure.* London: Penguin.

——. 1986. *The Care of the Self.* Harmondsworth: Penguin.

Gallop, Jane. 1982. *The Daughter's Seduction: Feminism and Psychoanalysis.* Ithaca: Cornell University Press.

Gayatri, BJD. 1997. *[Come] Outed but Remaining Invisible: A Portrait of Lesbian in Jakarta.* Unpublished ms. Jakarta.

Gevisser, Mark. 1995. "A Different Fight for Freedom: A History of South African Lesbian and Gay Organizations from the 1950s to the 1990s." In Mark Gevisser and Edwin Cameron, eds., *Defiant Desire: Gay and Lesbian Lives in South Africa,* pp. 14–89. New York: Routledge.

—— and Edwin Cameron, eds. 1995. *Defiant Desire: Gay and Lesbian Lives in South Africa.* New York: Routledge.

Grahn, Judy. 1984. *Another Mother Tongue: Gay Words, Gay Worlds.* Boston: Beacon Press.

Hall, Radclyffe. 1982. *The Well of Loneliness.* London: Jonathan Cape, 1928. Reprint, London: Virago Press.

Haraway, Donna J. 1988. "Situated Knowledges: The Science Question in Feminism as a Site of Discourse on the Privilege of Partial Perspective." *Feminist Studies* 14 (3): 575–599.

Harding, Sandra. 1991. *Whose Science? Whose Knowledge? Thinking from Women's Lives.* Buckingham: Open University Press.

Hartsock, Nancy. 1989. "Standpoint: Toward a Specifically Feminist Historical Feminism." In Nancy Hartsock, ed., *Money, Sex, and Power,* pp. 235–50. New York: Longman.

Healey, Emma. 1996. *Lesbian Sex Wars.* London: Virago.

Hekma, Gert. 1987. *Homoseksualiteit: Een medische reputatie, de Uitdoktering van de homoseksueel in negentiende-eeuws Nederland.* Amsterdam: SUA.

Herskovits, Melville. 1937. "A Note on 'Woman Marriage' in Dahomey." *Africa* 10 (3): 335–342.

Holland, Janet, Caroline Ramazanoglu, Sue Sharpe, and Rachel Thompson. 1994. "Power and Desire: The Embodiment of Female Sexuality." *Feminist Review* 46:21–38.

Jeffreys, Sheila. 1985. *The Spinster and her Enemies: Feminism and Sexuality, 1880–1930.* London: Pandora.

Karsch-Haack, Ferdinand. 1911. *Das Gleichgeschlechtliche Leben der Naturvölker.* Munich: Reinhardt.

Kennedy, Elizabeth Lapovsky and Madeline D. Davis. 1993. *Boots of Leather, Slippers of Gold: The History of a Lesbian Community.* New York: Routledge.

——. 1996. "Constructing an Ethnohistory of the Buffalo Lesbian Community: Reflexivity, Dialogue, and Politics." In Ellen Lewin and William L. Leap, eds.,

Out in the Field: Reflections of Lesbian and Gay Anthropologists, pp. 171–200. Urbana: University of Illinois Press.

Krige, Eileen Jensen. 1974. "Woman-Woman Marriage, with special reference to the Lovedu: Its Significance for the Definition of Marriage." *Africa* 44:11–37.

Kulick, Don and Margaret Willson, eds. 1995. *Taboo: Sex, Identity, and Erotic Subjectivity in Anthropological Fieldwork*. London and New York: Routledge.

Kumar, Ann. 1980. "Javanese Court Society and Politics in the Late Eighteenth Century: The Record of a Lady Soldier. Part 1, "The Religious, Social, and Economic Life of the Court." *Indonesia* 29:1–46.

Laqueur, Thomas. 1990. *Making Sex: Body and Gender from the Greeks to Freud*. Cambridge, Mass.: Harvard University Press.

Lewin, Ellen and William L. Leap, eds. 1996. *Out in the Field: Reflections of Lesbian and Gay Anthropologists*. Urbana: University of Illinois Press.

Loulan, JoAnn. 1990. *The Lesbian Erotic Dance: Butch, Femme Androgyny, and Other Rhythms*. San Francisco: Spinsters.

Malinowski, Bronislaw. 1989. *A Diary in the Strict Sense of the Term*. Stanford: Stanford University Press.

McNay, Lois. 1992. *Foucault and Feminism: Power, Gender, and the Self*. Cambridge: Blackwell.

Morgan, Tracy. 1993. "Butch-Femme and the Politics of Identity." In Arlene Stein, ed., *Sisters, Sexperts, Queers: Beyond the Lesbian Nation*, pp. 35–47. London: Penguin.

Myerhoff, Barbara G. and Jay Ruby. 1992. "A Crack in the Mirror: Reflexive Perspectives in Anthropology." In Marc Kaminsky, ed., *Remembered Lives: The Work of Ritual, Storytelling, and Growing Older*, pp. 307–50. New York: Pantheon.

Narayan, Kirin. 1993. "How Native is a 'Native' Anthropologist?" *American Anthropologist* 95:671–686.

Nestle, Joan, ed. 1992. *The Persistent Desire: A Femme-Butch Reader*. Boston: Alyson Pub.

Newton, Esther. 1984. "The Mythic Mannish Lesbian: Radclyffe Hall and the New Woman." *Signs: Journal of Women in Culture and Society* 9 (4): 557–576.

Reinfelder, Monika, ed. 1996. *Amazon to Zami: Towards a Global Lesbian Feminism*. London: Cassell.

Roscoe, Will. 1991. *The Zuni Man-Woman*. Albuquerque: University of New Mexico Press.

Rosenbloom, Rachel, ed. 1996. *Unspoken Rules: Sexual Orientation and Women's Rights*. London: Cassell.

Sankar, Andrea. 1986. "Sisters and Brothers, Lovers and Enemies: Marriage Resistance in Southern Kwangtung." In Evelyn Blackwood, ed., *The Many Faces of Homosexuality: Anthropological Approaches to Homosexual Behavior*, pp. 69–83. New York: Harrington Park Press.

Silvera, Makeda. 1992. "Man Royals and Sodomites: Some Thoughts on the Invisibility of Afro-Caribbean Lesbians." *Feminist Studies* 18 (3): 521–532.

Stein, Arlene, ed. 1993. *Sisters, Sexperts, Queers: Beyond the Lesbian Nation.* London: Plume.

Topley, Margaret. 1975. "Marriage Resistance in Rural Kwangtung." In Margery Wolf and Roxanne Witke eds., *Women in Chinese Society,* pp. 67–89. Stanford: Stanford University Press.

Vance, Carole. 1989. "Social Construction Theory: Problems in the History of Sexuality." In Dennis Altman et al., eds., *Homosexuality, Which Homosexuality?,* pp. 13–35. London: GMP Publishers.

Weeks, Jeffrey. 1981. *Sex, Politics, and Society: The Regulation of Sexuality since 1800.* Essex: Longman.

Whitehead, Harriet. 1981. "The Bow and the Burden Strap: A New Look at Institutionalized Homosexuality in Native North America." In Sherry B. Ortner and Harriet Whitehead, eds., *Sexual Meanings: The Cultural Construction of Gender and Sexuality,* pp. 80–116. Cambridge: Cambridge University Press.

Wieringa, Saskia. 1985. *The Perfumed Nightmare: Some Notes on the Indonesian Women's Movement.* The Hague: ISS, Working Paper.

——. 1987. *Uw Toegenegen Dora D.* Reisbrieven. Amsterdam: Furie.

——. 1989. "An Anthropological Critique of Constructionism: Berdaches and Butches." In Dennis Altman et al., eds., *Homosexuality, Which Homosexuality?,* pp. 215–239. London: GMP Publishers.

——. 1990. Van Monocausaliteit tot Diversiteit; een Persoonlijke Intellectuele Ontwikkeling. In Britt Fontaine, Peter Kloos, and Joke Schrijvers, eds., *De Crisis Voorbij: Persoonlijke Visies op Vernieuwing in de Antropologie,* pp. 165–182. Leiden: DSWO Press.

—— ed. 1995a. *Subversive Women: Women's Movements in Africa, Asia, Latin America, and the Caribbean.* London: Zed Books.

——. 1995b. "The Politicization of Gender Relations in Indonesia: The Indonesian Women's Movement and Gerwani Until the New Order State." Ph.D. diss., University of Amsterdam.

——. Forthcoming. "Sexual Metaphors in the Change from Sukarno's Old Order to Suharto's New Order in Indonesia." *Review of Indonesian and Malaysian Affairs* 32.

Williams, Walter L. 1986. *The Spirit and the Flesh: Sexual Diversity in American Indian Culture.* Boston: Beacon Press.

Wilton, Tamsin. 1995. *Lesbian Studies: Setting an Agenda.* London: Routledge.

10

Deborah A. Elliston

Negotiating Transnational Sexual Economies: Female *Māhū* and Same-Sex Sexuality in "Tahiti and Her Islands"

In this essay I examine same-sex sexuality among Polynesians living in the Society Islands of French Polynesia, an overseas territory of France in the South Pacific. My goals here are two-fold: first, to map some of the areas of the discursive field within which same-sex sexuality gains its meanings for many Polynesians; second, and in light of this, to analyze why and how some kinds of same-sex sexuality among Polynesians have emerged as locally problematic. At one level, my interest here is in the interactions between local and global signifying economies as these shape interpretive contests around same-sex sexuality in the Society Islands today: the ways the discursive field of sexuality in general, and same-sex sexuality more specifically, is shifting as new sexual ontologies and epistemologies become available for local uses—and by "uses" I mean that these sexual economies produce subject positions that are taken up by Polynesians today. This, then, is an analysis of the openings and recalibrations, challenges, uneasy negotiations, and contingent settlements between what I am glossing as Polynesian and transnational frameworks for interpreting same-sex sexuality. At another level, however, I want to use my analysis of these disjunctures to draw out some feminist lessons from Tahiti and her Islands for how to theorize same-sex sexuality, and particularly female same-sex sexuality, cross-culturally.

Interpretive Contexts

During my 1994–95 fieldwork in the Society Islands of French Polynesia, Polynesians I knew were relatively embracing of some configurations of same-sex sexualities, while they took stances ranging from ambivalence to animosity toward other configurations.[1] These evaluations relate to the rather substantial variety of categories that allow for the expression of same-sex sexuality in the Islands: the Tahitian-language gender categories *vahine* ("woman"), *tane* ("man"), and *māhū* (translated as "half-man, half-woman"); the Tahitian-language terms *raerae* and *petea* (see below), which are said to be of recent innovation; and the French-language terms *travesti* ("transvestite," used by Polynesians as a synonym for *raerae*) *homosexuel/homosexuelle* ("homosexual"), *pédé* ("pedophile," abbreviated, but in common use a colloquial term equivalent to "gay [male]"), *lesbienne* ("lesbian"), and *gouine* ("dyke").

The criteria for determining which same-sex sexualities Polynesians embrace today lie at the crossroads of multiple discursive formations, not all of which can be treated in this essay. In the larger project of which this essay comprises the initial analysis, I will analyze two other discursive formations in relation to which same-sex sexuality gains its current meanings among Polynesians. One of these is the Tahitian Protestant church's condemnations of same-sex sexuality. While church discourses on same-sex sexuality are available to Polynesians, I argue that they are of limited effect since these and other church teachings focusing on practices labeled "sinful"—sex outside of marriage, for example—are treated by Polynesians as largely impracticable edicts.[2] The second discursive formation is the French colonial contribution to the local meanings of same-sex sexuality. While these are complex and, like church teachings, lie beyond the scope of this essay, I want at least to note here that in a French "overseas territory" where most Polynesians are ambivalent about their rulers, it is not surprising that the same-sex sexualities associated with the French may also be met with some ambivalence.[3]

Along with those caveats about the margins around this essay, let me also convey something about the margins within it. Taking feminist critical work on epistemology seriously, as I do, includes addressing the ways in which knowledge claims are partial and situated (Haraway 1991; Mohanty 1987). I ask that the reader keep that partiality in the foreground as s/he considers the arguments and interpretations of this essay. While I take the position that all anthropological work is interpretive and grown from partial knowledges, it seems to me that because same-sex sexuality is oftentimes one of the more difficult subjects to investigate ethnographically, the interpretations anthropologists produce of same-sex sexuality may well be even less secure than our interpretations of other social practices. My analysis of same-sex sexuality in the Society Islands reflects the fact that I am not from those Islands, not Polynesian, and not māhū: I did not have privileged access to how same-sex sexuality is produced from those subject positions or to what same-sex sexuality looks like or feels like from those subject positions. The empirical basis of my knowledge claims about same-sex sexuality in the Society Islands, then, is located at a remove: it is based primarily on accounts and stories people told me about themselves and about others, and it is gleaned from my interpretations of the assumptions structuring those stories and accounts. It is also based on sexualized interactions and gendered performances I witnessed, but usually ones in which I did not participate in any substantive way. My knowledge claims, then, are filtered not only through my own partial perspective—that of a white Canadian/American lesbian anthropologist—but also through the situated perspectives of the Polynesians I knew. Given all of this, I situate my interpretations and analyses of same-sex sexuality in this essay as perhaps compelling but ultimately as speculative. I ask that the reader do the same.

With those caveats, my project in this essay is to examine, first, what I gloss as Polynesians' interpretive frameworks for understanding sexuality, and, more specifically, the logical and productive relationships Polynesians forge between gender and sexuality. Second, I examine the categories Polynesians have recently innovated in relation to translocal discourses of what I will gloss as queer sexuality. The argument of this essay is that the basis of the different (moral) evaluations Polynesians ascribe to the empirically identical "sex" practices that appear on each side of the line differentiating the morally unremarkable from the morally problematic categories lies in the disjuncture between the ontological and epistemological organizing premises of local as compared to translocal symbolic economies of sexuality. More specifically, I argue that these different organizing premises structure a conflict between Polynesians' privileging of practice or experience in adjudicating the ontological validity of same-sex sexualities, in contrast with the way the recently introduced and innovated same-sex sexualities are organized through an ontology of sexual essentialism (Rubin 1984) or "sexual identity."

Māhū

I focus on Polynesian māhū to begin my analysis of what I am glossing as Polynesian interpretive frameworks for conceptualizing same-sex sexuality.[4] The category māhū, which is indigenous to the Society Islands but is also found in the Hawaiian Islands, was translated by people I knew as meaning, "half-man, half-woman."[5] Unlike the other categories that allow for Polynesian same-sex sexuality (given above), references to māhū are found throughout early European accounts of social life in the Society Islands. These historical references to māhū, however, usually mention only male-bodied māhū: female-bodied māhū are largely absent from these historical accounts.[6] Gunson (1987) is one of the few scholars who has allowed that māhū historically could have been female as well as male, writing, "The relatively high proportion of transsexual or effeminate men, particularly in the Society Islands and Samoa, may well have been balanced by a similar phenomenon amongst women" (1987:145).[7] Most other scholars have assumed that such omissions mean that māhū has been a category available only to male-bodied Polynesians. I suggest, however, that such omissions do not preclude the possibility—indeed, the likelihood—that the category has also been available to females. In contrast to the scholarly presumption that māhū are exclusively male, during my research in the Society Islands I found the category māhū used by Polynesians to refer to both male-bodied and female-bodied persons. One vahine (woman) I knew explained the availability of the category māhū to both females and males by referring to the very meaning of māhū: "Māhū," she said, "that can be a man or woman because that's what it means, someone who's both."

My suggestion is that the logics that make the category māhū available to both males and females in the contemporary Society Islands have in all likelihood not changed substantially since the early contact period. While I detail those logics in subsequent sections, I want to note here the issue of the "visibility" of female-bodied māhū as a factor in their "notice-ability" for the ships' captains and other European and American men who narrated Polynesian social life in earlier periods and on whose narratives many ethnohistorical analyses depend. Even during my fieldwork, female-bodied māhū were far less visible, to me, than were male-bodied māhū. By "visible" I mean that relative to the performances of male-bodied māhū gender, the codes, cues, signs, and performances of female-bodied māhū gender were difficult for me to discern and certainly quite difficult for me to interpret as signifying female māhū gender performances. This is in part because the ways in which feminine gender is performed by Polynesian women varies substantially and, among adult and older women, is not stridently differentiated from masculine gender performances.[8] Female-bodied māhū, I suggest, extend the meanings of what Thomas (1987) has theorized as "gender misrecognition" and, in some important senses, may iconify the problems of reading the significances of gender differences (and their performances) not only in the past but in the present. Such gender misrecognition may well be the primary reason why female-bodied māhū have not only been largely absent from historical accounts of Polynesian social life, but also why female-bodied māhū have been absent from most ethnographic works on the Islands as well.[9]

As the translation "half-man, half-woman" may suggest, māhū is a gender category for persons who deploy and participate in complex combinations of masculine and feminine gender signs and practices. Māhū adopt styles of dress, work, and/or embodied expressions (gestures, stances, speaking styles, voice pitch) that, while incorporating both masculine and feminine associations, privilege one set of gender associations over the other. The set of associations privileged is, moreover, that of the gender opposite to the one coordinating with the māhū's own sexed-body status. Female-bodied māhū, for example, are thought to "behave in the manner of men," as the Polynesians I knew phrased it: some undertake work culturally coded as men's (working as drivers, for example, or working at *fa'a'apu* [subsistence gardening, cultivating work]); they may use embodied expressions and wear clothing culturally coded as masculine, and in a society where most Polynesian women grow their hair long, female-bodied māhū often cut their hair quite short.[10] Male-bodied māhū, in analogous form, are thought to behave "in the manner of women": they usually undertake work culturally coded as women's (sewing crafts, working at hotels, childcare); they move, talk, and/or gesture in stylized ways that are culturally coded as feminine and oftentimes slightly exaggerated beyond that, and most wear *pareu*, a form of dress worn predominantly by women.[11]

Polynesians' evaluations of māhū are, on the whole, accepting. People describe māhū as "natural" with the "naturalness" of māhū authorized largely through reference to the māhū's history of "being that way": māhū are thought to show signs that they are māhū at a very young age; that is, māhū are thought to begin demonstrating māhū styles of self-presentation or preferences for transgendered work when they are still children. Boys may be identified as māhū at the onset of displaying these behaviors; girls who are identified as "tomboys" (Fr., "*garçon manqué*") during their childhood or adolescent years may be perceived as likely to be māhū. The naturalization of māhū through appeals to the māhū's consistent personal history introduces the importance of experience for authorizing and explaining gender categorization among Polynesians and, more generally, points to the ontological primacy given to experience and behavior in the formation of the socialized Polynesian person. I return to this subject below.

While the gender-coded meanings attached to māhū were consistently foregrounded by the men, women, and māhū with whom I worked in the Society Islands, the sexuality of māhū was consistently backgrounded. Polynesians commonly assumed that male-bodied māhū have sex with men, and particularly with young men in the *taure'are'a* period of the Polynesian life cycle. (The *taure'are'a* period spans adolescence through young adulthood, roughly from the ages of fifteen to thirty.) Among male-bodied māhū I worked with and learned about, most took men (tane), and particularly young men (*taure'are'a tane*), as their lovers. But many of these male-bodied māhū had also had women (vahine) lovers; several were in long-term relationships with women when I knew them and fathers to the children borne of these relationships; still others were celibate.[12] Female-bodied māhū are generally assumed to have sex with women. Among female-bodied māhū I knew and learned about, most had taken women (vahine) as their lovers, but many had also at some time taken men (tane) as lovers; others were single and celibate.

The Heterosexual Matrix

Same-sex sexuality, between a māhū and a man (tane) or a woman (vahine), is culturally configured in terms of the māhū's gender categorization as "half-man, half-woman": it is, for example, through a female-bodied māhū's characterization as "half-man" that her sexual desires for women are rendered culturally intelligible. One of the corollaries of the complex relationship between gender and sexuality in the Society Islands is that the lovers of māhū are either men (tane) or women (vahine): māhū do not sleep with other māhū; that is, they do not take sexed-body-same māhū as their lovers. Female-bodied māhū behave, in Polynesian terms, "in the manner of men" and this means that, as for men, the focus of a female-bodied māhū's sexual desires may be a woman. The female lovers of female-bodied māhū are characterized socially and unproblematically as vahine or "women": they deploy the Polynesian signs of femininity—in styles of dress, work, and/or embodied expression—and they are considered by other people to be women (vahine). The women lovers of female-bodied māhū, then, unlike female-bodied māhū, are not linguistically or socially marked as anything other than women (vahine), even though they have sexual relationships with female-bodied māhū.[13]

This is a telling dimension of the ways in which gender and sexuality are both separate and interrelated in the Society Islands: māhū is primarily meaningful as a gender category. As a gender category, it is not tied to sexed-body assignment. Rather, gender and sexed-body status are disaggregated, with gender difference made contingent on gender performance—that is, on behavior. It is, then, the individual's participation in or practice of particular gendered codes and behaviors that determines her or his inclusion in the gender categories woman, māhū, or man.

This was made clear to me during a conversation I had with Aimata, a woman in her mid-thirties who had taken female-bodied māhū lovers as well as men (tane) as lovers. During a conversation about whether male-bodied māhū usually slept with men, Aimata rather impatiently told me, "If one dresses like a woman [vahine], of course it's someone who wants to sleep with a man [tane]: why would anyone dress like a woman [vahine] if he wasn't wanting to sleep with a man [tane]?" I want to draw attention to the series of logical links in Aimata's explanation between practice (dressing like a woman), gender (being like a woman), and sexuality (women have sex with men). Given Aimata's own sexual relationships with both female-bodied māhū and with men, her insistence on the unambiguous location of gender difference in determining sexual desire and practice becomes particularly compelling.

It is, moreover, and as Aimata's explanation suggests, the individual's practice-based participation in a particular gender category that most reliably and accurately produces the individual's sexual desires and practices. Gender, then, is not contingent on or derived from sexual practices; rather, gender produces sexuality, or, more accurately, Polynesians conceptualize gender difference as productive of sexuality. This suggests, and rightly I believe, that Polynesians' cultural configuration of both gender difference and sexuality is dynamically forged through and conceptually dependent on not only social practices but social contexts; that is, the emphasis on the place of gender difference in producing sexuality, in combination with the emphasis on practice/experience as productive of gender difference itself, requires that the cultural processes through which gender difference and sexuality are produced be foundationally tied to social contexts.[14] Further evidence of this lies in Polynesians' disinterest in marking—linguistically or socially—women who have sex with female-bodied māhū as different from women who have sex with men, or of marking men who have sex with male-bodied māhū as different from men who have sex with women. What set female-bodied māhū apart from women, and male-bodied māhū apart from men, are transgender-coded self-presentations and forms of work.

With the complex sets of masculine and feminine gender signs and practices that produce māhū gender difference come the possibility of taking lovers who are same-sex-bodied but of the "opposite" gender. The cultural intelligibility of māhū sexuality, then, lies in the māhū's designation as "like a man" or "like a woman." In more theoretical terms, māhū sexuality, I suggest, relies on a vision of heterosexuality as a particular configuration of sexual desires produced by and through gender difference, what I think of as a "heterosexual matrix." Māhū sexuality does not, then, rely on a configuration of sexual desires aligned with sexed-bodies, nor on a configuration in which sexual desires produce gender difference.

In other words, same-sex sexuality is configured within this matrix in gendered not sexed-body terms: same-sex sexuality, then, can never be same-gender sexuality. Instead, same-sex desire always relies on a gender difference between woman/man, man/māhū, māhū/woman. Given that, it becomes clearer why the women whose lovers are female-bodied māhū (and the men whose lovers are male-bodied māhū) are not marked by their same-sex sexual practices. Women who are lovers with female-bodied māhū are operating, in so doing, in the terms of and in accordance with the heterosexual matrix that coordinates sexual practice through gender difference. They are taking as their lovers persons who are of a different gender, persons who behave "in the manner of men" in a social context where gender is produced through behavior and experience, and not through sexed-body status.

Raerae, Petea, Lesbiennes

Compared to their acceptance of māhū and of tane and vahine who are the lovers of māhū, Polynesians register significant ambivalence about and even animosity toward the other categories circulating in the Society Islands today which allow for same-sex sexuality. By ambivalence I mean, for example, that people made disparaging comments—particularly about *raerae* and *petea*—as a matter of course. One day, for example, I was with three *tau-re'are'a* (youth in their early twenties) who were talking about a raerae they knew: during the conversation, the young man repeatedly told the two young women that in his view raerae and petea should be "exterminated." Or, to give another example, a middle-aged woman I worked with, who had raerae and petea friends with whom she regularly socialized, responded to my asking how she would feel if her eight-year-old son was raerae or petea, by saying, "I'd get a rope and tie it to a high tree branch, stick his neck in a loop at the other end, and that would be the end of him. . . . Not in my family." The subject of *lesbiennes* did not prompt such visceral reactions from people, but ambivalent and distancing statements—"I've never heard of that here," for example—were standard. The logics animating this ambivalence, I argue in this section, lie in the different ontologies structuring the meanings of these categories. In this section I focus on the categories raerae, petea, and lesbienne in order to explicate and analyze these ontological differences.

People privilege māhū as the older and in some sense more authentic category, relative to the other categories that allow for same-sex sexuality, and make reference to this category's availability to and use by their ancestors centuries ago. In contrast, people consider the other categories recent innovations or else recent arrivals (from France). When I asked Tefatua, a middle-aged married man I knew on Huahine, about the difference between a lesbienne and a (female) māhū, he answered, "Lesbienne is a universal thing, but māhū is just here, just in Polynesia. . . . It's only here you find māhū . . . we've always had them." Among other Polynesians, lesbiennes are viewed as completely foreign: lesbiennes are considered to be either French themselves, or to be Polynesians who have been influenced by the French—either way they are not considered "truly Polynesian." A married woman in her early thirties once reflected, "I think that lesbiennes didn't exist here in the old times. . . . It's since they brought porno films here that it's increased . . . now there are more. . . . I think that before, there were hardly any."

While lesbienne is interpreted as a category that has recently arrived in the Islands, the category petea is interpreted as a recent (Tahitian-language) linguistic innovation. Different people explained the meaning of the word *petea* as

> a white bird that runs away when you come up to it.
> A boy who's scared of things—scared to climb trees, scared of everything—cowardly.
> It's the name of a bird, really, but now it means—the person you call that, he sleeps only with men.

In Polynesians' usages of the term, petea is an exclusively sexual category for referring to any sexed-body male who has sex with other males; thus raerae are sometimes called petea, as are some māhū.

As with the recent innovation of the category petea, I was told that the category raerae had also not been around very long, "perhaps a generation or two" according to one man I knew. Many Polynesians I worked with felt that over the past generation specifically (the past fifteen to twenty years) there had been a substantial increase in the numbers of raerae, virtually all of whom are thought to reside in Papeete. "When I was growing up," a man in his late twenties told me, "you'd see raerae only rarely in Papeete, like at night, but nothing—nothing—like you see them now: all over Papeete, daytime, night time . . . it's really changed."

Raerae differ from māhū in several important respects. First, unlike māhū, who can be male-bodied or female-bodied, raerae are exclusively male-bodied: raerae is not a category used by females.[15] Relatedly, raerae are not only transgendered but sometimes transsexual: while only a few raerae have had sex reassignment surgery, many take hormones to grow small breasts. Moreover, unlike most māhū, raerae transgender practices are organized around what I might best describe as a specifically Eurocentric form of white femininity. For example, while a raerae might dress in a *pareu* around the house, in public s/he is most likely to wear European women's clothing. In particular, in public most raerae wear revealing European women's clothes: miniskirts, skimpy shorts, halter tops, high heels. Polynesian women I knew routinely admired raerae for their ability to wear these clothes well: one commented, "Raerae look better in women's clothes than we do." And the raerae's more proximate production of the kind of white European femininity idealized in mass media throughout this French territory (from advertisements on the state-run television station to billboards in Papeete to fashion magazines) enabled Polynesian women to make comments along the lines of what one young woman I knew said, in honest admiration: "They're very pretty, much prettier than us." A friend of hers made gestures of puffing her hair up on one side, in exaggerated imitation of a raerae's exaggerated imitation of this gesture: "They're more like women than we women are!" she said.

Second, raerae is both a gender and a sexual category. In addition to signifying transgender practices, the category raerae has explicit and unambivalent sexual meanings: raerae have sex with men (tane). In fact, most raerae work part-time as prostitutes, earning some of their money by having sex with men or stealing from their men clients. During the days, many raerae work, as did one raerae I knew, Taia, by providing their labor to the households in which they reside in exchange for being fed and cared for, a prevalent form of exchange.[16] When I asked Taia if all raerae work as prostitutes, for example, she responded: Yes, like me: I work for Mama Fa'atere [the head of the household] here [in Papeete] . . . sweep the floor, clean the house, do the laundry. . . . I work here, for Mama Fa'atere, and then in the evenings I do what I want." Raerae work as prostitutes, then, is only part-time: it is work they usually do at night, but not every night. When I knew her, for example, Taia, was going out most nights, but working as a prostitute only on some of the nights she went out, and often only for parts of the night. The rest of the night she socialized with her friends (many of whom were also raerae) at clubs and apartments and by driving around the island. Also, much of the money raerae prostitutes make appears to come not from prostitution but from raerae's renowned skill in stealing from their prospective and actual clients.

Third, raerae is a category that Polynesians, including raerae themselves, consider raerae as having chosen to take on. Taia, for example, who described herself as a raerae, told me she had "started off as a petea" and then "become a raerae." She had also, before and during these categorical transitions, fathered three children with a woman. In contrast to this, Polynesians do not talk about māhū as something they or others have chosen to be, nor changed into. Rather, they authorize māhū gender difference by reference to early signs that the māhū was "by nature" a māhū: that a girl was a tomboy as a child; that a boy showed early preferences for women's work. Being a māhū is premised on a set of practices and preferences that appear when the child is young and stay with the child: it is not something one changes, in part because as the child grows up she or he experiences and re-experiences her or his social world as a māhū and is treated by others as a māhū. As a result, people say that māhū "have always been that way." Produced through experience, māhū gender is fixed, in the same way that vahine and tane gender is fixed: these are gender categories authorized by and grounded in the gendered experiences of growing up, that is, in social contexts and practices.

My argument has been that vahine and tane are gender categories that produce sexuality through a heterosexual matrix organized around and through the gender difference tane/vahine (man/woman). In this matrix, gender structures sexuality: sexuality is produced through and is an outgrowth of the practices of gender difference. As a gender category, māhū also works within this matrix to produce māhū same-sex but opposite-gender sexuality. Because māhū are "half-man, half-woman" the sexuality their gender designation produces may be oriented toward either men or women: female-bodied māhū have at times had relationships with men; male-bodied māhū have at times had relationships with women. Whether a māhū engages in sexual relationships with a man or with a woman, māhū sexuality remains heterosexual in the sense that it is invariably directed at someone who is, in the heterosexual matrix, of the "opposite gender."

In contrast to the logics that naturalize māhū sexuality through gender, the variety of other categories circulating in the Society Islands that allow for same-sex sexuality and are ambivalently evaluated by Polynesians all organize gender and sexuality through a contrasting and Euro-American ontology. In these other configurations, sexuality is disaggregated from gender difference and located within the socially decontextualized individual and, perhaps, within the individual's sexed body. Raerae, for example, is both a gender and a sexual category: instead of gender producing raerae same-sex sexuality, however, both gender and same-sex desire are seen as producing raerae sexuality. This configuration, by giving equal ontological weight to gender difference and same-sex sexual desire, confounds the logical and unidirectional relationship in which gender difference produces sexuality. In addition, by conceptualizing people as being able to choose to become raerae, this configuration also confounds the logical and unidirectional relationship in which long-term experience produces gender categorization. Lesbienne is a sexual category forged in terms of sexed bodies (through sexed-body sameness): it is a category that has no necessary relationship to gender, let alone a relationship in which gender produces lesbian sexuality. Petea, lastly, has no necessary relationship to gender: like lesbienne, petea references sexuality and it does so in terms of sexed bodies, not gender difference. Sexuality, then, in each of these configurations, does not rely on gender for its meanings, nor for its production. Rather, it relies on a sexually essentialist understanding of the person.[17] In the Polynesian configuration, in contrast, I have argued that gender difference is itself productive of sexuality, and that gender difference is itself produced through practice or experience.

My analysis has been that māhū, vahine, and tane gain their contrasts with other gender and sexual categories (raerae, travesti, petea, lesbienne), first, through the productive relationship of experience to gender Polynesians elaborate (i.e., experience produces gender) and, second, through the productive relationship of gender to sexuality (i.e., gender produces sexuality). My argument is that it is through these contrasts that Polynesians' ambivalence about these other gender and sexual categories takes shape.

In some important sense, same-sex sexuality, to the extent that it is premised on a sexuality unmoored from gender difference, is not a culturally intelligible concept in the Society Islands. Of course, it is somewhat intelligible to the raerae, petea, and lesbiennes who use those categories to name or describe themselves. But even these Polynesians may voice ambiguity about the extent to which these categories apply to them: several lesbiennes I knew, for example, periodically referred to themselves as māhū; some raerae I worked with also on occasion referred to themselves and their friends as māhū. Such flexible forms of self-naming could be interpreted as attempts to borrow authority from māhū—a category that, as described previously, is relatively nonproblematic for Polynesians. Alternatively, or in addition, this flexible self-naming may point to these individuals' own ambivalence about the categories available to them and perhaps to their ambivalence about the ontologies those categories assume and promote.

Such ontologies, I suggest, produce ambivalence along several lines. My argument has been that the main source of ambivalence lies in the contrast between a Polynesian logic that constructs gender as produced by experience and gender as productive of sexuality, on the one hand, and an introduced logic—producing categories like raerae, petea, and lesbienne—that disaggregates and omits these necessary links between experience, gender, and sexuality. I am suggesting, then, that the ontological conflict stems from an introduced logic premised on a degendered reading of sexed bodies, one that locates sexuality within sexed bodies and as the product not of experience or gender difference but of presocial or socially decontextualized selves.

Lastly, māhū produce their gender difference (in relation to the categories vahine and tane) from an early age, and this practice helps to authorize their gender difference as "natural" and, in turn, to make intelligible their sexuality. Most raerae, in contrast, try to change their gender categorization later in their lives, a choice that is problematic because it violates an epistemological claim interlaced throughout this and other Polynesian social practice: the priority Polynesians give to behavior and experience for determinations of legitimacy. The introduced logic productive of petea, lesbienne, and raerae, in contrast, unties both gender and sexuality from social practice and social experience. My suggestion is that the untying of gender from practice and experience is a primary source of Polynesians' ambivalence toward these categories.

In conclusion, I want to offer several feminist lessons drawn from the foregoing analysis. First, the ethnographic arguments of this essay should serve both to reemphasize and to clarify a point made by other feminist anthropologists and feminist theorists: that, as Biddy Martin (1992:106) has succinctly written, "sexuality has no meaning outside of the cultural contexts in which it appears."[18] Sexuality, or "sex," is always about signs and signifying practices and is always the site of cultural interpretation; at the same time, cultural interpretation is itself always uneven and the site of contestation. In this essay I have analyzed one of the forms that contestation has taken by focusing on particular collisions between what I have glossed as Polynesian interpretive frameworks for understanding sexuality, and recently emerged uses, by Polynesians, of foreign sexual symbolic economies. Through such a focus I have tried to show that culturally specific ontologies, theories of the person, and epistemologies may be centrally involved in producing the meaningful interpretive frameworks not only for sexual practices and desires but for the moral standing of their practitioners.

This argument bears emphasizing not only for the project of developing frameworks for analyzing same-sex sexualities, but also in the context of recent academic fashions. Contrary to much work in queer theory, for example, and particularly work informed by poststructuralist and Lacanian frameworks, "sex" is not a free-floating signifier available for any social project that comes along: it is structured, embedded, and motivated. As a vital sign in divergent and oftentimes interacting sexual symbolic economies, the sign of sex is always simultaneously produced anew and motivated by the internal logics of the sign systems within which it is made to signify and through which it gains coherent cultural meanings. It is those logics that require ethnographic analyses if scholars are to develop not only more accurate but also politically accountable frameworks for analyzing same-sex sexuality.

Second, sexuality gains its meanings in relation to a varied range of discursive formations. Feminist anthropologists working on the cross-cultural study of sexuality have demonstrated that one of the more important of these is the nexus of discourses organized around gender difference. In other disciplines as well, feminist scholars have demonstrated the importance of gender ideologies for structuring women's sexual possibilities, as well as the nested links forged in variable forms cross-culturally between gender and other socially produced differences.[19] Building on their insights, I have tried to show another way in which gender may be involved in the production of same-sex sexuality: gender difference may itself mediate between culturally specific ontologies, epistemologies, or theories of the person, on the one hand, and, on the other, both the shape of legitimate same-sex sexualities and the framework within which people negotiate the local legitimacy of translocal sexual economies. I suggest, then, that gender may in yet another way prove to be one of the more salient sites of investigation for developing analyses of same-sex sexuality.

NOTES

Research for this paper was undertaken in the Society Islands of French Polynesia and funded by the Wenner-Gren Foundation for Anthropological Research (Predoctoral Grant, 1994–95), the Social Sciences and Humanities Research Council of Canada (Doctoral Fellowship, 1994–95), and New York University (Graduate School of Arts & Science Predissertation Research Grant, Summer 1993). Support during the writing of the dissertation out of which this essay has grown was provided by the Social Sciences and Humanities Research Council of Canada (Doctoral Fellowship, 1995–96) and New York University (Dean's Dissertation Fellowship, 1995–96; Department of Anthropology, 1996–97). I thank Fred Myers, Faye Ginsburg, and Annette Weiner for their intellectual fellowship, encouragement, and sustenance during the development of my analyses of Polynesian social life. My thinking on female same-sex sexuality in Polynesia has been consistently enriched by conversations with, in particular, Evie Blackwood and J. Kehaulani Kauanui. An earlier version of this paper was presented in the invited session "Queer Challenges" at the 1997 meetings of the American Anthropological Association.

1. I use the term "Polynesians" to refer only to Polynesians living in the Society Islands of French Polynesia and clarify in the text the few occasions when I mean the term in its more extensive sense (as referencing peoples from through-out the Polynesian triangle). My decision to use this term articulates Polynesians' preferences in self-naming. The more common scholarly term for people of the Society Islands is "Tahitians." Yet island of origin is a vital and powerful reference point for these Polynesians' senses of themselves (see Elliston 1997). Thus the generalization from Tahiti Island to all other Society Islands (embedded in the term "Tahitians") was regarded by the people with whom I worked as both inaccurate and problematic.

2. See chapters 5 and 6 in Elliston (1997), for analysis of the practical significance of Protestant church teachings about sexuality and marriage.

3. For analysis of the meanings of continuing French colonialism in the context of the contemporary Polynesian nationalist struggle, see Elliston (1997); see, especially, chapter 2 for an overview of the histories of missionization, French colonialism, and Polynesian resistance in the Islands.

4. I have opted not to anglicize Tahitian-language nouns; that is, not to mark plurality or singularity through the manipulation of a final "s." In the Tahitian language, as in the other reo Ma'ohi languages, plurality is usually deduced from a noun's context of use. I leave it to the reader, then, to deduce a noun's singularity or plurality from its context of appearance and use: in the footnoted sentence, for example, māhū is plural.

5. See Morris (1990) on the possibility that Kanaka Maoli (Hawaiians) borrowed the term māhū from the Society Islands. Other societies in the Polynesian triangle have gender categories the meanings and practices of which scholars have usually analyzed as similar to māhū: *fa'atama* (for females) and *fa'afāfine* (for males) in Samoa (Mageo 1992); *fāfine tangata* or *fakatangata* (for females) and *fakafefine* or, more recently, *fakaleitī* (for males) in Tonga (James 1994). Besnier (1993) examines these Polynesian categories as a group under his coined term "gender liminality." Linguistically, however, the causative prefixes in these words—the "*fa'a*" prefix in Samoan, for example, or the "*faka*" prefix in Tongan—render the meanings of these categories more along the lines of "to become male" or "to become female." Neither the Tahitian nor Hawaiian languages have constructions paralleling these Samoan or Tongan terms; in Hawaiian, for

example, a comparable construction would be *ho'ohine* or *ho'okane*, but these words do not exist. In Tahitian, the causative prefixes *fa'a* or *ha'a* (enabling the terms *fa'avahine* or *ha'avahine, fa'atane*, or *ha'atane*) would be the likely candidates—but as with Hawaiian, these words do not exist. Rather, in the Hawaiian and Tahitian languages speakers use a linguistically and etymologically distinct word: māhū. This suggests that māhū should probably not so easily be treated as a gender category on par with these other Polynesian gender categories. I thank J. Kehaulani Kauanui (personal communication) for pointing out these distinctions to me and clarifying their import.

6. I should clarify the meanings I am attaching to some of the terms I use in this essay. The terms "male" and "female," for example, and the phrase "sexed bodies" are terms I deploy for purposes of analytical clarity and in recognition of the predominantly American audience for this essay. These terms distinguish particularly marked bodies from the gender categories in which those bodies participate and comprise a necessary analytical clarification in order to draw out the significances of sexuality, gender, and desire in their Polynesian forms to an American readership. My use of these terms draws attention to the ways genitals and what is known in the clinical literature as "secondary sexual characteristics" may be given primacy for gendering bodies among Americans. Their meanings for Polynesians, however, are more ambiguous.

7. I would caution the reader, however, about accepting the premises and terms embedded in Gunson's suggestion: first, that transsexuality and effeminacy are accurate descriptive terms for māhū; second, that it is useful or meaningful to quantify māhū as a "proportion" of a population (a move also made by Levy [1971] in his assertion that there is always one and only one [male] māhū in a village); third, that it is meaningful to speak of a "relatively" high number of effeminate and/or transsexual persons; and, fourth, that one can draw clear links between the presence of transgender males and the likelihood that there are transgender females. See Elliston (forthcoming, a) and Rorbakken (n.d.) for accounts of transgender females and same-sex sexuality between females in Polynesian societies, including female māhū in Hawaii and the Society Islands; see Blackwood (1983), Elliston (forthcoming, b) and Hall and Kauanui (1994) for treatments of female same-sex sexuality in societies throughout the Pacific.

8. Relatedly, as I have argued elsewhere (and see below), the gender performances of some male-bodied māhū and most (male-bodied) raerae seem to be modeled after a specifically Eurocentric vision of white femininity (Elliston 1997, chapter 5). The close match between Eurocentric ideal and locally real in the feminine performances of male-bodied raerae and some māhū was not lost on the Polynesian women I knew: as one woman put it, "They're more like women than we women are!" (quoted in Elliston 1997:310). My point is that Polynesian females could and did engage in a wide range of behaviors, many of which fell well outside the narrow ideal of white European femininity. The avail-

ability and practice of a wide range of gendered behaviors by female Polynesians made it difficult for me, as someone from a Eurocentric society, to see which behaviors were relevant to "recognizing" someone as a female-bodied māhū rather than as a woman (vahine). Such recognitions did not, however, seem to be a problem for Polynesians.

9. Levy (1973:141), for example, has written, "Māhū is considered by many to be misused for describing female homosexuals." My research suggests that Levy is both right and wrong. He is right to identify it as a misuse to translate "māhū" as "female homosexual," since, as I argue subsequently, the meanings of māhū for males and for females revolve not around homosexuality but around gender. He is wrong, however, to imply that females do not identify as or are not recognized by other Polynesians as māhū: if they "behave in the manner of men" people I knew recognized female māhū as māhū.

10. Long hair is a potent symbolic form Polynesians associate with femininity and with sexuality. Most adolescent and adult women have hair that falls down to their waists, although most wear their hair braided as a rule, particularly outside of the household: loose hair connotes, I was told, a kind of loose womanhood as well. It is associated, for example, with the sexuality of Polynesian dance, and while it is entirely appropriate (and enjoyable for the audience) for young women to wear their long hair loose when dancing, this may shade into the risqué and even the morally compromised in other public contexts. For a comparative case, see Mageo (1994) on the symbolics of hair in Samoa.

11. Polynesian *pareu* are a sarong-type garment similar to others found throughout the Pacific—in, for example, Samoa and Fiji, as well as in Indonesia—and historically related to the barkcloth (*tapa*) sheets Polynesians wore as draped garments in the early contact period. In the contemporary Society Islands, *pareu* are most often worn by women (vahine), but they are also worn by some men (tane): for example, cultural activist men may wear *pareu* as a statement of cultural pride.

12. My reference to "long-term relationships with women" indicates common-law marriages and should not be interpreted as a form of marriage that is in any sense qualified: most Polynesians practice common-law marriage and are reluctant to formalize their marriages (i.e., make them legal and church-sanctioned) for reasons discussed in Elliston (1997).

13. One of the more difficult dynamics within relationships between female-bodied māhū and their women partners, however, stems precisely from the ways gender and sexuality are disaggregated and coordinated: the sexuality of the women (vahine) in these relationships may be viewed, by their female-bodied māhū partners especially, as insecurely tied to the female-bodied māhū—because women who desire female-bodied māhū as their lovers are culturally understood as equally capable of desiring men (tane) as their lovers. Female-bodied māhū, on the other hand, view themselves and are viewed by others as more likely to desire

women sexually than they are to desire men sexually; that is, as having their sexuality more securely focused on women. As my phrasing might suggest, and as I describe in more depth subsequently, none of these sexual dynamics is set in stone: the only constant across the gender categories of tane, māhū, and vahine is that of gender difference between the sexual partners.

14. See Elliston (1997, chapter 6) for further analysis of the context-dependencies of sexuality and its links to Polynesian concepts of the person; on the context-dependencies of personhood and social action in Samoa, see Shore (1982); in the Marquesas Islands, see Kirkpatrick (1983); see also White and Kirkpatrick (1985) on personhood in the Pacific.

15. During our conversations about māhū and raerae, two people I worked with each independently offered variations on the term raerae that created a female variant of the term. One offered *tamahine raerae* (*tamahine* is a Tahitian-language term meaning "girl" or "daughter") as the female version of raerae; the other said she had heard "women who sleep with women" referred to as "*vahine raerae*" (women raerae). I do not include these terms in my main analysis, however, because neither appears to be widely known, or used: other people I worked with were not familiar with the terms these women offered.

16. Giving labor in exchange for being cared for or "fed" is the predominant framework within which, and through which, Polynesians conceptualize relationships within a household: it structures kinship (for example, relationships between parents and children), as well as (in the case of Taia) relationships between "patrons" and "clients" in a household. See Elliston (1997), Finney (1965), Levy (1973), and Oliver (1981).

17. See Elliston (1995) for an analysis of Euro-American theories of the person and their relationship to sexuality, developed as part of a critique of the concept of "ritualized homosexuality" and an argument for a reconfigured anthropology of sexuality.

18. The feminist anthropological scholarship on the social construction of sexuality is at this point extensive; see, for example, the anthologies by Altman et al. (1989), Caplan (1987), and Vance (1984b). Useful theoretical formulations on this subject in feminist anthropology include, among others, Blackwood (1984, 1986), Rubin (1975, 1984), and Vance (1984a). For a range of possible points of entry into the substantial feminist ethnographic work in this field, see Alexander (1997), Frankenberg (1993), Kennedy and Davis (1993), Lewin (1993, 1996), Morris (1994), Ortner & Whitehead (1981), Stoler (1989), and Weston (1991); see Kulick and Willson (1995) and Newton (1993) for feminist ethnographic works which privilege reflexivity in the cultural analysis of sexuality.

19. On the interrelationships between gender and same-sex sexuality see, for example, Blackwood (1984, 1986), Lewin (1993), and Weston (1993). On the interrelationships between gender, sexuality, and race see, for example, Anzaldúa (1987), Collins (1990), Hammonds (1997), Lorde (1984), and Moraga (1983). On

the interrelationships between gender, same-sex sexuality, and class, see, for example, Kennedy and Davis (1993).

REFERENCES

Alexander, M. Jacqui. 1997. "Erotic Autonomy as a Politics of Decolonization: An Anatomy of Feminist and State Practice in the Bahamas Tourist Economy." In M. Jacqui Alexander and Chandra Talpade Mohanty, eds., *Feminist Genealogies, Colonial Legacies, Democratic Futures*, pp. 63–100. New York: Routledge.

Altman, Dennis, Carole Vance, Martha Vicinus, and Jeffrey Weeks, et al., eds. 1989. *Homosexuality, Which Homosexuality? Essays from the International Scientific Conference on Lesbian and Gay Studies*. London: Gay Men's Press.

Anzaldúa, Gloria. 1987. *Borderlands/La Frontera: The New Mestiza*. San Francisco: Spinsters/Aunt Lute.

Besnier, Niko. 1993. "Polynesian Gender Liminality Through Time and Space." In Gilbert Herdt, ed. *Third Sex, Third Gender: Beyond Sexual Dimorphism in Culture and History*, pp. 285–328. New York: Zone Books.

Blackwood, Evelyn. 1983. "Lesbian Behavior in the Cultures of the Pacific." *Anthropological Research Group on Homosexuality* 4 (1/2): 13–17.

——. 1984. "Sexuality and Gender in Certain Native American Tribes: The Case of Cross-Gender Females." *Signs: Journal of Women in Culture and Society* 10 (1): 27–42.

——. 1986. "Breaking the Mirror: The Construction of Lesbianism and the Anthropological Discourse on Homosexuality." In Evelyn Blackwood, ed., *The Many Faces of Homosexuality*, pp. 1–18. New York: Harrington Park Press.

Caplan, Pat, ed. 1987. *The Cultural Construction of Sexuality*. New York: Tavistock Publications.

Collins, Patricia Hill. 1990. *Black Feminist Thought: Knowledge, Consciousness, and the Politics of Empowerment*. New York: Routledge.

Elliston, Deborah A. 1995. "Erotic Anthropology: 'Ritualized Homosexuality' in Melanesia and Beyond." *American Ethnologist* 22 (4): 848–867.

——. 1997. "En/Gendering Nationalism: Colonialism, Sex, and Independence in French Polynesia." Ph.D. dissertation, Department of Anthropology, New York University.

——. Forthcoming, a. "Māhū." In Bonnie Zimmerman, ed., *Encyclopedia of Homosexuality*. 2d ed. Vol. 1: *Lesbian Histories and Cultures*. New York: Garland, forthcoming.

——. Forthcoming, b. "Pacific Islands." In Bonnie Zimmerman, ed., *Encyclopedia of Homosexuality*. 2d ed. Vol. 1: *Lesbian Histories and Cultures*. New York: Garland, forthcoming.

Finney, Ben R. 1965. "Polynesian Peasants and Proletarians: Socio-Economic

Change among the Tahitians of French Polynesia." *The Journal of the Polynesian Society* 74 (3): 269–328.

Foucault, Michel. 1990. *The History of Sexuality*. Vol. 1: *An Introduction*. New York: Vintage Books.

Frankenberg, Ruth. 1993. *White Women, Race Matters: The Social Construction of Whiteness*. Minneapolis: University of Minnesota Press.

Gunson, Niel. 1987. "Sacred Women Chiefs and Female 'Headmen' in Polynesian History." *The Journal of Pacific History* 22 (3/4): 139–173.

Hall, Lisa Kahaleole Chang and J. Kehaulani Kauanui. 1994. "Same-Sex Sexuality in Pacific Literature." *Amerasia Journal* 20 (1): 75–81.

Hammonds, Evelynn M. 1997. "Toward a Genealogy of Black Female Sexuality: The Problematic Silence." In M. Jacqui Alexander and Chandra Talpade Mohanty, eds., *Feminist Genealogies, Colonial Legacies, Democratic Futures*, pp. 170–182. New York: Routledge.

Haraway, Donna. 1991. "Situated Knowledges: The Science Question in Feminism and the Privilege of Partial Perspective." In *Simians, Cyborgs, and Women: The Reinvention of Nature*, pp. 183–202. New York: Routledge.

James, Kerry E. 1994. "Effeminate Males and Changes in the Construction of Gender in Tonga." *Pacific Studies* 17 (2): 39–69.

Kennedy, Elizabeth Lapovsky and Madeline D. Davis. 1993. *Boots of Leather, Slippers of Gold: The History of a Lesbian Community*. New York: Routledge.

Kirkpatrick, John. 1983. *The Marquesan Notion of the Person*. Ann Arbor: UMI Research Press.

Kulick, Don and Margaret Willson, eds. 1995. *Taboo: Sex, Identity and Erotic Subjectivity in Anthropological Fieldwork*. London/New York: Routledge.

Levy, Robert I. 1971. "The Community Function of Tahitian Male Transvestism: A Hypothesis." *Anthropological Quarterly* 44 (1): 12–21.

——. 1973. *Tahitians: Mind and Experience in the Society Islands*. Chicago: University of Chicago Press.

Lewin, Ellen. 1993. *Lesbian Mothers: Accounts of Gender in American Culture*. Ithaca: Cornell University Press.

Lewin, Ellen, ed. 1996. *Inventing Lesbian Cultures in America*. Boston: Beacon Press.

Lorde, Audre. 1984. *Sister Outsider*. Trumansburg, NY: The Crossing Press.

Mageo, Jeannette Marie. 1992. "Male Transvestism and Cultural Change in Samoa." *American Ethnologist* 19 3): 443–459.

——. 1994. "Hairdos and Don'ts: Hair Symbolism and Sexual History in Samoa." *Man* 29 (2): 407–432.

Martin, Biddy. 1992. "Sexual Practice and Changing Lesbian Identities." In Michèle Barrett and Anne Phillips, eds., *Destabilizing Theory: Contemporary Feminist Debates*, pp. 93–119. Stanford: Stanford University Press.

Mohanty, Chandra Talpade. 1987. "Feminist Encounters: Locating the Politics of Experience." *Copyright* 1:30–44. Reprinted in Michèle Barrett and Anne

Phillips, eds., *Destabilizing Theory: Contemporary Feminist Debates*, pp. 74–92. Stanford: Stanford University Press, 1992.

Moraga, Cherríe. 1983. "A Long Line of Vendidas." In *Loving in the War Years*, pp. 90–149. Boston: South End Press.

Morris, Robert J. 1990. "*Aikāne*: Accounts of Hawaiian Same-Sex Relationships in the Journals of Captain Cook's Third Voyage (1776–80)." *Journal of Homosexuality* 19: 21–54.

Morris, Rosalind C. 1994. "Three Sexes and Four Sexualities: Redressing the Discourses on Sex and Gender in Contemporary Thailand." *Positions* 2 (1): 15–43.

Newton, Esther. 1993. "My Best Informant's Dress: The Erotic Equation in Fieldwork." *Cultural Anthropology* 8 (1): 3–23.

Oliver, Douglas L. 1981. *Two Tahitian Villages: A Study in Comparison*. Honolulu: Institute for Polynesian Studies.

Ortner, Sherry B. and Harriet Whitehead, eds. 1981. *Sexual Meanings: The Cultural Construction of Gender and Sexuality*. Cambridge: Cambridge University Press.

Rorbakken, Sharon. n.d. "Lesbianism in Polynesia: Tolerance or Abstinence." Unpublished manuscript, November 11, 1991.

Rubin, Gayle. 1975. "The Traffic in Women: Notes on the 'Political Economy' of Sex." In Rayna R. Reiter, ed., *Toward an Anthropology of Women*, pp. 157–210. New York: Monthly Review Press.

Rubin, Gayle. 1984. "Thinking Sex: Notes for a Radical Theory of the Politics of Sexuality." In Carole S. Vance, ed., *Pleasure and Danger: Exploring Female Sexuality*, pp. 267–319. London: Pandora Press.

Shore, Bradd. 1982. *Sala'ilua: A Samoan Mystery*. New York: Columbia University Press.

Stoler, Ann Laura. 1989. "Making Empire Respectable: The Politics of Race and Sexual Morality in 20th-Century Colonial Cultures." *American Ethnologist* 16 (4): 634–660.

Thomas, Nicholas. 1987. "Complementarity and History: Misrecognizing Gender in the Pacific." *Oceania* 57 (4): 261–270.

Vance, Carole S. 1984a. "Pleasure and Danger: Toward a Politics of Female Sexuality." In Carole S. Vance, ed., *Pleasure and Danger: Exploring Female Sexuality*, pp. 1–28. London: Pandora Press.

Vance, Carole S., ed. 1984b. *Pleasure and Danger: Exploring Female Sexuality*. London: Pandora Press.

Weston, Kath. 1991. *Families We Choose: Lesbians, Gays, Kinship*. New York: Columbia University Press.

Weston, Kath. 1993. "Do Clothes Make the Woman? Gender, Performance Theory, and Lesbian Eroticism." *Genders* 17:1–21.

White, Geoffrey M. and John Kirkpatrick, eds. 1985. *Person, Self, and Experience: Exploring Pacific Ethnopsychologies*. Berkeley: University of California Press.

PART IV

Nationalism, Feminism, and

Lesbian/Gay Rights Movements

11

Margrete Aarmo

How Homosexuality Became "Un-African":
The Case of Zimbabwe

It is a common perception among many Africans that homosexuality[1] or same-sex behavior does not exist in African cultures. It is believed to be something that was imposed on Africa by foreign people. If black people engage in same-sex relations at all, they allegedly have been seduced by white people and are said to do "it" (sex) only for the sake of money.

In this chapter I will highlight the phenomenon of homosexuality in Zimbabwe, which is almost unknown beyond the local context. Until recently very little anthropological fieldwork was done on issues concerning same-sex behavior and relations in sub-Saharan African countries. I will also contextualize the story of the gays and lesbians within the framework of Zimbabwean nationalism. I shall focus on the discourse utilized by those holding the power in Zimbabwe in what I see as an attempt to reinforce a national identity constructed by means of culture. This was set in motion by President Mugabe's opening speech at the Zimbabwean International Book Fair 1995, in which he attacked gays and lesbians.

Nationalism and Culture

Yuval-Davies (1997) distinguishes between two different modes of constructing nationalist projects. One is constructed along the dimension of the common origin of a people. The other is the cultural dimension in which "the symbolic heritage provided by language and/or religion and/or other customs and traditions is constructed as the 'essence' of the nation" (Yuval-Davis 1997:21). In a multiethnic country like Zimbabwe, it is problematic to build the national project on myths of common origin because it would favor one ethnic group at the cost of others (Shona is the largest ethnic group [70% of the population]; the Ndebele constitute 25%, and Tonga, Venda, and other small groups make up the rest. Each group has its own language and traditions.). In Zimbabwe the nationalist project was built along a cultural dimension. I shall investigate this dimension and the notion of culture it requires.

Anderson (1991) says that nationalisms are built on an idea of a horizontal comradeship, the fraternity, which takes the form of a passionate comradeship between men. This kind of homosocial male bonding has to be distinguished from homosexual relations. The image of the nation is gendered.[2] A nation is often referred to in female terms and when threatened likened to a female body that needs protection from intruders, who violate and penetrate it, both physically in war and also ideologically through imposition of ideas, belief systems, and modernization processes (Thaiss 1978:6). The male is symbolized by the soldier, who is willing to die for the nation, the "imagined community" in Anderson's term. Women's task in the nation is to reproduce it, both biologically and symbolically. They are celebrated as mothers and carriers of the cultural tradition, and men as protectors and providers for the family and the nation. Within the nation men and women have never had the same privileges. "The idealization of motherhood by the virile fraternity would seem to entail the exclusion of all nonreproductively oriented sexualities from the discourse of the nation. Indeed, certain sexual identities and practices are less represented and representable in nationalism" (Parker et al. 1992:6–7). Since nationalism in this sense requires specific heterosexual gender relations, homosexuality is not representable for the idea of the nation. This will be elaborated in the following description of the "case" of Zimbabwe, which offers an opportunity to understand how the homophobia of nationalistic projects works. We find this kind of homophobia within most nation states, but perhaps especially in the former colonies, where homosexuality is often conceived of as an aspect of colonialism and Western imperialism.

In the first part of this essay I describe the Zimbabwean International Book Fair 1995, which is the historical event that triggered the public debate on homosexuality and put it on the political agenda. This public airing is remarkable since issues related to sexuality are considered taboo and not appropriate subjects for public discussion. I give examples of the discursive practices used and attempt to understand the logic in which gays and lesbians became such a "useful" symbol in the Zimbabwean political context.

In the second part of this essay I shall present empirical examples that illuminate aspects of the lives of black, feminine gays and lesbians and contextualize their experiences within the framework of black Zimbabwean culture. I shall also give examples of how the informants reflect and meet with their culture. The reason for bringing in feminine men is to illuminate the "problem of femininity" in nationalist ideas.

A major concern in this article is the notion of culture. Clifford Geertz described culture as a web of significance man himself has spun (Geertz in Keesing 1984:161). Scholte's answer to that was "that one cannot merely define men and women in terms of the webs of significance they themselves spin, since . . . few do the actual spinning while the . . . majority is simply caught" (1984:140, quoted in Keesing 1987). We need to ask: Who shares these ideas and meanings, who has the power to define them, and what happens to those who do not share them? Keesing says that cultures as systems of meanings "constitute *ideologies*, disguising human political and economic realities as cosmically ordained" (Keesing 1987:161). I shall try to show how culture was used by those in power as an ideological tool in processes of exclusion or inclusion of members of the moral collectivity of the nation. I also look at how the informants engage and relate to this culture, and in what ways culture can be experienced as an obstacle to those who do not "fit in." In the last part of this essay I discuss the body as a site for individual experience and negotiation of cultural, social, and personal identities. I conclude with a discussion of bodies and sexuality as sites for struggles over gender.

Field Situation

I did my field research in Zimbabwe between September 1995 and July 1996 and arrived shortly after the book fair had taken place. I left just before the next one was about to take place. I came to Zimbabwe to start a field project designed to deal with the local conceptualizations of AIDS in a village in the rural area in the southern part of the country. While I was in the village, I got some newspapers and magazines and discovered the debate on homosexuality and homosexuals, a discussion derived from the incidents at the book fair just a month prior to my arrival. Knowing that homosexuality is regulated by law in this country and that homosexuals are kept "invisible," I wanted to investigate the reasons for this sudden visibility and interest in the media.

Being a lesbian myself, I was tired of pretending to be heterosexual in the village and felt lonely. I didn't actually "pretend" anything, but the "normal" is always taken for granted everywhere, and people tend to address and include everybody as if one were one of them, while in fact one is not. I feared that "revealing my identity" might affect the collection of data. I decided to take advantage of my sexual orientation and turn it into an option. I was confident that this would open up a field for me that might otherwise have been closed. Thus I decided to study the impact of the book fair on the lives of gays and lesbians, and to learn about their lives and backgrounds in general.

Gays and Lesbians in Zimbabwe (GALZ)

GALZ was formally founded as an association at the turn of the 1980s and the early 1990s. It was a result of gay and lesbian activities in a variety of clubs and scenes that had existed since the 1970s. From the beginning it was a mixed group consisting of whites, coloreds, and blacks, but problems existed due to the colonial past based on racial segregation. Small personal networks in Harare and other towns slowly transformed themselves into a community structure through the work of activists who formed GALZ. One of GALZ's aims was to reach out to isolated black gays and lesbians in high density areas. Another aim was to offer counseling and AIDS awareness to those black gays and lesbians who, due to poor living conditions, were known to obtain an income through a variety of illegal activities. At the time of the founding of GALZ the lesbian community consisted mainly of white women, but the goal was to try to include black lesbians, who lived in isolation in their local areas.

Whites dominated the association, but the number of black members grew, especially in the wake of the Book Fair 1995. In 1995–96 GALZ membership varied from between 75–150 registered members. Though small, GALZ constitutes a conglomerate of people representing all colors, genders, classes, and ethnic groups in the country. Most of the blacks come from the lower social strata, whereas the white members come from middle and upper strata. In GALZ "race" and class seem to coincide.

Members of GALZ describe their aims in the following way:

> As a support group for the homosexual and lesbian community, GALZ's aims are to try to provide services such as counseling, access to literature and films, AIDS awareness, providing opportunities for the community to meet and try to better the conditions under which they are forced to live. One of the primary aims of GALZ is to educate the public about the realities of gay life and explode some of the more damaging myths concerning homosexuals and lesbians. GALZ aims at a national situation where gay men and lesbians can enjoy full human rights. GALZ will and does at all times operate within the currently existing laws, and does not encourage in any way actions by gay men and lesbians that are not legal. (GALZ pamphlet)

The Book Fair and the Homosexuals

In August 1995, during the Zimbabwean International Book Fair (ZIBF), gays and lesbians in Zimbabwe became visible in public in a way never seen before. The ZIBF is a big and prestigious event, drawing local and international participation and interest. GALZ had applied for and been granted a stand at the book fair to distribute information about safe sex and the counseling service of GALZ. Since all public media communication lines had been closed to GALZ by the authorities, this was an important opportunity to spread information. The theme of the book fair was "Human Rights and Justice."

A few days before the opening a letter from the government, signed by the minister of information, barred GALZ from participation in the book fair. The reason given was that "whilst acknowledging the dynamic nature of culture, the fact still remains that both the Zimbabwean Society and Government do not accept the public display of homosexual literature and material. The Trustees of the Book Fair should not, therefore, force the values of gays and lesbians onto the Zimbabwean culture."

The stand had to be left empty, but other participants at the book fair put up flyers in support of GALZ, and balloons and flowers soon filled the empty stand. "It became like a shrine," one informant put it. Slogans like "gay rights are human rights" and "human rights are indivisible" were displayed on the stand. Despite the barring, GALZ operated informally. More black than white GALZ members were deliberately sent to hang around the stand, to counter the myth that homosexuality is a "white thing." GALZ wanted to show that blacks also could be gay. The presence of GALZ members attracted a lot of attention; they answered questions from the curious audience, and were interviewed about their conditions by international media.

The President's Speech

President Mugabe opened Book Fair '95 with a speech in which he attacked gays and lesbians. He called them perverts, offenders against the law of nature and against the moral and religious beliefs of the country. "If we accept homosexuality as a right, as is being argued by the organization of sodomists and sexual perverts, what moral fiber shall our society ever have to deny organized drug addicts or even those given to bestiality the rights they might claim and allege they possess under the rubrics of individual freedoms and human rights, including the freedom of the press to write and publicize literature on them" (tape-recorded version of his speech). To a question from the press whether gays and lesbians were not also entitled to human rights, Mugabe replied: "Oh, we don't think they have any rights at all. And I hope time will never come when men can bear children by having wombs."

Mugabe here expresses the common perception of homosexuality as an inversion of sex and gender roles, which is at the base of the stereotype of the effeminate gay man, as I will argue below.

International Protests and Mugabe's Replies

The exclusion of GALZ and Mugabe's attacks led to international condemnation of the president and support for GALZ. Members of the U.S. congress, international aid, donor, and human rights organizations like the United Nations and Amnesty International sent their protests against what they saw as a serious violation of human rights.

Mugabe's response to his international critics was: "Let the Americans keep their sodomy, bestiality, stupid and foolish ways to themselves, out of Zimbabwe. . . . Let them be gay in the U.S., Europe and elsewhere. . . . They shall be sad people here" (Dunton and Palmberg 1996:13). Specifically addressing the U.S. congress he sneered, "Their own political positions are more important than our humanity."

Consequences for GALZ

GALZ members became scared and went underground. They did not know what to expect, and some feared for their lives. GALZ's material and membership and mailing lists were split up and spread all over town to protect them in case of police raids. A few members were followed by the CIO (Central Intelligence Office), and even though they needed support from other GALZ members in this situation, they stayed away from their friends so the police would not trace the latter also. Some moved out of their private homes for a while and went to stay in safer places. Nobody knew what the government was up to. A black lesbian told me that when she heard Mugabe's speech she got so shocked that she immediately obtained a false passport and identity papers, so she could flee to a neighboring country "if conditions would turn out to be the worst." So although GALZ had "come out" at the book fair, gays and lesbians were not out during the next months. But the "worst" did not happen, and after a while gays and lesbians "surfaced" again. Many of the black members who had been at the book fair said that for the first time in their lives they felt they had an opportunity to really express themselves. They felt proud despite the fear Mugabe and the government had spread.

Ironically, Mugabe's attacks put the "gay issue" on the political and public agenda, and many people heard about it for the first time. People with same-sex preferences throughout the country who had never known of GALZ's existence, now had an opportunity to get in contact with the association, through popular magazines that printed GALZ's contact address.

The incidents at the book fair led to a politicalization of GALZ, a turn many members did not favor. At a meeting held in September many members, especially many white gays, feared that the new visibility would rupture their options and reputations in careers and businesses. Many of them went back into the "closet" and resigned from GALZ. But a large number of new black members joined. They claimed they had nothing to loose and that they wanted to fight for their rights to be both gays/lesbians and black. This brought about a change in the "racial" hierarchy in GALZ.

Legal Position of Homosexuality in Zimbabwe

In Zimbabwe homosexual conduct is regulated by common law. This law is not indigenous but an adoption of the Roman-Dutch law, which remained unchanged on the issue since the beginning of colonial rule. There is no law preventing people from *being* homosexual, but some homosexual acts are illegal and thus punishable: sodomy and "unnatural offenses." Anybody can participate in acts classified as an "unnatural offense" except the combination of a man and a woman. What may be lawful sexual acts between male and female may be criminal acts between people of the same sex. The law is not clear on sexual conduct between women. But the law against "unnatural offenses" is vague. I met lesbians who were not sure whether sexual acts between women were included in this law.

In Zimbabwe there is a general constitutional right of freedom of association. No law prevents an association being formed to enable homosexual men and women to meet and discuss matters of concern to them, though laws could be made that may limit this right on the grounds of public morality. But as there is no such law, there is no lawful reason why the police should attend or try to prevent such a meeting (GALZ pamphlet "Homosexual Conduct: The Legal Position").

GALZ is thus a legal membership-based organization. This means that the authorities could not prevent GALZ from participating in the book fair according to the law. As already mentioned, GALZ was barred on "cultural

grounds." When the parliament in September 1995 debated "the Evil and Iniquitous Practice of Homosexualism" an MP stated that it was the duty of the
president and the government to prevent national contamination by the gays
and lesbians, who the MPs saw as "cultural prostitutes."

The Heroes Day

On August 11 Zimbabwe celebrates "Heroes Day." This is the memorial day
of the freedom fighters who died in the Zimbabwean Liberation War[3] in
which the white regime of Ian Smith in what was then called Rhodesia was
overturned. On Heroes Day 1995 the president told thousands of people who
had gathered at the "Heroes Acre," the burial ground for the fallen heroes,
that homosexuals were "worse than pigs and dogs," who know their mates.
He added that animals do not copulate with mates of the same sex but turn
to the opposite sex in order to procreate. Mugabe also claimed that homosexuality is alien to black, African culture.

Mugabe thus deployed a black, national symbol, the Heroes Acre, in the
construction of a distinction between those who belong to the nation and
those who do not "fit in," the homosexuals. The soldiers and heroes are associated with the masculinity of the male gender role required in the idea of
the nation. By contrast homosexuals are characterized as feminine, "men
with wombs." Feminine men contest the ideology of the nation and its hierarchical divisions between the male and female gender. To homosexuals is
ascribed behavior that goes beyond both humans and animals. In addition,
homosexuality is defined as un-African, thus clearly homosexuals must be
excluded from the moral community. Following this logic, gays and lesbians
can never be granted any rights in Zimbabwe.[4]

Custodians of the Heritage

The Zanu (p., f.)[5] Women's League refer to themselves as "mothers and cus-
todians" of their cultural heritage. At a demonstration against gays and lesbians in 1995 these women carried banners with slogans such as "We are people, not animals; what are we going to teach our children about posterity? We
cannot stand back watching foreign behaviors infiltrate our society to destroy it. We now have incurable diseases and endless suffering due to foreign
bodies being allowed to play havoc with our sons and daughters."[6]

Again we find the dichotomization between human and nonhuman. The
women emphasize their own, preservative role within the nation as carriers
of children and of the cultural tradition. This role is contrasted to foreign

elements identified as evil forces causing damage to the children and the future of the nation.

Several members of parliament share these views. They asked how people will be able to procreate if they do not do it the "right way." In order for Zimbabwe to remain as a nation with its own dignity, one MP said, the homosexuals should be eradicated, like witches used to be eradicated. It is the duty of the president and the government to spearhead and promote the Zimbabwean national identity. What this identity is, is not made clear, though, but the conclusion of the parliamentary debate seems to be that Zimbabwe "as a nation should condemn it [homosexuality] totally." However, as another MP concluded, this would require an openness in discussing sexual matters that are regarded a taboo in Zimbabwe.

In one of the parliamentary debates Mr. Chigwedere presented homosexuality as a threat to the society as an organism: "When your finger starts festering and becomes a danger to the body you cut if off. . . . The homosexuals are the festering finger." And Chief Mangwende used an analogy to animal life: We can see that animals are behaving in a better way. Cows know that they have to go to bulls only and the bulls know that they have to go to the cows (Dunton and Palmberg 1996:14–15).

The vast majority of Christian churches, which hold tremendous power in the country, also supported the president. They seem preoccupied with the purpose of man and woman multiplying on earth according to the word of God. Since homosexuals are not believed to procreate, homosexuality is regarded as being against both the laws of nature and the laws of God and therefore unnatural and unchristian. Circular arguments dominated the debate: the family is the natural unit for procreation; procreation is the purpose of life; hence the family is a natural unit.

The Media Debate

The Zimbabwean public picked up these "messages" and a heated debate on homosexuality started in articles and letters to the editors in newspapers and magazines. (It was mainly the literate urban population that contributed to this debate.) Although there were letters in support, most letters were hostile in tone.[7] Much of the argument focused on the homosexual threat to the institution of the family, because homosexuals allegedly do not beget children. Black homosexuals were accused of "doing it for money," and of being seduced by white people. They were lumped together with child abusers, rapists, serial killers, and other kinds of people performing perversions and crimes. Homosexuality was described as a taboo in "our cherished culture," and further as "sinful, dirty, shameful, unchristian, alien to African culture." It was said to be a white "thing" imposed on blacks, contributing to the damage and decay of black culture and its values, a result of colonialism and the "Western" influence of today. (All citations are from Zimbabwean print media. See bibliography for references.)

To some extent statements like this must be understood in relation to colonial times when the social organization of families was disrupted and changed through the reorganization of work. Black men were employed on farms and in mines and stayed in "men's" camps, while their families were left behind in the rural areas. This is said to have deprived men of a natural sexual life with their wives, and thus they engaged in homosexual behavior out of need (Gevisser and Cameron 1994:59). Nobody seems to have considered what the wives did back home! This reflects the common notion that men have "natural" sexual drives, whereas women are not seen as sexual beings in themselves.

Zimbabwean Culture

Black Zimbabwean culture presents a complicated picture. Zimbabwe is a multiethnic country with a variety of local cultural traditions and influences introduced by colonial administration and Christian missionaries that intersect and parallel each other. The culturalist dimension of nationalism in Zimbabwe is a postcolonial project in which black traditional culture becomes part of the modern, postcolonial discourse on black national identity. The cultural "essence" that became the basis for the construction of anti-homosexual arguments can be found in folk models of fertility and regeneration of life common to most Bantu-speaking peoples in the region (Jacobs-Widding in Tumo-Masabo and Liljeström 1994:144). The conceptualization of sexuality, procreation, and gender roles found in this tradition "fits" the definitions of gender and sexualities required in Zimbabwean nationalism. Christian sexual morality and the value of children in traditional society is used to exclude homosexual practices.

Traditional Zimbabwean culture was centered on the cult of fertility and regeneration of life. Society was organized in patrilineal groups with male leaders, who controlled both the distribution of land and of wives. The purpose of marriage was not romantic love but to produce children. "Marriage was a social act, the primary purpose of which was to produce children for the husband's lineage. As such it was not a contract between individuals, but between two kin groups" (Schmidt 1992:16–17). The continuation of a man's lineage was vital to his wealth and power. He had the right to return a barren woman to her father's lineage if she could not give birth. Within this type of social organization the control of women's reproductive capacities becomes crucial; women's sexuality and bodies are under the jurisdiction of men and, to some extent, of elder women past menopause. Whereas a woman's sexual life is linked to her reproductive capacities, a man must be sexually active his whole life. His prestige depends on his capacity to produce offspring. A man's value as a human being is dependent upon his permanent potency, which secures him status as an ancestral spirit (*mudzimu*) in his lineage after death. Although this cultural knowledge is now more implicit than explicit, it is still paramount for men to prove their potency, which is a sign of masculinity (Liljeström and Tumo-Masabo 1994:146; Schmidt 1992).

Despite the strength of the Christian churches, ancestor beliefs hold a strong position in the consciousness of many Zimbabweans, more so in rural than in urban areas. According to tradition, ancestor spirits protect their descendants and secure rain if the descendants honor the ancestors by following the cultural rules. "The belonging to an ancestral clan constitutes the ideological basis of notions of personhood and identity" (Jacobson-Widding and van Beek 1990:34). There will always be some people who do not "fit" into the cultural norms. Such a person is suspected of being possessed by an evil spirit or of being a witch. Rituals must be performed to make the person conform to the norms. If this is not successful, the person must be evicted from the community or killed because she or he poses a threat to the collectivity.[8] Homosexuality is explained as possession by a spirit of the opposite sex. Some of my male informants had been subject to such explanations from elders in the rural areas, but they said that even if deviance can be explained, it is not necessarily accepted.

In a tradition where the production of children is paramount, to be childless is surrounded with fear. The sign of being different is to be childless. People who die without children will not become ancestor spirits. People who are murdered or otherwise die an unnatural death can turn into evil spirits, *n'gozis. N'gozis* are much feared, because they come back for revenge. They are the opposite of the lineage ancestors who represent the fertility and regeneration of life (Lan 1985).

According to the myths of a major ethnic group in Zimbabwe, the Shona, the fertility of a woman is often linked to the fertility of land, which in turn is linked to rain and rainbringing spirits, symbols of male principles. Rainmaking ceremonies and views on life and death are filled with sexual symbolism. A man must be potent when he dies, otherwise he will not become an ancestor who "rains" his semen to fertilize the soil (Jacobson-Widding in Liljeström and Tumo-Masabo 1994:146; Schmidt 1992). Barrenness in humans and infertility of land are symbolically connected. Both pose a threat to men's wealth and position in this life and in the next.

Lan (1985) describes how the rainbringing ancestral spirits, *mhondoro*, cooperated with the guerrilla soldiers through spirit mediums to help the Zimbabwean people win the liberation war. He elaborates the strong connections between land, fertility, sexuality, and the new nation. In the public debate gays and lesbians were blamed by some religious leaders for the droughts.[9] Religious resistance to homosexuality can be interpreted within the framework of ancestor beliefs and rain symbolism. Procreation and reproduction are a matter not for the individual, but for the lineage, the collectivity, and the nation. Mugabe's speech on Heroes Day, in which he compares pigs and dogs with gays, suggests the following logic: the animals represent fertility and symbolize the natural order of things, while gays represent infertility, which symbolizes danger and death.

These cultural beliefs form part of a framework people use to interpret acts and events as natural or unnatural, normal or abnormal. Delaney says that " 'nature' and the 'natural' come imbued with gender associations that are embedded in a particular religious or cosmological system" (1995:182). These systems benefit some people, usually men in power, at the cost of others, usually women. A black lesbian said that women do not gain from the traditional values because these values secure the power of men while keeping women in a subordinated position.

Ideally the collective has priority over the individual, and it is crucial to fulfill one's social obligations and take on the preordained social roles associated with being male or female. Patrilineal social organization and the gender roles it produces are legitimized through notions of nature (biology) and religion, the "laws of nature" and the "laws of God," both referring to procreation and the "multiplying of man." In this way inequality is constructed as "natural," leaving no space for ambiguity in gender roles based on the "naturalness" of the dimorphic two-sex system of male and female (Herdt 1993).

The Sociopolitical Context: Change and Culture

The attacks on gays and lesbians by the government must also be seen in a broader social and political context. At the macro level Zimbabwe has within a short historical period (about twenty years) gone through times of rapid change: from apartheid through socialism to market liberalism.[10] Zimbabwe is today struggling with a whole range of problems due to the ESAP (Economic Structural Adjustment Program), initiated by the IMF and the World Bank (the "West"), an unemployment rate of more than 50 percent, droughts, and AIDS, to mention just a few. Despite the liberation from the white regime, the economy is still controlled by the small, white minority (industry and commercial farming).[11]

The government is implementing an indigenization program in order to empower black people economically, but so far this has not resulted in any considerable changes in the economic sphere. The ESAP and market liberalism have led to a deepening of the gap between a small, emerging black elite and the mass of the poor black population. Living conditions are deteriorating and families can no longer function as they used to. What was built up in the first decade after independence in 1980—such as schools, health clinics, water supplies, and roads—is not maintained because of lack of money or mismanagement of it. Corruption, bribery, and factionalism between different ethnic groups as well as in governmental circles are seen as obstacles to development in the country. The government has not been able to deal with the problems satisfactorily, and people feel neglected. There is a growing dissatisfaction with the government and the ruling party among people. Many agree that there is a need for political change, but the opposition, like a variety of civil rights' groups, is effectively oppressed by the government. At the presidential election in 1996 only 29 percent of the enfranchised bothered to vote. Although Zimbabwe is a formal democracy with several political parties, those parties are of no political importance, insofar as they cannot threaten the position of the ruling party.[12] The president is in fact ruling a one-party state, which is not a unified nation.

Culture and Ideology: The Motivating Force of a Symbol

When the nation is "falling apart," those in power have a growing need for a unifying identity that goes beyond all immediate internal political, economic, and social crises and divisions among people of different classes and ethnic groups. Where there is no homogeneous national identity, it must be "invented." Notions of culture become a powerful means to this end. Cultural values are being romanticized, and culture is made to function as ideology. To produce meaning, the culture and the nation must appear as a whole, as a "we." This can only be done by establishing an other, a "they." Nations are thus constituted through the production of difference. The boundaries of the nation must be clear. In this process there is no room for ambiguity and alternatives. It is crucial to pick the "right" other, one most people can identify as other and would not protect.

Nationalism is an ideology that requires a reified, essentialist notion of culture in order to establish the boundary between "us" and "them." The promotion of cultural homogeneity is an ideological project. The discourse on the homosexual issue in the media reveals that people do not know much about either same-sex relations or the lives of gays and lesbians. It is also apparent that very few people are able to define what Zimbabwean culture is. Cultural values and norms usually are experienced as given and hence appear natural. In the national/cultural identity-building project of the government it is irrelevant whether people actually are able to define what culture is. What is crucial is that people are made to believe that they "have" a culture, which is distinctively different from other peoples' cultures. "Ideologies derive their potentially mobilizing force from their ability to organize and make sense of immediate experiences of their adherents" (Eriksen 1992:50). Notions of fertility, reproduction, and collective values were used in this sense, I believe.

Those in power must find a symbol that works in legitimizing the power of the state. The actual meaning of a symbol is arbitrary and multivocal (Turner 1967). The same symbol can take on different meanings for differently positioned people in various contexts. It is the ability of symbols to evoke emotions and rouse people to action that is crucial. In the Zimbabwean context homosexuality came to work as a symbol, I believe, because it was posed as a simple, binary opposition to the extended family, the heterosexual, patrilineal institution that constitutes the "cultural backbone" of the cultural tradition in Zimbabwe.

The meaning and social function of this kind of family has partly vanished and changed due to colonialism and processes of modernization and globalization. But one's family is part of everyone's experience and makes sense to most people. In debates people bemoaned the deterioration of the family. It was as though only restoring the institution of the family could solve the social problems caused by unemployment, crimes, and moral decay. Despite the profound changes, "family" can be seen to work as a symbol in the imagining of an authentic, black, and noncontaminated culture. Gays and lesbians are constructed as the opposite of families because they are believed not to procreate, and hence they come to represent the forces that disintegrate the family.

Nationalism defines cultural and social boundaries for a community and excludes those who do not fit in. The government and the president constructed a boundary between homosexuals and Zimbabwean society. The moral decay symbolized by the deterioration of the family is blamed on the lack of good moral values. Homosexuals are seen as a threat to the family institution. By defining gays and lesbians as inversions of nature and thus ascribing to them the role of "moral aliens," they are excluded from the moral community of the majority, i.e., from the nation.

Gays' and Lesbians' Stories

In the project of building a nation, gays and lesbians are used as a symbol and hardly have a voice themselves. In the following section I shall give voice to gays and lesbians themselves and try to grasp the way in which they represent themselves and their individual concerns. The harsh attacks and accusations against them caused a search for explanations, which led to a great deal of reflection about their lives. The examples will illustrate problems related to the definitions of black culture in Zimbabwe, gender roles, and notions of femininity and masculinity as well as to the experiences of black, lesbian women.

The women and men I talked with have moved away from their families in many parts of Zimbabwe to settle down in Harare. In the big city there is a potential for them to meet equals. The big city offers a degree of anonymity as well as the possibility of being "out," which is not offered in smaller places.

Since black gays are the main target of the government and in other debates on culture, I present examples of black informants only. In public debate gay men were attacked more than lesbians. The contested masculine role seems to be one major turning point in the discussion. This is why I chose to present feminine gay men[13] as well as lesbian women.

A White Thing?

Evershine is one of the black lesbians who condemned Mugabe's outbursts against homosexuals. "But still I admire the president for his courage to tell the West to go to hell!" Evershine is very conscious of the colonial period and what the "West" did to Africa. As a black Zimbabwean, she supports Mugabe in his contempt for the "West," but as a lesbian she is scared of the attacks concerning her sexual orientation. This paradox runs through large parts of the black community and illustrates that gay/lesbian identities are made up of complex and disparate "domains" and sometimes cause conflicts of loyalty. The black gays and lesbians frequently refer to their culture both as an obstacle to the expression and enactment of their same-sex desires and also as the source of their identities as blacks.

They counter the myth that they adopted a white sexual practice. "You can't adopt feelings!" They emphasize that they belong to the black culture and that they do not identify with anything "white." (Some dream about going abroad to get a better life, though). They were born in Rhodesia, which was a state based on racial segregation. They have grown up in "black" environments, for example, in townships or in rural areas, and were raised in the black culture. They have had little, if any, contact with white people. Nevertheless, they realize that they felt desire for partners of the same sex at an early age, between the ages of six and eight. So how can homosexuality be "white?" Most claim to have been born gay/lesbian. They see their sexual orientation as their destiny and explain their desires in essentialist terms.

Most informants said they have always felt that they do not "fit in." Thinking back to their childhood, they recollect that they did not like to do what had been expected of them according to their gender roles. The feminine gays had preferred to be with their sisters and mothers in the women's places doing "girl things" like cleaning, cooking, and fetching water. This is accepted when a boy is small, but when he reaches the age of adolescence, he is supposed to take up male activities. There is an indigenous expression for a boy like this: *n'gochani*. It refers to a bull with only one testicle, who is therefore unable to mount a cow in order to procreate. Within the last couple of years, especially after the book fair in 1995 *n'gochani* has come to mean "homosexual man" (Shire 1994:155). (I did not come across an indigenous term denoting homosexual women in the same way). In the public debate some implied that homosexuality does not exist in Zimbabwe because there is no word that literally means homosexual. Others claimed that since the term *n'gochani* exists, homosexuality must exist.

Taylor is a very feminine man. He has a soft voice and what is usually conceived of as feminine body movements. He says he feels like a woman, and he takes his femininity as a proof of being born gay. When he grew up in the rural areas he enjoyed doing "girl things." When he did not seem to take interest in male activities, like herding the cattle, at the age he was supposed to, his grandmother wanted to take him to the *n'anga* (traditional healer) to cure him and turn him into a "proper" man. Taylor said: "If they think the *n'anga* has a cure against homosexuality, it means that it must exist in our culture!"

Ncube refers to himself as a woman. He says that he has never penetrated a man and that he would never be with a man who lets himself be penetrated. He wants "real men" to penetrate him. He puts himself in the traditional position of a woman. He thus copies and adopts the traditional gender role. The same roles that oppress him also supply him with models for his own life.

Several of the very feminine gays claim that if they had the money they would go through a sex change operation. "In our culture it is too difficult to be gay. Maybe it would be easier for them [society and family] to accept me if I became a woman." These men dress in drag at gay parties. It makes them feel comfortable to expose their femininity. But they also say that "when a man dresses like a woman, he puts himself down to nothing." They know from their own experiences that women do not enjoy much respect in Zimbabwe. It is hard to understand, especially for heterosexual men, that some men voluntarily denigrate themselves to the position of women. They cannot imagine any male who gives up the prerogatives and prestige more or less vested in the Zimbabwean male role.

Lovemore used to work as a secretary, but now he is unemployed. It is difficult for him to get a job as a secretary, because, as he says, he is a man. Lovemore is feminine and at job interviews he has sometimes been questioned by employers about his sexuality. He wears clothes of his own design, and both design and colors stick out as different from the way other men dress. Since "it is quite obvious that I am gay, I don't get the job." Secretarial work is conceived of as a female occupation appropriate for women, not for men. This illustrates how gendered and sexed ideologies structure both occupations and workplace. Cultural notions of gender roles structure body language and behavior. As a secretary Lovemore has an "unmanly" profession. Since he is a man, he can't get a female job. As a feminine gay, he is an "unmanly" man. He represents ambiguity, "dirt."[14] The paradox is that in fact Lovemore has a big, muscular body, with a strong growth of body hair, i.e., traditionally masculine attributes.

Many gays work as hairdressers and stylists. Even though this is an "unmanly" occupation, an informant said that "people *expect* gay men to be hairdressers! That's the only job they can do." That does not imply that it is "appropriate" to be gay. None of the gay hairdressers I met were explicitly "out" at work.

The problems these gay men face have to do with their femininity. It creates ambiguous male roles, which society generally does not accept; there is no space to act out these roles without risking moral sanctions. The gays' experiences as being too feminine and gay to them are an explanation for why they don't get a job, or why they lose a job, or are thrown out of the place where they live. Tawana was harassed by a crowd of Zanu (p., f.) supporters who gathered in front of the block were he lived. The crowd yelled that this gay man should move out. The same group also came to his workplace to demonstrate against him. He had to leave his room and keep a very low profile at work.

These black gay men have an irregular or low income. They rent small rooms in crowded places. This makes it difficult for them to have any private life at all. "We cannot take lovers home," they say. So they go out. But it is risky to have sex in public places, because one can get "caught in the act" and get arrested. They all dream about a good job and income so they can get a flat and some private space. But as we have seen, gender and sexuality are made relevant in the social context and influence their opportunities to get a job and an income and hence a good place to live.

Black Lesbians

It was a common perception among all gays and lesbians I met that within the gay and lesbian communities it was the black lesbians that faced the most severe difficulties and constraints among homosexuals in Zimbabwe. Black gays said that many black lesbians have no opportunities to come out because they are so controlled by their families and by society. Despite the new visibility due to the Book Fair, black lesbians remained fairly invisible. Those who had come out and lived as lesbians today paid a high price for insisting on living out their same-sex desires.

Some of the black lesbians said they had been "tomboys" as children, and had fantasized about changing their biological sex. Shikaye is one of them. When she was a girl, she did not want to become a woman, because "as soon as a girl gets her period her freedom is limited. She is told not to screw around, and can't move around like men do." Shikaye looked at her mother and the women in her neighborhood. They seemed to live a life for others; for husbands, children, and family. A life as a man seemed so much easier, but to enjoy the prerogatives of a man was unthinkable for a woman. So Shikaye wanted to become a man, which would imply a physical change of her biological sex. She felt attracted to women, a feeling that furthermore contributed to the thought of changing sex, because only men could love women. She could not name the attraction for women and she would not accept it. Shikaye's social context contained only two acceptable roles, that of a man and a woman, essentialized and fixed in their content. Her ideas changed, however, after she came out to herself. The coming out situation took place in a European capital. Shikaye had been invited by an expatriate friend, and together they explored the gay life in the city. They also went to lesbian sex shows, and "then I understood what I was," she said. She now understood what it was that she had felt toward women before but had been unable to name or accept because she thought she was the only one in the world. After this experience when Shikaye understood and accepted for herself that it was possible for a woman to love another woman, she stopped fantasizing about being a man. The lesbian role (which is of course not fixed) offered her new potentialities as a woman as well as a kind of freedom in her life because she could choose not to marry a man. But even if her lesbian identity eased some pressure at a personal level, living as a lesbian woman in Zimbabwe causes lots of problems and risks. Shikaye has lost many friends. She is scared of losing her job if her identity is revealed, and she is not known as a lesbian to her family. "I love them too much to risk to lose them." Shikaye considers becoming pregnant and having a child, although that is not what she wants. But "life would be easier, because as a mother people would stop thinking that I am a lesbian."

Tendai is a mother. She lived with her parents, her husband, and their three children for five years. Then she realized that she was attracted to women and that she could no longer pretend to be heterosexual. She learned about GALZ (via a friend in South Africa). She became a member and started to receive the quarterly GALZ magazine. Her father found the magazines, got suspicious, and pressed Tendai until she admitted she was one of "them," a lesbian. Her father yelled at her to get out of the house immediately and never to come back. The children were to remain with their father. She was no longer a member of the family. The next three years she was denied any contact with her children. "It was so painful! But I can't change." Although Tendai had fulfilled her social obligations by being a mother, her lesbian identity was considered more important. She was denied access to her children as she had not fulfilled her proper role as a wife.

On another occasion it was her identity as mother that became relevant. Tendai was taken in by the police who questioned her about her sexual orientation. (Gays and lesbians are not often harassed by the police in this way, but nobody knows when it might happen.) In the course of the interrogation she told the officers that she was the mother of three children and showed them the pictures. She asked the officers whether they would drag a mother through court in front of the eyes of her children. The police released her, doubting that this mother, so concerned for her children, could be a lesbian after all.

The importance of becoming a wife and mother is illuminated in the next example. When Joice's parents realized she did not want to marry any of the young men they presented to her, they forced an old man on her. She was locked up in a room of the house with the old man, who raped her in order to make her pregnant. Joice said that in this way her parents wanted to force her to marry. Joice became pregnant. She ran away from home, and she had an abortion. She almost bled to death and had to spend four weeks in the hospital. Her parents sent the police to search for her. She was found and brought back to her parents, who beat her up so badly that she was severely injured. Once Joice had recovered, the parents sent in the man to rape her again, and Joice became pregnant. This time she kept the child as she was afraid of another abortion. In the sixth month she had a miscarriage. "Maybe I lost it because I hated it so much." Joice fled from home, went underground, and lived on the street for a while, constantly on the run.

Joice's parents used brute force to make her return to "normality" and to make her conform to the cultural norms of the collectivity, norms she felt she could not adjust to. I think we have to take into account the values of the black culture described earlier if we want to understand the violent reactions of families toward their "deviant" children. "Fitting in" is considered more important than the personal interests of the individual.

Today both Joice and Tendai live alone in small rooms in black, high-density areas. They are unemployed, but like so many other Zimbabwean women they try to make a living by trading in neighboring countries.

Rose has scars on her body. She was raped several times by a male family member. He cut her with a knife to make her shut up about it. She did not tell anybody, because "people tend to believe it is the woman's own fault." She tried to kill herself. The rape and the sexual harassment she has been subjected to have affected her relation to her own body. She hates her breasts because "they stick out, and I hate when men stare at them. They always stare at women's bodies and get sexual pleasure out of it." She wishes she could get her breasts to droop, like the hanging breasts of an old woman, because then they would not arouse men's desire. The rape is literally carved into her body, and she wants to change her body physically, from the attractive and feminine body that appeals sexually to men into the mature look of an older woman, who has another, more respected status after menopause. As these examples show, the pressure on women in their reproductive age is tremendous.

The Extended Family: The Individual and the Collective

All my black informants stressed the importance of the family in black culture. Since the Economic Structural Adjustment Program (ESAP) was introduced in the country, social welfare and medical services have been cut dramatically in order to stabilize the economic situation. Thus the family unit has gained a renewed meaning as the safety net for its members. Without a family it is hard to survive. "If the family is not going to help you, who is?"

Those who have been ostracized and who become unemployed have nowhere to go for help. This causes economic as well as emotional problems.

One dimension of the strong position of the extended family in the lives of black gays and lesbians is its size. "When you come out it does not only concern you and your mother and father. It is a concern of the whole extended family! It means the involvement of thirty to forty people! That is why it is so difficult for us blacks to come out. It is not an individual concern."

The importance of the collective values was also given as an explanation by blacks for why it allegedly was a different matter for blacks and whites in GALZ to fight for "gay rights as human rights." The "Western" notion of human rights concerns the political and civil rights of the individual. In the "African Charter for Human and Peoples' Rights" these rights are acknowledged, but there is also an emphasis on cultural rights and on the rights of peoples. These are rights concerning the African collectivities, and individual rights must not work against the rights of the collectivity. Norms and values concerning the family unit are to be protected by the state as the basis of society. Given this ideology of family values, gays and lesbians are perceived as individualists who break out of the collectivity. They represent the opposite of the values of traditional black culture, on which the modern state is built.

Since there are no acceptable social roles nor places for gays and lesbians within the social contexts in Zimbabwe, they have to create them for themselves.[15] Through their social practices and activities such as drag shows, gays and lesbians do create both spaces and roles that enable them to come to terms with a life as "deviant" human beings in a hostile environment.[16] To be gay/lesbian has to be described in terms of a process of becoming, rather than as a fixed identity. No identity is entirely defined by sexuality. The examples I have presented show that other factors, such as race/color, class, and gender come into play as well.

Zimbabwean lesbian women and gay men do not fulfill their preordained social roles, thus they will never be "proper" Zimbabweans. In this regard they are deemed socially dead, and this makes them feel excluded from many parts of society. However, they do express a strong identification with black society. It is as *black Zimbabweans* that they try to create an identity as gay/lesbian. But they are aware of the paradox of belonging to a society that excludes them, and the government's hostility creates a great deal of fear.

Their stories tell us that sexuality is a powerful symbol and a profound boundary marker. At a macro level it is used by those in power for political ends in an ideological struggle over national identity. At the level of experience, the examples show that the body is a social space and is acted upon according to the values of the hegemonic discourses of gender and sexuality. Sexuality is experienced through the body, but it is not a private matter; the body does not belong to the individual. The body is a site both for struggle and resistance. The conflict between the ideology of the "right" genders and bodies and the social practices and experiences of the gays and lesbians I spoke with indicate that gays and lesbians are developing new ways of being male and female. Culturally accepted genders do not fit all bodies.

Within this hostile environment essentialist explanations of being homosexual seem to be the only plausible ones. My informants do not conceive of their sexual orientation as a choice. They claim to have been born gay and that since it is in their blood, they cannot change it. They thus naturalize their "deviance," just as the government and the church naturalize power and inequality. What they can change, though, is their bodies. I suggest there is a connection between the rigid classification of the sexes into only two acceptable gender categories (man and woman), and the constructed appropriate sexual and bodily behavior "applying" to these, and the experience of the total oppression of the gay identity as an acceptable alternative. The fantasies concerning sex change indicate that the dichotomy between the two gender roles "man" and "woman" is experienced as absolute. By their mere existence the gays and lesbians counter these absolutes. Their experiences and social practices show empirically that gender is fluid.

The study of homosexuality and the experiences of gays and lesbians touches upon a whole range of topics, each a study in itself. In Zimbabwe homosexuality is "alien," and gays and lesbians are "other." In public rhetoric black gays and lesbians come to represent the "ultimate transgressors" of culture. Gay men and lesbian women contest the naturalness of masculinity and femininity as defined in the traditional male gender role. They "betray" the "laws" that demand procreation. By not conforming to the cultural ideology with its emphasis on collective values, they come to represent individualism, which in turn has come to stand for the "West," modernity, and the dissolution of traditional values. They thus serve as the "perfect other" in a context where definitions of culture seem to be crucial for the construction of the modern Zimbabwean national identity.

NOTES

I am currently working on my thesis for the dissertation in social anthropology. This essay is a working paper that touches on only a few aspects of a very complex reality. It is a revised version of a paper presented at the conference "Beyond Boundaries: The First International Conference of the Crosscultural Study of Sexuality," held in Amsterdam 1997. I would like to thank Saskia Wieringa and Evelyn Blackwood for encouraging me to contribute the paper to this book and for their comments. My research was funded by the Research Council of Norway.

1. I am aware that the use of categories and notions like "gay," "lesbian," "feminine" and "masculine" are problematic analytical tools because they do not mean the same to everybody and are not fixed in content. But for the sake of convenience I shall use the category "gay" and "lesbian" to denote men and women who engage in same-sex relations. Both gays and lesbians refer to themselves as "gay" in Zimbabwe. Lesbians also frequently use the term "dyke" and less often "lesbian." I shall refer to the women as "lesbians" and the men as "gays." I use the English terms instead of indigenous ones because GALZ (Gays and Lesbians in Zimbabwe) was founded by white gays and lesbians whose language is English. Any information about them and GALZ has been written in this language. GALZ constitutes a multiethnic and multilingual network of people, so English is the "public" language here as well as in the country as a whole. GALZ has started to publicize information in the Shona and Ndebele languages. "Homosexuality" is an emic term used by the participants in the public debates.

2. Anderson (1983) does not elaborate an analysis of gender although his work points to the sexualized and gendered aspects of nationalisms.

3. The war ended in 1979. Zimbabwe was proclaimed an independent state on April 18, 1980.

4. People in general seem now to be indifferent to the "worshipping" of the war heroes. Many see this as a way by the government to cling to heroic past and legitimate the hegemonic position of the ruling party since the Liberation.

5. The Zanu, Zimbabwe African National Union (patriotic front), is the ruling party.

6. This is a reference to AIDS.

7. Many liberal and radical whites and blacks did support GALZ's right to participate in the book fair.

8. This was explained to me by a government secretary when I interviewed him about "cultural arguments against homosexuality."

9. Zimbabwe has been plagued by severe droughts throughout the 1980s and 1990s. The worst was in 1992, when people lost their cattle and starved. The country has still not recovered from these droughts. The "book fair year" did not look promising either but the rain came at last.

10. Before Independence in 1980 Zimbabwe was ruled by Ian Smith and his apartheid regime. The economy was in white hands. In the subsequent decade the political system of Zimbabwe was a mixed capitalist and planned socialist system, with strong ties to the communist and socialist countries. Mugabe has

been in power all these years, first as prime minister, then as president. In the name of reconciliation, whites kept their rights to property and continued to control the economy through industry and commercial farming, and this is the case even today. The First Five-Year Plan was a failure. Conditions in the world market, mismanagement, and inflation had serious consequences for the economy. In 1990 the Zimbabwean government decided to implement the IMF-World Bank Structural Adjustment program in order to revive the economy. This meant a farewell to socialism and the introduction of market liberalism. The economy has thus to a very large extent been a "white thing" throughout the history of Zimbabwe. For further readings on ESAP see Chakaodza (1993).

11. Some 70–80% of the fertile land is controlled by only 4,000–5,000 white commercial farmers.

12. A political scientist I interviewed held that the leaders of these two other parties were paid by Zanu (p., f.) to "play fools" in the election, i.e., to act as opposition.

13. Many gays define themselves as masculine and do not like feminine men. These categories must be investigated empirically, of course.

14. A notion of order implies a notion of dirt. What cannot be classified is called dirt. Dirt is disorder, and disorder must be reordered. See Douglas (1966).

15. GALZ now has a center in a house in Harare.

16. At the Book Fair 1997 GALZ was allowed to distribute information and publications. GALZ did not have a stand but shared one with other human rights groups.

REFERENCES

African Charter for Human and Peoples' Rights. Adopted by the Eighteenth Conference of Heads of State and Government of the OAU, June 1981, Nairobi, Kenya.

Anderson, Benedict. 1991. *Imagined Communities: Reflections on Origin and Spread of Nationalism.* New York: Verso.

Beek, Walter van and Anita Jacobson-Widding. 1990. "Chaos, Order, and Communion in African Models of Fertility: Introduction." In Walter van Beek and Anita Jacobson-Widding, eds., *The Creative Communion: African Folk Models of Fertility and the Regeneration of Life.* Uppsala.

Chakaodza, Austin M. 1993. *Structural Adjustment in Zambia and Zimbabwe: Reconstructive or Destructive?* Harare: Third World Publishers.

Delaney, Carol. 1995. "Father State, Motherland, and the Birth of Modern Turkey." In Sylvia Yanagisako and Carol Delaney, eds., *Naturalizing Power: Essays in Feminist Cultural Analysis*, pp. 177–199. New York: Routledge.

Douglas, Mary. 1989. *Purity and Danger: An Analysis of the Concepts of Pollution and Taboo.* London: Ark.

Dunton, Chris and Mai Palmberg. 1996. *Human Rights and Homosexuality in Southern Africa.* Uppsala: Scandinavian Institute of African Studies.

Eriksen, Thomas Hylland. 1992. *Us and Them in Modern Societies: Ethnicity and Nationalism in Mauritius, Trinidad, and Beyond.* Stockholm: Scandinavian University Press.

Gevisser, Mark and Edwin Cameron, eds. 1994. *Defiant Desire: Gay and Lesbian Lives in South Africa.* Johannesburg: Ravan Press.

Herdt, Gilbert, ed. 1993. *Third Sex, Third Gender: Beyond Sexual Dimorphism in Culture and History.* New York: Zone Books.

Jacobson-Widding, Anita. 1994. Interview for "Looking for Men" by Rita Liljestrøm and Betty Komba-Malekela. In Rita Liljestrøm and Zubeida Tumo-Masabo, eds., *Chelewa, Chelewa: The Dilemma of Teenage Girls*, pp. 144–148. Uppsala: Scandinavian Institute of African Studies.

Keesing. Roger M. 1987. "Anthropology as Interpretive Quest." *Current Anthropology* 28 (2): 161–162.

Lan, David. 1985. *Guns and Rain: Guerrillas and Spirit Mediums in Zimbabwe.* Harare: Zimbabwe Publishing House.

Liljestrøm, Rita and Zubeida Tumo-Masabo, eds. 1994. *Chelewa, Chelewa: The Dilemma of Teenage Girls.* Uppsala: Scandinavian Institute of African Studies.

Mosse, Georg L. 1985. *Nationalism and Sexuality: Middle-class Morality and Sexual Norms in Modern Europe.* Madison: University of Wisconsin Press.

"Homosexualism and Lesbianism Motion. Fourth Order read: Adjourned Debate on Motion on the Evil and Iniquitous Practice of Homosexualism," September 28, 1995.

Parker, Andrew, Mary Russo, Doris Sommer, and Patricia Yaeger, eds. 1992. *Nationalisms and Sexualities.* New York: Routledge.

Schmidt, Elizabeth. 1992. *Peasants, Traders, Wives: Shona Women in the History of Zimbabwe, 1870–1939.* Harare: Baobab.

Shire, Chenjerai. 1994. "Men Don't Go to the Moon: Language, Space, and Masculinities in Zimbabwe." In Andrea Cornwall and Nancy Lindisfarne, eds., *Dislocating Masculinity*, pp. 147–158. New York: Routledge.

Thaiss, Gustav. 1978. "The Conceptualization of Social Change through Metaphor." *Journal of Asian and African Studies* 13:1–13.

Turner, Victor. 1967. *The Forest of Symbols: Aspects of Ndembu Ritual.* Ithaca: Cornell University Press.

Yuval-Davis, Nira. 1997. *Gender and Nation.* London: Sage.

Newspapers referred to, issues dating from 1995–1996:

The Herald
The Chronicle
The Sunday Gazette

The Financial Gazette
The Independent

Magazines referred to, issues dating from 1995–1996:

Horizon
Mahogany
Moto
Parade
Read On!

12

Tan beng hui

Women's Sexuality and the Discourse on Asian Values: Cross-Dressing in Malaysia

The decade of the nineties has witnessed the emergence of a disconcerting trend in Malaysia: the unprecedented public scrutiny and regulation of female sexuality, particularly that of young women. This has coincided with a period of apparently increasing social ills for which women, and to a lesser extent men, of the younger generation have been blamed. By attributing the cause of these perceived social ills to the decaying moral fabric of society, the state has initiated a specific discourse on Asian values, implicit in which is the assumption that women have either failed in their duty to uphold the traditional family unit and/or that they have not lived up to the expected norms of female self-representation and behavior. It is a discourse that justifies the regulation of women's bodies in the name of returning to the harmonious and well-ordered society of the past.

In light of the above, this essay is an exploration of the patterns of domination and resistance that prevail in the regulation of young women's sexuality in Malaysia. In arguing that the practice of controlling women's bodies is problematic and needs to be contested, my objectives are twofold. First, to understand how the dominant discourse on female sexuality—in this case, the Asian values discourse—defines and determines the category "woman"; and second, to explore the implications for women who do not live up to constructed gender norms. More concretely, I question the methods of "targeting" women and their sexuality and the motivations underlying them. Why is it that a disproportionate emphasis has been placed on the need to regulate female (as opposed to male) sexuality? How is this control being exercised? Which types of women are most susceptible to being attacked? I will demonstrate how the debates on Asian values—rife in the country since the early 1990s—can be considered a form of nationalist and fundamentalist discourse. However, rather than denying the validity of Asian values per se, my intention in problematizing this subject stems from a concern as to how the ideology of the powerful uses cultural values like these to impose controls over women. In the final section I introduce the case study of Azizah and Rohana, two women who managed to wed because the former had successfully passed as a man. I use this to illustrate the extent of controls used to ensure that women live up to certain imposed standards of womanly appearance and behavior.

Nationalism and Fundamentalism

In the era of globalization, there is an added pressure on many postcolonial states to reassert their national identities against the homogenizing tendencies of global capitalism. The defense of these "local" identities has led to an intensification of nation-building efforts through the invocation of different nationalist discourses that at times can be, and have been, fundamentalist in nature (Guibernau 1996:135). The notion of nation building itself should be understood as a dynamic and open-ended process of fostering group identity and loyalty (Bloom 1990:71–75), in which an "imagined community" is created (Anderson 1987).

To retain the power to unite the people under their rule, state-led nationalist discourses often aim at projecting the impression that common values, symbols, and a national culture exist, and for this they employ a selective use and interpretation of tradition (Guibernau 1996:47, 149). For example, in Malaysia what has come to be defined (and promoted by the rhetoric on Asian values) as the common national identity is not a product from any shared "genetic pool" or tradition, but rather the result of carefully juggling different class and ethnic interests over the years. In its latest formulation, there is now even to be one *bangsa Malaysia* (Malaysian race).

All nationalisms rely on feminine imagery to construct the nation, and through this they dictate a very specific definition of what being a woman is all about (Heng 1997:359, n. 2; Pettman 1996:48). Women are typically assigned a dual function: one, as symbolic bearers of the nation's future and two, as boundary markers of the group to differentiate its members from the "Other." In sorting people into "us" versus "them" categories, difference becomes hierarchized: being different from what has been dictated as the norm is posited as either being inferior or a threat to the common collective "good." Excluded are not only those who stand outside the defined boundaries of the group but also those within the group who are perceived as socially different (Pettman 1996:46).

Because women are used as the maintainers and reproducers of group identity, they and their sexuality are targets for control and regulation by members of the same community (Peterson 1994, cited in Pettman 1996:59). By constructing the nation on the bodies of women, efforts to defend women can also be justified in the name of keeping the national identity intact, most especially when a nation is perceived to be under threat. Neither explicit conflict nor external threat are necessary for such "protection" to be justified since the nation can also be perceived as being threatened by the enemy within, for instance, by women who refuse to live up to the norms of motherhood and femininity. In the name of "protecting" women and thus the community's interests, the line between protecting and controlling the female body is often trespassed.

Today, after a marked growth in the number of fundamentalist movements all over the world, the term "fundamentalism" is more commonly used in reference to "modern political movements which use religion as a basis for their attempt to win or consolidate power and extend social control" (Sahgal and Yuval-Davis 1994:7). As with nationalism, several writers (e.g., Sahgal and Yuval-Davis 1992; Hardacre 1993) have correctly cautioned against treating fundamentalism as a monolithic entity.[1]

The emergence of fundamentalist movements is often explained as a response to a threat--real or imagined--that they define in antifaith terms. Topping this list of threats are secularized modernity, imperialism, and Westernization. Protests against these take place in several ways whereby reverting to a set of original values belonging to a glorified past, to a "golden age of purity" is the most common (Marty and Appleby 1993:3). However, though fundamentalist movements appear to want to turn back the clock by calling for adherence to "traditional values" or the "return to original sources" (e.g., religious texts or scriptures), it is necessary to recognize that what fundamentalists really do is "use the legitimacy of past ideals to reshape the present and postulate the future. . . . Their historical discourse is not merely intended to set the record straight; it is geared towards correcting the present deviation from the true path" (Gerami 1996:26–27).

Central to all fundamentalist projects of returning to tradition is the reconstruction of gender relations. In envisioning the past, strong emphasis is placed on the roles of women and (to a lesser extent) men within the idealized family. The basic message is that both have different but complementary roles that are strictly not equal or interchangeable. In this relationship men are vested with authority while women's role is to obey and give in to this authority. It is this principle of male dominance and female submission fundamentalists wish to use to construct their new social order. Women feature in this configuration as the ones chiefly responsible for the domestic sphere. They are to derive fulfillment from motherhood, homemaking and attending to the well-being of all those in the family (Hardacre 1993:131–132, 138–139). Even if they need to work outside the home, their primary duty should remain that to the family.

Fundamentalists are also concerned with controlling the observable aspects of women's lives, e.g., the way they dress, look, or behave, their choice of relationships, sexual activity, and reproductive options (Papanek 1994:45). As in nationalist discourses, women are seen as boundary markers and as biological and ideological reproducers of the group. Since they are seen as carrying culture and values into future generations and their behavior is used to distinguish those belonging to the group from others, a high degree of control over women's bodies is deemed necessary (Yuval-Davis and Anthias 1989, cited in Saghal and Yuval-Davis 1992:8). The desire to control women is also said to stem from the inability of fundamentalists to deliver their promises of redressing the problems they associate with Westernization. Precisely because they have failed in this respect, they turn to effecting change in a more manageable domain--the domain of interpersonal relations (especially within the family)--by exercising control over women: be it wives, mothers, daughters, sisters, or any other female relative (Hardacre 1993:138).

For fundamentalists who engage in anti-Western rhetoric, women who do not conform to the predetermined codes of feminine behavior--women who strive to be "modern" as opposed to "traditional"--are often branded as having been influenced by the (evil) West. Yet it is important to recognize that fundamentalists are not necessarily against Western modernity per se. Rejecting all things Western does not include rejection of modern instrumentalities, such as the media; instead, these are seen as crucial in the propagation of fundamentalist ideology.

Asian Values: The State-Led Discourse on Women's Sexuality in Malaysia

Malaysia has a multiethnic and multireligious society where Malays form the largest ethnic group and Islam is recognized as the national religion.[2] Since 1957, when British colonialists handed over power, the country has been ruled by the coalition *Barisan Nasional* (BN) party. Comprising different ethnically based political parties, the composition of which has changed over the years, the BN has essentially been led by the Malay-based UMNO (the United Malay Nationalist Organisation) party and been unwaveringly supported by the subordinate MCA (Malaysian Chinese Association) and the MIC (Malaysian Indian Congress) parties. Although a system of parliamentary democracy formally exists, the fact that the opposition has never been in power indicates that it is extremely weak and unable to function as a "check and balance" mechanism, let alone to significantly challenge the authority of those in government.

Indeed, if the criteria for a "democracy" include the right to vote, a responsible government, freedom of expression and association as well as protection from being arbitrarily arrested, then the Malaysian political system is better described as a "restricted democracy" (Munro-Kua 1996:6), where a plethora of laws exists to curb certain fundamental rights of all Malaysians. However, unlike their counterparts in the region, those in authority appear to have perfected the art of achieving mass compliance without resorting to violent means. In day-to-day life, the knowledge that such laws might be used, combined with subtle and not-so-subtle warnings that are periodically sent out, instills enough fear in Malaysians to prompt them into regulating their own social behavior.[3] The existence of repressive legislation has been justified, if at all, in the name of maintaining political stability and racial harmony, goals the government promotes as the two vital ingredients for national unity and the country's continuing economic success.

A survey of local press reports will show that as early as 1994 a concerted state-generated discourse on values has been rife in Malaysia.[4] In its earliest form, this discourse was posed in terms of Eastern (Asian) versus Western values. It posits that contemporary Western, mostly Christian, societies have witnessed a breakdown in social relations and in previously revered institutions, such as marriage and the family, because materialistic, selfish, and greedy desires of individuals have overtaken the needs of their communities.[5] As such, the key to social order lies in the successful preservation of the traditional family unit where "filial piety is the supreme virtue and . . . individual happiness is de-emphasized" (Tanji and Lawson 1997:144). By drawing parallels between loyalty to one's family and obedience to the authority of political leaders,[6] the discourse on Asian values insists that certain differences within a country's peoples have to be sacrificed in the name of the common national or collective "good."

While the discourse on Asian values is clearly geared toward building a Malaysian nation, it also shares many features with fundamentalism. More important, it is also gendered and assigns women very specific roles and spaces in society. For example, they are allowed, and sometimes even encouraged, to seek work in the public sphere but when upon demand they are expected to prioritize the interests of the family over all else. This explains why often the disintegration of the family unit—which in fundamentalist discourses augurs the collapse of social order—is blamed on women's assertiveness in the public realm. With women's role defined in terms of natural and biological givens, the question of why women should be solely assigned to safeguard the morality of society is conveniently avoided.

In many ways the contradictory demands that have accompanied women's active participation in national development plans and industrialization projects have been inevitable. Crucial for economic growth, women's pursuit of education, employment, and political participation meant that they simultaneously defied certain cultural norms. The very creation of a young Malay female wage-earning labor force—perceived as indulging in "individualistic ideas, behavior, and modern forms of consumption"—has drawn Islamic pronouncements on the weakening of morality, which is feared as threatening Malay culture (Ong 1994:378). With Malaysia being predominantly Malay and Muslim, the state is to some extent influenced by the interests of this group, more so in light of the increasing challenges to UMNO's legitimacy by various fundamentalist elements. At the same time, however, the state has to ensure that it does not appear too extreme to the non-Malay population or to the foreign investors it seeks to woo (Nagata 1994:85), nor does it want to abandon its plans for economic expansion. The process of juggling these different demands has not been easy, but it seems that for now the way out of the contradictions that have arisen with modernization is through greater regulation of female sexuality.

Good or Bad? Ramifications of the Asian Values Discourse

The whole idea of juxtaposing Eastern and Western values sorts Malaysians into "us" and "them" categories. Anti-Western rhetoric is specifically generated to construct "good" Asian values against "bad" Western ones. By intentionally glossing over its heterogeneous nature, this rhetoric portrays the West as a source of danger, contamination, and disease. The point here is that what constitutes "good" and "bad" is carefully constructed to suit the objective at hand. In this case, those who qualify as having "good" Asian values are considered part of the national "us" and accordingly receive the recognition that comes with this; those who do not are stigmatized, isolated, and sometimes even persecuted. By extending this line of argument further, one can thus see the fate of women (and men) who do not adhere to the norms promoted by this discourse. Depicted as the brokers of sexual morality and familial harmony, women in the Asian values discourse are not given space to present themselves as anything that might threaten the fragile social order for which they are made responsible. What is more, this discourse also sets the general standards of sexual morality for all Malaysians by using female sexuality as its yardstick, thus giving further justification for its regulation. I am not arguing that there exists some kind of conspiracy by the state to do so. I am inclined to Foucault's (1978) understanding of power as diffused and not concentrated in the hands of any particular group in society. This means that although the state regulates--according to the interests of those groups that have access to its power or whose support is necessary for its continued legitimacy--it does so within the constraints of its location in the discursive networks that operate in society (Sharp 1996:105).

Although on one level the Asian values discourse may be potentially repressive in the resultant patrolling of women's sexuality, on the other hand, precisely because power is productive, the same discourse can generate a starting point for opposing strategies. By being entrusted with upholding sexual order, women "are empowered to threaten the values of the discourse" (Evans 1997:214). This also explains why efforts to control female sexuality remain so persistent. Yet there is already evidence that even within the dominant Asian values discourse, there are competing interests. This may be a state-led discourse, but since the State is not a monolithic entity with uniform interests, clashes between the different players are inevitable.

Similarly, the discourse on Asian values has also "benefited" the homosexual (female and male) community in Malaysia. The constant cautions against homosexuality and other forms of social "evil" have given these various phenomena--as well as the actors behind them—a prominence never before seen in Malaysia. The Asian values discourse has inadvertently ended up publicly acknowledging and naming the presence of homosexuality in Malaysian society. Furthermore, the very idea of needing to contain homosexuality and to "get rid" of it is premised on a recognition that homosexuality not only exists but that it can also be promoted. This is extremely significant since it implies that sexual identities are not natural, fixed, and immutable as they are commonly made out to be (see also Stacey 1991).

Transgressing Sexual Boundaries

The Construction of "Woman" in Malay Society

Today the dominant discourse on female sexuality in Malaysia insists that being "female" is synonymous with being "feminine." Through this equation, particular characteristics of femininity are essentialized and often promoted as qualities that all "good" women should naturally possess. Frequently marriage is glorified as an incentive for women to adhere to the strict standards of femininity. Furthermore, displays of female sexuality outside the perimeters of marriage are represented as a "source of disorder and danger" (Evans 1997:213).

According to a study on Malay kinship by David Banks, in traditional Malay society marriage was morally required of all Muslims, including those individuals who may not have been interested (1983:93). A similar observation is made by Ingrid Rudie who researched gender relations in Kelantan. She writes that the informants in her fieldwork insisted that in Islam there was no leeway for a person to remain single. In the case of women, marriage was also seen as a means of protecting a woman's reputation and, further, of ensuring that she would not grow old alone. Thus even if religion did not dictate so, the concern that women should have some sort of family attachment was reason enough to get married (1994:142). Perhaps an even greater incentive to get married and have children is to gain recognition, which is reserved specially for those who fulfill this obligation. As Lenore Manderson contends, "until she married and had borne children, a [Malay] woman was essentially without status" (1980:17).

With marriage set as the ultimate goal in life, young single Malay women are expected to possess certain qualities that will fetch them a husband. Brought up differently from her male counterpart, the young Malay woman learns how to behave herself in the "demure, refined, and respectful manner befitting that of an unmarried woman" (Manderson 1980, quoted in Lie and Lund 1994:33). The Islamic ideals of female chastity and virginity remain important virtues[7] even in—or perhaps *especially* in—current times where the number of sexual encounters between single male and female youth is on the rise. It is more common, though, for young women to be discouraged from flaunting their sexuality. Thus, even if it is claimed that Islam applies the rule of modesty equally to both sexes (Doi 1990:12), it is still much more common today for women to be burdened with the responsibility of preventing men from lusting after their bodies (Sisters in Islam 1993:80).

Over the past few years women's styles of dress have taken center stage in determining levels of morality and acceptable feminine behavior in

Malaysia. Among urban middle-class women, this has especially become an issue, and many of them resort to *dakwah* (Islamic) dress styles that do not emphasize the curves of their bodies and include the wearing of *tudungs*.[8]

Malay society is often referred to as an example of a Muslim society where relations between the sexes are fairly equal (Ong 1990:260), but once married the "ideal" Malay woman is still expected to be subordinate to her husband, the head of the household.[9] The stress on obedience stems from the Islamic cosmogony's insistence that a woman's function and duty is to obey, otherwise the hierarchy of order will be threatened (Mernissi 1996:111). Lenore Manderson argues that like Islam, the other major influence on Malay culture--*adat* (custom)—also encourages women's subservience to their husbands (1980:17). Writers like Karim (1995) and Ong (1990) disagree. To them, traditionally *adat* and Islam have served female and male interests differently; the former is said to be more advantageous to women's control over domestic resources and the latter gives more control to men (Ong 1990:260).[10] However, such views either ignore that economic power is only one of the many facets of power operating in society or assume that it is always a marker of social status.[11]

Repercussions for "Deviant" Women: The Case of Azizah and Rohana

In December 1996 the Malaysian press reported that a twenty-one-year-old Malay woman in the state of Kelantan had impersonated a man in order to marry her lover, another woman.[12] Hailed as the first incident of its kind in Malaysian history, the case drew much attention for well over three months and even up to today is considered newsworthy. The accused Azizah Abdul Rahman was said to have fooled her bride, the local *imam* (religious leader), the district registrar of marriages, and the witnesses at her wedding by successfully passing herself off as a man. All professed that they had no idea that Azizah was a woman because she not only looked and behaved like a man but had also assumed a man's name and possessed a male identity card. Within three weeks of her arrest, she was indicted and sentenced by the magistrate court to two years imprisonment on two counts; the first and more severe charge was for impersonating a man and the second for using another person's identity card.[13]

Despite her arrest and conviction, the Azizah and Rohana episode continued to feature in the local newspapers as reporters pursued all possible angles of this story. At first it persisted as a dramatic account of "a woman who shook the nation." The initial reports thus concentrated on explaining how she managed to dupe those around her into believing that she was a man, and how she was able to get married and sustain her facade. This required presenting first impressions of how she looked ("more like a teenage boy," "just like a man") and what she wore ("only a chocolate-colored pair of slacks and a purple t-shirt"), as well as alluding to her character ("Thai citizen who is a permanent resident in Malaysia," "used a false identity card," "detained in a squatter house," "paid a man RM75 to conceal her real identity and become her marriage witness," "tarnished the image of Islam," "the demonic son-in-law," "tricked her victim"). Specific mention was also made of the police finding "a dildo and a bottle of semen . . . in the house where the couple were staying" and of the registrar of marriages saying that perhaps this incident was "a sign that the world is coming to an end."

Once public curiosity had been sufficiently stirred, the press moved on to paint a picture of Azizah as a woman who had gone "wrong" and of Rohana as the helpless victim. This necessitated isolating Azizah and her actions from all around her, including her family, Rohana, and even the bought-off witness. Each one vehemently denied abetting the crime. The first person interviewed, Azizah's sister, publicly denounced Azizah's actions and implored her to repent and never repeat them. She claimed that from an early age Azizah had behaved like a boy, and despite advice by her family and neighbors to change her ways, she had never paid any heed. The sister also explained that she had been tricked into being at Azizah's wedding[14] but despite everything she would still accept her sister as part of the family after her release from prison.

Threatened with court action by Rohana's father, the witness also denied having anything to do with Azizah and said that he was even willing to testify in court that he had never taken money from her.[15] Instead of being an accomplice, he insisted that as soon as he had realized what was happening, he had gone straight to the *imam*'s house to reveal Azizah's real identity. For her part, Rohana professed that she had never suspected Azizah's true identity because from the time they first met Azizah had already assumed a male identity, and more important, she had never expected Azizah to betray her trust. In her interview headlined "I did not marry Azizah because I am a lesbian,"[16] Rohana—in her father's presence—admitted that although they had had intercourse[17] she had remained unaware that Azizah was a woman because not only was the room always dark, but also because the latter did not appear to have breasts and was always clothed in bed. The implication was that had she known better, she would not have been part of this entire wrongdoing. Yet in an unpublished interview (i.e., information never made publicly known), Azizah claims that she only married Rohana after the latter had issued an ultimatum to get married or to end the relationship.[18] In any case, after being portrayed as surviving an ordeal, Rohana was elevated to a martyrlike position, fit to caution other young women not to be tricked like she had been: "Let me alone suffer such a tragic fate." Little was made of the fact that it was Rohana's father and not she, who had publicly exposed Azizah and insisted that their marriage be annulled.

In large part the case continued to have a life in the news because of the press-generated responses. For instance, several religious leaders, whose opinions were solicited, were quoted as unanimously agreeing that women who married other women were still considered virgins because a real marriage could only take place between a man and a woman. Furthermore, they claimed that even though penetration with a dildo was not considered intercourse—perceived as "real" sex--what had taken place between Azizah and Rohana could still be deemed a *zina* (sex-related crime).[19] Following this, the chief *kadi* (religious judge) in Kelantan threatened to charge Azizah--even if she was already serving her sentence by the magistrate court--and all those involved in making it possible for the marriage to take place under *Shariah* laws. The PAS government,[20] although having failed earlier to implement *Hudud* laws, which would penalize women who have sex with other women,[21] now announced that the state government would tighten the Islamic Family Enactment to prevent marriages between women from recurring. All these actions not only demonstrate the importance religious fundamentalists place on virginity, but also the extent to which they will go to ensure that what they have constructed and defined as "woman" remains intact.

While the court was deciding on Rohana's father's application to annul the still legally recognized marriage, the press turned to presenting Azizah's side of the story. Already in prison for over a month, the first press encounter with Azizah was entitled "Azizah returns to womanhood." Citing the effect of her prison sentence in returning her to normality, Azizah was depicted as a feminine woman--complete with a *tudung* (headdress) who not only regretted her erroneous ways but even accepted the possibility of marrying again (to a man) in the future. When questioned about her motives for marrying Rohana, Azizah is quoted as saying that she did so out of love. She refuted the rumor that she had wanted to sell Rohana into prostitution once they were married.[22] Although she knew that what she was doing was unacceptable in Islam and in the eyes of the law, and that these would eventually catch up with her, she claims to have married Rohana to prevent the latter from "slipping through her hands into somebody else's." She pursued her ambition believing that this was an unavoidable "matter of the heart" and moreover, that "love would conquer all [difficulties]."

Subsequent prison interviews delved into her past to show that she was a "genuine woman" who had previously been married to a man and had a seven-year-old son. Her interest in being like a "tomboy" apparently surfaced after her marriage ended and when she decided that she would no longer allow herself to be supported by men. Instead, she resolved to have relationships with women. According to Azizah, even though they never discussed the matter, it was impossible for Rohana not to know that she was a woman.[23] Furthermore, the love she had with Rohana was mutual and another reason why she could not turn away was because the latter cared deeply for her. Azizah also highlighted the fact that "[feminine] women usually prefer tomboys because they do not ill-treat them but instead are always willing to support them financially and cater to their every wish."

One of the final news reports on this incident appeared as late as August 1997. Based on an interview with Azizah's mother, the article is written as a warning to parents on how important good guidance and a religious upbringing are for their child's future. Three points were highlighted. First, Azizah's mother's relief and hopes that her daughter had a chance of leading a "normal" life after her time in prison. Second, the revelation that Azizah's tomboyish characteristics emerged when she was being brought up by an aunt and not when she was with her mother. And third, that despite all her misdeeds, deep down Azizah was a good daughter who cared very much for her mother.

The Function of Media Discourse

The mass media in Malaysia are tightly controlled by the government so that "a direct form of mediation between the executive and the *rakyat* [the people]" is possible (Munro-Kua 1996:123). Bearing this in mind, and to get a better picture of the government's position on such matters, it is useful to further analyze how the media attempted to represent the case of Azizah and Rohana to the public. Specifically, I want to investigate more deeply why it gave so much publicity to Azizah and Rohana's marriage. How did they succeed in depicting Azizah as a "deviant" woman? I also wish to show that after a certain point the press attempted to "normalize" Azizah's actions. How did they do this and to what end?

The news reports on Azizah and Rohana's marriage had three main functions: first, depicting the abnormality of a woman who had dared to transgress sexual boundaries; second, to deter others from following suit, a message also had to be conveyed that such behavior was against the norms of femininity, the family, and religion; and third, her behavior had to be explained and Azizah herself had to be "normalized." In the first instance, spiced-up reports--focusing on her manly appearance and behavior as well as on her prison sentence--contributed to presenting a picture of unnaturalness and perversion. By airing critical voices--her sister, her lover, her mother, and religious leaders--all of whom deplored her actions, the message clearly stood out that such behavior would not be tolerated and certainly not accepted by the dominant discourses in society.

The ultimate success in showing her deviancy was dependent on setting Azizah apart as distinctly different from "good" Malaysians in general and from the "ideal" Malay woman in particular. To create an effective "Other," "us" versus "them" sentiments had to be generated. This was done, for example, by pointing out Azizah's Thai and lower-class origins. Against the archetypical affluent Malaysian, her foreign background and apparent lack of middle-class aspirations set Azizah apart as the "Other." By picturing her as a despicable woman who was willing to cheat on her family and society, and whose actions no one condoned, she and her shady character were further distanced from that of the "good" respectable Malaysians who, according to the discourse on Asian values, had strong morals and family values. The media obsession with her masculine appearance was also necessary to show how different she was from the "normal" woman. Far from the expected ideal, Azizah displayed all the characteristics that made her the polar opposite. She was masculine, not feminine; she displayed initiative, not obedience; and what is more, she was seen as bold and courageous enough to try and become a man.

However, once Azizah's actions had been firmly established as evil, there was a shift in the tone and angle of media reports. Around the time of her prison interviews, press reports became more sympathetic although no less righteous or moralistic. From here on it appears that there were attempts to "normalize" Azizah by searching for possible explanations for her actions. It was almost as though her character and wrongdoings had been sufficiently chastised, so now it was time to put together the pieces and reconstruct a woman who could lead a "normal" life again. Why else was it necessary to point out her transformation back into womanhood after a month in prison? What was the purpose in bringing up Azizah's failed marriage, or in trying to explain her marriage to Rohana as a ploy to sell the latter into prostitution? Why get her mother to tell the public that despite her stubborn ways, Azizah was essentially a filial child who cared for her elders?

Even mentioning Azizah's hopes of getting married (to a man) again and discarding her masculine ways—these were all attempts to paint a picture of potential "normality."

"Normalizing" Azizah

But what exactly was the purpose of trying to make Azizah appear "normal"? Marjorie Garber's discussion of the case of Billy Tipton, a married jazz musician who was discovered to be a woman upon his/her death provides some possible answers to this question. As in Azizah's case, there were attempts to normalize the story of Billy Tipton. According to Garber:

> This normalization of the story of the transvestite is all too typical of the way in which cross-dressing is treated, explained, and explained away, sometimes in very sophisticated and theoretically ingenious ways. Whatever discomfort is felt by the reader or audience is smoothed over and narrativized by a story that recuperates social and sexual norms, not only reinstating the binary (male/female) but also retaining, and encoding, a progress narrative: s/he did this in order to (a) get a job, (b) find a place in a man's world, and (c) realize or fulfill some deep but acceptable need in terms of personal destiny, in this case, by becoming a jazz musician. (1992:69)

Although never explicitly referred to as a transvestite, in Azizah's case it is clear that the media discourse sought to attribute her behavior to her misguided youth--robbed of her real mother's love--and her failed marriage, at the same time emphasizing the possibilities for her to discard her past and look forward to the future as a "normal" human being; essentially, the treatment of her actions was the same as in the case of Billy Tipton.

One can also see the relevance of Garber's argument that "cross-dressing can be 'fun' or 'functional' so long as it occupies a limited space and a temporary time period: after this . . . the cross-dresser is expected to resume life as he or she was, having, presumably, recognized the touch of 'femininity' or 'masculinity' in her or his otherwise 'male' or 'female' self'" (1992:70). In pointing out that her daughter used to work in all kinds of odd jobs to survive in her youth--including jobs that required her to be "like a man" and to carry heavy objects--Azizah's mother was trying to justify Azizah's masculine behavior so that even though cross-dressing as a man was certainly not "fun," at least for a period of time it was "functional" in Azizah's existence.

Whatever the justifications, one of the more important conclusions from the months of press coverage is that cross-dressing behavior, if it happens at all, should only be a passing phase. By publicizing that Azizah's male impersonation extended to the possession of a dildo,[24] the press conveyed the message that women can never be men--regardless of whether or not this was really Azizah's intention—because no matter how hard they try, they will never have the defining feature of manhood: a penis. Precisely because femininity and heterosexuality are assumed to be innate features of women, all other forms of "deviant" behavior that are attributed to an unfortunate past are meant to be temporary phenomena that can, and must, be corrected. In short, "deviancy" can be changed for the better if those guilty have the right guidance (e.g., Azizah in prison) and "good" family support. "Deviant" women can be "saved" after their "deviancy" is punished and rectified. Women who insist on going against the standard "ideal" are then cast as truly evil and unnatural, sources of societal disorder and decay. These are the women who deserve condemnation and prosecution.

Before concluding this section, I wish to briefly return to how Azizah's previous marriage was treated by the press. I think it is very significant that her first marriage was merely mentioned even though the reports claimed that this was because Azizah had refused to comment further on it. From the above-mentioned unpublished interview with Azizah in prison, I discovered that at the age of thirteen Azizah had eloped to Thailand to get married because she was pregnant. Not long after that she left her husband because of abuse (Alynn, July 22, 1997). Given this, I believe that the press did not persist in publicizing Azizah's previous marriage because it did not serve well as a picture of blissful heterosexual union that was meant to be the counterpoint to the "wrong" marriage Azizah had with Rohana.

Fauzi and Zakaria

At this juncture, it is also relevant to examine if there are similarities or differences between the way male and female cross-dressers are treated in Malaysia. In doing so, we might see if and how women's sexuality is differently regulated than that of men. Whether or not it was a coincidence, just over a month after Azizah was convicted by the magistrate court judge and two weeks before the Kelantan *Shariah* court finally decided to annul her marriage to Rohana, a similar incident was reported in the papers. This time however, the marriage was between two men in the neighboring state of Terengganu.

The offender was described as a fifteen-year-old, illiterate Malay shop assistant who had been brought up by a foster father. Like Azizah, Fauzi Yakub was originally from the south of Thailand and had been so successful in passing himself off as a woman that he purportedly had five previous marriage proposals. The same precision we saw in the description of Azizah's physical appearance was visible also when Fauzi was arrested (i.e., dressed in a red shirt and jeans and wearing a pair of women's shoes with two earrings in his left ear). Even though their offenses were slightly different,[25] similar charges with equivalent sentences were levied against both offenders since ultimately, the crime was that of transgressing sexual boundaries through cross-dressing.

Despite the parallels, there were several conspicuous differences between the two cases. First and foremost, the duration of Azizah and Rohana's media coverage stretched well over three months while Fauzi's lasted for five days. Basically, after Fauzi had been detained, newspaper coverage ceased. Furthermore, although the final verdict remains unclear to me[26] this in itself is a significant difference since in the case of Azizah, her crime and punishment were not only made clear from the beginning but also reiterated each time any reference to her case was made in the press. It is also interesting to note that just before his final arrest, Fauzi had already been picked up not once but twice by the police, and in both instances had been released again. Why were the cases handled differently?

Here I am not arguing that male "deviants"--cross-dressers, transvestites, or homosexuals--are necessarily treated better than their female counterparts. It is a well-known fact that in Malaysia male homosexuals have traditionally been more susceptible to government crackdowns against indecent behavior in public. This would explain why Fauzi was threatened with a penalty twice the magnitude of Azizah's although both he and she were prosecuted by their respective state religious authorities for behaving against the laws of Islam. However, the difference in treatment is better attributed to the fact that for so long women who do not conform to heterosexual norms have been made invisible in public discourses on female sexuality. This means that they have existed alongside their male counterparts but have never been regarded the same way. In comparison, even as male homosexuals and transvestites are being persecuted, to some extent they have continued to have more opportunities to lead public and visible lives.

Azizah's experience with the law shows that when women cross-dressers finally receive public recognition, immediate measures are taken to curb their "deviant" behavior because it directly challenges the reproduction of the "ideal" Malay woman. Female cross-dressing appears to be a greater threat than male cross-dressing because of the roles that have been assigned to women within their communities.[27] As agents of sexual morality and familial harmony, women are not meant to deviate from the norms of the "ideal" woman, which is seen as threatening the very identity of their community. In short, women's bodies and sexual behaviors need to be controlled more because of all the chaos unregulated female sexuality stands for.

On another level female cross-dressing is also problematic because women are not allowed to cross into the terrain of male privilege. The message conveyed by the press coverage when Azizah was jailed was meant as a warning to others like her to change their ways or risk being stigmatized, ostracized, and/or prosecuted. In a way, the increasing visibility of women like Azizah is a good thing as it questions how realistic the notion of the "ideal" woman is in society. But the problem is that as soon as Azizah's actions had made visible the lives of other women like her, stern measures were taken to outlaw such behavior on the part of females. When "deviant" women receive public acknowledgment of their existence, they are told that they have to become "normal," and measures to return them to "normality" are invoked. Taking the Johor state government's introduction of a new law that prohibits lesbian behavior[28]--hitherto unmentioned in any legal document—as an indicator, I believe that the episode of Azizah and Rohana has precipitated the start of more legal restrictions on the lives of women who transgress sexual and gender boundaries.

Still, it is important to note that not all female cross-dressers have been problematized. Azizah is far from being the only woman in her community to go against the norms of the "ideal" Malay woman. Many more women who dress in male clothes and adopt masculine characteristics can be found, especially in the urban areas throughout the country (Nur and A. R. 1996:72–74). Yet their existence has not been emphasized as a public menace the way Azizah's was. It would thus seem that there was something special in her case that warranted the intense public attention. I suggest that the dominant discourse on female sexuality barely tolerates masculine traits in women when they are limited to imitating male appearance and behavior, and even less so when this boundary is crossed. By assuming the male role in marriage, women like Azizah stand accused as having trespassed into the forbidden territory of heterosexual male privilege and in so doing are seen as challenging and rebelling against the laws of gender, the fundamental aspect of the social order.

The Significance of "Deviant" Women

So far, I have shown how "deviant" women are subjected to control and regulation through state-led discourses on female sexuality. To end the story on this note would be oversimplifying the complex relations at hand, unfairly negating women's experiences, and denying that they might have the ability to resist the power that is imposed on them. To see women like Azizah as helpless victims implies that ridding themselves of domination is not possible. Hence in this section I would like to propose that women "deviants" like Azizah are significant exactly because they are much more than victims of state regulation.

Whether or not the effect is intended, one of the most important aspects of cross-dressing "is the way in which it offers a challenge to easy notions of binarity, putting into question the categories of 'female' and 'male'" (Garber 1992:10, in Weeks 1995:108). Accepting that "definitive [gender] categorisation brings relief," the hostility Azizah provoked can be seen as a response to the unsettling ambivalence caused by her actions (Lau 1996:226). At the very least then, women like her are feared because they "mess up" gender identities and show them for what they really are: fluid and alterable.

However, these women are perceived as a threat as well because their actions also demonstrate that sexual identities, especially heterosexual ones, are extremely unstable. After all, if heterosexuality was as natural and permanent a condition as it is claimed to be, why then did one religious leader feel compelled to say that Azizah and Rohana had to be separated? What was the reason to fear a marriage between two women if such a concept cannot be real or exist? Alan Sinfield proposes that one way to explain this contradiction is to understand that heterosexuality's aggressiveness lies in its insecurity (1993:22, cited in Valentine 1996:148). Subsequently this insecurity takes shape in "regulatory regimes that constrain the possible performances of gender and sexual identities, in order to maintain the 'naturalness' of heterosexuality" (Valentine 1996:148).

As it stands, it is not easy for women to go against explicit norms of social behavior. However, more often than not, the norms controlling such behavior are implicit. Unless the norms are violated, they are unnoticed (Arthur 1993:68). Taking into account that "it is very much harder to question norms which are not articulated at all" (Hutter and Williams 1981:10), Azizah can be said to have done all women a service by exposing the controls that dictate the norms of the "ideal" woman. What the above also illustrates is that since forms of domination are diverse and contradictory, opportunities for resistance and change exist. Attempts to control and repress can produce the opposite effects (Weeks 1985:205). Women like Azizah, although defined as "unnatural" by the dominant discourse on female sexuality, are simultaneously empowered through their ability to name themselves, and this allows them to identify with others like themselves (Bland 1996:78), thus potentially sowing the seeds for greater social change.

By conflating biological sex with socially constructed gender, the official discourse on women's sexuality in Malaysia insists on certain characteristics and codes of behavior as the natural possession of all women. As stated, failure to comply means risking being labeled "abnormal" at best or, at worst, ostracized and jailed. However, while Azizah's persecution reveals the strength of the dominant discourse, she also promotes (as do women like her) a counterdiscourse that exposes how the naturalized category of "woman" is in fact socially constructed. In pointing to the performativity of gender, "strong" social constructivists like Judith Butler have correctly highlighted the instability of this category. Yet her assumption that all women who cross-dress are necessarily taking part in a parody disregards the fact that sometimes, especially in oppressive settings, cross-dressing is much too serious to be considered play. Women like Azizah, far from indulging in the parody of gender, do not always have the choice that Butler implies they have. Otherwise they would surely not pursue relationships with women, knowing full well the dire consequences of such actions.

If such women are persecuted for what they represent, it is essential that others take up the challenge to contest the dominant discourse. It would seem that nongovernmental organizations already working on issues of women's rights and/or questioning practices that stereotype women are in the best position to meet this challenge. However, their response was disappointing to say the least. As I have argued elsewhere (see Tan 1997), their silence throughout the duration of Azizah's case can be attributed to a range of factors, including fear of repercussions by the state, homophobia, and heterosexism. Whatever the reasons, it is more important to note that with the position Malaysian feminists took, the overall silence generated by the dominant discourse on Asian values was complete.

The imagining of the Malaysian nation in this decade has been done on and through women's bodies, and it is this that requires that women's sexuality be controlled. The inability to deal with the contradictions and pressures that have emerged between wanting to pursue policies of rapid economic growth on the one hand and presenting an image of Islamic correctness on the other, has contributed to a state-led discourse on Asian values that constructs a particular type of Malaysian woman to satisfy both demands.

This "ideal" Malaysian woman is expected to participate fully in efforts to build the nation, but at the same time she should never forget that her primary responsibility lies in the domain of the family. In turn, her assigned roles in society require her to possess certain traits. By claiming that femininity—the state of being passive, obedient, and subservient—are biologically determined, the dominant discourse on female sexuality promotes an essentialist perspective of gender that naturalizes these characteristics and idealizes them as the only way for Malaysian women to be. And because such characteristics and mannerisms are supposedly "natural," and by extension "good," any woman who does not live up to or, even worse, appears to have chosen to go against them, is stigmatized as abnormal and evil. This also means that it is easier to justify the persecution of such "deviant" women. Indeed, nationalist discourses may not always be reactionary and repressive, but the one formulated and articulated in Malaysia through the discourse on Asian values is problematic because by naturalizing women's roles and duties, it legitimizes control and domination of women.

On another level, it should also be recognized that the norm of the "ideal" woman is not always explicitly stated. Instead, it often operates unnoticed until its standards have been contravened. Such defiance, however, is immediately countered to insure further compliance. At least this is what my case study of Azizah and Rohana reveals. By disguising as a man and crossing into the terrain of male privilege by marrying her lover Rohana, Azizah showed how resistance and alternatives to the "ideal" woman are possible, that women are not just passive "victims" of discourses that control their sexuality but are able to act under their own power. However, such assertions are not well received by the dominant discourse. The high-handed treatment Azizah received can largely be attributed to the fact that her actions challenged the dominant definition of "woman." Both this and the way she was subsequently disciplined and expected to return to "normality" after rehabilitation showed that in the final analysis, the naturalized discourse on female sexuality is not all that "natural." Precisely because gender categories and roles are constructed by nationalist and fundamentalist discourses, they are open to change; this also means that it is even more important to invoke measures that will ensure its appearance of "naturalness."

Social construction theory is extremely useful in highlighting the fallibility of fixed gender identities. However, "stronger" social constructionist positions like Judith Butler's, which view gender as performance, cannot adequately explain why Azizah took the risk of impersonating a man knowing full well the repercussions that would ensue. Although by subverting existing gender categories she destabilized the dominant discourse's construction of "woman," in the repressive circumstances of her "performance," Azizah's "doing" masculinity cannot be simply seen as just a "performance." Remembering that she herself claimed that she cross-dressed to pursue her desires,

it is obvious that for her drag was a sign of desperation and much more serious than parodying gender. It is this inability of Butler's position to explain
the persistence of bodily desires that leads me to conclude that further research into this matter is still necessary.

NOTES

This essay is a shortened version of a research paper written for the Women and
Development programme at the Institute of Social Studies (ISS) in The Hague,
The Netherlands. It has benefited greatly from the comments of my supervisor,
Saskia Wieringa, as well as from the encouragement and financial support pro-
vided by the Women's Development Collective (WDC), Malaysia, and the
Frauen Anstiftung (FAS), Germany.

1. See also Sayyid (1997) and Nederveen Pieterse (1994).

2. Out of a population of 20 million, half of whom are women, 61 percent are
*bumiputera*s (literally meaning "princes of the soil"), a term referring to Malays
and indigenous tribal people of the peninsula and the states of Sabah and
Sarawak, 30 percent are Chinese, and 8 percent are Indians while the remaining
one percent of the population are minority ethnic groups (Arabs, Eurasians, Sin-
halese, and Portuguese, among others) (Gomez 1996:1). The right of the non-
Malay populace to hold their respective religious beliefs is also enshrined in the
Federal Constitution.

3. See Barraclough (1985) and Case (1995) for details.

4. Calling the same phenomenon the "Pan-Asian rhetoric," Miyume Tanji
and Stephanie Lawson write that it all began when a number of political leaders
in Asia used "selected cultural symbols to construct an overarching 'Asian identity'" (1997:146). Indeed, this discourse is not restricted to Malaysia and has been
put to similar use in other Asian nations, e.g., Singapore.

5. The prime minister also often uses the same rhetoric to explain how the
West has come to "be riddled with single-parent families which foster incest,
with homosexuality, with cohabitation, with unrestrained avarice, with disre-
spect for others and, of course, with rejection of religious teachings and values"
(quoted in "East Meets West" 1995:42).

6. By emphasizing the need to inculcate values that prioritize harmony, consensus, community, and the family, national leaders who invoke the Asian values
rhetoric have been able to justify their authoritarianism as *the* Asian brand of
democracy (Tanji and Lawson 1997:147).

7. In some cases, whether or not a woman is a virgin determines the bride-
price she commands when getting married. For instance, at the time of this writing, Banks claimed that the bride-price for a virgin could be at least eight times
more than that for a previously married woman (1983:94).

8. This usually takes the form of head-scarves or mini-*telekungs*: a headdress

comprising a veil or shawl that hides a woman's hair, neck, and shoulders but leaves the face uncovered (Rudie 1994:312).

9. This is not the same as saying that Malay women are powerless, especially since in many instances wives have an important say in the major decisions made in the household (Banks 1983:96).

10. It is said that Malay *adat* provides women with "a keen sense of independence, mobility, entrepreneurship and (with seniority and age) prestige," but this is countered by the influence of Islam, which when formulated in a patriarchal and fundamentalistic form, results in Malay women being subject to increasing domination by men (Karim 1995:44).

11. For instance the status of a male head of household in Indonesian batik-producing areas does not derive from the amount of income he brings into the family but rather from the occupation he has. If he were a servant of the royal court, earning virtually nothing, his status would still be higher than that of his money-earning and batik-producing wife (personal communication of Saskia Wieringa).

12. The following account and analysis are based on the reports featured in three main daily newspapers: the *Berita Harian* (BH) and *Utusan Malaysia* (UM), two Malay newspapers that dominate the Malay readers market, and *The Star*, which is widely read among the English-speaking middle class. Almost all of the twenty-six reports on the case of Azizah and Rohana (*Star* seven, UM nine, and BH ten) and the additional eleven reports in relation to the case of Fauzi and Zakaria (*Star* five, UM three, and BH three), were published between December 21, 1996 and March 6, 1997. The final article I located on the former episode was published on August 4, 1997.

13. On the first count, out of a maximum sentence of seven years' imprisonment she was sentenced to twenty-four months, and the second, out of a maximum two years imprisonment, she received another three months. The presiding judge instructed that the prison sentences be served concurrently.

14. Initially, Azizah's sister denied having any knowledge of the wedding but later confessed that she had been there and was the one who placed the wedding ring on Rohana's finger (!).

15. He maintained that he was merely the taxi driver who had taken Azizah to the *imam*'s house and had agreed to be her witness only because she had approached him as a customer.

16. Most likely this reference to lesbianism was made since the previous day the Grand *Imam* of the National Mosque had accused Azizah and Rohana of having had a lesbian relationship, which was strictly forbidden by Islam.

17. She actually tried to qualify her statement by saying that because she was a virgin, she was not able to tell otherwise, i.e., she would not really have known if what she experienced was intercourse or not.

18. According to the same source (Alynn, July 22, 1997), after having been together for eight years, Azizah found herself in a bind when Rohana told her that because of family pressure they either had to get married or end their relationship.

19. However, it would fall under the classification of a sexual offence involving other bodily parts (e.g., hands) or other sex implements (e.g., dildos).

20. Out of thirteen states, Kelantan is the only one governed by an opposition Islamic party, PAS, that has had a history of mass appeal in the predominantly rural Malay east coast region (where Kelantan is located).

21. In 1993 the PAS government enacted the Islamic *Hudud* laws, but the implementation of these laws has been stalled by the federal government. Under clause 19 of part 1 *Hudud* offenses, the "act of sexual gratification between females by rubbing the vagina of one against that of the other" would have been considered an offense (cited in Ismail 1995:116–117).

22. "Why else" she asks "would I have saved RM10,000 as the payment for the bride-price?"

23. "I know she realized I was a woman. How could she not when I used to *mandi berkemban* [a method of bathing with a piece of cloth tied just above a woman's breasts in order to cover her body]?" asked Azizah. Moreover, she maintains that Rohana used to caress her body.

24. The report that quoted Azizah as saying that she had to obtain a dildo because she realized that to be a "husband" she would need to be a "complete" man, i.e., with a penis, reinforces the myth that sex between women has to involve dildos or "penile substitutes" because such women are really pseudomen (Richardson 1992:192).

25. Unlike Azizah, Fauzi never succeeded in marrying his lover since his plans were abandoned after his disguise was discovered.

26. After Fauzi's arrest I was unable to locate any more references to this case in the newspaper websites on the internet. I realize that this may not necessarily mean that there were no more reports on the case, but I find it also a significant contrast to the media exposure Azizah received.

27. Michael Peletz has suggested that in traditional Malay society men who cross gender boundaries (*pondan*) are more tolerated and accepted than female cross-dressers (1996:120, 123).

28. The law is included under the Johor state's *Shariah* Criminal Offenses Enactment 1997 and imposes a RM5000 fine, six strokes of the *rotan* (whip), or a jail sentence of up to three years, or any combination of the penalties upon conviction. It is also applicable to others categorized as sex offenders under this law: prostitutes, pimps, and those who have sexual intercourse outside wedlock (*Star Online*, "Department to can sex offender," June 8, 1997; http://www.jaring.my/~Estar).

REFERENCES

Alynn (anon.). Personal communication, E-mail reply to query from author, July 22, 1997.

Anderson, Benedict. 1987. *Imagined Communities: Reflections on the Origin and Spread of Nationalism.* London: Verso.

Arthur, Linda Boynton. 1993. "Clothing, Control, and Women's Agency: The Mitigation of Patriarchal Power." In Sue Fisher and Kathy Davis, eds., *Negotiating at the Margins: The Gendered Discourses of Power and Resistance.*, pp. 66–84. New Brunswick: Rutgers University Press.

Banks, David J. 1983. *Malay Kinship.* Philadelphia: Institute for the Study of Human Issues.

Barraclough, Simon. 1985. "Malaysia in 1985: A Question of Management." *Southeast Asian Affairs* 1985:185–207.

Bland, Lucy. 1996. "The Shock of the Freewoman Journal: Feminists Speaking on Heterosexuality in Early Twentieth-Century England." In Jeffrey Weeks and Janet Holland, eds., *Sexual Cultures: Communities, Values, and Intimacy*, pp. 75–96. London: Macmillan Press.

Bloom, William. 1990. *Personal Identity, National Identity, and International Relations.* Cambridge: Cambridge University Press.

Butler, Judith. 1993. *Bodies that Matter: On the Discursive Limits of "Sex."* New York: Routledge.

Case, William. 1995. "Malaysia: Aspects and Audiences of Legitimacy." In Muthiah Alagappa, ed., *Political Legitimacy in Southeast Asia: The Quest for Moral Authority*, pp. 69–107. Stanford: Stanford University Press.

Doi, Abdur Rahman I. 1990. *Women in Shariah.* 3d ed. Kuala Lumpur: F. S. Noordee.

"East Meets West." 1995. "Inside Story." (Book Excerpt) *Asiaweek* 8:40–43.

Evans, Harriet. 1997. *Women and Sexuality in China: Dominant Discourses of Female Sexuality and Gender Since 1949.* London: Polity Press.

Foucault, Michel. 1978. *The History of Sexuality.* Vol. 1, *An Introduction.* Trans. Robert Hurley. London: Penguin Books.

Garber, Marjorie. 1992. *Vested Interests: Cross-Dressing and Cultural Anxiety.* London: Penguin.

Gerami, Shalin. 1996. *Women and Fundamentalism: Islam and Christianity.* New York and London: Garland.

Gomez, Edmund Terence. 1996. "Privatised Patronage: The Economics and Politics of Privatisation in Malaysia." Unpublished manuscript, Department of East Asian Studies, University of Leeds.

Guibernau, Montserrat. 1996. *Nationalisms: The Nation-State and Nationalism in the Twentieth Century.* Cambridge: Polity Press.

Hardacre, Helen. 1993. "The Impact of Fundamentalisms on Women, the Family, and Interpersonal Relations." In Martin E. Marty and R. Scott Appleby, eds., *Fundamentalisms and Society: Reclaiming the Sciences, the Family, and Education*, pp. 129–150. Chicago: University of Chicago Press.

Heng, Geraldine. 1997. "A Great Way to Fly: Nationalism, the State, and the Varieties of Third-World Feminism." In M. Jacqui Alexander and Chandra Talpade Mohanty, eds., *Feminist Genealogies, Colonial Legacies, Democratic Futures*, pp. 30–45. New York: Routledge.

Hutter, Bridget and Gillian Williams. 1981. "Controlling Women: The Normal and the Deviant." In Bridget Hutter and Gillian Williams, eds., *Controlling Women: The Normal and the Deviant*, pp. 9–39. London: Croom Helm.

Ismail, Rose, ed. *Hudud in Malaysia: The Issues at Stake*. Kuala Lumpur: SIS Forum.

Karim, Wazir Jahan. 1995. "Bilateralism and Gender in Southeast Asia." In Wazir Jahan Karim, ed., *"Male" and "Female" in Developing Southeast Asia*, pp. 35–74. Oxford/Washington, D.C.: Berg.

Lau, Gail Ching-Liang. 1996. *White Skins/Black Masks: Representation and Colonialism*. London: Routledge.

Lie, Merete and Ragnhild Lund. 1994. *Renegotiating Local Values: Working Women and Foreign Industry in Malaysia*. Richmond: Curzon Press.

Manderson, Lenore. 1980. *Women, Politics, and Change: The Kaum Ibu UMNO Malaysia, 1945–1972*. Kuala Lumpur: Oxford University Press.

Marty, Martin E. and R. Scott Appleby. 1993. "Introduction." In Martin E. Marty and R. Scott Appleby, eds., *Fundamentalisms and the State: Remaking Politics, Economics, and Militance*, pp. 1–9. Chicago and London: University of Chicago Press.

McClintock, Anne. 1995. *Imperial Leather: Race, Gender, and Sexuality in the Colonial Context*. New York and London: Routledge.

Mernissi, Fatima. 1996. *Women's Rebellion and Islamic Memory*. London: Zed Books.

Munro-Kua, Anne. 1996. *Authoritarian Populism in Malaysia*. London: Macmillan Press.

Nagata, Judith. 1994. "How to be Islamic Without Being an Islamic State: Contested Models of Development in Malaysia." In Akbar S. Ahmed and Hastings Donnan, eds., *Islam, Globalization, and Postmodernity*, pp. 63–90. London and New York: Routledge.

——. 1995. "Modern Malay Women and the Message of the 'Veil.'" In Wazir Jahan Karim, ed., *"Male" and "Female" in Developing Southeast Asia*, pp. 101–120. Oxford/Washington, D.C.: Berg.

Nederveen Pieterse, Jan. 1994. "Fundamentalism Discourses: Enemy Images." In *Women Against Fundamentalism*, pp. 2–6. London:WAF.

Nur, Rais and A. R. 1996. "Queering the State: Towards a Lesbian Movement in Malaysia." In Monika Reinfelder, ed., *Amazon to Zami: Towards a Global Lesbian Feminism*, pp. 70–86. London: Cassell.

Ong, Aihwa. 1990. "State Versus Islam: Malay Families, Women's Bodies, and the Body Politic in Malaysia." *American Ethnologist* 17 (2): 258–276.

——. 1994. "Colonialism and Modernity: Feminist Re-presentations of Women in Non-Western Societies." In Anne C. Herrmann and Abigail J. Stewart, eds., *Theorizing Feminism: Parallel Trends in the Humanities and Social Sciences*, pp. 372–381. Boulder: Westview Press.

Papanek, Hanna. 1994. "The Ideal Woman and the Ideal Society: Control and Autonomy in the Construction of Identity." In Valentine M. Moghadam, ed., *Identity Politics and Women: Cultural Reassertions and Feminisms in International Perspective*, pp. 42–75. Boulder: Westview Press.

Parker, Andrew, Mary Russo, Doris Sommer, and Patricia Yaeger. 1992. "Introduction." In Andrew Parker, Mary Russo, Doris Sommer, and Patricia Yaeger, eds., *Nationalism and Sexualities*, pp. 1–18. New York: Routledge.

Peletz, Michael. 1996. *Reason and Passion: Representations of Gender in a Malay Society*. Berkeley: University of California Press.

Pettman, Jan J. 1996. *Worlding Women: A Feminist International Politics*. London: Routledge.

Rich, Adrienne. 1983. "Compulsory Heterosexuality and Lesbian Existence." In Ann Snitow, Christine Stansell, and Sharon Thompson, eds., *Powers of Desire: The Politics of Sexuality*, pp. 177–205. New York: Monthly Review Press.

Richardson, Dianne. 1992. "Constructing Lesbian Sexualities." In Ken Plummer, ed., *Modern Homosexualities: Fragments of Lesbian and Gay Experience*. London: Routledge.

Rudie, Ingrid. 1993. "A Hall of Mirrors: Autonomy Translated Over Time in Malaysia." In Dianne Bell, Pat Caplan, and Wazir Jahan Karim, eds., *Gendered Fields: Women, Men, and Ethnography*, pp. 103–116. London: Routledge.

——. 1994. *Visible Women in East Coast Malay Society: On the Reproduction of Gender in Ceremonial, School, and Market*. Oslo: Scandinavian University Press.

Saghal, Gita and Nira Yuval Davis, eds. 1992. *Refusing Holy Orders: Women and Fundamentalism in Britain*. London: Virago Press.

——. 1994. "The Uses of Fundamentalism." In *Women Against Fundamentalism*, pp. 7–9. London: WAF.

Sayyid, Bobby S. 1997. *A Fundamental Fear: Eurocentrism and the Emergence of Islamism*. London and New York: Zed Press.

Seda-Poulin, Maria Luisa. 1993. "Islamization and Legal Reform in Malaysia: The Hudud Controversy." *Southeast Asian Affairs* 1993:224–242.

Sharp, Joanne P. 1996. "Gendering Nationhood: A Feminist Engagement with National Identity." In Nancy Duncan, ed., *Bodyspace: Destabilizing Geographies of Gender and Sexuality*, pp. 87–108. London: Routledge.

Sisters in Islam. 1993. "Of Dress and Muslim Women." *Islam, Gender, and Women's Rights: An Alternative View*, p. 80. Kuala Lumpur: SIS Forum.

Stacey, Jackie. 1991. "Promoting Normality: Section 28 and the Regulation of Sexuality." In Sarah Franklin, Celia Lury, and Jackie Stacey, eds., *Off-Centre: Feminism and Cultural Studies*, pp. 284–304. London: Harper Collins Academic.

Tan, beng hui. 1997. "Dressing Like a Man: The Discourse on Asian Values and the Regulation of Women's Sexuality." Master's thesis, Institute of Social Studies, The Hague.

Tanji, Miyume and Stephanie Lawson. 1997. "'Democratic Peace' and 'Asian Democracy': A Universalist-Particularist Tension." *Alternatives* 22:135–155.

Valentine, Gill. 1996. "(Re)negotiating The 'Heterosexual Street': Lesbian Productions of Space." In Nancy Duncan, ed., *Bodyspace: Destabilizing Geographies of Gender and Sexuality*, pp. 146–155. London: Routledge.

Vance, Carole. 1989. "Social Construction Theory: Problems in the History of Sexuality." In Dennis Altman et al., eds., *Homosexuality, Which Homosexuality?*, pp. 13–34. London: GMP Publishers.

Weedon, Chris. 1997. *Feminist Practice and Poststructuralist Theory*. 2d ed. London: Blackwell.

Weeks, Jeffrey. 1985. *Sexuality and Its Discontents: Meanings, Myths, and Modern Sexualities*. London: Routledge and Kegan Paul.

——. 1995. *Invented Moralities: Sexual Values in an Age of Uncertainty*. Cambridge: Polity Press.

Yuval-Davis, Nira. 1997. *Gender and Nation*. London: Sage Publications.

13

Norma Mogrovejo

Sexual Preference, the Ugly Duckling of Feminist Demands: The Lesbian Movement in Mexico

Analyzing the history of the Mexican lesbian movement is no simple task. The political dynamics of Latin America are heterogeneous, varied, and changing. They are mixed with elements of Catholicism, authoritarian regimes, exclusive political systems, and a truncated modernization. All this is linked to a multicultural society, ethnic pluralism, growing economic crisis, and poverty. This creates a mosaic that is difficult to assemble. Nonetheless, the principal problem that we face in attempting to analyze the history of the lesbian movement in Mexico is not solely based on the complexity of political dynamics but also on the difficulty of finding the right pieces of the puzzle.

The lack of opportunity to publish and the virtual absence of archives makes recording the movement's history all the more difficult. It has been preserved in an oral tradition that is lost when it is forgotten or denied. The few that manage to organize themselves and develop a political consciousness with respect to their identity lead a semiclandestine existence for fear of reprisals from family and colleagues. For this reason throughout the history of the lesbian movement in Latin America there have been few lesbians who have declared their sexuality openly and have come out publicly.

It is because of this that the task of rewriting the history of the lesbian movement in Latin America is not only a historical, anthropological, sociological, or political task, it is also an archaeological task. It implies reconstruction of personal archives, which may have been destroyed or are on the verge of disappearing. Hence the importance of the oral stories of the protagonists, some of whom we have already lost (such as Nancy Cárdenas in

1993). We have the historical obligation to save these stories in order to understand our own history.

Gay, Feminist, and Lesbian Movements: Between Equality and Difference

The Latin American feminist movement began in the 1970s in most countries. The United Nations and its development programs after 1975, when the First World Conference for Women was held in Mexico City, provided an institutional impulse. Feminism was an important influence on the gay and lesbian movements because it started the debate on issues such as sexuality and reproduction. We can, however, assert that there was reciprocal influence.

The biannual Latin American and Caribbean feminist conferences that took place in different countries led—initially with some difficulty—to the discussion of the subject of sexual preference, as one of the conflicts the feminist movement had to take on. This made room for a generation of new autonomous groups of lesbians and the appearance of feminist discourse within mixed homosexual groups. Some of these groups, which had analyzed sexual preference from a purely gay standpoint, introduced a gender perspective into their analysis and called themselves lesbian/gay. Furthermore, some political parties, principally those with Trotskyite tendencies, were taken with this new political presence and gave both theoretical and militant support to the homosexual struggle.

The presence of lesbians and the lesbian movement in Latin American political life has been intrinsically linked to gay and feminist struggles, principally to the latter, due mainly to the lack of a distinct lesbian theory that could guide an autonomous militant activity and also because feminism gave the lesbian movement a space in which to work and survive. Many feminist lesbians who have done lesbian or hetero-feminist work in the feminist movement have preferred to back hetero-feminist demands, believing that these include lesbian ones too. This has reinforced a profound, internalized lesbophobia in the feminist movement, an issue that will be explored in this essay.

The lesbian movement in Latin America developed in three distinct historical phases. These were closely linked to the three theoretical positions posited by the European feminist movement. Despite belonging to different historical moments, these positions are not in opposition to one another but coexist and mutually reinforce each other in the context of ongoing feminist debate (Kristeva 1981; Golubov 1993). The three theoretical positions are

1. Women demand equal access to the symbolic order. Liberal feminism. Equality or the moment of universality.
2. Women reject the masculine symbolic order in the name of difference. Radical feminism. The search for the "feminine essence."
3. Women reject the difference between what is masculine and what is feminine as metaphysics (Moi 1987).

This essay studies the Mexican case in the context of these theoretical positions. I will consider the Mexican lesbian movement as it relates to the gay movement, the feminist movement, and as an autonomous movement within the above-mentioned positions.

Gays and Lesbians in Search of Equality

The first generation of feminists aspired to win a place in history. They fought to integrate themselves into the logic and values of the dominant rationale, that of the nation-state. In Europe these feminists were mainly the suffragettes. In the Latin American context the second wave of feminism appeared in the 1970s,[1] together with the "new left," in the form of rebellious middle-class women who questioned the traditional molds. Most were intellectuals who—inspired by the philosophy of modernism—demanded universality and equality for women. This would allow women to become social subjects and would signify the first step toward neutralizing sexual difference (Vargas 1991).

The rise of homosexual organizations fighting for their political and civil rights in the beginning of the 1970s was closely connected to the struggles of the Latin American Left against capitalism and imperialism and for social justice, the transformation of the social system, and the "socialist fatherland." For homosexuals the goal of social change was the transformation of social relations and acceptance of sexual preference as a political right. In their search for universality and equality, lesbian organizations were initially formed within homosexual groups, hence one of their first slogans was "socialism without sexism." The significant participation of feminist lesbians led to a change in the movement's name from "Movement for Homosexual Liberation" to "Movement for Lesbian-Homosexual Liberation," a movement characterized by feminist and socialist discourse.

During its infancy the Mexican homosexual liberation movement was influenced by the events of 1968,[2] the radicalization of youth, and the incidents of Stonewall, all of which resonated in the consciousness of Mexican homosexuals. The history of the Mexican homosexual movement goes back to 1971. On August 15, 1971, a group of students and artists who took part in the movement of 1968 formed the Mexican Homosexual Liberation Front, a pioneering gay and lesbian organization that served as a training ground for the future leaders of the Mexican gay and lesbian movement.

One of the most important events in the history of the movement was Nancy Cárdenas's participation in a television broadcast. At the end of January 1973 a North American man accused the Nixon government of dismissing him from the civil service simply because he was gay. Nancy Cárdenas was invited to take part in a television program that enjoyed the highest viewing rates in Mexico. The program discussed the equality of homosexuals, their legal position, their systematic persecution and repression, and the distorted view psychoanalysis and psychiatry have of homosexuality. The interview, as one of the first serious attempts by the mass media to deal with homosexuality, had a great impact on the national consciousness in general and on homosexuals in particular. It provided the greatest impulse for the creation of an organized mass homosexual movement.

The Homosexual Liberation Front lasted approximately a year and a half, and until 1978 a variety of men's, women's, and mixed groups openly showed their adherence to feminist and socialist causes. Lesbos, the first lesbian organization in Mexico, was set up in 1977 and experienced persecution by both the police and the feminist movement. The experiences of Yan María Castro with the Coalition of Women and of Luz María Medina in a bar paved the way for this to happen.

> In the coalition I realized that the demands that were being fought for responded only to the needs of heterosexual women. When I said to them "I'm a lesbian," they found it very shocking. At first they said to me: "We love you very much anyway." Or they would say: "It is OK for you to be like that. We respect all women here. But maybe it is best if you do not make this known to the outside world." I got in touch with Cristina, another lesbian feminist. We both wanted to get the first lesbian group underway, but we had no means to do it and no idea how. We had no methodology and had no theoretical material to support us. We did not know where to find lesbians. We thought we were the only Mexican lesbians in the entire country.[3]

> I went to "Topo," a gay bar close to the Revolutionary Monument also frequented by heterosexuals. There was a raid at about eight o'clock at night. Uniformed and judicial police arrived and behaved in a violent manner. They used tear gas in the bar. I was near the entrance when they burst in. Those of us who were on the edges managed to get out, but we did not run away. We saw from afar how the police were beating people and were taking them away, mainly men but also some lesbians and one or two heterosexual couples. Those of us outside protested, and as we were uncertain as to what would happen, we agreed to meet in "Sanborns" in Aguascalientes.[4]

The feminist movement was the closest reference point for the women from Lesbos. They attempted to join it as a lesbian-feminist group.

> We got in touch with other lesbians in the Coalition of Women, but they were not prepared to fight for lesbian causes. We learnt that often our worst enemies were lesbian feminists who were not openly lesbian and who fought from inside the closet. One of the leaders of the coalition who is a known lesbian was our strongest opponent. She put forward a theory as to why it was not convenient for lesbians as a group to be present within the coalition. We kept quiet as we lacked the documentation, the means, and the theoretical base for a political analysis to establish our cause. We even felt guilty about forming a lesbian group. Some asked us why we wanted to be apart and told us we should stay together with them. Others said that it was good that we lesbians were together because this meant we were separated from them. Others again believed that it was dangerous politically that we should get together because then we would insist that we be included in other feminist organizations. We were unable to enter the Coalition of Women as a group and always remained isolated and apart.[5]

After this, relations with the feminist movement became strained because of an internalized lesbophobia, both on the part of heterosexual feminists and of closet lesbians, and because of a permanent demand on the part of lesbians for the recognition of their existence as lesbians within the feminist movement and the recognition of their demands as feminist demands.

In its work for consciousness-raising and self-affirmation, Lesbos asserted the need for a "coming out of the closet." This was one of the central aspects of the lesbian movement and implied a transformation into an organization showing its real face to society. For a majority of the members the risk was seen as too great, and this lead to a split and the formation of OIKABETH.

The name OIKABETH comes from the Mayan words *Olling Iskan Katuntat Bebeth Thot*, which mean "movement of warrior women who open the way and scatter flowers." This group was initially formed in close association with the gay group FHAR but soon went its separate way, due to the misogynist attitudes of the latter.

> We split and formed OIKABETH as part of FHAR, but we only lasted about four months. A homosexual man from the group Black Butterflies assaulted us verbally: "You stupid, useless macho women, soon we will no longer need women, not even in order to reproduce, thanks to technological developments." We were very angry and Luz María said: "we need to be an autonomous group." We then separated from FHAR and formed an au-

tonomous lesbian group called OIKABETH. Then the "traveling women" started to arrive, many women (up to sixty) from Europe and the USA. It was a movement of women who traveled the world, especially the third world, in the 1970s, as part of the hippie experience. They brought with them a strain of European and American radical feminism which we absorbed. Apart from being radical lesbians they were separatists and OIKABETH became a very radical separatist group.[6]

Subsequently a variety of lesbian groups came into existence. OIKABETH gave way to "Socialist Lesbians," "Marxist-Leninist Seminar of Feminist Lesbians," "Ambar" and others, which were generally set up by Yan María Castro.

The participation of lesbians in the homosexual movement was very important. Their double militancy in the feminist movement encouraged the discussion of gender issues with male homosexuals. The first public appearance of the lesbian and gay movement took place on July 26, 1978. A small contingent of some thirty homosexuals made Mexican gay history by joining a public demonstration. Militant members of FHAR took part in a commemorative march to celebrate the Cuban revolution. Following this, in mid-August, *Lambda*, FHAR, and OIKABETH took part together in the march to commemorate the tenth anniversary of October 2.[7] The demonstrators made a public statement of their sexuality and supported the predicament of the politically "disappeared."

In 1979 the lesbian-homosexual movement organized its first important event: the first Gay Pride March. The organization of the march highlighted the divisions between FHAR and Lambda as to the character the march should adopt. Should the march, as a tactical move, take on board the stereotypical characterization of homosexuals? FHAR felt that this would be the most radical way to change the sexist beliefs about gays and the image that people had of them. Lambda, on the other hand, believed that a demonstration along these lines would play into the hands of the oppressive dominant ideology. This conflict was the beginning of an irreconcilable difference that created two currents within the lesbian-homosexual movement. FHAR prioritized work among the more marginalized sectors such as transvestites, *tibiris*—men who attend popular parties where transvestites are present—and bar homosexuals, who were known as the "lumpen proletariat." Lambda took a more traditional political stance, even going as far as identifying with the opposition party PRT. In spite of the differences, approximately one thousand homosexuals and lesbians participated in the march.

The second march in 1980, the largest in the history of the lesbian-homosexual movement, developed into a political celebration. Between five and seven thousand people took part with the support of left-wing political organizations. With hundreds of colored balloons, violet flags, and posters bearing the message "neither sick nor criminal, merely gay," the demonstrators demanded an end to illegal raids and condemned the abuse of homosexuals and transvestites.

There was a lot of political activity that year. Public demonstrations took place outside the Cuban and Iranian embassies, denouncing the sexist policies of these countries. The lesbian-homosexual movement was also involved in various conferences, congresses, and publications. The results of all this activity soon became visible. The left-wing organizations began to soften their opposition to the lesbian-homosexual movement as their struggle transformed itself into an attractive movement that had the possibility of mass appeal.

The preparations for the third Gay Pride March in 1981 were initially held back somewhat by the reluctance of the authorities to grant the necessary permits. Despite police intimidation, two thousand people took part in the march under the slogan "Like it or not, we are here to stay!" There were contingents from Oaxaca, Veracruz, Aguascalientes, Toluca, Puebla, and Ciudad Nezahualcoyotl. With slogans such as "Workers' rights for homosexuals," "Sexual freedom for all," "Fight, fight, fight for the freedom to love" and "Lesbians and homosexuals are everywhere," lesbians and homosexuals asserted their existence.

During the rally, FHAR called for scientific and objective sex education in schools in order to demystify homosexuality and teach children about alternative sexuality. Lambda questioned the labeling of homosexuals and lesbians as either sick or immoral, introducing a new concept of love, while OIKABETH warned against the march becoming an established annual tradition, stating that it should instead form part of a movement for democratic renewal. The socialist lesbians asserted the impossibility of forming a revolutionary movement and of bringing about change in society without an accompanying sexual revolution. During this third march speeches were also given by the well-known politician Mrs. Rosario Ibarra de Piedra, representatives of the FNCR, feminist groups, and left-wing individuals.

Although the atmosphere was positive, the various lesbian and gay groups began to feel the effects of the crisis in their ranks. Members were beginning to feel disenchanted as the movement proved incapable of providing answers and viable alternatives to their followers. The groups recognized the low level of consciousness among the militants and the lack of internal solidarity. This crisis led to several groups leaving FHAR to make way for various autonomous cultural and discussion groups.

Homosexuals Enter the Electoral Campaign

In 1982 there were presidential elections in Mexico. Lesbians and homosexuals gave their support to Rosario Ibarra, the PRT candidate and first female presidential candidate in the history of Mexico. They formed the National Coalition of Lesbians and Homosexuals aimed at setting up a Lesbian and Homosexual Committee in Support of Rosario Ibarra (CLHARI). This group formed an alliance with the PRT and put up seven gay candidates for district offices in Mexico City, Guadalajara, and Colima. This historic event had considerable impact on society and led to an increase in the political credibility of the movement. CLHARI fought a strong campaign within the gay community under the motto "Don't vote for your exploiters." Although none of the candidates in the election won a seat, the campaign was seen as a success because it provided the lesbian-homosexual movement with mass media coverage of its new image.

The fourth Gay Pride March in 1982 took place under the shadow of the unfolding electoral campaign. It was, nonetheless, a mass event with groups from Puebla, Guadalajara, and Colima and included delegations from Christian groups such as Fidelity and the United Fraternity of Churches. The march demanded an end to the national macho culture, social marginalization, police corruption, and sexual harassment of homosexuals in the workplace and in society at large. It also called for nonsexist sex education, an end to sensationalist media coverage and discrimination in general, and demanded employment and housing. It also called for the arrest of the murderers of two homosexuals in Colima and the release of two comrades who, under torture, had admitted to being guilty of the crime.

Until that time the political parties had not felt the need to take a stance on the issue of homosexuality and sexual freedom, but this changed following the CLHARI campaign. The widespread mobilization of the lesbian-homosexual movement forced the political parties to make statements on these issues. For example, during the Nineteenth Congress of the Mexican Communist Party, the Communists decided to give their support to the homosexual struggle and the ideal of sexual liberty: "each individual must have the right to realize their sexuality as they best understand it, to make free use of their body and to claim pleasure as a human attribute, without legal, political or moral pressures" ("Sexualidad y Política" 1989).

The fifth Gay Pride March on June 26, 1983, was badly affected by the political differences within the movement, and it split into two distinct processions. The first section was organized around the defense of civil and political rights for homosexuals and was led by groups from Lambda, OIKABETH, Guadalajara Gay Pride Group (GOHL), Fidelity, and contingents from the provinces and the Mexican Institute of Sexology. The second section was a politico-carnival procession, headed by a group of transsexuals, the Lesbian and Homosexual Network, autonomous groups, and the LHOCA network. The march ended in a rally denouncing violence against transvestites and calling for an end to raids (Fratti and Batista 1984).

The Difference Between the Masculine and the Feminine: The Fight Against Phallocentrism and Misogyny

By 1984 both OIKABETH and Lambda were worn out though still active to some extent. They called for the organization of a sixth march, the last of this first phase. The march was to have a mournful character and a coffin was to be carried representing the deaths of lesbians and homosexuals as a result of violence and repression. Some felt that the lethargy that had taken hold of the movement meant that it no longer attracted attention from the press and that its actions were no longer newsworthy. They hoped that the mournful march would increase the movement's profile.

The sixth Gay Pride March took place on June 30, 1984. Lambda, OIKABETH, GOHL, Gay Community, Fidelity, Horus, New B of Mexico, Unification, and the Metropolitan Community Church took part, carrying a coffin. From the other side LHOCA Net, the Sun Collectives, Black Butterflies, the magazine "The Guillotine," a group of transvestites, and a group of punks participated. Some homosexuals in this second group brought enormous phalluses made of plastic, with which they wanted to visually express the language of denigration as well as present a controversial image. The Sun Collectives handed out a famous document they called "Euthanasia to the Lilo Movement" in which they argued that tolerance and social recognition had obliterated the most subversive demands of the movement, which was currently integrated, demobilized, and nonexistent. With the document they called for euthanasia by decree for the lesbian-homosexual movement.

A description of the march by the Masiosare Gay Collective, in response to an article by Juan Jacobo Hernández and Rafael Manrique (1988), former leaders of the FHAR, stated:

> On the one side there were the self-declared radicals, the revolutionaries, led by the ex-militants from FHAR. On the other side there were the reformists,

headed by Lambda. Their march had a mournful character. That of the "radicals," on the other hand, proclaimed the "difference" and attempted to bring together gays, gangs, prostitutes (though none attended as far as I can remember), *tibiris* and the whole amalgam of weirdos in the capital. On the occasion our comrades from the Sun Collectives handed out the legendary "Euthanasia to the Lilo Movement" flyer, in which they clearly described the Lesbian-Homosexual Movement as "*chimuelo*"—toothless. In it they also denounced the coalition between Lambda and OIKABETH with groups on the right of the political spectrum, "listed the mistakes" made by gay groups and deplored the mournful character of the reformist march. All this led them to call for the death of the lesbian-homosexual movement. When the marches arrived at the Hemiciclo a Juárez—the traditional end point—the radicals, accompanied by a group of gangs and headed by comrades from the Sun Collective and Guillotine, prevented the reformists from holding their planned meeting, broke the coffins they were carrying, pushed, shouted abuse[8] and even resorted to physical violence to force a retreat by Lambda and its allies. Other boys had made phalluses of foam and were playing around with them. Some people from Guillotine told us to go and annoy members of Lambda, but they never told us to hit them. They claim that we hit them, but no one ever touched them, not even with a rose petal.[9]

The presence of women in the lesbian-homosexual movement, particularly in the group Lambda was another cause of tension. According to some of the militant women, members of FHAR, reflecting their misogynist attitudes,[10] accused Lambda of being influenced by women. In this context the march had greater significance for women. The phalluses were interpreted as direct aggression toward lesbians.

That bloody march was very aggressive from the moment that the boys arrived with those things; it looked like a carnival of the phallus. They arrived with those great big pricks. I think they belonged to the Black Butterflies. Many members of FHAR also branded us as reformists because we were a mixed group. Patria came with the people from OIKABETH and when we arrived at the Hemiciclo she threw a paper airplane which she had set alight at one of the pricks and it caught fire. The boys felt attacked in the same way that we girls had done earlier. It was obviously an ideological aggression against us, because within Lambda feminist ideals were defended.[11]

The marches were a kind of celebration. It was going out into the streets and saying "I'm gay and I'm proud." In this march boys from Guillotine, former members of FHAR and transvestites came to attack us with those phalluses, to goad us with them. I was angry because it was our own people who were attacking us; it wasn't even the police. The only thing I felt was that I didn't want to know anything about them and the people who did this, I no longer wanted to share the streets with them.[12]

For many women this march was the moment in which the differences became explicit and led to a split from the men. Some returned to the feminist movement and others set up autonomous lesbian groups. The rejection by lesbians of the phallocentric[13] attitude as a system of power became clear after the sixth march. The cult of the phallus by homosexuals led to a rupture in the militancy and activism of lesbians. The rejection of the phallocentric stance did not imply androphobia, it simply denied a system of power in which the phallus symbolizes an instrument of dominance and violence, and marks women as "incomplete" and thus lacking in power.

After 1984 and 1985 the militants in the movement were concerned with one of the major problems to affect the movement: AIDS. They formed NGOs (nongovernmental organizations), self-help groups, provided services, and so on. During the later years of the crisis, attempts were made to analyze the situation that had weakened the lesbian-homosexual movement and to see what steps could be taken to solve the conflict. During the preceding six years the lesbian-homosexual movement had denounced sexism, political persecution, sensationalism by the mass media, and worker exploitation and had struggled for legitimacy in various political spheres. It had failed to achieve more tangible successes. Political persecution, raids, and prejudices had still not been eradicated. At the legislative level lesbians and gays are still second class citizens and their rights in relation to the family, work, housing, and social security are not recognized. The movement has not even succeeded in creating an autonomous gay community, however small, as exists in other countries. Even if these are criticized for being ghettos, they are necessary as places for social and political reference.

Feminists and Feminist Lesbians:
The Struggle Against Lesbophobia and Hetero-Feminism

The second theoretical position of "difference" focused on the specificity of female psychology and its symbolic expressions. Feminists searched for an irrefutable feminine identity without an equivalent in the opposite sex (Cixous 1991; Irigaray n.d.). In the Latin American case, however, modernity was cut short and did not give women full rights as subjects. "Totality did not include them, universality made them invisible" (Vargas 1991). For the Latin American feminist movement, the phase of difference focused primarily on the search for autonomy within the Left. In the context of the lesbian movement, lesbians focused on their difference in relation to homosexual men and on the construction of an individual and collective identity where the phallus is absent. Hence the separation from the homosexual movement and later from the feminist movement.

In the initial stages of the feminist movement in Latin America, its proximity and adherence to the Left and Marxist categories of analysis diluted the recognition of gender specificity as the point of departure and central focus of the movement. Some Marxist feminist opinions valued work connected to economic issues (workers and/or the masses) while neglecting demands relating to the personal sphere, the body, and sexuality. They labeled these as bourgeois themes. The theme of homosexuality was the cause of many conflicts.

In its first phase (1971–1975) the feminist movement was characterized by expansion and by the reproduction of ideas and basic concepts from North American and European feminism. Under the influence of these ideas the movement grew. Middle-class women with a higher than average level of education came together in small groups dedicated to reflection and action. During this phase the concerns about strengthening and expanding the feminist movement in popular sectors grew. It was a phase of enormous growth, with some groups having more than one hundred members. Abortion became the most significant issue for some of the groups. The movement made a great effort to bring these issues to public awareness through talks, debates, newspaper articles, and so on. School textbooks were revised and sexist language in legislation was questioned. Demands were made for the modification of laws that discriminated against women and for the recognition of domestic work (González 1987).

In the second stage of the feminist movement's development (1975–1984) the main concerns were to integrate the efforts of the different groups toward joint actions that would give the movement strength and a public image as an "alternative social movement" for women.

For the homosexual liberation movement this period was, to a large extent, one of cultural dissemination. Through artistic activities such as theater, music, literature, and the press as well as through discussion groups, the religiously sanctioned traditional concepts concerning sexuality in Mexican society became less rigid. This exercise of dissemination was not a mass movement, nor was it a particularly public one, and it was therefore unable to provide a point of reference for the great majority of gays and lesbians who lived a clandestine lifestyle.

The presence of foreign lesbians during the First World Conference for Women of the International Women's Year 1975 brought lesbian issues to the fore although they were not openly debated there. This caused such commotion that the capital's press reported the event on the front pages. Nancy Cárdenas came out in front of a multitude of journalists. She emphasized the lack of public security that made declarations concerning homosexuality difficult, due to the fact that the law allowed for the penalization of statements made in favor of homosexuality. Nonetheless, with the backing of a group of lesbians, for the first time in Mexican history, the "Declaration of Mexican Lesbians" was brought into the open.

For Nancy Cárdenas and her group of Mexican lesbians the meeting between the Mexican lesbians and the foreign lesbians was like a meeting between two worlds. As Nancy Cárdenas remembered:

> We got all the foreign lesbians together and I invited them to a meeting in my house to introduce Mexican lesbians to them. I brought them lesbians who felt they were men trapped in women's bodies, those who were in their sixties and had not accepted gay militancy, and young girls of twenty; I wanted them to see everything. I asked what they would have done with the men versus women problem? I felt crushed at not having been able to overcome this obstacle. When they told me that they too had been unable to overcome it, a feeling of relief swept over me. It was not my personal clumsiness. Up to that time the issue of male and female roles was a difficult one. You felt equally ridiculous breaking them as adhering to them. We asked them how they dealt with that. Their reply was very helpful. "Let's see, which one is having her period? She will be the passive one. What mood are you in?" It was scandalous and marvelous at the same time to know that you could change your preference in this way. It gave us a new perspective in which on top or under are equally delicious and in which all orifices are equally sacred to communicate love energy.[14]

After the International Women's Year the public arena for lesbians began to shrink once more. For lesbian discussions—as yet not organized—the feminist arena provided an option, even if from the closet, in the form of a subtext, or, as Nancy would say, as an indiscretion.

In 1976 and 1978 the Coalition of Women and the National Front to Struggle for the Liberation and the Rights of Women (FNALIDEM) were formed. The first was an organization coordinated by six of the feminist groups dedicated to the struggle for the right to unrestricted and free abortion, the fight against rape, and for support for battered women. At the same time, FNALIDEM brought together feminists and committees of women from political parties and unions. The objective was the struggle for the achievement of complete civil and political rights for women. FNALIDEM gave its full support to the demands of voluntary maternity (including the decriminalization of abortion) and to the protection of women against rape. The participation of political parties (in particular PERCENT and PRT) diverted FNALIDEM from its initial objectives. Nonetheless it is important to mention that together with the coalition this organization contributed to creating a political arena for Mexican feminists.

As the feminist movement adhered so strongly to Marxist analysis, lesbians found it hard to link up with feminists. Instead they initiated a separatist current with groups such as Lesbos and OIKABETH. For lesbians the attempts to find an arena among feminists has been exhausting and painful.

> When the summons was made to form FNALIDEM, all female, unionist and political organizations came together. We, as OIKABETH, asked to join, together with lesbians from Lambda and FHAR. But the National Union of Women of the Communist Party stated that it was not possible for us to join a serious organization which was fighting for women from a proletarian and popular perspective, saying "if these women are allowed in, then alcoholics, prostitutes, and criminals will follow." Marta Lamas and the women from the PRT countered this argument. The UNM then decided to leave FNALIDEM because of us. It was a very important loss, especially as far as the contacts at the international level with socialist countries were concerned. For me, as a Communist, it was very painful that comrades left because of us. Since the foundation of the first lesbian group, our experience has been very painful.[15]

Lesbians became integrated in all activities of FNALIDEM and fought jointly for the demands the front was making at that time. All of them worked from a hetero-feminist perspective as it was not possible to integrate lesbian demands with feminist ones. "They did not accept lesbianism. If we had not previously taken part in the party political and unionist struggles, I think it would have been very difficult to include lesbian issues in the women's struggle. We always had an anti-imperialist and nonclass outlook, we took part in union congresses and the forums of popular culture."[16] The lack of discussion about the way "heterosexual identity" was constructed meant that the lesbian movement was unable to introduce lesbian demands into the feminist movement. Lesbians, nonetheless, carried on working within the feminist movement, preferring to do so rather than to struggle for "sexual liberation."

> During the marches of the 1980s our participation as lesbians in favor of voluntary maternity was strong. The issue of maternity did not appear to have much to do with us. It does not mean that lesbians cannot be mothers, but we argued that it was an issue of freedom to use one's body and saw that this had parallels with our own demands, even if many of us did not see ourselves as

ever becoming mothers. The feminist movement in Mexico has always carried out its discussion from a heterosexual perspective. Some companions even say "why talk of lesbianism when the problem is one of gender?" This is false. As long as there is discrimination and repression it is necessary to specify that there are lesbians.[17]

The Rapprochement of the Hetero-Feminists

During this period, the lesbian movement moved closer to the feminist movement. In December 1978 the first meeting of lesbians and feminists took place in Nancy Cárdenas's house in Cuernavaca. The results of the meeting, even if they did not lead to joint activities, managed to open a channel for discussion. During the meeting those present questioned the theories of sexuality and the social institutions that regulate and set the conditions for sexual exchanges such as the family, marriage, the state, compulsory heterosexuality, the productive system, and the social division of sexually structured work ("Primer Encuentro" 1979).

The second meeting, which also took place in Cuernavaca, on June 23, 1979, was attended by lesbians from various groups, independent lesbians, and heterosexual feminists, primarily members of GAMU (Grupo Autónoma de Mujeres Universitarias, Autonomous Group of University Women). Its purpose was to inform each other of the work each group was carrying out and to intensify the discussion on the issues that had been brought up at the first meeting ("Il Reunion" 1979).

A third meeting was organized in return by GAMU in the house of one of its members. The participants discussed the issue of sexual preference and argued for an understanding of it as a political position that defied normative ideas and institutions. The meeting also served to strengthen relations between the groups and especially between lesbians and heterosexuals who began to question their sexual preference.

> Nancy proposed that some meetings be held. We talked about repression (both internal and external) and its costs, the raids, the lack of an arena for women—a recurring theme which I think is still relevant today. About sixty women would attend each event, chatting away. The meetings were very fruitful because the hetero-feminists began to lose their fear of being branded lesbians because they were feminists. GAMU became close friends with the lesbian groups Lambda and OIKABETH. The meetings had both a political and a personal nature. We would stay over and eat, sleep, and play around at night. These activities were seen by the feminists attending them purely in the context of feminism and not of lesbianism, which was what most of them feared and some, perhaps, desired.[18]

We came to the lesbian meeting and saw lesbians in flesh and blood, talked to them, saw they were like us. We saw that there were all types of women: very feminine, very masculine. From that moment on we decided, as a group, to start talking and reading about the topic, and we began to have conferences everywhere in the university. Prior to this meeting GAMU had never really thought about the subject of lesbianism. We invited psychoanalysts. The trouble came when a lot of us started to have homosexual experiences. Many of the women who were the least forthcoming with their thoughts were those who at some time in their lives had had homosexual experiences, but resisted because they came from the left, the PRT, and the PERCENT.

The leaders were mostly heterosexual but almost ninety percent of the women at that time had had homosexual experiences. Some of us, up until this very day, are lesbians, others remained bisexual or have a stable heterosexual relationship while still having homosexual experiences. None of us erased it from our lives.[19]

Amid the rapprochements between lesbians and hetero-feminists, the differences between them came to the fore as well.

Once the meetings got underway, a heated argument arose that there was a hetero-feminism and lesbian-feminism. The extreme position was that we lesbians are not interested in maternity and hence abortion could not be a central issue of the lesbian feminist movement. Others stated that rape was not a lesbian issue but most of us countered this argument by saying that "as women we are all vulnerable in the same way."[20]

These discussions within the feminist movement brought into the open one of the most stigmatized of topics: lesbianism as sexual determination or political option. For lesbians who had come to terms with their identity at a very young age and for those to whom *The Well of Loneliness*—one of the first books to deal with the issue of lesbianism—had reinforced the idea that homosexuality was imposed on some people by nature at birth, the entry of new lesbians to the ranks of the "scene" opened up the possibility of a new political position, in which lesbianism would not simply be an erotico-affective possibility but a political alternative.

There were also lesbians who said "I have come to be a lesbian through a political decision," textbook lesbians. Coming out took place in many different ways. Some became lesbian through a one-night stand, others through a serious, strong relationship who, when they split up, returned to being heterosexual, whilst some remained lesbian or declared themselves bisexual.[21]

The discussion about lesbian determination has been a recurring theme in the feminist movement—the idea that lesbianism is a transgression of the taboos of an authoritarian society and an affirmation of women. Hence the lesbian movement called for a political choice. The words of Ti-Grace Atkinson, "Feminism is the theory and lesbianism is the practice," were used to affirm that lesbianism is not reduced to sexual behavior but is instead a psychological rebellion specific to women against the role assigned to them by a macho society (Linhoff 1978).

Autonomous Lesbian Movement:
From Exclusive Purism to Coming out of the Closet

The third theoretical position argues for a coexistence with the separatist women's movement due to the fact that women still have to demand their place as equals in society. In the history of the feminist movement the first two phases are clearly defined. The first is that of equality and universality, in which the movement identified itself with the social struggles the Left was engaged in at the time. The lesbians of the homosexual movement recognized in these feminist demands a source of strength. They brought the issue of gender to the homosexual arena. In the second historical phase represented by the ideas of difference and separatism, the reaffirmation of lesbian identity was rooted in the rejection of the masculine symbolic order, phallocentrism, and the heterosexual exclusiveness of the demands of the feminist movement. In the third phase, in contrast to the feminist movement, the lesbian movement—due to its separatist tendencies—did not open new forms of interrelation with gay men and masculinity. The separation from the homosexual movement was radical. As the latter was greatly affected by AIDS from the mid-1980s on, it channeled much of its energy to fighting this disease. Nonetheless, in relation to the arenas of power, a representative bureaucracy has emerged in the lesbian movement—as it has in the feminist movement—one that aims to find ways to communicate with the patriarchal arena and assumes regional representation (Mogrovejo 1995). With the feminist movement lesbians struggled to create for themselves a space as women and feminists, fighting for a theoretical space to analyze their repression as an oppressed sexual minority.

Gender analysis, which feminists of the third phase adhere to, aims to explain social relationships based on the fact that human bodies are not the same and that women have a subordinate position; hence the interaction between men and women is the central issue in the category gender (Barbieri 1996). But it does not analyze the social organization of sexuality or the basic power relations in the sexual arena in which lesbians, homosexuals, transvestites, transsexuals, voluntary sadomasochists, and prostitutes share many sociological traits and, consequently, many of the same social punishments. Lesbians are also oppressed due to the characterization of homosexuals as perverts and to sexual stratification unrelated to gender (Rubin 1989). This position argues for the need to elaborate a radical theory of sexuality that will analyze the political persecution of dissident sexual groups, harassed because of their image as erotic objects.

Lesbianism is seen as politically subversive; according to some views, men simply are irrelevant. This point of view deconstructs the masculine/feminine binary (Kristeva 1981; Lauretis 1991). The concept of gender in the binary male-female relationship is inadequate to explain the dynamics of lesbian relationships where the "other" is not an "other" but an "equal," a "same." This is why the third phase of the lesbian movement is one of searching for an individual logic, language, and interpretation. Nonetheless there are dangers, as looking into the mirror can become the ghetto that excludes not only the Other but also the image one's own mirror reflects, the similar one, the lesbian sister. This problem makes it difficult to account for differences among lesbians. This stage has its antecedents in the Latin American feminist conferences.

The beginning of the lesbian current within the feminist movement in Latin America took place in Colombia during the first Latin American Feminist Conference, held from July 18 to 21, 1981. The Committee for Sexuality and Daily Life organized discussions on the subjects of rape and lesbianism. In the forum on lesbianism, discussions were held on the need to make theory and practice coherent, the traditional heterosexual couple, the conditioning of social roles, and patriarchal society in general. This caused many hetero-feminists to identify themselves with lesbianism ("Foro sobre Lesbianismo" 1982).

During the second Latin American Conference, held in Peru in 1983, lesbians made their presence felt when they turned the miniworkshop "Patriarchy and Lesbianism" into "The Workshop" of the Conference. Approximately 350 women from all over the continent and of all sexual persuasions took part. The public "coming out" of many feminists was one of the greatest events of the conference. It showed the need to bring out into the open an issue that appeared to be personal. This "coming out" gave rise to the lesbian-feminist current within the Latin American feminist movement. Many lesbians returned to their countries from "The Workshop" motivated to set up a group of lesbian feminists. After the second conference, the

Lesbian Feminist Self-Awareness Group (GALF) was founded in Peru, Ayuquelén in Chile, Crescent Moon in Mexico, and Mitilene in the Dominican Republic.

During the third Feminist Conference in Brazil in 1985 lesbianism and relationships between women were part of the agenda. At the same time, GALF-Brazil and GALF-Peru set up a workshop entitled "Lesbian Organization."[22] The discussions in this workshop focused on the demands lesbians had of the feminist movement, on the criticism of the dominant heterosexual model, which denied the sexuality of women and centered on procreation, and on lesbian desires as a possible desire for all women. If these demands were not achieved, they argued, the feminist movement would only be partially successful. A proposal was developed during this conference to set up a lesbian movement at the continental level in Latin America and the Caribbean, independent from the feminist conferences. The need to set up a support and information network between lesbians on the continent was also noted.

In March 1986 nine Latin American lesbians received an invitation from the Dutch-based International Lesbian Information Service (ILIS) to take part in their ninth conference, which would take place in Geneva, Switzerland. For the first time ILIS included women from the second and third worlds in their conferences.

The Geneva conference is important as it helps explain the development of the autonomous lesbian movement in Mexico and Latin America. It was in this phase that ways of exercising political power were first developed by those who were chosen as leaders in their respective countries. This was also the phase in which political definitions that were fashionable in Europe, such as separatism, purism, and exclusion, began to spread. The Latin American Network consisted of a system of communication between lesbians and lesbian groups aimed at keeping everyone informed and distributing reports concerning the violation of lesbian rights. The idea was to create an institution similar to the IGA, the International Gay Association (which later included lesbians and became the ILGA).

The ILIS conference agreed to the formation of the Latin American Network and of the First Latin American, Caribbean, and Mexican Lesbian Feminist Conference. The only groups that fulfilled the requirement laid down by the Geneva Conference were those that had been present at ILIS because at that time—and even today—most lesbians lacked organizations and the few that were organized were in mixed groups (homosexual and feminist).

The Organization of the First Lesbian Feminist Conference of Latin America and the Caribbean (First ELFALC)

On their return, the Mexican representatives called on Mexican lesbians to collectively organize the First ELFALC. In spite of Mexico's organizational experience, there were only three groups, namely MULA, Crescent Moon, and the Marxist Leninist Seminar of Lesbian Feminists. Most lesbians who had at some stage been militant were not part of any specific group.

With the Latin American Lesbians (LAL) in Mexico and with the participation of both organized and independent lesbians, the organizing committee for the First ELFALC was set up. There were many conflicts within LAL:

> From the start there were differences between the groups. For the members of MULA it was a humorous, friendly, and aesthetic meeting while we, members of the Seminar, wanted to define strategies for joint struggle by Latin American lesbians. For us, MULA represented the reactionary wing, while the Seminar was the left, radical wing. These two sides, MULA and the Seminar, were fixed and many of the independent newcomers would take sides. MULA controlled finance and external contact while we had food, press, and propaganda under our control. Alma O. and I made the same mistake we had made earlier: while we did the groundwork and put the infrastructure in place, others began to take political power.[23]

The suggestion to include nonlesbian sectors, gay men, political groups, and unions in the organization and the event caused conflict inside the organizing committee. One section strongly defended the autonomy of the organization. Its organizers excluded those who were identified as not meeting the proper requirements of "lesbian feminists." The vetoes also reflected personal vendettas between committee members.

The growing politics of exclusion began to affect the members of LAL. Under the guise of purism, expulsions took place, or members were pressured to leave of their own accord. "There were different registration categories for the conference. Marta Lamas wanted to participate in the conference but was prevented from doing so on the grounds that she was heterosexual. Yan said people had to prove that they were lesbians. How? Through a lesbianometer?"[24] The atmosphere became aggressive. The desire to invalidate "the others" sometimes took on sinister forms. This was the background of the First National Lesbian Conference, which had been called for by LAL in order to bring all lesbians together, to discuss the need to strengthen the autonomous lesbian movement, and to interest lesbians in the great event. The group Patlatonalli, from Guadalajara, organized the event, and even though they did very well, conflicts had already arisen and spread to the national conference.

One of the main objectives of the conference was the formation of a network, as discussed in Geneva. Information about this issue was either incomplete or had not been given due consideration during the organizational stages by LAL because of internal conflicts.

> We all, including the Chicanas, thought that at the conference we were going to set up a Latin American lesbian organization, but this network already existed. It already had its tactics, strategies, and defined objectives, but most of us did not know about this. If the Seminar had known about the aims and objectives of the network, we would not have taken part in the conference; it had a separatist nature influenced by Silvia Borren from ILIS in Holland. We are not separatists. On the contrary, separatism in Latin -America and the third world is a reactionary philosophy. Lurdes, Carmelita, GALF Peru, GALF Brasil, Nicaragua, and Ayuquelén did not want us to join, especially not the Chicanas. Silvia Borren did not want the Chicanas to join because they were from North America and were very politically active. We were told this by a comrade who was our spy and was present at these secret meetings. With the conditions imposed by the network almost all lesbian organizations in Latin America were excluded, as they almost all worked with gay or heterosexual feminist groups. This is because the Latin American reality is different to that in Holland.[25]

The discussion of the network turned the conference into a powder keg. It was impossible to carry out workshops or plenary sessions. As Yan remembers:

> It was a terrible experience. We were unable to carry out any discussions on activities which lesbians living under dictatorships and totalitarian regimes could organize. We did not manage to discuss what we could do and how we could coordinate our activities living in situations of extreme conservatism, as was the case in all Latin American societies. It had been our objective to find a stance that lesbians could take in the face of public debt, inflation, unemployment; to find a way of forming part of the national reality. All this was not discussed. Nothing was done. There was a bloody self-defense workshop given by some Europeans; we found this insulting as it seemed far more important to us to discuss what strategies we were going to pursue in Latin America. The lively party and fun and games prevented any meaningful discussion.[26]

The conference marginalized some people and groups and left others demoralized and disillusioned. The lesbian movement lost its initial momentum, and participants went home with a sour taste in their mouths.

One agreement reached at the conference concerned the creation of a Latin American network in which independent lesbians, as well as those belonging to autonomous lesbian groups and mixed groups, the Chicanas, and Latin Americans living abroad, would participate. At the conference there was an important presence of Chicanas and Latin Americans who lived in the United States or Europe, either in exile or voluntarily, and who asked to join. After a heated debate, this conflict was finally resolved in their favor. The network was to start with a bulletin in the form of memoirs to be published in Mexico. In reality, the network never did work. A "satellite" network was active in an informal manner between some of those who had been present at the conference in Geneva and others who later joined. They made decisions in the name of the entire Latin American lesbian movement (Mogrovejo 1995).

Immediately thereafter the Fourth Feminist Conference was held in Taxco. On three of the four days of the conference, workshops were held that were closely linked to lesbian concerns. These were: "Myths, Roles, and Sexuality," "Lesbianism and Repression," "Lesbianism and Politics: The Relationship Between the Lesbian-Feminist and the Hetero-Feminist Movements," and "Lesbian Mothers." The discussions in these workshops focused on the relationship between the feminist movement and the lesbian movement. The feminist movement was forced to consider lesbian demands and thus to confront its own fears of being considered lesbian by the outside world.

The workshops asserted that "the feminist movement is neither exclusively heterosexual nor exclusively lesbian, but it has portrayed, albeit in different ways, a heterosexual image." Faced with this fact, lesbians felt the need to strengthen their struggle inside the movement through discussions and the creation of more groups. They did not, however, wish to turn the feminist movement into another lesbian movement but wanted instead to pressure the feminist movement to fight for a sexual politics that was not limited to the narrow margins of heterosexuality and sexual puritanism (Ramos et al. 1987). One of the most direct attacks of the lesbian movement on the feminist movement was in a paper presented by Trinidad Gutiérrez. In it she asserted that it had been a long and difficult task for lesbians to be recognized within the feminist movement in Mexico and that in spite of the active participation of lesbians in the struggles of the feminist movement, the latter had not looked beyond its heterosexual analysis of feminism. The paper accused the feminist movement of seeing lesbianism as a separate struggle, to be dealt with solely within the parameters of sexuality. This limited analysis of lesbianism was due not to lack of lesbian involvement in the feminist movement but to heterosexual "blindness." This resulted in lesbianism remaining "in the closet" of feminist analysis, thus reduced to leading a marginal and invisible existence within feminism (Gutiérrez 1987).

In 1990, in a final attempt to unify the feminist movement, there was a call for the formation of a Mexico City Feminist Union. In the discussions preceding its formation, three basic demands for participation were set out: free and voluntary motherhood and abortion, action to prevent violence against women, and support for free sexual preference. Adherence to these demands was the condition for participation in the union; this was an important precedent in the history of the feminist movement. After ten years of effort by the lesbian movement, the feminist movement had finally taken on lesbian demands.

In spite of everything, the lesbian-homosexual movement has attained several achievements. The growth and expansion of the lesbian-homosexual movement allowed the spread of new ideas concerning sexuality and its unbreakable link with politics. It gave rise to a counterargument that opposed the images and characterizations presented by the tabloid press, traditional psychiatry, psychoanalysis, medicine, law, and religious morality. This counterargument portrayed the sexual movement as a revolutionary one that took its place alongside the struggles for those on the periphery of society and for democracy. The lesbian-homosexual movement allowed thousands of gays and lesbians to develop a sense of pride and security in their own sexuality, reducing the feelings of guilt and fear. It managed to change political ideals that had been cast in iron and ensured the acceptance of homosexual and lesbian demands by political parties. In some instances this went as far as their inclusion in political manifestos, as was the case with the Mexican Communist Party and the PRT. It organized sex education among the young and in broad sections of society in general. The mere presence of the lesbian-homosexual movement strengthened civil society, shook up social inertia, and promoted the representation of the demands of other marginalized sectors of society (see also Hernández and Manrique 1988). The struggle of the lesbian-homosexual movement allowed an important number of artists and intellectuals to declare themselves in favor of lesbian and gay demands.

In spite of the unconditional adherence of the lesbian movement to the feminist struggle and its demands, for a decade the issue of sexual preference remained taboo within the feminist movement. Although criticism of the social and cultural determination of gender and sexual roles was the point of departure for both movements, the different political actions taken by them led to a split. The feminist movement gave priority to its political activities in the popular sectors. The search for institutional legitimacy took second place, which led to the prioritization of those demands that would not harm its image. This is why its theoretical analysis and its actions were limited to a heterosexual framework. The lesbian movement, on the other hand, carried out its political activities within the space provided first by the homosexual movement and later by the feminist movement. There are subtle and veiled forms of misogyny in the homosexual movement and lesbophobia in the feminist movement that prevent both from taking on the demands of the lesbian movement as their own. The lesbian movement was unable to create its own space for political activity. This could have been achieved after 1987, when an autonomous movement was created. Nonetheless, the search for the historical subject was not carried out in the broader lesbian sectors. The work of the autonomous Mexican lesbian movement was limited to its own constituent groups, creating an arena of internal consumption, atomization, and saturation. This led to exhaustion and a subsequent crisis in the movement.

The greatest achievement of the lesbian movement, both as an autonomous movement and as part of the feminist movement, has been (and still is) the permanent questioning of the feminist movement with respect to the construction of its identity. "The feminist movement cannot assume a heterosexual identity," the lesbian movement has argued, and it thus sees itself as an integral part of the feminist movement. It asserts that a discussion of sexuality and the roles derived from it is crucial in order to achieve more democratic changes in society.

At the Latin American level there is still great difficulty in consolidating a lesbian movement. There is still a large gap between the theoretical and organizational levels of the feminist movement and the lesbian movement. While the feminist movement has held seven conferences at the Latin-American and Caribbean level, the lesbian movement's conferences have been problematic. The growing political crisis and violence, together with an increase in gay and lesbian repression, made it difficult to organize international conferences. The characteristics of the two movements are different. The lesbian conferences have been subjected to repression and direct political violence. Furthermore, global political strategies that would make the lesbian movement's conferences massive and regular events have not been developed.

The dynamics of exclusion and intolerance in the internal relations of the lesbian movement made a program of plural coordination impossible. This reflects an internalized lesbophobia on the part of the militants. The conflicts between small groups have made the advancement of the movement increasingly difficult. As is the case in most of the small political opposition groups, the struggle for survival has produced a dynamics of atomization and self-destruction. Within the lesbian movement it has always been very difficult for different groups and currents to coexist and interact at the political level. For many, the worst enemy of the lesbian movement has not been the state, nor the political right, nor the church, but the lesbian movement itself.

Within these internal dynamics the lesbian movement has shown certain historical characteristics. First, complex political relations are mixed with amorous ones. Infidelity causes a realignment of forces, new passions give way to new alliances. This shows the strong influence of internal dynamics on social ones, reaffirming the strong link between political and sexual relations. Second, the struggle for power and the personality cult has strengthened the image of leaders who were able to open themselves up to the public in general. Third, the lesbian movement is characterized by a contradictory and neurotic practice, which was probably the result of leading double lives, an internalized lesbophobia, and/or a lack of social and political security to come out of the closet. Finally, the lesbian movement tended toward institutionalization and the formation of small elites with pretensions of being representative.

The fact that a movement demands the right to freely exercise sexual preference goes much further than the preference itself, as it leads to a social questioning of sexuality, a fundamental part of peoples' lives (Guattari 1986). Sexuality is the target of repression and authoritarian conduct. In this context the number of people that take part in this struggle is irrelevant. What matters is the effect this struggle has on society.

NOTES

1. Second-wave feminism is the term used for the feminism that appeared in the 1970s. The suffragist struggles of the first decades of the century are referred to as the first wave.

2. On October 2, 1968, a student revolt ended in a massacre at the "Square of the Three Cultures" of Tlatelolco. This "massacre of Tlatelolco" was a watershed in Mexican political life. It gave rise to most new Mexican social movements, such as the urban popular, the feminist, and the homosexual movements.

3. Interview with Yan María Castro, February 9, 1995.

4. Interview with Luz María Medina, December 3, 1994.

5. Interview with Yan María Castro, ibid.

6. Interview with Yan María Castro, ibid.

7. The anniversary of the massacre of Tlatelolco, in which many students were killed.

8. Slogans were shouted such as "The dead stink" and "Put the dead in a hole, put the living in my hole."

9. Interview with Juan Jacobo Hernández, December 18, 1995.

10. Misogyny is hate or contempt of women. The focus of erotic desire and interpersonal relations of homosexual men on the phallus has developed in many cases into contempt for women, even if they are lesbians.

11. Interview with Eugenia Olson, January 19, 1995.

12. Interview with Chave, October 1995.

13. Phallocentrism is the term given to the cult of the phallus. Patriarchal society has centralized the image of power and violence in the phallus. In the case of the homosexual movement it is the centralization on the phallus of an allegedly erotic-transgressor or anticultural discourse.

14. Interview with Nancy Cárdenas for "Otro Modo de Ser Mujer," 1990.

15. Yan María Castro, ibid.

16. Yan María Castro, ibid.

17. Trinidad Gutiérrez. Interview for "Otro Modo de Ser Mujer," 1990.

18. This interviewee wanted to remain anonymous, so we have called her Carmelita. Interviewed in October 1995.

19. Interview with Norma Bands, member of GAMU, October 1994.

20. Interview with Emma and Gina for "Otro Modo de Ser Mujer," 1990.

21. Emma and Gina, ibid.

22. Lesbian groups that took part in the workshop included the Ayuquelén Collective from Chile, the Victoria Mercado Lesbian, and Gay Brigade from the U.S., Crescent Moon from Mexico, the Gay Consciousness Collective from Puerto Rico, GALF from Brazil, and Peru as well as independent lesbians.

23. Interview with Yan María Castro, ibid.

24. Interview with Nayeli, August 28, 1995.

25. Carmelita, ibid.

26. Yan María Castro, ibid.

REFERENCES

Barbieri, Teresita. 1996. "Certezas y Malos Entendidos sobre la Categoría de Género." IIDH Serie Estudios de Derechos Humanos Vol. 4.

"Boletin No. 2 de la Red de lesbianas latinas y del Caribe." Peru, August 1989.

Cixous, Hélène. 1991. "The Laugh of the Medusa." In Sonja Gunew, ed., *A Reader in Feminist Knowledge*. London: Routledge.

Foro sobre Lesbianismo. "Cuentame tu vida." Revista de Mujeres No. 6, Cali, Colombia 1982.

Fratti, Gina and Adriana Batista. 1984. *Liberación Homosexual.* Mexico: Posada.

Golubov, Nattie. 1993. "Delo colectivo alo individual: La crisis de la teoría literaria feminista." *Los Cuadernos del Acordeón* 5 (24).

González, Cristina. 1987. "El Movimiento Feminista: Aproximaciones para su Análisis." Master's thesis, Facultad de Ciencias Políticas y Sociales. UNAM.

Guattari, Felix. 1986. *Nuevos Movimientos Sociales.* Revista Desvios No. 5. Brazil.

Gutiérrez, Trinidad. 1987. "En el Feminismo desde el Closet o Acerca del Trabajo de las Mujeres Feministas Lesbianas en el Movimiento Feminista." Essay presented at the Fourth Latin American and Caribbean Feminist Conference. Taxco, October 1987.

Hernández, Juan Jacobo and Rafael Manrique. 1988. "10 Años de Movimiento Gay en México: El Brillo de la Ausencia." Unpublished manuscript. Mexico, August 29, 1988.

II Reunion de Mujeres. "Documento de Trabajo, Grupo Lambda." Cuernavaca 23 de June 1979.

Irigaray, Luce. n.d. "El Cuerpo a Cuerpo con la Madre: El Otro Género de la Naturaleza." In Catherine Belsey and Jane, *Otro Modo de Sentir*, pp. 115–132. Barcelona: La Sal.

Kristeva, Julia. 1981. "Women's Time." *Signs: Journal of Women in Culture and Society* 7 (1): 13–35.

Lauretis, Teresa de. 1991. "Problemas, Conceptos, y Contextos." Transl. Gloria Bernal. In *El Género Como Perspectiva.* México: UNAM.

Linhoff, Ursula. 1978. *La Homosexualidad Feminina.* Barcelona: Anagrama.

"Memorias III: Encontro Feminista Latinoamericano e do Caribe." Brazil, 1985.

Moi, Toril. 1987. "Feminist, Female, Feminine." In Toril Moi, ed., *French Feminist Thought: A Reader.* Oxford: Blackwell.

Mogrovejo, Norma. 1995. "Burocracias Representativas y el IV Encuentro de Lesbianas Feministas de América Latina y el Caribe." *La Correa Feminista* 12:58–60.

"Primer Encuentro de Lesbianas y Feministas." In "Política Sexual." *Cuadernos del FHAR*, vol. 1, no. 1, May 1979.

Ramos, Juanita, Alma Oceguera, et. al. 1987. "Resument de las Conclusiones y Propuestas de los Tallere Lésbicos Feministas de IV Encuentro Feminista Latinoamericano y del Caribe." Unpublished manuscript. Taxco, October 1987.

Rubin, Gayle. 1989. "Thinking Sex: Notes for a Radical Theory of the Politics of Sexuality." In Carole S. Vance, ed., *Pleasure and Danger: Exploring Female Sexuality*, pp. 267–319. Boston: Routledge and Kegan Paul.

"Sexualidad y Política: Ponencia Presentada por el PRT al Foro de Derechos Humanos." Unpublished manuscript, Cuidad Universitaria, October 1989.

Vargas, Virginia. 1991 "El Movimiento Feminista Latinoamericano: Entre la Esperanza y el Desencanto (Apuntes para el Debate)." *El Cielo por Asalto* 2:59–60.

ABBREVIATIONS

CLHARI: Comité de Lesbianas y Homosexuales en Apoyo a Rosario Ibarra (Lesbian and Homosexual Committee in Support of Rosario Ibarra)

CNL: Coordinadora Nacional de Lesbianas (National Coordinator of Lesbians)

ELFALC: Encuentro Lesbico Feminista de América Latina y el Caribe (Lesbian Feminist Conference of Latin America and the Caribbean)

FHAR: Frente Homosexual de Accion Revolucionaria (Homosexual Front for Revolutionary Action)

FNALIDEM: Frente Nacional de Lucha por la Liberación de los Derechos de las Mujeres (National Front for the Struggle for the Liberation of Women's Rights)

GALF: Grupo de Autoconciencia de Lesbianas Feministas (Lesbian Feminist Self-Consciousness Group)

GOHL: Grupo Orgullo Homosexual de Guadalajara (Gay Pride Group of Guadalajara)

ILIS: International Lesbian Information Service

ILGA: International Lesbian and Gay Association

LAL: Lesbianas de América Latina (Latin American Lesbians)

OIKABETH: Olling Iskan Katuntat Bebeth Thot (Movement of Warrior Women who Open the Way and Scatter Flowers)

PRT: Partido Revolucionario del Trabajo (Revolutionary Labor Party)

Red LHOCA: Red de Lesbianas y Homosexuales, Colectivos Autónomos (Network of Lesbians and Homosexuals, Autonomous Collectives)

UNAM: Universidad Nacional Autónoma de México (Mexican National Autonomous University)

Index

BETWEEN MEN ~ BETWEEN WOMEN

Lesbian and Gay Studies

Lillian Faderman and Larry Gross, Editors

Corinne E. Blackmer and Patricia Juliana Smith, editors, *En Travesti: Women, Gender Subversion, Opera*

Don Paulson with Roger Simpson, *An Evening at The Garden of Allah: A Gay Cabaret in Seattle*

Claudia Schoppmann, *Days of Masquerade: Life Stories of Lesbians During the Third Reich*

Chris Straayer, *Deviant Eyes, Deviant Bodies: Sexual Re-Orientation in Film and Video*

Edward Alwood, *Straight News: Gays, Lesbians, and the News Media*

Thomas Waugh, *Hard to Imagine: Gay Male Eroticism in Photography and Film from Their Beginnings to Stonewall*

Judith Roof, *Come As You Are: Sexuality and Narrative*

Terry Castle, *Noel Coward and Radclyffe Hall: Kindred Spirits*

Kath Weston, *Render Me, Gender Me: Lesbians Talk Sex, Class, Color, Nation, Studmuffins . . .*

Ruth Vanita, *Sappho and the Virgin Mary: Same-Sex Love and the English Literary Imagination*

renée c. hoogland, *Lesbian Configurations*

Beverly Burch, *Other Women: Lesbian Experience and Psychoanalytic Theory of Women*

Jane McIntosh Snyder, *Lesbian Desire in the Lyrics of Sappho*

Rebecca Alpert, *Like Bread on the Seder Plate: Jewish Lesbians and the Transformation of Tradition*

Emma Donoghue, editor, *Poems Between Women: Four Centuries of Love, Romantic Friendship, and Desire*

James T. Sears and Walter L. Williams, editors, *Overcoming Heterosexism and Homophobia: Strategies That Work*

Patricia Juliana Smith, *Lesbian Panic: Homoeroticism in Modern British Women's Fiction*

Dwayne C. Turner, *Risky Sex: Gay Men and HIV Prevention*

Timothy F. Murphy, *Gay Science: The Ethics of Sexual Orientation Research*

Cameron McFarlane, *The Sodomite in Fiction and Satire, 1660–1750*

Lynda Hart, *Between the Body and the Flesh: Performing Sadomasochism*

Byrne R. S. Fone, editor, *The Columbia Anthology of Gay Literature: Readings from Western Antiquity to the Present Day*

Ellen Lewin, *Recognizing Ourselves: Ceremonies of Lesbian and Gay Commitment*

Ruthann Robson, *Sappho Goes to Law School: Fragments in Lesbian Legal Theory*

Jacquelyn Zita, *Body Talk: Philosophical Reflections on Sex and Gender*

Evelyn Blackwood and Saskia Wieringa, *Female Desires: Same-Sex Relations and Transgender Practices Across Cultures*

William L. Leap, ed., *Public Sex/Gay Space*

Larry Gross and James D. Woods, eds., *The Columbia Reader on Lesbians and Gay Men in Media, Society, and Politics*

Marilee Lindemann, *Willa Cather: Queering America*

George E. Haggerty, *Men in Love: Masculinity and Sexuality in the Eighteenth Century*

Andrew Elfenbein, *Romantic Genius: The Prehistory of a Homosexual Role*

Gilbert Herdt and Bruce Koff, *Something to Tell You: The Road Families Travel When a Child Is Gay*

Richard Canning, *Gay Fiction Speaks: Conversations with Gay Novelists*

Laura Doan, *Fashioning Sapphism: The Origins of a Modern English Lesbian Culture*

Mary Bernstein and Renate Reimann, eds., *Queer Families, Queer Politics: Challenging Culture and the State*

Richard R. Bozorth, *Auden's Games of Knowledge: Poetry and the Meanings of Homosexuality*

Larry Gross, *Up from Invisibility: Lesbians, Gay Men, and the Media in America*

Linda Garber, *Identity Poetics: Race, Class, and the Lesbian-Feminist Roots of Queer Theory*